ISLAMIC LAW AND FINANCE
RELIGION, RISK, AND RETURN

Arab and Islamic Laws Series

Series General Editor
Dr. Mark S.W. Hoyle

This book will be published
as the sixteenth volume in the Series.

The titles published in this series are listed at the end of this volume.

Arab & Islamic
LAWS SERIES

ISLAMIC
LAW AND
FINANCE

Religion, Risk, and Return

by
Frank E. Vogel and Samuel L. Hayes, III

KLUWER LAW
INTERNATIONAL

The Hague • London • Boston

Library of Congress Cataloging-in-Publication Data on File

COVER DESIGN

Calligraphy "al-mīzān" or "the balance" is by Muhammad Zakariya, executed on January 2, 1998. The term "al-mīzān" occurs nine times in the Qur'an in verses exhorting fairness in dealings among humans (6:152, 7:85, 11:84-85) and as a metaphor for the divine standard of right and wrong revealed by the prophets: "We bestowed on them [Our messengers or prophets] from on high the revelation and the balance so that men might behave equitably" (57:25; see also 42:17, 55:7-9).

Copyright since 2003 by Koninklijke Brill NV, Leiden, The Netherlands.

ISBN 9041105476 (hardcover)
ISBN 9041106243 (softcover)

ISLAMIC LAW AND FINANCE
RELIGION, RISK, AND RETURN

DETAILED TABLE OF CONTENTS

CHAPTER 3

Qur'an and Sunna on Contract and Commerce   53

CHAPTER 4

Islamic Laws of Usury, Risk, and Property   71

CHAPTER 7

Islamic Financial Instruments: A Primer   181

Preface

The impulse for the writing of this book came some four years ago, when in meetings with Wellington Management Company of Boston, Harvard University's Center for Middle Eastern Studies (CMES) identified the need for an objective cross-disciplinary study of Islamic banking and finance addressing both its origins and its future potential. Thomas Mullins, Associate Director of CMES, and Professor Frank Vogel, Director of the Harvard Law School's Islamic Legal Studies Program and a faculty member of the Law School and CMES, recruited Professor Samuel Hayes of the Harvard Business School as well as a group of faculty scholars and interested graduate and undergraduate students to undertake the Harvard Islamic Finance Project. Together with Wellington, the National Commercial Bank in Jedda and Goldman Sachs in London generously agreed to support the Project. The National Commercial Bank, under the far-sighted leadership of Sheikh Mohammed Bin Mahfouz, provided us not only the major financial support but also valuable research support and introductions to scholars and information sources around the Islamic world.

This book, the work of two members of the Project, is one of the expected fruits of this extraordinary initiative. Our work has benefited much from the travel, research assistance, and editorial support afforded us by the Project.

We were assisted in our research for this book by a great many individuals and institutions. First among them is the Islamic Development Bank of Jedda and its associated Islamic Research and Training Institute (IRTI). The Bank's two successive Presidents, H.E. Dr. Osama Faquih and H.E. Mohammad Ali, both gave their warm support to our exchanges with the Bank. IRTI scholars, especially Dr. Sami Homoud, Dr. M. Fahim Khan,

Dr. Omar Hafiz, and Dr. Munawar Iqbal, gave us much instruction and insight into this subject, and were willing sounding boards for our hypotheses and financial product ideas. We exchanged several visits with them, in Cambridge and in Jedda. Special thanks go to Dr. Sami Homoud, who, with IRTI's sponsorship and support, came to Harvard in April 1995 to offer us a three-day intensive lecture series on Islamic finance. Interviews with officials of the Bank itself, including particularly Vice President, Finance, Dr. Fuad A. Al-Omar, General Counsel Dr. M. Al-Fatih Hamid, Dr. D. M. Qureshi, and Dr. Beshier Omer Fadlallah, gave us a great many insights and ideas. Many Bank officials and IRTI scholars took part in a most illuminating two-day workshop on a draft of the book held in Jedda in September 1996.

Islamic banks as well as other financial intermediaries cooperated in the research effort, giving generously of their time and expertise. At NCB, Dr. Said Al-Martan, Abdullah Al-Darwish, and Sami Barmah in Jedda and Kiril Coonley in London; at Goldman Sachs, Brace Young and Roy Salameh in London; at Wellington Management, Nicholas Greville and George Lodge in Boston and Ronald Strunck in London; at the Islamic Investment Bank of the Gulf (DMI), Mr. Iqbal Ahmad Khan; at Citi Islamic Investment Bank, Mr. Mohammed E. Al-Shroogi and Mr. Usama Mikdashi; at the International Investor in Kuwait, Mr. Adnan Al-Bahar; at Al-Baraka Investment and Development Co. in Jedda, Dr. Saleh J. Malaikah; at DMI International (Geneva) and Faisal Finance (Switzerland), Dr. Mohammad El-Helw; and at the National Bank of Kuwait, Mr. Al-Tayeb Al-Dajani, were all extremely helpful. Prince Amr bin Mohammed Al Faisal Al Saud was a valuable resource, as was Sheikh Khalid Alturki, Chairman of ABC International in London, and Samer S. Khanachet, Managing Director of United Gulf Management in Boston.

Among academic colleagues, we are particularly indebted to Dr. Mohamed Elgari, Director of the Center for Islamic Economics at King Abdulaziz University, Jedda, who spent two snowy weeks with us at Harvard Law School in January 1996 giving us the benefit of his learning and experience. Professor Zuhayr Mikdashi of the University of Lausanne contributed at several points in our research. Our colleagues at the Harvard Law School and the Harvard Business School made many useful suggestions which found their way into the book.

At the Center for Middle Eastern Studies, the successive Directors, Professors William A. Graham and E. Roger Owen, have strongly supported both the Project and this book. Tom Mullins deserves immense credit for launching the overall Project and shepherding it along. Project research has been coordinated by Dr. Don Babai, with assistance from Zahir Asmayl, Tim Buthe, Helen Al Mallakh, Elaine Murphy, Elizabeth Papp, Said Saffari, and Tarik Yousef, all Harvard students.

The Islamic Legal Studies Program at Harvard Law School played a central role in the work toward this book. Barbro Ek, Associate Director of the Program, and Denise Heintze, Staff Assistant, helped administer the multiple activities supporting our research and writing.

We received much valuable help from our research assistants. These included Indrajit Garai, Hashem Montasser, Abdullah Binladen, Dr. Hassan Osman, Newell Cotton, and Walid Hegazy.

Editorial assistance was provided by Deborah Kreuze, Richard Luecke, and Rachel Vargas.

Needless to say, while acknowledging the invaluable help of so many, the authors take full responsibility for the content of this book.

Frank E. Vogel
Samuel L. Hayes, III
Cambridge, Massachusetts

CHAPTER 1

Introduction

This book describes the field of Islamic banking and finance as practiced in the modern era. The dramatic growth of this unique form of commerce over the past twenty years coincides with expanding wealth in the Middle East and parts of Asia and with a turning away from secular Western practices. In Iran, Pakistan, and Sudan, Islamic banking is now the law of the land. In many other states, such as Egypt, Malaysia, and Brunei, it coexists and competes with Western-style institutions.

The commercial potential of this new field has not gone unnoticed; a number of major Western, Middle Eastern, and Asian financial institutions recognize Islamic banking as an important new opportunity for growth. These firms have established Islamic practices to serve this growing market. Mutual funds have also sprung up that — like socially responsible funds in the West — invest client monies in ways that do not conflict with the conscience or practical interests of Muslims.

To do business with Muslim clients, and to engage in cross-border financing, they need to be familiar with current Islamic financial practices and potential avenues of innovation. Students and scholars of Middle Eastern and Islamic culture will likewise benefit from understanding this important aspect of Islamic life.

What Is Islamic Banking and Finance?

The structure of Islamic finance is firmly rooted in the Qur'an and the teachings of Muhammad, and the interpretations of these sources of reve-

1

lation by his followers. In various forms it has been a constant of Islamic civilization for fourteen centuries. In the last three decades it has emerged as one of the most significant and successful modern implementations of the Islamic legal system, and a test case for future Islamic legal innovation and development. Nonetheless Islamic finance remains subject to a variety of misunderstandings by both Muslims and non-Muslims. For example, it is widely known that Islamic finance prohibits the charging of interest on loans. But most do not know that Islamic law does not reject the notion of the time value of money. The capital provider is permitted an adequate return. For instance:

- If money is committed to another party to use for a period of time, compensation for the financing may not be a predetermined amount guaranteed by the other party to the contract; instead, it should be a share in the actual profits of the venture. Money is not treated as a commodity, as in the West, but as a bearer of risk, and therefore subject to the same uncertainties as those borne by other partners in the enterprise.
- If investors finance the acquisition of tangible goods by sale or lease, they may legitimately compensate themselves for foregone opportunities. Profits deriving from lease payments or from credit sale may reflect, even explicitly, a time factor.

Given these ways in which finance is legitimately compensated, the term "profit banking" is a useful way to describe the system of credit extension in the Islamic world.

Islamic rules do permit businesses to utilize credit, and do not prescribe that all businesses be financed entirely with equity capital. Islamic businesses can and do utilize financial leverage in their capital structures, thereby exposing their owners to both the potential enhancement of returns on equity if things go well and to value reduction if results are disappointing.

There are many similarities between Islamic and conventional finance, since both deal with a common set of operating business realities. In most cases, Islamic and conventional finance simply travel different paths toward the same goal, but there are important differences. Consider these examples:

- Most businesses need long-term financing. In conventional finance, this is accomplished through some mix of long-term debt and owners' capital. In one Islamic solution, passive partners contract for a certain share of the profits, with another share going to the entrepreneurs who manage the business. This solution meets the concept of partnership required by doctrine and is similar to a conventional preferred shareholder contract. If the business does not want to dilute its ownership by bringing in partners, other options exist, such as leasing. A lease does not involve formal interest or a partnership stake, yet satisfies the business's need for long-term financing of plant and equipment and the investor's need to earn a fair return.
- Inventory financing is a requirement common to both Islamic and conventional commerce. An Islamic business in need of short-term inventory financing can purchase the inventory on credit, that credit being supplied either by the inventory supplier or a bank. The bank can purchase the inventory for the business based on the business's promise to buy the inventory later for cost plus a fair markup.
- Many businesses find it necessary to supply credit to their customers through accounts receivable. An Islamic business can do this but is not permitted — as in conventional finance — to refinance by pledging or selling those receivables because they are not real assets. Under Islamic law, financial assets cannot be sold or used as collateral. So the Islamic business either has to finance its credit extensions from internally-generated funds or arrange for a third party to buy the goods on behalf of its customers and resell them to those customers with a markup — just as the Islamic business would finance its own purchases from suppliers.

These are some of the simpler Islamic alternatives to conventional finance. These and a number of others are examined in detail in this book. To the outsider, some of these arrangements may seem to be elaborate subterfuges for conventional financial transactions. This conclusion would ignore a number of important subtleties with respect to intentions, the detailed legal incidents of the various transactions, the religious and secular constraints on banking practices, and the limited number of financial contracts currently available to practitioners of Islamic finance.

Even if in some cases variation from conventional practice is only nominal, one should not forget that in all religions even purely formal accommodations to piety can be of crucial importance. In any event, Muslim investors, religious advisers, and finance managers are expressing increased dissatisfaction with purely nominal or concessionary practices, and demanding more genuine investment vehicles. These demands are stimulating innovations that promise to make Islamic finance more robust and in step with the requirements of modern commerce. The prospects for these innovations are assessed later in this book.

THE ORIGINS OF ISLAMIC FINANCE

Islamic finance is not an invention of this century's Islamic extremist political movements but stems from injunctions found in the Qur'an and the sayings of the Prophet Muhammad. These inspired central tenets in the religious law of Islam concerning commercial dealings are as much part of the religion as is marriage. Islamic law has derived from revealed texts a web of interrelated norms prohibiting interest-taking and undue speculative practices. In medieval times, these were considered both sinful and illegal, and were duly avoided. The centuries-old practice of finance in Islamic form was largely eclipsed during the period of the European colonial empires, when almost the entire Islamic world came under the rule of Western powers. Under European influence, most countries adopted Western-inspired banking systems and business models and abandoned Islamic commercial practices. Thus, the modern period of Islamic finance traces its beginnings to the independence of Muslim countries after World War II.

The earliest recorded Islamic financial institution, the Mit Ghamr project, was established in Egypt in 1963, soon followed by the Nasser Social Bank in 1971. The next milestone is the founding, under the Organization of the Islamic Conference, of the multinational Islamic Development Bank in 1973. During the seventies many Islamic financial institutions were established in a number of countries — some public, some partly government-owned, and some private.[1]

The more recent surge of Islamic self-identity has provided another positive push for adopting Islamic principles in business and finance. Re-

---

[1]See Abdullah Saeed, *Islamic Banking and Interest* (Leiden: E.J. Brill, 1996), 5-16.

pelled by the politics and culture of the West, and inspired by religious piety, a growing number of devout Muslims seek greater conformity between their lives in the modern world and the precepts of their faith. Islamic banking makes that conformity possible in the realm of commerce.

The end of colonialism and a rising tide of religiosity may have sparked the revival of Islamic finance, but the great wealth generated through the oil boom fueled its growth. Dramatic increases in oil revenues throughout the 1970s brought an unprecedented degree of affluence and surplus savings to the populations of a number of oil-rich Middle Eastern states. Prior to that, only a handful of ruling families and the merchant elite had significant investable funds, most of which were directed to conventional Western investments that did not square with traditional religious principles. Since these practices were limited to a few individuals and largely unnoticed by the broader population, little was said about them, even by religious leaders.

The oil boom changed this situation dramatically. Quite suddenly, much more money was in many more hands, and the question of how believers should invest these funds became pressing.

GROWTH IN ISLAMIC FINANCING ACTIVITY

The actual size and rate of growth in the Islamic financing pool worldwide is difficult to measure. Size estimates range from $50 billion to more than $100 billion, excluding the financial assets of the three totally Islamic economies, Pakistan, Iran, and Sudan. One approach to measuring the size of the Islamic savings pool would be to aggregate the balance sheets of the important Islamic banks. Despite a number of complications which make this route unpromising, a comparison of the balance sheet footings for the leading Islamic banks for which numbers can be obtained shows a growth of more than 15 percent per year for the past five years. Furthermore, large sums of Islamically-directed savings in the hands of individual investors are not channeled through banks at all, but are invested directly in businesses. It would not be unusual for a bank in London (a major market center for Islamic finance) to place $100 million or more on behalf of a single wealthy individual.

There is general agreement that the funds currently handled by Islamic banks represent ready money — i.e., the funds of individual investors with strong personal commitments to religious principles. Ten or twenty years earlier, many kept their funds idle in non-interest-bearing accounts in Western banks. Others circumvented the conventional banking system altogether, keeping money in their homes. With this easily attracted money now accounted for, some bankers we interviewed believe that the current pace of growth will be difficult to sustain. In their opinion, future growth will depend on the industry's ability to attract the funds of savers and investors who currently opt for the superior returns and risk characteristics of conventional bankers and investment bankers.

There is, indeed, a rich lode of Muslim savings to tap; the experience of the Gulf War makes this clear. One knowledgeable observer estimated that more than $50 billion of savings fled the Gulf region during the Gulf War crisis of 1990-91. Most went to Swiss banks, which have long provided wealthy Middle Easterners with safety, discretion, and competitive returns. Little of that money had reportedly returned to the Gulf by the end of 1996. Attracting these and other funds will require the development of Islamic investment opportunities that offer competitive rates of return at acceptable levels of risk.

In the opinion of many, this will not happen within the context of the Islamic financial transactions as now practiced. Subsequent chapters will describe the current universe of these transactions. These are few in number and in many cases create difficulties for investors and capital users that conventional financial arrangements do not. Nevertheless, many anticipate innovations in these and other Islamically valid contracts that may surmount these difficulties.

FINANCIAL INTERMEDIARIES

As described earlier, the potential of the Islamic capital market has not gone unnoticed by financial institutions — either indigenous or foreign-owned — operating in countries with Muslim populations. A handful of large Gulf-owned Islamic banks (which often omit "bank" from their names to emphasize their Islamic character) dominate the current market. These include al-Rajhi, DMI (for Dar al-Mal, or "treasury" in Arabic), al-Baraka, and Kuwait Finance House. In addition, some indigenous and Western commercial banks have substantial Islamic operations, including National Commercial Bank, Saudi American Bank, Citibank, Kleinwort

Benson, Grindlays, the recently-merged Chase Manhattan Bank, and Bankers Trust. A number of these were initially reluctant to initiate Islamic deposit programs with profit-sharing structures for fear of cannibalizing their conventional account base in which some Muslim depositors were accepting no interest. This fear later proved to be justified. While the indigenous institutions appear to have the dominant share of Muslim deposits in the Gulf region at this time, fortunes may be looking better for some Western banks. Notable scandals and failures — and the political impact of the Gulf War — have cast a cloud over some domestic institutions. By comparison, Western operators enjoy an aura of deep pockets, geographic diversification, and reputations for sophisticated, reliable, and innovative banking.

It seems likely that Islamic bankers will continue trying to move away from the banking model of accepting short-term deposits and extending Islamically-acceptable commercial credit, toward more of an investment management role. This trend would certainly be supported by Islamic law, which generally favors equity investments over credit arrangements.

CURRENT BANK PRODUCTS

Compared to conventional investors, Muslim savers today have relatively few acceptable investment contracts from which to choose. These are covered in considerable detail elsewhere in this book. Our research indicates that most Islamic funds are confined to short-term, low-risk investments, principally in the form of trade financing for inventory accomplished through the markup (*murabaha*) contract described earlier, in which the bank buys inventory from the supplier to resell it to the customer at a price covering the bank's cost plus a markup. Investments are also scattered in profit-sharing partnerships called *mudaraba* and *musharaka*, and in leasing arrangements called *ijara*, but these represent a small portion of the total investment pool and historically are concentrated in the portfolios of more innovative vendors.

Although Islamic banking and finance are often referred to by Islamic economists and others as profit-sharing finance, it has already been noted that the bulk of Islamic funds are aimed at short-term markup deals with slim profit margins. A variety of explanations for this can be drawn from both field interviews and the existing literature. Perhaps the most frequently cited explanation is the fact that an Islamic bank has no central bank discount window to turn to when it needs quick liquidity, and no deposit insurance program to reassure savers and help prevent panic bank runs. Thus, longer-term investments (which are typically more profitable) create a worrisome mismatch between assets and liabilities, despite the formal requirement of advance withdrawal notice that Islamic investment depositors are supposed to give. As a practical matter, many Islamic investors expect the same instant liquidity (and yields) as conventional banks. Field interviews suggest that Islamic investors in the Gulf (including the Islamic banks) are more averse to risk than investors elsewhere. This may be attributable in part to shocks such as the collapse of the Souk al-Manakh (the Kuwait stock exchange) and the failure of BCCI, in which a number of Islamic banks and other investors maintained large deposits. Banks in these regions do sit on lots of nervous money, but their concern for liquidity seems overblown in light of the facts. During the Gulf War in 1991, for example, the Islamic banks in that region lost 40 percent of their deposits, yet in 1996 these same banks maintain 80-90 percent of their assets in short-term investments — twice their worst historical withdrawal experience.

Another explanation for caution is the limited capacity of these institutions to undertake the rigorous credit analysis required for more aggressive investing. It is understandable that they would be reluctant to enter into long-term investments unless they were confident that they understood the risks; lacking this confidence, it is natural to stick with short-term deals.

This short-term investment strategy of Islamic banks may be a dead-end, however. Profit margins in these contracts are simply too thin to support overhead and produce sufficient bottom-line profits to satisfy both depositors and bank owners. Typically, 70 percent of these profits go to depositors and 30 percent to bank owners, but in the current atmosphere, depositors at some Islamic banks have only been able to earn returns comparable to those offered by conventional banks at the expense of the bank's owners. A number of Islamic banks have had to subsidize profit distributions to depositors out of the bank owners' share of profits or, in some cases, out of additional capital infusions by owners, a situation which is clearly unsustainable.

If this bleak scenario is not sufficient motivation for bankers and investors to move to higher-yielding but riskier investments, recent pronouncements by respected Islamic scholars may provide it. A number of scholars have recently cast doubts upon the acceptability of one of the most widely used forms of Islamic finance: the type of *murabaha* trade financing practiced in London. These transactions involve, for the most part, trade financing deals between Islamic investors and well-known multinationals seeking lowest-cost working capital loans. Although these multi-billion-dollar contracts have been popular for many years, many doubt the banks truly assume possession, even constructively, of inventory, a key condition of a religiously acceptable *murabaha*. Without possession, these arrangements are condemned as nothing more than short-term conventional loans with a predetermined interest rate incorporated in the price at which the borrower repurchases the inventory. These "synthetic" *murabaha* transactions are unacceptable to the devout Muslim, and accordingly there is now a movement away from *murabaha* investments of all types. Al-Rajhi Bank, al-Baraka, and the Government of Sudan are among the institutions that have vowed to phase out *murabaha* deals. This development creates difficulty: as Islamic banking now operates, *murabaha* trade financing is an indispensable tool. It makes it possible for Islamic businesses both to make credit sales to customers and to obtain credit from suppliers for their own inventory and equipment purchases. There is currently no alternative investment contract that provides Islamic investors with the high liquidity and low risk profile they have been demanding. Because of this, Islamic businesses would be severely crippled if *murabaha* trade financing were prohibited.

So where will Islamic investors turn? To the extent that they opt for longer-term, higher-yielding investments, they show a preference for leases (*ijara*) over other contracts. Leases have some of the same advantages as sale in allowing recognition of the time factor in setting prices, and investors may regard leases as incorporating lower risks because the investor retains title to the property until the end of the contract. If there is a default, the property can be repossessed, thereby avoiding the cumbersome and debtor-partial rules that accompany a default under *shari'a* law.

THE IMPACT OF RELIGIOUS SCHOLARS

Islamic scholars have a profound influence on the day-to-day practice of finance; to our knowledge there is no equivalent in other religious cultures. For example, Islamic financial institutions generally maintain boards of scholarly advisors, called *shari'a* boards, to review all proposed transactions for conformity with religious law. The judgment of religious scholars is neither absolute nor uniform. In Sunni Islam four schools of Islamic jurisprudence apply Islamic teachings to business and finance in different ways. Disagreements on specific points of religious law occur both between these four schools and within them. Furthermore, *shari'a* boards sometimes change their minds, reversing earlier decisions.

The sophistication of *shari'a* boards has visibly increased as they have gained experience with modern financial concepts and their applications in contemporary commerce. In the early years, religious scholars were less familiar with the dynamics of financial markets and the impact of finance on business organizations and portfolio investment strategies. Not surprisingly, their pronouncements were cautious and often looked more to the form of financing arrangements than to intent or outcome. All parties to these contracts, in fact, were feeling their way along an unfamiliar road, and the terms of the financings were typically spelled out in elaborate detail, often with frequent referrals back to the *shari'a* board for clarification and approval on particular points of religious law.

Today, *shari'a* boards are more knowledgeable about modern finance and the practical requirements of investors and businesses, and they increasingly consider the intent as well as the letter of situations brought before them. The length and degree of detail included in many of these contract documents have shrunk, undoubtedly reflecting, at least in part, the scholars' enhanced understanding of the workings of the financial markets, and their increased comfort level with frequently-used Islamic contracts.

The more familiar Islamic scholars become with the actual workings of real-life finance, and the more knowledgeable business and investment professionals are about Islamic religious principles, the more likely that their collaboration will produce acceptable and innovative Islamic solutions to financial needs. Greater training for both *shari'a* board members and financial professionals will advance this collaboration.

GOVERNMENT INFLUENCE

Although the raison d'être for the practice of Islamic finance is undeniably religious, politics and national government policy also play important roles in determining how it manifests itself in the Islamic world. Government stances can be divided into several categories:

- those that have transformed their entire internal financial systems to an Islamic form (Iran, Pakistan and Sudan);
- those that embrace Islamic banking as a national policy while supporting dual banking tracks (Bahrain, Brunei, Kuwait, Malaysia, Turkey, United Arab Emirates);
- those that neither support nor oppose Islamic banking within their jurisdictions (Egypt, Yemen, Singapore, and possibly Indonesia); and
- those that actively discourage a separate Islamic banking presence (Saudi Arabia and Oman).

Following the revolution in 1978-79, the theocratic Iranian government called for an immediate transformation of the country's economy to one run according to Islamic principles, including a switch to a wholly Islamic banking and finance structure. The process has been difficult and has involved often cumbersome arrangements.

In Malaysia, civil disturbances in the late 1960s by Muslim ethnic Malays protesting the ethnic Chinese dominance in the commercial sector prompted a government program to redistribute wealth and concentrate more political power in the hands of Muslim Malays. Islamic traditionalists also inveighed against aspects of Western culture that had become part of the Malaysian scene. To placate these activists, the government initiated Islamic banking in parallel with conventional banking on a trial basis. Ten years later, it made Islamic banking a permanent part of the financial structure, and increasingly takes pride in its Islamic banking sector.

The tiny Sultanate of Brunei followed Malaysia's example in 1985 when the Sultan decreed an Islamic banking option. Although the government did not actually put an Islamic bank into operation until 1992, it has actively supported that bank and has provided subsidies that permit it to pay competitively attractive dividends to depositors. A profitable Islamic insurance sector has also been established.

In Turkey, President Ozal initiated Islamic banking in 1982 as a way of attracting deposits from Muslims in the oil-rich Gulf states. Turks have shown little enthusiasm for this Islamic alternative — less than 5 percent of total deposits are channeled there, and neither have the Turkish

Islamic banks attracted significant deposits from other parts of the Muslim world.

Egypt is usually credited with being the cradle of Islamic banking, since much of the earliest financing activity was centered there, but insufficient government regulation helped create conditions that led to massive fraud by certain "Islamic investment companies" in the 1970s, resulting in huge depositor losses. Since then, both government and savers tread a cautious path regarding Islamic banks.

In the last category of Islamic countries, Saudi Arabia provides an instructive example. It has actively discouraged a distinct Islamic banking sector, despite the fact that Saudi Arabia is a highly traditionalist Islamic religious state, and is the fountainhead of much of the private sector savings that fuel Islamic banking elsewhere in the Gulf. Its official position is that since it is an Islamic state, all of its banks are as Islamic as is feasible. To single out certain of them as Islamic would imply that the others are not Islamic. In reality, none of the Kingdom's principal banks follow the principles of contemporary Islamic banking and finance, except where they have been permitted to open Islamic windows to accommodate religious depositors. Some observers suggest that, in contrast to Malaysia which encourages Islamic banking as a constructive outlet for Islamic religious fervor, the Saudi leadership may fear that Islamic extremists would turn an Islamic banking base into a political weapon to disrupt the country.

One important government regulatory issue related to alternative banking systems is the relationship between bank liquidity needs, profitability, and the appropriate composition of the capital structure. Liquidity concerns have caused Islamic banks to be particularly cautious in their investment policies, to the detriment of bank profitability. The Bank for International Settlements has established minimum capital levels for conventional commercial banks around the world, but no such standards have been established for Islamic banks. Reserve requirements in Turkey, for instance, are set at 1 percent for Islamic investment deposits in contrast to the 10 percent reserve required for conventional bank deposits. This level may be insufficient.

In Malaysia, the Central Bank has set up a formal interbank lending facility along Islamic lines to deal with liquidity questions. Thus far it has not been tested because most of the banks taking Islamic deposits already have a surfeit of liquidity. In some other Islamic countries, governments have established informal means to provide assistance to Islamic institutions in a liquidity crisis.

THE POTENTIAL OF ISLAMIC BANKING AND FINANCE

No irreducible obstacles exist to the continued development of Islamic finance. This is not to suggest an absence of challenges. An important deterrent to continued growth in the Islamic banking sector is a shortage of investment outlets with acceptable risk/reward tradeoffs. Unlike conventional investors who can choose from a broad menu of debt and equity investments, Islamic investors who follow their religious principles have considerably fewer choices. We therefore give much attention to existing Islamic contracts and ways to expand their uses in either their original or modified forms, ways which in our opinion have good prospects for receiving the approval of *shari'a* boards.

One almost indispensable resource for accomplishing this is a secondary market capable of providing acceptable liquidity for investors. There is much debate about what kinds of investments can be traded in a secondary market. Islamic law forbids the sale or trade of financial contracts, which explains why financing of accounts receivable is difficult. On the other hand, if a contract or security represents a direct claim on a real asset, it may be sold or traded. Thus, if a common share is understood as a undivided share in the ownership of a company's assets, it may be eligible to be traded under Islamic law. An interest in leased property can also be traded because it represents a direct claim on an asset.

Given such interpretations, a number of Islamic securities could even now be traded. So why is there now no viable secondary market for any instruments in any part of the Islamic world? Interviews with bank executives and others suggest various explanations. For one thing, there is no generally accepted set of Islamic religious principles which can assure that such traded securities will meet the religious standards for all groups of Muslim investors. Additionally, a variety of accounting issues need to be clarified to establish just what an investor is paying for when he buys a publicly-traded instrument. Then, too, Islamic vendors appear reluctant to commit the capital and the overhead required to create such a market.

Thus, among the most obvious impediments to the future growth of Islamic banking and finance are lack of liquidity, a limited set of approved instruments, cumbersome transactional arrangements, and no ready provisions for risk management. But as the following chapters will show, none of these impediments is insurmountable. Innovation, driven by growing demand for Islamically-approved capital outlets, has the potential to create new forms that would satisfy capital users, investors, and religious requirements.

GOALS AND METHOD OF THIS BOOK

This book aims to give a fresh description of Islamic finance. We do not claim that this description is comprehensive. We do not attempt, for example, an institutional analysis of the industry, which would describe both Islamic financial institutions and the regulatory setting in which they operate in various countries. The focus of this book is largely at the micro level. Here we examine individual Islamic financial transactions using the disciplines of finance and of law, seeking to bridge between Islamic legal and financial theories and practices and those employed in conventional or Western law and finance.

While we try to portray the motivations and conceptions of Islamic banking and finance, this is no summary or abridgement of the existing literature. We do not attempt to make the final statement of either fact or interpretation on any issue. Rather we attempt to pose and seriously pursue a series of thought-provoking questions about Islamic finance — questions chosen for their power to reveal some of its differences and similarities, both conceptual and factual, with conventional law and finance.[2] Though our coverage is therefore partial, we hope that insights drawn from our study will enhance comparative knowledge of Islamic law, commerce, and finance.

Our sources include the available literature of Islamic finance (in Arabic and English) and empirical research. Given the nascent state of the field, statistical sources are frustratingly limited. We conducted extensive interviews with individuals involved in Islamic finance — in both private and public sectors, in both Islamic and non-Islamic financial institutions, in a number of countries — asking them for details about actual transactions, including documents, where possible. In some cases we were permitted to examine extensive in-house files on Islamic financial transactions. We also received helpful comments on drafts of this book from a number of persons, including those mentioned with gratitude in the preface.

We hope that responses to our work — now that it emerges in published form — will not only bring to light any mistakes of fact, interpretation, or evaluation we may have made, but more importantly lead to increasing the exchanges, still meager, between the insiders and outsiders to Islamic finance, both scholars and practitioners.

---

[2]Our method is further discussed in Chapter 3, 53–55.

This book seeks to maintain a respectful attitude toward Muslims' efforts to implement their faith and law. The last thing we wish is to cause offense in such grave matters, and we apologize for any lapses in this respect. This does not prevent us, however, from commenting as fairly and factually as we can on the successes and failures of Islamic banking, usually by reference to the field's own standards and aspirations. As religious sciences, Islamic jurisprudence and economics do not shun but seek the light of objectivity and fact. We trust, therefore, that participants and supporters of Islamic finance will not dismiss or mistrust our efforts, even as outsiders, to add something to that light. Again, we hope that this book at least makes the argument for enhancing objective, thorough-going exchange between participants in Islamic finance and outside observers.

PLAN OF THE BOOK

The rest of this book is divided into three parts. Part I (by Frank Vogel) is a comparative description of the Islamic law relevant to finance. While these chapters are a basic introduction to this subject, they also include detailed explorations of several issues that are on the controversial cutting edge of Islamic finance innovation. Part II (by Samuel Hayes) examines the relevance of a number of concepts, theories, and practices of conventional finance to Islamic finance, highlighting similarities and differences between the two bodies of practice. Part III draws on all the foregoing material to offer illustrations of possible future innovations in Islamic finance. These innovations serve as case-studies for testing the findings and conclusions of the book. Part III is followed by a conclusion.

PART I

The Islamic Law of Finance

Frank E. Vogel

CHAPTER 2

Islamic Finance as the Application of Islamic Law

One of the more striking facts about the rise of Islamic banking and finance is that it represents an assertion of religious law in the area of commercial life, where secularism rules almost unquestioned throughout the rest of the world. Even as adherence to Western-derived commercial laws is becoming more commonplace and advantageous, Islamic finance challenges these laws in two key respects: first, it challenges the presumption that modern commercial mores are per se more efficient or otherwise superior; and second, it challenges the secular separation of commerce from considerations of religion and piety. Islamic economics raises similar issues for the modern science of economics.

From the middle of the nineteenth century, nearly every Muslim country, under direct or indirect pressure from the newly dominant West, adopted laws and legal systems based on Western models, particularly in the civil and commercial sphere. Only a few (such as the future Saudi Arabia and other countries of the Arabian peninsula) were able to avoid the Westernizing tide and retain their traditional legal systems. As Muslim countries gained independence from Western powers in this century, they usually adopted codes paying deference to Islamic law. Even these, however, remained close in form and substance to Western codes. Only in family matters did Islamic law remain in force.

Far-reaching Westernizing changes in the laws and legal systems of Islamic countries were accepted by most Muslim religious scholars, but only on grounds of necessity. The scholars refused to lend them their prestige and cooperation, and struggled to preserve the principle of Islamic law's sovereignty over all spheres of life — even as practice flaunted the principle more and more. To a large extent, the scholars succeeded, and Islamic law remains — in faith if not in legal reality — the criterion for right action in Muslim life. Today, after further gains in independence, many Muslims call for restoring Islamic law as the law of the land. While for the religious this call is an expression of piety, it also reflects, among both religious and non-religious persons, a desire for authenticity and independence, and a rejection of Western "isms" in favor of the ideals through which Islamic civilization achieved past greatness. Even the non-religious can appreciate the need for laws that reflect the convictions of the people and engage their support. Islamic jurisprudence (*fiqh*) is one of the greatest achievements of Islamic civilization, and many believe that Muslims may retain it and still find their own way in the modern world. They can adopt from the West what is useful, but not at the cost of their cultural identity.

Best known for the call to reinstate Islamic law are the activist Islamic political movements, called "fundamentalist" in the West. Few in the West, however, recognize that the trend toward Islamic legal authenticity is far wider than these movements; it is a cherished wish even among many who reject or distrust the various political movements that rally beneath the Islamic banner.

The question of whether law should be secular or religious can represent a false dichotomy to the Muslim. To the believer, Islamic law is not merely an obligation of conscience, which if observed earns eternal reward; the law is also the best guide to human welfare in this world. To believers, God legislates for their well-being in this world and the next. As a law instilled by God in man and nature, obedience to it leads to social and individual success and happiness. Muslims often conclude that their current social, economic, and moral weaknesses are a consequence of their deviation from divine law in favor of Western ways.

Calls to return to the application of Islamic law emerged into prominence during the 1970s, seizing the world's attention most forcefully with the 1979 Iranian Revolution. Many Muslim rulers and governments responded to these calls with promises to bring domestic legal systems into accord with Islamic law, but progress has been slow, particularly in the fields of contract and commercial law. Concrete indications of legislative movement toward Islamic law are found chiefly in constitutional provisions recognizing *shari'a* as a "principal source of legislation," new civil codes in Jordan and the UAE hewing closer to Islamic legal doctrine, and statutes banning interest-lending between individuals. But no country —

not even Iran or Sudan where radical Islamic regimes rule — has abolished or revised all, or even most, of its West-derived laws and legal institutions. Clearly, if recognition by Muslim states of Islamic contract and commercial law is to continue to advance, it will do so gradually and without wholesale break with Western-style legal norms and methods.

Inertia in these matters of profound legislative change intensifies attention on those spheres of obedience to Islamic law that are voluntary, private, or individual. Observers report increased compliance with religious norms — prayer attendance; fasting; religious studies; abstinence from forbidden alcohol, dancing, and music; and modest dress and veiling for women. To Westerners, these behaviors are easily understood as indicators of religious piety. But Islamic law also lays demands on believers in spheres most Westerners no longer associate strictly with religion: family interactions (courtship customs, inheritance rights, gifts to heirs); social security and public welfare (alms-tax, strengthening religious education); social interactions (separation of the sexes, women not working); and, most importantly for our purposes, contract. Classical Islamic law offers a complete corpus of commercial and contract law intimately linked with fundamental religious precepts. Courts in most parts of the Muslim world have not applied that law for nearly a century and a half, but its precepts retain a claim on the Muslim religious conscience. Muslims are now turning in large numbers to Islamic banking and finance as the application of Islamic law by voluntary means, accomplished through contract and business association.

Indeed, as we shall see in the next section, the strictures of Islam in matters of commerce and finance are emphatic and far-reaching. The religious person cannot be unmoved by them, and one cannot overestimate the reserves of piety driving the desire for full compliance with them.

In sum, the surge in Islamic banking and finance is part of the much larger phenomenon of Islamic reassertion. Since the tenets of Islamic banking derive from fundamental principles of Islamic law, one may expect Islamic banking and finance to endure, as Muslims continue working out the significance of their faith for modern life.

Driven by these forces, Islamic banking and finance are the areas in which contemporary Islamic law is undergoing its most rapid and fertile development. A great many impressive advances have been made, and the pace appears to be increasing. Gains include:

- the training of a practical-minded cadre of scholars;
- new institutions and methodologies for legal development;

21

- new channels of international cooperation in Islamic legal research and opinion;
- new familiarity and respect for Islamic law in non-Muslim societies.

Work in this field provides a model for development in other difficult areas — politics, international law, and Islamic social sciences. The potential for long-range success in Islamic finance has great significance for assessing the potential of Islamic law to continue to shape the worldly life of Muslims.[1]

Many worldly interests propel the advance of Islamic finance. Here, money and power intersect forcefully with religion. A sense of impropriety or incongruity in such a conjunction is felt far less by Muslims than non-Muslims. After all, Islamic law is supposed to operate at the heart of struggles for worldly goods and authority, regulating them toward justice; it is not supposed to be some other-worldly ideal or purely personal value. As is proper, in Islamic finance, legal scholars and practitioners are not just irrelevant clerics; they are called on to decide real-world issues. Such demands invigorate and vindicate them and their work.

Legal development in Islamic finance advances also because of its relative distance from politics. Admittedly, Islamic banks have been drawn into political alignments, such as alliances with the Sudanese Islamic Front prior to the 1989 coup. In other instances, as in Pakistan or Malaysia, they are made to symbolize a degree of Islamization in the larger political and social order. But generally Islamic banking and finance infringe little on local politics. Islamic banking is advancing in countries of all political and religious colors: from total state-mandated systems in Pakistan, Iran, and Sudan; to Saudi Arabia where it is an unheralded but growing sector of the banking community; to Malaysia, Brunei, Jordan, Bahrain, UAE, Egypt, and a dozen other countries where Islamic banking is a specialty alongside interest-based banks; to Turkey, where it is expanding despite official secularism; to Denmark, where an Islamic retail bank has been chartered; to Europe and the United States, where Islamic banks from abroad carry out many forms of non-retail banking and business, and where conventional

---

[1] See Frank E. Vogel, "Islamic Governance in the Gulf: A Framework for Analysis, Comparison, and Prediction," in *The Persian Gulf at the Millennium: Essays in Politics, Economy, Security, and Religion*, ed. Gary G. Sick and Lawrence G. Potter (New York: St. Martin's Press, 1997), 249-295.

banks and investment firms increasingly compete to develop Islamic products. Only a handful of Muslim countries, notably Iraq (until the Gulf War) and Syria, are fearful of the symbols of Islamic identity, and only in these places has Islamic banking been wholly absent.

RELIGIOUS LAW (*SHARI'A* AND *FIQH*)

Islamic banking and finance seek to apply the Islamic religious law (*shari'a*) to a sector of modern commerce. This law — more than business organization, economics, politics, theology, or history — shapes Islamic banking and finance and differentiates it from its conventional counterparts.

Since the time of the Prophet, Muslims have understood that the means by which the believer earns God's favor, and with it salvation, is through obedience to the Divine Command as conveyed for all time in the words of the Qur'an, the divine book, and the Prophet's Sunna, or example. The latter, when conveyed by authenticated reports of the acts and words of the Prophet, is also taken as revealed, since God corrected the Prophet whenever he was in error. The Sunna is embodied in a great many written reports about the Prophet's lifetime (individually called *hadith*), each subjected to a careful process of authentication in various degrees. Thus the Sunna, like the Qur'an, ends up as a written text. From these two texts Islamic jurisprudence arises by interpretation, the interpretation carried out by persons considered sufficiently learned, called the "scholars" (*'ulama'*). The scholars labor to derive from the texts specific rules of behavior, indeed rules to govern all spheres of human life — from inward (e.g., worship, personal morality, family life) to outward (e.g., buying and selling, communal relations, political life, and international relations).

Islamic legal rules encompass both ethics and law, this world and the next, church and state. The law does not separate rules enforced by individual conscience from rules enforced by a judge or by the state. Since scholars alone are capable of knowing the law directly from revelation, laypeople are expected to seek an opinion (fatwa) from a qualified scholar on any point in doubt; if they follow that opinion sincerely, they are blameless even if the opinion is in error.

Note that a distinction is possible between the perfect, immutable Divine Law itself as revealed in the Qur'an and the Sunna, called *shari'a* (literally "the Way"), and the sum of human efforts to apprehend that law, some of which may be in error or at least in dispute, called *fiqh* (literally "under-standing"). For example, while God knows His perfect Law in its last detail, human beings often differ about that Law, particularly in details. Many schools of thought see little point in differentiating between *shari'a* and *fiqh*, since they believe that *fiqh* is the only valid means to know the *shari'a* and that any apparent flaws in *fiqh* are divinely intended. Yet the distinction remains useful and valid. The outsider who wishes to comment on Islamic legal phenomena in history without questioning either the perfection of Divine Law or the truth of Muslim beliefs may find it indispensable.

In what follows, when we refer to Islamic law we nearly always mean *fiqh*, not the *shari'a*. Within *fiqh*, moreover, we are usually concerned only with classical *fiqh*, by which we mean the law as constituted in the immense corpus of legal writings by religious scholars from the eighth to the eigh-teenth century (before the westernizing transformations). This law pro-vides a constant, in the sense of being authoritatively knowable. But, by using the term "classical" we do not imply that classical *fiqh* is hopelessly out-of-date; this would be to deny out of hand the very validity of the en-terprise that is the subject of this book. We also discuss modern *fiqh*, i.e., novel interpretations and applications of the *shari'a*, which undeniably differs from classical *fiqh*. It not only differs in content, such as in dis-cussing matters like heart transplants or commodities options, but also in method or process. For many traditionalist scholars, *fiqh's* methodology (*usul al-fiqh*), schools of thought (*madhahib*), and scholarly disciplines (e.g., deference to past scholars' views) continue without change, but a great many others recognize change even in these. We therefore need a term by which to distinguish modern and contemporary legal writings from writings predating the vast Westernizing transformations in Muslim law and legal systems.

RELEVANCE OF THE RELIGIOUS LAW TO BANKING AND FINANCE

Classical legal rules that appear to prohibit categorically this or that mod-ern practice — such as paying interest on bank deposits — pose a quandary for the devout Muslim. Are these rules out of date? Should a modern practice such as interest-based banking be assessed anew and per-haps declared benign? Indeed, should not Muslims live in the modern world with naturalness and common sense, without disfiguring their lives with antiquated rules? Or is the prevalence of a practice like interest-taking a modern corruption, a sign of the decadence and religious error of modern society? By indulging in the practice, is one not committing a sin with one's eyes open? One's only excuse may be the compulsion exerted by life in a system shaped by alien values.

Many Muslims have moved beyond this quandary, concluding that modern financial practices are not irreligious in and of themselves, even if they involve interest, insurance, pure speculation, and other practices not countenanced in the classical law. For such Muslims, the Qur'an and Sunna must be reinterpreted on these matters, and the teachings of the classical law not applied literally. Literal application of the classical law today is, for them, a denial of reality, a hopeless turning to the past, a reinforcement of reactionary tendencies, and a diversion of energy from genuine Islamic causes.

But such Muslims, though numerous, appear to be in the minority. A much larger number, supported by a near-unanimity of traditionalist scholars, seem certain that modern bank-interest falls within the revealed prohibitions and entails a major sin, tolerable only in the throes of necessity. For many Muslim societies, the case for excuse from strict rules due to necessity is compelling; for at least a century interest has been central to the blueprint of economy and society. But in other countries, notably the newly modernized Gulf states, such claims of necessity are less powerful, and have not dispelled a consciousness of sin. In Saudi Arabia and other countries, many bank customers refuse interest on their large cash deposits, producing a windfall for the conventional banks that hold those deposits. Similar concerns inhibit use of other modern commercial contracts, such as life insurance, which is banned in several parts of the Muslim world due to concerns over religiously prohibited risk-taking (*gharar*) and the belief that death is predestined.

But if some Muslims are certain what Islamic commercial morality demands, a great many others are not sure. Perhaps they have been partly swayed by the fact that a few '*ulama*' have declared bank interest permissible. A key concern for this group — and not an irrelevant one religiously — is whether banking and finance without interest are practicable in today's world. Whatever they believe, this is a swing group, which will embrace Islamic banking if it succeeds materially, but desert it if it fails.

Here one sees the failure of the Westernizing elites to convince the masses of the Islamic permissibility of imported laws and legal practices.

Islamic banking as we know it today would never have arisen if the classical law did not still command overwhelming authority and prestige. The growth of this new form of commerce is driven by the desire not to *replace* the classical law but to *apply* it. There is a feeling that the law has never been given a fair chance in modern times. This line of thinking dictates a legal conservatism in Islamic banking and finance, a conservatism probably greater than could be explained by the methodological tenets of its practitioners. Why revise Islamic law, as has been tried so extensively and in times of political and religious weakness, when its original provisions may be more desirable? Therefore the determinant in Islamic finance is, and is likely to remain, the classical law itself.

Islamic banking and finance are straightforward in asserting their differences with conventional forms. If a drastic liberalizing reinterpretation of the Qur'anic ban on interest and other strictures were broadly accepted by religious Muslims, Islamic banking and finance would have little purpose. Advocates do not dream of a future alignment with conventional practice, but of successfully asserting their difference with it. If necessary, they will create a permanently distinct sphere of finance. If their ways convert the rest of the world, well and good; otherwise Islamic finance will go its own way. In any event, if its interpretation of God's law is correct, Islamic finance should experience great worldly success, yielding moral, financial, and social rewards, thus proving to the world the superiority of Islamic norms. Its successes should not only be individual, but social, leading to a more just society, enjoying a fairer distribution of wealth, greater support for the poor and needy, and less corruption and dishonesty.[2]

---

[2]Many authors anticipate such benefits from adopting Islamic finance and related aspects of Islamic economy. See, e.g., Umar Chapra, *Towards a Just Monetary System* (Leicester, UK: The Islamic Foundation, 1985). Some of these authors must be disappointed by the mundane commercial nature of actual Islamic banks. Though the banks and their employees certainly profess aspirations to Islamically guided, socially responsible investment, it is doubtful how much more is done than is demanded by good community image. See, regarding the Jordan Islamic Bank, Fuad Al-Omar and Mohammed Abdel-Haq, *Islamic Banking* (London: Zed Books, 1996), 52-56. Some ordinary Muslims believe Islamic banks to be discredited when they are shown in practice to be not "religious" or "charitable" institutions but mere profit-making businesses.

At their deepest, these unresolved clashing perspectives on Islamic banking — profit-making under Islamic law versus agent for advancing Islamic virtue and welfare, — may align with two strains in contemporary "Islamism," i.e., activism to-

That Islamic finance is expected to lead to this-worldly benefits points up a nuance in how outsiders and insiders use the term "Islamic bank," "Islamic finance," and so forth. To Muslims, it can seem inappropriate, even offensive, that outsiders wish to term every novel finance and banking procedure engaged in by Muslims "Islamic." Even the terms "Islamic bank," "Islamic finance," or "Islamic investor" can seem unsuitable. Ideally, they would be replaced with "profit bank," "equity investor," and the like. If the Islamic laws that dictate norms for everyday conduct are truly God's, they reason, then they must reflect the true nature of man and the world and would benefit Muslims and non-Muslims alike. A non-Muslim labelling novel modes of finance "Islamic" (e.g., "an Islamic lease," "an Islamic stock option") implies a rejection of the rational and utilitarian arguments offered in their favor by Islamic economists and lawyers, and betrays a view that they arise only from the arbitrary dictates of an alien religion. Despite these objections, however, such terms are in frequent use. But when Muslim bankers, economists, and lawyers use the term "Islamic" for their financial techniques and institutions, the nuance is usually different. They are not saying that their banks or instruments should be associated with religious life in the same manner as, for example, prayer or almsgiving; they are saying that these activities, while practical and mundane, do not, unlike

---

ward achieving a more "Islamic" society and politics. One strain is utopian, radical, communitarian, populist, dismissive of things Western; in its extremes it can be violent, as in Egypt, Saudi Arabia, or Algeria, and revolutionary, as in Iran. Another strain is socially and politically conservative, seeking individual piety and social mores built around traditionalist compliance with *fiqh*, and looks to social and political improvements mainly as a result of that. Islamic banking outside Iran is far more characterized by the latter strain than by the former.

Noting this fact, one Western commentator sympathetic with the first strain denounces Islamic banking as mere marketing designed to enrich further a business elite born of government influence and largesse. It demonstrates the falsity of the second strain's promises to reform society, these being based solely on calls for individual virtue while ignoring socioeconomic realities. Olivier Roy, *The Failure of Political Islam*, trans. Carol Volk (Cambridge, MA: Harvard University Press, 1994), 140-46. The comment is apt in pointing to the micro, individualizing, conservative, traditionalist tenor in Islamic banking's approach to *shari'a*; it is not apt in failing to notice the degree to which this approach has enduring historical, social, cultural, ethical, religious, and even political significance for Muslim societies. For more on these differing strains of Islamism and the relevance of Islamic banking to them, see Vogel, "Islamic Governance."

their conventional counterparts, conflict with Islamic law. Any added flavor to the term reflects a call to community solidarity: that "Islamic banks," being enlightened by Islamic norms, should enjoy Muslims' support and patronage.

In sum, for many Muslims, Islamic financial institutions offer an invigorating escape from one of the more difficult quandaries of modern life. If they succeed economically, they relieve the practitioner of pangs of conscience while benefiting him financially. The success of Islamic financial institutions would be the harbinger of a host of other advances toward a more integrated Islamic way of life.

OBSTACLES TO THE APPLICATION OF THE ISLAMIC LAW

It is easy for the uninitiated to underestimate the difficulty of applying the classical Islamic law to modern commercial transactions. Some believe that the law's dictates can be summed up in a set of vague and general ethical and moral precepts, which do not entail any precise system of legal rules. In contrast, others expect that the legal restrictions are few, concrete, specific, and easily accommodated, leaving the rest of the field free for innovation and development. In either case, the outsider may expect to adapt Islamic finance easily to Western practices, simply by observing a short list of do's and don'ts.

Instead, on closer examination the outsider finds the applicable classical jurisprudence (*fiqh*) extraordinarily rich and complex. While this law does harbor profound general principles, it is not stated in those terms but as innumerable detailed rules. The rules and the principles are interconnected at a level rarely made explicit. Moreover, the rules and principles offered are not only legal but moral, defeating at times any hope of a legalistic precision.

These are some of the difficulties of grasping the classical law; others will be mentioned presently. But first consider the inherent difficulty of applying to modern phenomena a system of law that emerged in a wholly different time and social setting. (We emphasize that here we are discussing the system of the classical jurisprudence or *fiqh*, not the *shari'a* or Divine Law. To Muslims the Divine Law is timeless and always in application, if only in the fora of God's judgment and the believer's conscience.) In most parts of the Islamic world, Islamic law has been separated from legal practice and application in all but personal and private affairs for one hundred and fifty years. It is found in writings usually at least 500 years old. Even if it were to be applied at present, knowledge of how to apply it has entirely lapsed, among both laypeople and specialists — no one now alive has ever observed or used the classical commercial law in its entirety in actual commerce. Moreover, the scholars charged with interpreting the law no longer hold the influential positions held by scholars in the past — legislators, judges, officials, social leaders, and merchant-notables.

The societies and economies of all Muslim countries have been utterly transformed in the modern era. Most of the banking and financial transactions that now must be evaluated religiously did not even exist as such when the classical law held sway. The form and substance of every transaction is either altered or entirely new. Many concepts we take for granted today have no direct parallels from the past: the corporation, artificial personality, the share, the option contract, the bank deposit, documentary credits, non-possessory security interests, insurance, and many other tools of modern finance. Not only are the transactions novel, but the contexts in which they are applied are light-years distant from the contexts of the classical law. Consider changes such as the speed and security of modern communication and transportation; widespread monetary inflation; worldwide markets for commodities, currency, and securities; the anonymity of many commercial relationships; vastly increased governmental and regulatory power in the economy; or the transition from personal and confessional legal regimes to territorial and national ones. Were the classical scholar transported to our world, how many of his judgments (fatwas) would remain the same? Would not many of them be affected fundamentally by the surrounding system and context?

Clearly, adapting classical Islamic law to the modern financial world is a huge task. While a great deal has been achieved — for which a great many brilliant and hard-working scholars deserve immense credit — the legal elaboration of Islamic finance is still at a beginning stage. But the pace of progress is increasing. Finance is presently the most innovative area of contemporary Islamic law.

ISLAMIC LAW AND ISLAMIC ECONOMICS

Islamic legal thought about modern finance proceeds largely along two approaches, Islamic law and Islamic economics, neither of which solves all the difficulties just described. Both approaches are in a sense survivals of the classical law.

The first, Islamic law or *fiqh*, seeks to evaluate modern behavior in terms of the classical legal rules. The classical law arises from the advice of private scholars to individuals on particular events of their lives, and thus has an intrinsic private and micro focus. It is ultimately concerned with concrete individual actions, since it is these that have prime religious significance.[3] The classical law largely delegates concern for welfare at large, and all of the more systemic or macro aspects of Islamic life, to the state or ruler, who has a religious duty (*siyasa shar'iyya*) to pursue the public good within general Islamic principles. Modern legal writings on finance also view questions from a micro perspective, focusing on the particular terms of particular contracts (e.g., may an Islamic bank in its installment sales contract impose penalties on defaulting but solvent debtors?).

The second approach to Islamic finance, that of Islamic economics, is a novel discipline that seeks to develop from Islamic teachings an alternative to conventional Western economics — one that produces more beneficial economic outcomes, even as judged by the non-Muslim economist. Much of the concern of Islamic economics is with developing Islamic macroeconomic models, distant from the transactional focus of Islamic law. In contrast to legal scholars, Islamic economists usually mine the classical law corpus for fundamental Islamic principles: general legal rules (such as the prohibition of interest on debt), general moral precepts (such as opposition to fraud or corruption; approval of markets, trade, and commerce), and basic legal institutions (such as the alms-tax). Many areas in classical writings are instructive from this perspective: the rules as to charity (*sadaqa*), alms-tax (*zakat*), charitable trusts (*waqf*), supervision of markets (*hisba*), the fisc (*bayt al-mal*), public revenues, taxation, price-fixing, expropriation in the public interest, and social security (many of the these falling under the general heading of political governance [*ahkam sultaniyya, siyasa shar'iyya*]). From investigating such rules economists derive recommendations on macro matters (e.g., the institutional structure of banks or regulatory agencies; traits of an interest-free economy; modern Islamic taxation or social security; an Islamic stance toward consumerism).

---

[3]Most classical legal scholars do consider aggregate economic effects, but to a limited extent. First, they generally lack the tools to appreciate these effects, tending to see them only as individual benefits multiplied; and second, according to their formal methodology, utility or welfare (*maslaha*), individual or collective, is only a subsidiary consideration, helping to choose between two opinions deriving from other sources. Classically, most scholars decline to use utility as an independent basis for legal rules: either they reject it theoretically or delegate it to the ruler.

While Islamic law and Islamic economics operate in very different ways, both draw on the classical legal corpus. Insofar as Islamic economics addresses phenomena at the state, macro, and social level, instead of just the behavior of particular individuals, it fills gaps in the classical law and its characteristic method.[4] The two disciplines are becoming better acquainted, and even now are enriching and disciplining each other. Someday they may yield a single, fertile discipline governing Islamic economic activity. Islamic economics may develop theories and observations correlated closely enough to the reasoning, principles, rules, and particular judgments of the law as to provide legal scholars guidance and security in venturing reinterpretations of the classical sources. For the present, however, it is the classical law, with its micro, formal, transaction-based perspective, that most influences practices of Islamic banking and finance. It alone concerns us in this and the following four chapters.

STRUCTURE AND METHOD OF CLASSICAL LAW IN THEORY AND PRACTICE

Since classical Islamic law dictates the most distinctive traits of Islamic banking and finance, and most influences their innovation and development, it is useful to discuss its basic characteristics.[5] In the following discussion, and indeed throughout the book, we shall consider only the majority Sunni division of Islam.

---

[4]For a meditation by an economist on the relation of the two sciences, in which a fact-value distinction plays the key role, see Muhammad Anas Zarqa', "Tahqiq islamiyyat 'ilm al-iqtisad," *Majallat Jami'at al-Malik 'Abd al-'Aziz* 2 (1990): 3-40.

[5]There are several basic introductions to Islamic law, including Noel J. Coulson, *A History of Islamic Law* (Edinburgh: Edinburgh University Press, 1964); Joseph Schacht, *An Introduction to Islamic Law* (London: Oxford University Press, 1964); M.A. Abdur Rahim, *Principles of Muhammadan Jurisprudence* (London: Luzac & Co., 1911). A very clear, brief description of *ijtihad* and *usul al-fiqh* is Bernard Weiss, "Interpretation in Islamic Law: The Theory of Ijtihad," *American Journal of Comparative Law* 26 (1978): 199-210. The particular points made in this section are considered in more detail in Frank E. Vogel, *Islamic Law and Legal System: Studies of Saudi Arabia* (forthcoming, 1998).

Ijtihad, or Derivation from Revealed Sources

In Islamic conception, all law must be ultimately rooted in the Qur'an and the Sunna. While God is thus the true and only law-giver, in worldly terms those who determine the law are those skilled in interpreting the re-vealed sources, namely religious scholars (*ulama'*). According to these scholars, the Islamic law is to be found from the Qur'an and the Sunna by a qualified scholar employing the interpretive effort called *ijtihad* (literally, "effort"). *Ijtihad* observes a particular methodology, called "the roots of the law" (*usul al-fiqh*). In what follows we examine various aspects of the sys-tem of laws built on the conception of *ijtihad.*

Shari'a and *Fiqh*; Divergence of Opinion; Schools of Law

The English term "Islamic law" is ambiguous, translating two Arabic terms, *shari'a* (the divine law) and *fiqh* (human comprehension of that law). As explained above, *fiqh,* unlike *shari'a,* can be faulty, multiple, uncer-tain, and changing. Indeed, since the revealed texts are only finite and are often ambiguous, the norm is that *fiqh* rulings are uncertain and merely probable suppositions as to what God's law truly is. Indeed, on most points of doctrine *fiqh* writings record multiple opinions, all from qualified schol-ars. *Fiqh* rulings are taken as truly and certainly God's law only when they are established by a literal revealed text or when they have been agreed upon unanimously by all Islamic scholars of an age. The latter agreement is called "consensus" or *ijma'.*[6]

The theoretical prerequisites for *ijma'* are stringent, meaning that the doctrine lends certainty to relatively few rules, leaving almost everything no more than probable. In practice, however, scholars accord presumptive truth to propositions to the degree that past scholars have reached agree-ment, partial or complete, on them, with the result that the law has a work-able stability. While this was the classical practice, nowadays the authority of the past is less tenacious, and less conservative writers feel free to depart from the views of even a majority of bygone scholars.

---

[6]Scholars' constructions of *ijma'* differ. For some, no qualified scholar's view can ever be overridden by a later agreement. This gives more scope for variation than other positions on *ijma'* holding that an *ijma'* in a later generation disproves all the contra-dictory views of earlier generations.

This discussion yields two points useful in understanding and evaluating *fiqh* rulings:

- although there is general agreement on the general methodology and on many principles and basic conceptions of the law, the various schools of law (not to mention individual scholars) disagree frequently on particular rules; and
- where they disagree, none of their views can be declared wholly wrong.

While *fiqh* harbors a multiplicity of views on an issue, most scholars do not think this means that God Himself embraces multiple truths, or that the revelation is inadequate to guide humans to the single Truth. Instead, human beings simply fall short of finding the one truth due to the inherent difficulty of correct interpretation or *ijtihad*. Only one view is right, but no one except God knows with certainty what it is.

Such is the situation in theory. In practice, and to enable the application of the law, classical Islamic legal scholars introduced institutions and conceptions to narrow — for purposes of application of the law — the range of acceptable rulings. For the majority Sunni division of Islam, the most important such idea is the doctrine of universal "conformism" (*taqlid*) or the "closing of the door of *ijtihad*," the idea that scholars are no longer qualified to practice *ijtihad* (to interpret the Qur'an and Sunna for themselves) but must simply follow past scholars' views. This idea originated in the ninth century and became increasingly widespread as centuries passed. In practice, all scholars joined one or another of the established schools or "ways of thought" (*madhhab*). Sunni opinion became confined to four "schools of thought," the Hanafi, Maliki, Shafi'i, and Hanbali, all named after scholars living in the period roughly between 700 and 850 CE. These schools in turn progressively narrowed their positions over time, until at last in any one time and place one could know what position each school espoused on any issue. Thus, on a proposition of Islamic (Sunni) law one can usually list four positions, taking the most accepted one from each school.

The duty of conformism was not as absolute, however, as it is often represented. In every age eminent scholars continued to practice *ijtihad*, whether they or their contemporaries acknowledged it or not, and many scholars declared, against the trend, that *ijtihad* is a perennial duty for all who possess learning. Moreover, the scholars never claimed that school authority assures ultimate truth. As proper *ijma'* doctrine requires, all views on which there is no *ijma'* remain technically available and unrefuted. In recognition of this, and in order to make the record for *ijma'*, each school carefully preserved and handed down the opinions of earlier scholars, even when these were abandoned in favor of other views. Each school developed mechanisms to invoke weaker, abandoned, or minority views as alternatives to the standard views, usually when a view agreed with custom or the general welfare.

The Muslim layperson has always dealt with this diversity by following the rules traditionally followed in his or her family on ordinary matters, and by consulting the scholar he or she most respects on other matters. Institutions committed to Islamic law — including financial institutions — follow a similar approach, adhering to generally accepted views when possible, and consulting a particular scholar or board of scholars on all other matters.

So far we have described the law as it was handed down from medieval times. Modern law has introduced many changes in outlook. For one thing, the long-standing controversy over *ijtihad* and *taqlid* has drastically shifted ground. Nowadays most scholars agree with the medieval critics of conformism, and insist that the "door of *ijtihad*" is not closed and never was. Indeed, moderns do not think it necessary today to belong to a single school, in the sense of invariably following its precepts (although most have a single school in which their training was concentrated and in which they are most skilled). They argue that a scholar may adopt whatever opinion seems best on the grounds of its proof.

Four Methods of Elaborating the Law: Interpretation, Choice, Necessity, and Artifice

The legal rulings applied in today's Islamic banking and finance are, generally speaking, developed using one or the other of four different techniques.

The first and metaphysically most pristine technique is *ijtihad*, or derivation directly from the revealed texts of the Qur'an and the Prophet's Sunna, as discussed above. This method is increasingly being used in Islamic banking and finance, particularly when a legal instrument or ruling is considered novel, never considered by scholars of the past. For example, the scholars have found that the option contract has no counterpart in classical law, and so must be evaluated afresh using *ijtihad*. Indeed, the need for *ijtihad* is increasing as scholars move from everyday transactions to newer and more complex ones.

But the scholars animating modern Islamic banking are conservatives, and reluctant to diverge from *fiqh* on points of past broad agreement. As long as a new approach can be subsumed by a legal conception from the past (for example, if it can be understood as a lease or a sale), the rules of the past tend to be applied. Practically any new contract will overlap substantially with one or more contracts from the classical law, which after all incorporates the basic building blocks of commercial and contract law: property, sale, lease, loan, pledge, and so forth. In the case of options, after practicing *ijtihad* scholars declared them invalid and improper on the grounds that: 1) an option is more similar to sale than to any other contract type; 2) in the classical law of sale what is sold must be "property" (*mal*); and 3) the option right is not property according to the classical definition.[7]

Clear departures from old rules are extremely rare. Scholars rarely invent new terms, alter the definition of old ones, introduce new legal constructions, or criticize the methods or thought processes of the old scholars. They do not systematically refer to specific intervening changes in technology, institutions, economics, or law as guides or motives to review, amend, or replace old rules. They are mostly content to work with existing rules in ways that would be largely familiar to scholars of the past. Devotion to basic "principles" (*qawa'id*) of the Islamic law lends further stability. *Qawa'id* are general legal rulings, often stated as maxims, some found in Prophetic sayings, that classical scholars have identified, by a process of induction from many *fiqh* rulings, as sound generalizations about the law. Scholars consider these to be innate, systemic characteristics of *fiqh* which can hardly be altered without changing the whole edifice.

In Islamic finance *ijtihad* has not usually been employed for fresh inventions anyway, but for evaluating and modifying existing conventional financial or banking practices (such as the option contract above). In such cases *ijtihad* often takes the form of deciding whether the transaction can

---

[7]Decision 65/1/7, seventh session (1992), *Majallat Majma' al-Fiqh al-Islami* [Journal of the Islamic Fiqh Academy] 1: 711, 715 (hereafter cited as *Fiqh Academy Journal*). (Note: There is another Islamic Fiqh Academy of a similar name organized under the auspices of the Muslim World League, with its headquarters in Mecca. This Academy has not taken as prominent a role in *fiqh* deliberations on Islamic finance as has the OIC [Organization of the Islamic Conference] Academy.)

Options are further discussed in Chapters 5, 6, 9, and 10.

be reconciled with Islamic revealed texts and *fiqh* principles. As an example, by *ijtihad* the modern company or corporation with artificial personality and limited liability — an entity wholly novel to Islamic law — has come into common use.[8] Only in rare instances have concepts new to both Islamic and Western law arisen in response to the needs of modern Islamic transactions. One example is the provision of "Islamic insurance" by a sort of mutual aid society, to which Muslims make common "donations" agreeing to aid each other in the event of loss.

When faced with tough questions, scholars seek strength in numbers. They realize that to gain more acceptance for their opinions, and to deal with the many complexities of questions submitted, they must act in groups. The result is a modern innovation called "group *ijtihad*" whereby scholars gather in convocations to deliberate collectively and decide questions by majority vote.

A second method by which to reach opinions, instead of *ijtihad* directly from the Qur'an and Sunna, is the method of choice (*ikhtiyar*) among views already propounded by past scholars. This method has the advantage of aligning the modern scholar's view with that of a great scholar of the past, which at a minimum lends assurance that nothing about the opinion fundamentally offends *shari'a*, that no disastrous innovation is afoot. There are various subcategories of this method, according to the criteria of choice employed. One criterion, the most ambitious, reverts to the Qur'an and Sunna and to basic *fiqh* principles to decide which view offers the best or strongest interpretation of the revealed texts. A second criterion evaluates an opinion by the rules of decision internal to the school which espouses it, such as the degree of support from the school's founder or its consistency with other school holdings (e.g., there are "stronger" and "weaker" Hanafi views). A third criterion examines which view best serves the general welfare (*maslaha*, a conception including religious welfare), sometimes because it conforms to prevailing practices or customs. One argument for this last approach is that *fiqh* delegates freedom to act to those responsible for the general welfare as long as they do not offend fundamental principles of *shari'a*.[9] Note that this last approach is much less ambitious metaphysically than *ijtihad*, since its immediate choice of doctrines

---

[8]This although debate continues on some of the difficult *ijtihad* issues it poses. See Imran Ahsan Khan Nyazee, "Corporations and Islamic Law" (manuscript on file at Islamic Legal Studies Program, Harvard Law School).

[9]The classical term for this delegation of power is *siyasa shar'iyya*.

follows not from revelation but from changing temporal circumstance. Let us call this sub-method "utilitarian choice."

Quite often, a question cannot be answered simply by deploying the method of choice among single views of past scholars. Transactions are often complex, and to approve them scholars need to combine views of different schools on different parts or aspects of transactions. This can accentuate the need for independent *ijtihad*, since, as views are combined, issues never addressed by any past scholar come to the fore. Also, since schools do differ in their approaches to contract law, combining their views willy-nilly can distort or negate the chains of reasoning by which the schools justified their views, requiring the modern scholar to look again at the underlying justifications for the composite positions using the revealed sources and *fiqh* principles. The result can be a method halfway between *ijtihad* and choice, in which a modern scholar's *ijtihad*, immensely respectful of the past, tries to weave appropriate modern solutions from the threads of old opinions. Such a scholar may draw simultaneously on all the three sub-methods of choice just noted. If this is done improperly, merely mechanically, it is referred to disparagingly as "patching" (*talfiq*). To give an extreme (but historical) example of patching, one might combine one scholar's view prohibiting X, and another scholar's view permitting X, to yield a novel third view by which X is allowed only under certain conditions.

In Islamic banking and finance, choice is the method most commonly in use. Usually modest in their claims to practice *ijtihad*, scholars most often say they practice only utilitarian choice.[10] They use this technique across all the four Sunni schools, and sometimes beyond. They claim not to practice "patching," though they sometimes accuse each other of this.[11]

Paradoxically, choice, especially utilitarian choice, is more likely than *ijtihad* to liberalize, because of scholars' conservativism in using *ijtihad*. It has sanctioned changes that from a comparative legal perspective hold the potential to transform Islamic contract and commercial law. Note that if

---

[10]The religious consultant of the Kuwait Finance House, Badr 'Abd al-Basit, affirms that he never offers an opinion of his own as long as a classical view "whether from near or far" is available. When nothing in classical opinions is relevant, he turns to general principles (*qawa'id*) of Islamic law, particularly the pursuit of welfare. He says nothing about *ijtihad*. Oddly, this discussion is preceded by mention of how many modern economic transactions are novel and unknown to past scholars. Bayt al-Tamwil al-Kuwayti [Kuwait Finance House], *al-Fatawa al-shar'iyya fi al-masa'il al-iqtisadiyya 1979-1989* (Kuwait: Kuwait Finance House, n.d.), 1: 5-13.

[11]E.g., as to *murabaha li-amir bi-al-shira'*. See 140-143 and referenced sources.

one were systematically to single out the scattered opinions of past Islamic legal scholars that align with Western contract law, removing them from context, one might construct, "patch" together, a *fiqh* of contract identical to Western contract law. Adopting extraordinary views can erode the Islamic system's internal logic, making it increasingly susceptible to the pull of conventional legal theory and practice. This has not as yet occurred, but the force of this seemingly modest method should not be underestimated. In Islamic and other legal systems, minor steps such as small shifts of definition, or uses of legal fictions to cast novel practices as old laws, have wholly transformed the law in practice and eventually in theory.[12]

We shall see a number of instances of potentially radical change in the following sections. For example, respect for the opinions of Ibn Taymiyya, a fourteenth-century Hanbali scholar with strikingly modern-sounding views, is a pervasive influence on the modern law. If his opinions were adopted without reservation, especially as he emphatically states them, the results would be revolutionary. Similarly, modern *fiqh* opinion is strongly attracted to the idea of the binding promise, a concept basic to Western laws but recognized only exceptionally by classical Islamic law. This might provide a basis for contractual obligations independent, and subversive, of the classical law's regime of contract types. Another example is the idea, in play already, of importing into contract law tort conceptions of damages for wrongful acts to create liabilities for breaches of representations or promises that classically are not binding.

A third method of deriving rulings, still lower in metaphysical status, permits one to adopt as a ruling any position, even one contravening a categorical *shari'a* rule, when one is compelled by stark necessity (*darura*). The necessity must be of great severity, usually life-or-death. The basis for this approach is the Qur'an's frequent recognition that a person driven by necessity may eat otherwise forbidden food (e.g., 2:173), and also its disavowal of any divine intent to cause mankind hardship or to press it beyond its capacity (e.g., 2:286). A version of the doctrine holds that a mere "need" (*haja*), if it affects many, may be treated like a dire necessity affecting only one.

Scholars in Islamic finance and banking have invoked necessity to permit exceptional relaxations of rules. They have issued fatwas (opinions) allowing Islamic banks to deposit funds in interest-bearing accounts, par-

---

[12]See Lon Fuller, *Legal Fictions* (Stanford, CA: Stanford University Press, 1967); Baber Johansen, *The Islamic Law on Land Tax and Rent* (New York: Croom Helm, 1988).

ticularly in foreign countries, because these banks have no alternative investments at the necessary maturities. Typically, however, they place conditions on such fatwas, such as requiring that the unlawful gains be used for religiously meritorious purposes such as charity, training, or research. Such fatwas are particular to the circumstances in which they are issued. If conditions change, or if an alternative to the necessary evil arises, the scholars require that the practice end.

Classical Islamic law indulged in a fourth method of attaining desired legal outcomes: the legal artifice (*hila,* pl. *hiyal*). The foundation of this method is a formalistic approach to contract, in the sense of a concern for the external form of transactions instead of the parties' substantive intentions. All classical scholars found *hiyal* acceptable when they were merely clever uses of law to achieve legitimate ends. For example, a landlord, worried about a tenant cancelling unfairly, might stipulate payment of the bulk of the rent early in the lease term. But other *hiyal* were frank subversions of the law's basic rules and principles. A famous example is the ancient double-sale (*'ina* or *mukhatara,* in Europe called *mohatra*). In this deal a borrower and a lender arrange to sell and then resell between them a trivial object, once for cash and once for a greater sum on credit, with the net result being a loan with interest.[13] In another example, a lender sells a borrower an object for an exaggerated price and then immediately lends him money.[14] A third example, quite widely accepted classically, is the "sale with right of redemption," or *bay' al-wafa',* by which the borrower, who owns certain property, sells that property to the lender, leases it back, pays rent on it (equalling interest), and then invokes a right to repurchase the property for the original sale price.[15] Schools vigorously differ on these subversive artifices, their views falling across a spectrum: the Hanafis and Shafi'is often declare them valid although immoral (in many cases scholars declare them not even immoral), but the Malikis, and even more consistently the Hanbalis, condemn them altogether.[16]

---

[13]In the Hanafi school the dominant position was that such a sale is permissible. See *al-Fatawa al-hindiyya* (large compendium of Hanafi law legal opinions current in India, compiled in 17th century) (Beirut: Dar Ihya' al-Turath al-'Arabi, 1980), 3:208; Muhammad Amin Ibn 'Abidin (d. 1836), *Hashiyat radd al-muhtar 'ala al-durr al-mukhtar sharh tanwir al-absar* (Cairo: Mustafa Babi al-Halabi, 1966), 5:273.

[14]*al-Fatawa al-hindiyya,* 3:202-203.

[15]*al-Fatawa al-hindiyya,* 3:209.

[16]Yvon Linant de Bellefonds, "Volonté interne et volonté déclaré en droit musulman," *Revue internationale de droit comparé* 10 (July-Sep. 1958): 510-521.

In modern Islamic banking, artifices of the latter type are in acknowledged use mainly in Pakistan, where the most common transaction of all ("markup" financing) is the *'ina* sale. For example, a firm seeking inventory financing sells its inventory to the bank for cash and simultaneously repurchases it on credit; the parties never even bother to identify the inventory.[17] Apparently Islamic banking in Malaysia employs the same approach.[18] Despite condemnation by the OIC Fiqh Academy,[19] *bay' al-wafa'* has reportedly seen use even in the Gulf. Contemporary scholarly opinion disapproves of such techniques. Nevertheless, deals distinguished from conventional counterparts by little but their form do take place, leading one to ask whether the classical religious debate about *hiyal* needs to be reopened. In any event, it is sometimes difficult to decide if a particular artifice merely overcomes inconvenience in the law or wholly defeats its purposes, or when certain technical differences between one transaction and another unlawful one should preserve the former from condemnation. Such line-drawing exercises are hardly unknown in other legal systems, as, for example, in lawyerly schemes to get around obstacles or burdens under tax or securities laws.[20]

The above techniques describe a hierarchy of responses a scholar may make if asked to legitimize a transaction useful for Islamic banking or finance. First, the scholar may evaluate the transaction exercising his *ijtihad*, his own best understanding of the divine law of contract. Since, however, the authoritative scholars tend to be conservative in their use of *ijtihad*, they use this approach only for wholly novel elements of contracts, where *ijtihad* is unavoidable. The second level in the decision hierarchy is to choose from among past opinions ones that, without deviating from fundamental principles of the law, advance the interests or utility of Muslims in financial transactions. Third, if a transaction cannot be rendered lawful

---

[17]National Bank of Pakistan contracts on file with Harvard Law School, Islamic Legal Studies Program.

[18]Ismail Onn, "Development of the Islamic Capital Market in Malaysia," in *Symposium of the Malaysian Experience in Islamic Banking* (Kuwait: High Consultative Council for the Completion of the Implementation of the Islamic Shari'a, 1996), 7.

[19]Decision 68/4/7, seventh session (1992), *Fiqh Academy Journal*, 557.

[20]A good example is the difficulties for tax purposes of drawing lines between leases and installment sales. See, e.g., US Internal Revenue Service, Rev. Proc. 75-21 (Jan. 1975) on leveraged leases (with gratitude to Prof. Reuven Avi-Yonah, Harvard Law School).

under prior opinion, and if necessity still demands its use, there is the alternative of allowing it, but only to the extent and for the duration of the necessity. The fourth approach, that of artifice, is generally condemned, though practiced in Pakistan and Malaysia.

Given all these options, in evaluating a report that a scholar (or board of scholars) has permitted transaction X, one should not conclude that transaction X is "Islamic" for all parties and for all time. The *ijtihads* of different scholars may legitimately vary. Moreover, if the fatwa is based on utilitarian choice, assessments of utility can change with place and time. And, lastly, a fatwa might rest on nothing more than temporary, and changeable, necessity.

One result of these diverse and often changeable opinions is that Islamic financial institutions differ in the practices they follow. These institutions would certainly benefit from greater uniformity of scholarly opinion, for example, in enhancing cooperation in secondary financial markets, joint investments, or syndications; consumer confidence (religious and secular); and full disclosure. The diversity of opinion probably is due less to specific disagreements in legal reasoning than to differing degrees of strictness in general; for example, one bank is well known for charging customers penalties for late payments, but other banks consider this practice usurious. Strictness varies strikingly with geographical region; for example, practices in Saudi Arabia are reputed to be far stricter than practices in Malaysia or Pakistan.

Ethical and Legal Consequences of Islamic Legal Rulings

Another point essential to understanding Islamic legal opinions is that Islamic law is the arbiter of not only legality but also virtue and vice. An Islamic judgment falls into a scale of five values: 1) prohibited (*haram*), 2) reprehensible (*makruh*), 3) indifferent (*mubah*), 4) meritorious (*musta-habb*), and 5) obligatory (*wajib*). All these values have consequences both in worldly legal matters and in the reckoning of the Hereafter. Values 2, 3, and 4, from a worldly legal standpoint, entail permissibility and are given their legal effect. Values 2 and 4 do have additional moral consequences, but these are left to the Hereafter. Value 1 acts are not only sins, but are in this world ordinarily legally invalid or void, as well as punishable. Value 5 acts are not only virtuous acts, but are also ordinarily not only valid and enforceable but also compulsory, their neglect being punishable. But there are some exceptions to all these results. Some prohibited acts (value 1) are legally valid (e.g., in some schools, employing subversive artifices [hiyal]), while some obligatory acts (value 5) are denied legal validity and recognition (e.g., in some schools, a wife refusing to cohabit with a man who, as she knows but cannot prove, established marriage with her by procured witnesses). Many deeds are obligatory in conscience but cannot be enforced by a judge (e.g., unilateral promises; certain alms-tax obligations; atonement for vows and oaths). The moral and the legal in Islamic legal rulings is sometimes difficult to disentangle.

In what follows, transactions declared "invalid" or "void" are usually also "prohibited" (haram) and a sin. (In our contexts the reasons for invalidity and sinfulness are usually violations of revealed prohibitions against either usury [riba] or risk or uncertainty [gharar] or both.) Morally, gains from such a contract should not be put to one's use; at best they can be given away in charity. In secular legal terms, the most common consequence of a violation of Islamic law is that the contract between the parties is or becomes void and unenforceable. At the suit of either party (usually a party disappointed by the outcome of a deal), an Islamic court will give a judgment that, to the extent feasible, restores the parties to their state before the contract was made, by returning their respective performances or payments. Sometimes not the whole contract but only a single term is voided. This sometimes results in a shift in the balance of the bargain between the parties. For example, a party may bargain hard for a particular term in a contract, e.g., a guarantee by the other party of a level of profits. If that term is later declared void by an Islamic court or arbitrator, the losing party ordinarily gets no compensation for its loss, such as by an adjustment in the price.

The Casuistic Style of Classical Islamic Legal Reasoning

The way the classical law grounds its rulings in the Qur'an and the Sunna is key to understanding many aspects of Islamic banking and finance. A problem the law addresses is that the style of the revealed texts does not lend itself to promulgating general legal rules or principles. Qur'anic verses were revealed in relation to specific events during Muhammad's prophethood. Most of the legally significant verses declare certain actions prohibited or obligatory in general terms (e.g., drinking wine, paying alms-tax), posit general moral principles (e.g., "do justice," "be true to your trusts"), or lay down a few specific rules (e.g., how an inheritance is to be divided).

The Sunna, far more voluminous, contributes enormously to the interpretation of the Qur'an, but follows a similar style. Legal utterances of the Prophet are mostly either very general or very specific, and often relate to a particular event. Perhaps because of the concreteness of so much of this legal material, Islamic law decided not to treat the specific revealed rulings as mere implementations or instances of other more general laws that God intended to reveal through them. Taking such an approach would, in almost all scholars' view, introduce too great a human element into the divine message. Rather, the law strove to take the literal rulings as the divine law, and to minimize the role of fallible human reasoning in elaborating and applying them.

How to do this awakened much controversy in early centuries, but in the end scholars settled on analogy (*qiyas*) as the most defensible legal method. According to this doctrine, a divine law revealed for one event can be applied to another event only if some common feature is found to exist in both events. Of course, analogy can become a powerful tool for rationalization, potentially equal to reasoning by induction to general rules or principles which, we have noted, Islamic law has rejected. Muslims endorsed only a modest analogical method, merely the linking of a particular novel case to a particular revealed judgment on the grounds of some shared external trait. Such a method results in a casuistic law — i.e., one elaborated as a series of rulings for each imagined case — rather than in a rational or hierarchical system of rules. For example, from the Qur'anic ban on drinking "grape wine," various scholars selected the following traits as the basis for analogies: grape beverage; grape, date, or raisin beverage; drink from steeping fruits; drink after fermentation and settling; intoxicating liquid. Only a few scholars identified as the rule the one which is most general and most rational: intoxicating substance. Other human sources of law, such as utility or custom, are in formal theory subordinate to analogy, invoked only to choose one possible analogy over another. Note that wholly absent from this schema is any notion of legislation by the state or other worldly authorities.

It is likely that many all-embracing general legal theories and conceptions were employed in the early development of the law. But after the formalization of the law's methodology such forms of interpretation retreated to the background, yielding pride of place to strict analogical method. Only in specialized works (e.g., *qawa'id*, *furuq*) were general inductive propositions discussed at length. In such works principles are not presented as the law, or even as its source, but as mere useful generalizations about the law.

The result of all this is that the legal method of the classical law is daunting to the outsider — atomistic, multifarious, scholastic. These traits hobble comparison with modern laws based on Western models. Westerners studying the classical law may feel perplexed by its multiplicity, and conclude that behind the details there must be some fixed system that instead is "the law." They are wrong; such a system does not exist.

Modern Reinterpretations

Intensive efforts have been made in the last two centuries to reform and renew the classical law, departing from new intellectual bases and using different methods.[21] Important in all of them is an increased interest in the utility and legal rationality of law.

Simplification and Rationalization. One form of reinterpretation of Islamic law is simply to restate its rules and principles in the fashion of Western law (particularly the civil legal systems of Europe), using Western terminologies and Western intellectual tools and methods. For decades, writers — among them lawyers, economists, and bankers — have made major contributions to this comparative legal task. Famous lawyers, whose work has been critical for modern Islamic finance, include 'Ali al-Khafif, 'Abd al-Razzaq al-Sanhuri, Muhammad Abu Zahra, Mustafa al-Zarqa', Subhi Mahmassani, and others.

While such restatements generally do not seek to change the law, but merely to simplify access to, and to generalize about, its holdings, less diligent work along these lines, usually by non-lawyers, does introduce many misunderstandings. Some authors seem to think that the complexities of

---

[21]See, e.g., A. Merad, "Islah," pt.1, *Encyclopedia of Islam*, 2d ed.

the classical *fiqh* can be replaced with a few basic rules or principles, or that *fiqh* is just the wordy elaboration of a handful of general propositions. Among the propositions — *all wrong* — often presented as summing up the Islamic law on banking and finance are the following:

- rules on usury (*riba*) are to prevent exploitation of the weak;
- Islamic law denies the opportunity costs of capital, or denies the value of time;
- the prohibition of "risk" (*gharar*) is to prevent "speculation";
- gain is lawful only when accompanied by substantial risks.

Again, as statements about the classical law, these propositions are *incorrect*. They cannot be taken as the law itself or as adequate predictors of scholarly opinions. To endow them with legal force would be to replace the classical law with something else, and also to disregard the great wealth of interpretation found in the classical writings.

Not all such simplifying reinterpretations undermine Islamic banking and finance. Many of them are used daily by practitioners of Islamic finance as rules of thumb to guide and organize their work, and to attempt to predict and understand the workings of their *shari'a* review boards. Others are invaluable to economists as the tools from which to construct theories about the as-yet-unrealized Islamic economic system. Still others offer potential sources of critique of Islamic banking, should its micro-legitimated practices lead to macro injustices, such as the aggrandizing of the wealth of a few or increasing the cost or difficulty of credit for the poor.

At present in Islamic banking circles there are two highly divergent understandings of Islamic finance: one, a simplified and rationalized system employing Western economic and financial conceptions and a highly generalized understanding of Islamic law; and the other, the classical legal method. The two approaches correspond to the background and persona of their users: respectively, Western-trained experts in finance and economics, and traditionally-trained *ulama* or religious legal scholars. (Only a few famous leaders can combine the two areas of expertise.) A certain cacophony results when discussions go on simultaneously in both idioms. At its worst, the methodological divide between them engenders a communication gap that blocks progress and perpetuates certain mistaken ideas about *fiqh*. Narrow interests of the group can also cause gaps: for example, bankers may wish to keep *shari'a* review abstract and distant from nuts-and-bolts while scholars may want to preserve *fiqh* from manipulation by the uninitiated.

Change in the Law. Modern reinterpretations of *fiqh* also seek to make changes in the contract law. A central topic has been reinterpretation of the Qur'anic ban on usury, which is fundamental to everything that follows. In the 1930s, Syrian scholar Marouf al-Daoualibi suggested that the Qur'an bans interest only on consumption loans, not investment loans,[22] and in the 1940s Egyptian jurist al-Sanhuri argued that the Qur'an sought chiefly to ban interest on interest.[23] A more extreme and recent example is the opinion of the mufti of Egypt, Shaykh Muhammad Sayyid Tantawi, who in 1989[24] declared that interest on certain interest-based government investments was not forbidden *riba* (because the gain is little different from the sharing of the government's profits from use of the funds or because the bank deposit contract is novel), thus joining the thin ranks of prominent religious figures who have issued fatwas declaring clear interest practices permissible.[25] This fatwa aroused a storm of controversy, with opposition from nearly all traditional religious scholars and warm praise from secular modernizers. Later he went even further, saying that interest-bearing bank deposits are perfectly Islamic, and more so than "Islamic" accounts that impose disadvantageous terms on the customer. Laws should change the legal terminology used for bank interest and bank accounts to clarify their freedom from the stigma of *riba*.[26]

It must be recognized, however, that no such reinterpretations have as yet gained a mass following among Muslims, and all have been rejected by

---

[22]M. Daoualibi, "La Théorie de l'usure en droit musulman," in *Travaux de la semaine internationale de droit musulman*, ed. L. Milliot (Paris: Receuil Sirey, 1953), 139-142.

[23]'Abd al-Razzaq al-Sanhuri (d. 1971), *Masadir al-haqq fi al-fiqh al-islami* (Cairo: Dar Ihya' al-Turath al-'Arabi, 1967-1968), 3: 234-244. On the genesis of this opinion, see Chibli Mallat, "The Debate on Riba and Interest in Twentieth-Century Jurisprudence," in Chibli Mallat, ed., *Islamic Law and Finance* (London: Graham & Trotman, 1988), 69-88.

[24]*al-Ahram*, 8 Sept. 1989.

[25]Chibli Mallat, "Tantawi on Banking Operations in Egypt," in *Islamic Legal Interpretation: Muftis and their Fatwas*, ed. M. Khalid Masud, Brinkley Messick, and David Powers (Cambridge, MA: Harvard University Press, 1996), 286-296.

[26]See, e.g., *Akhbar al-yawm*, 22 Feb. 1997, 1, 3.

the overwhelming majority of religious scholars. In the short term, these reinterpretations may afford some ease of conscience for those forced (or eager) to follow conventional practices. In the longer term, they provide precedents for other scholars of permissive views. But the Islamic banking and finance industry vehemently rejects such attempts, since that industry is built, as noted above, on the idea of applying the classical law, not replacing it.

THE CONTEXT FOR ISLAMIC LEGAL DEVELOPMENTS IN ISLAMIC BANKING AND FINANCE

Modern Islamic Legal Institutions

We noted earlier that the Islamic legal system was dismantled during the eighteenth and nineteenth centuries and replaced by systems drawn mainly from the West. This transformation had two far-reaching effects on the context in which Islamic law operates. First, and most obviously, Islamic law is no longer recognized as the law of the land in many Islamic countries. Outside the sphere of family law, Islamic law is now enforced chiefly through personal or communal means, and not by the state. Second, the transformation weakened or abolished the institutions governed by Islamic legal scholars, official and private, through which Islamic law was authoritatively taught and studied and through which legislating (by giving fatwas and judgments and by advising the government) was achieved. Even the "schools of law" that once dictated legal thought and action are now important chiefly as vehicles for organizing legal education and for the study of past views. Thus, one of the challenges to the persistence of Islamic law is the absence of institutions that could lend stability and authority to its prescriptions.

With their institutions weakened, their worldly sway greatly eroded, their expertise seemingly remote from much of contemporary life, Islamic scholars have lost much of their means to exert authority, and this at a time when Islamic law faces greater challenges than in any era since its early centuries. Though many scholars enjoy great respect among the religious, and a few have international renown and huge followings, they cannot claim for their opinions on law any conclusive effect, even among the faithful. One problem is that few scholars have expertise in both the classical law and in modern sciences and arts, and this often shows in their opinions. Indeed, what is often most cherished about a scholar is his firm resistance to modern ways, even at the cost of familiarity with them.

Scholars have made many adaptations to cope with these difficulties. One is to acknowledge the need to consult with experts in other fields before reaching any decision to which those fields are relevant. A second response is the convening of groups of scholars for *ijtihad*, as mentioned above. These two ideas have contributed to important institutional innovations, particularly the creation of *fiqh* convocations or academies, both national and international. There are now three or four *fiqh* academies of major significance, the most important of which is the Islamic Fiqh Academy in Jedda formed under the auspices of the Organization of the Islamic Conference (OIC).

The Academy meets annually in various locations; its members are scholars appointed by member-states of the OIC. The Academy itself appoints a number of consultants, among them scholars of Islamic law as well as specialists in areas relevant to decisions, such as the natural sciences, law, economics, finance, and banking. In advance of the meetings, members and experts prepare studies for subjects on the agenda, which they then present. After debate, a decision by majority vote of those present states the Academy's Islamic legal opinion or fatwa on the issue. The reports and debates, as well as the fatwas, are published in the journal of the Academy.[27]

The Academy concentrates on pressing Islamic legal issues, most of them involving modern scientific, technological, and institutional innovations. The topic most preoccupying the Academy in recent years has been Islamic finance and banking; second most important has been medical practices, such as organ transplant and in vitro fertilization. The publications of the OIC Academy are invaluable, indeed without equal, for the study of the development of the law of modern Islamic finance.

The concept of group *ijtihad* is important also within individual Islamic financial institutions. After initially relying on single scholars for fatwas, Islamic banks now form *shari'a* review boards of several scholars to facilitate research and enhance credibility. These review boards sometimes collaborate by holding international conferences on Islamic finance issues, sometimes under the auspices of international Islamic finance companies and organizations. These collaborative activities are helping to increase the momentum and the coherence of intellectual work in the field of Islamic finance.

---

[27]*Fiqh Academy Journal.*

The institution of the *shari'a* review board is important for the study of Islamic finance, because it has become standard practice for Islamic financial institutions to obtain a fatwa to support any new product or amendment to an old one. Supportive fatwas are an important component of a product, and potential investors or customers often inquire about them. Some banks have published fatwa collections. Scholars of repute are sought after by banks to serve in providing fatwas, and customers inquire as to their identities when reviewing the "Islamicity" of products.

Nearly every institution has regularized the fatwa process through the creation of its own permanent *shari'a* review board. Many review boards have progressed beyond provision of fatwas, which are purely advisory, to degrees of control and audit of Islamic propriety. Some boards employ techniques borrowed from financial audits to enforce *shari'a* compliance. Boards report periodically to shareholders on the Islamicity of procedures. The institution of *shari'a* boards is likely to see much elaboration and development in the future.[28]

A recent survey of *shari'a* review boards of fifteen Islamic banks in various countries asked a number of questions related to board structure and function.[29] Forty-one board members responded. The surveyed boards varied in size from one scholar (three respondent banks), to seven or more. Ninety-two percent of the board members had Islamic law training, while 60 percent instead or in addition had studied modern non-religious law. Boards most often (49 percent) meet quarterly, though many meet monthly (7 percent) or weekly (24 percent).

Respondents differed in their understandings of the functions of *shari'a* control boards. Almost all (98 percent) felt that board opinions were compulsory for the bank, to the extent that if the board rejected a transaction it would not be performed. Most felt that their authority derived from the shareholders (75 percent) rather than from the board of directors or management (25 percent). Salaries of respondents were most often fixed by the shareholders in the annual meeting (66 percent), rather than by the board of directors (29 percent) or the management (4 percent). The great majority, however, characterized their relationship with directors and management in terms of coordination and advice, not authority. Most

---

[28]See, e.g., Muhammad Bahjat, "Nahwa ma'ayir lil-riqaba al-shar'iyya fi-al-bunuk al-islamiyya," *Majallat buhuth al-iqtisad al-islami* 3 (1994): 1-60.

[29]Faris Mahmoud Abumouamer, "An Analysis of the Role and Function of Shariah Control in Islamic Banks" (Ph.D. diss., University of Wales, 1989).

(71 percent) would report any unlawful practice to the shareholders, as well as to management or the board.

The great majority of *shari'a* boards perform some degree of auditing. While a great majority (85 percent) stated that they "audit" the balance sheet, nearly as many perform an "audit" of key accounts. On the other hand, most members of boards (66 percent) stated that they rely on statements by management to learn of the "financial" practices followed by the bank before issuing fatwas, without consulting records. Thirty-two percent of respondent members of *shari'a* control committees believed that 100 percent of their bank's activities were Islamically legal; another 51 percent considered them at least 90 percent legal; 10 percent, less than 90 percent legal.

While responses from management attached great importance to the boards, responses from bank clients indicated less attention to them. Only about one-third of the clients stated that they learn of Islamic lawfulness of bank transactions from the *shari'a* boards, as opposed to management or bank publications, and a similar fraction stated they did not even know or understand the role of the boards.

Islamic Legal Application in a Western Legal Environment

Although parties may agree by contract to abide by Islamic precepts, they cannot alter the surrounding legal system which in the end enforces their agreements. In nearly all Muslim countries today, civil and commercial codes are greatly influenced by European laws, most commonly French, next most commonly English. Egyptian law and jurisprudence, inspired by French and other continental European law, are widely emulated in Arab countries. The legal institutions and laws of procedure in most Muslim countries are also taken from Western models. Only in Saudi Arabia, Oman, and a few other countries of the Arabian Peninsula do legal rules and institutions resemble those of classical periods, but even in these countries, Western patterns have made strong inroads. In Saudi Arabia, the world's most traditionally Islamic country, the laws applied in explicitly commercial matters, such as companies, banking, and commercial paper laws, strongly resemble French and Egyptian laws. But the general Saudi legal environment, including the general civil law regime, is that of the classical Hanbali school. All laws are applied by judges trained in Islamic law using largely Islamic procedures and rules of evidence.

When classical Islamic law is applied in an alien environment, even if parties structure their agreements according to a classical Islamic legal form, the laws that govern the interpretation and enforcement of these agreements usually are wholly ignorant of that form. It is simply impractical for parties to incorporate into their agreement all the relevant Islamic rules, but many of the rules which are omitted are just as much the outcome of Islamic principles as are the bans on interest and excessive risk. For example, Islamic law does not allow recovery of lost profits, seeing such claims as both speculative and unearned. But a national law may award such damages, even against a losing party's protests that the contract is "Islamic." Note also that if the parties have agreed on terms that are questionable under Islamic law but allowed under local law, such as a contract to sell in the future, the local legal system will almost certainly enforce it, enabling parties to push the limits of, or even evade, the Islamic law.

The only way by which Islamic finance contracts can avoid such outcomes is by opting out of local law and courts through choice-of-law and dispute-settlement clauses, which are very common in Islamic finance contracts. An (unscientific) survey of all the sample contracts in our possession shows that many contracts still do not choose Islamic law (or, e.g., Saudi Arabian law) but rather the law of one or another non-Islamic system. This can be due to the insistence of a non-Islamic, or even Islamic, party to the contract, who desires to avoid either the impracticalities or the uncertainty of applying classical Islamic law in any respect beyond affording the basic model for the contract. Some contracts, including those of the Islamic Development Bank, choose as applicable law the "principles of the Islamic shari'a," a term that allows flexibility as to the details of Islamic legal rules. Still other contracts adopt a compromise position: "Subject to the principles of the Glorious shari'a, this Agreement shall be governed by the laws of England."

Finally, some contracts do choose "Islamic law" as the applicable law. When they do so, according to our survey, virtually all also include a provision for commercial arbitration. If the arbitrators have expertise in Islamic law, it is possible that the award would fully reflect the classical law. Such an award would then be enforceable in most countries, as long as no offense is given to the fundamental national values called "public policy." Presumably these contracts provide for arbitration, and not adjudication in national courts, because the latter courts likely could not apply Islamic law fully or successfully. Islamic law is not applied in toto by any national system, can be known only from scholarly texts in Arabic or by expert testimony, is often in dispute, and does not possess analogues to many institutions of modern law. Indeed, courts might declare some of the law's provisions unenforceable and against public policy — its use of corporal punishment and imprisonment to secure payment, for example, and possibly its denial of certain damages.

CHAPTER 3

Qur'an and Sunna on Contract and Commerce

This chapter acquaints the reader with the primary revealed texts on the chief themes of commerce and contract. We present here all vital Qur'anic verses, but only a few of the most important Sunna reports, since the Sunna is much larger and more complex than the Qur'an. The next chapter addresses the contract law deriving from these verses and reports.

Any attempt to give a brief introduction to Islamic law relating to banking and finance is beset with difficulties, especially if we want to learn something of that law's religious and cultural context. Simply stating the law's ethical and general principles would provide a glimpse of the religious wellsprings of the law and the moral logic of particular outcomes. It would not, however, help the reader to predict legal results or show how they are derived. On the other hand, a codified statement of basic rules would make the law seem much more fixed, mechanical, and categorical than it is, and would convey little of the religious and ethical background. Neither approach would indicate the methods by which the law is developed and justified.

Despite these difficulties, our approach aims to give the uninitiated outsider an appreciation at once of the religious nature, the detailed content, and the legal methods of the law. It hopefully will also suggest something of the dynamics of the field: its inner tensions, the choices it faces, and its likely trends of future development.

The first step in this outsider-based approach is to acquaint the reader with translations of the central scriptural texts that shape Islam's unique approach to finance and commerce, giving a glimpse into the very heart of the religion and religious law relevant to our subject.[1] The second step, taken up in Chapters 4 and 5, is to learn something of the most authoritative interpretations of these texts — namely, the rules and principles of the classical contract and commercial law (*fiqh*) propounded by medieval scholars. The third step, in Chapter 6, is to see how modern scholars, lawyers, and bankers apply both the revealed texts and the classical rules and principles to modern problems of finance and banking.

As represented by the tetrahedron in Figure 3-1, our approach juxtaposes, but keeps distinct, four stances from which to understand the Islamic law. Three of the vertices of this tetrahedron represent the three viewpoints on Islamic law just mentioned: the Qur'an and Sunna; the classical Islamic law (*fiqh*); and the modern Islamic law. The fourth vertex represents the stance of the outsider, who, we assume, holds conventional, largely Western ideas of law, finance, and economics. The purpose of this book is, in a sense, to explore the relationships among these four vertices.[2] The three vertices other than the Qur'an and Sunna — those that define a single plane or face (A) of the tetrahedron — represent human, interpretive, relative, truth. These three we constantly interrogate and compare as interpretations and realizations of the revealed texts. A second face (B) of the tetrahedron is defined by the three Islamic expressions of the law. The outsider's viewpoint, having no Islamic authority, stands outside this plane, but remains relevant to Muslims' interpretations of the law, if only because Islamic law and finance interact intensively with non-Islamic law and finance, are categorized and judged by it, and are under immense pressure to conform to it. A third face (C) is defined by the three expressions of the law observable in our time. Since the classical law and its practice can no longer be fully recaptured, any enactment of them must be a reenactment, a modern interpretation. If we confined ourselves to the fourth face (D), we would be improperly ignoring the Islamic validity and authority of mod-

---

[1]The translations given here are my own, drawing on two works: Muhammad Asad, *The Message of the Qur'an* (Gibraltar: Dar al-Andalus, 1980); and Saudi Arabia, Presidency of Islamic Researches, Ifta, Call, and Guidance, *The Holy Qur'an* (Medina: King Fahd Holy Qur'an Printing Complex, 1992).

[2]Of course, each of the vertices of this tetrahedron has complexities and multiplicities: for example, for each of classical Islamic, modern Islamic, and modern Western law, we face multiple rules and multiple legal systems.

ern Muslim interpretation and practice of Islamic law and harshly opposing a "true" Islam of the past with the modern West. Such an approach is taken in common by the classic Orientalist and the ultraconservative Muslim. The hard reality is that even were Muslims to seek to apply nothing but classical law, under present circumstances they could not do so without constant comparison among all the four vertices.

Our treatment of the Qur'an and Sunna in this chapter is not scientific in Islamic terms. First, we use translations, and, as Muslims properly insist, no translation is the Qur'an. Second, inevitably English translations offer a modernizing commentary. Third, we cannot delve into the full commentarial and historical depths of each verse (or Sunna report). Our goal is, however, not sophisticated internal Islamic appreciation of these texts, but only an outsider's fresh and inquiring first acquaintance. (In other words, it is to do an initial trace of the line between the top and the leftmost vertices of Figure 3-1.) This step is necessary for the work of subsequent chapters.

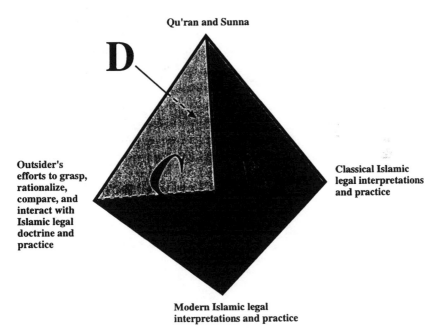

Qu'ran and Sunna

Outsider's efforts to grasp, rationalize, compare, and interact with Islamic legal doctrine and practice

Classical Islamic legal interpretations and practice

Modern Islamic legal interpretations and practice

Figure 3-1. Comparative Method

PROPERTY OR WEALTH

"The earth belongs to God," says the Qur'an in many places. "He gives it as a heritage to those whom He wills of His servants." [7:128]

The Qur'an repeats more than twenty times that "His is the dominion over the heavens and the earth; and all things return to God." [57:5] Dominion on earth is delegated to man as God's vicegerent.

> It is He who has created for you all that is on the earth . . . And lo! Your Lord said to the angels: "Behold, I am about to establish on the earth a *khalifa* [inheritor, successor, or vicegerent]." [2:29-30][3]

We thus find *fiqh* statements that everything is God's property, and that man deals with it only as agent. Every worldly benefit comes to mankind from God, as his providence. God taught mankind all arts that lend comfort to their life,[4] and encourages industry to gain his bounty.

> When the prayer is ended, disperse through the earth and seek something of God's bounty... [62:10]

Unlike Christian teaching, the Qur'an discourages asceticism and rejection of the world. All things are good, except for those things which God specifically forbids, such as pork and wine.[5]

> O Children of Adam! Adorn yourselves beautifully for every time and place of prayer; eat and drink; but do not waste. . . . Who is there to forbid the beautiful things which God has brought forth for His servants, and the good things from among the means of sustenance? [7:31-32][6]

> God wills for you ease, and does not will for you hardship. [2:185]

Nevertheless, God has deliberately created disparities in the distribution of goods in this world. But no one may claim more than he has earned.

> Do not covet the bounties which God has bestowed more abundantly on some of you than on others. Men are allotted what they earn, and women are allotted what they earn. Ask God for something of His bounty. [4:32]

---

[3]See e.g. 6:165; 7:129; 27:62; 35:39.
[4]See, e.g., *sura* (chapter) 16.
[5]2:172-3.
[6]See also 5:87.

God urges all to do charity, to "spend [on others] out of the sustenance We have granted them." [2:3] Indeed, charity devolves from man's status as vicegerent,[7] and is no mere gift but a right of the dispossessed:

Behold, the pious [who] in their property acknowledge a due share [right, *haqq*] to those who ask and to those who are deprived. [51:15-19; see 70:24-25.]

One of the "five pillars" of Islam is the alms-tax, levied on various forms of wealth in fixed percentages annually.[8] The Qur'an describes charity as a "good loan" to God, which he will "repay many times over."[9] Spending from God's sustenance is enjoined; hoarding is condemned.[10]

Property rights are sacred.

As for the man who is a thief and the woman who is a thief, cut off their hands in requital for what they have reaped, and as an exemplary punishment from God. [5:38]

Consider the following reference to property from reports of the Prophet's famous Farewell Pilgrimage sermon:

'O people! Do you know what month you are in, and what day you are in, and what town you are in?' They said, 'In a sacred day, a sacred month, a sacred town.' He said, 'Then your persons, your property and your honor are as sacred [forbidden] to you as the sacredness of this your day in this your month in this your town, until the day you meet Him.' Then he said, 'Hear me, O my nation! Live together, but do not do wrong, do not do wrong, do not do wrong! For [taking] the property of a man is not permissible except by his finding it good [*bi-tibi nafsin minhu*].'[11]

---

[7]57:7, 10.
[8]9:60; see also 59:7.
[9]2:245; 64:17; 30:39.
[10]9:34.
[11]Ibn Hanbal and Ibn Maja. As noted in Chapter 2, the Sunna, Prophet Muhammad's words and deeds, is constituted from reports called *hadith*. In the earliest centuries of the Islamic era, particularly in the third (the 9th century CE), specialized collections of authenticated *hadiths* emerged considered authoritative by later generations. *Hadiths* are normally cited to these collections. Six of these collections are the most relied upon, each named after its author: Bukhari, Muslim, Abu Dawud, Tirmidhi,

Many Qur'anic verses condemn the wrongful taking (lit., eating or consuming) of property. These verses afford guidance on matters of fundamental significance for contract law — the rightful and the wrongful means of acquiring property from others.

> Do not devour one another's property wrongfully, nor throw it before the judges [i.e., to influence them corruptly] in order to devour a portion of others' property sinfully and knowingly. [2:188]

> Behold, those who unjustly devour the property of orphans but fill their bellies with fire; they will soon endure a blazing flame! [4:10; see 4:2]

> So, for the wickedness of the Jews, We prohibited them certain of the good things of life which had been allowed to them; and [We did this] for their having turned many away from the path of God, and their taking usury [*riba*] which had been forbidden them, and their wrongful devouring of others' property. [4:160; see also 9:34]

> Do not devour one another's property wrongfully — unless it be by trade based on mutual consent [*taradin*] — and do not kill [or destroy] yourselves [or one another] . . . . One who does this with rancour and wickedness — him shall We make to endure fire. [4:29-30]

Thus, we see this phrase — wrongfully devouring property — associated with taking property by legal artifice, consuming property of orphans entrusted to one's care, usury, and trade without ready consent. The last two of these associations will be discussed below. Classical Qur'anic commentaries explain the term "wrongfully (*bi-al-batil*)" as all that is unlawful under the *shari'a*, like usurpation, usury, gambling, theft, perjury, or deception.

These verses have had profound repercussions in Islamic culture, stir-

---

Nasa'i, Ibn Maja. We shall cite *hadiths* — as here — simply by naming the collections in which they can be found, omitting exact citations to any particular edition. We also cite to several other famous collections: Ibn Hanbal, Hakim, Bayhaqi, etc. (Bibliographic information about editions of these collections can be found in the bibliography.) Ibn Hajar al-'Asqalani (d. 1449), *Bulugh al-muram min jam' adillat al-ahkam* (Beirut: Dar al-Kutub al-'Ilmiyya, n.d.) was employed as a useful collection of relevant and authoritative *hadiths*.

ring pious anxiety about the sacredness of property,[12] and about whether one's property is honestly earned (*halal*). For example, Qur'an and Sunna texts condemn rulers who take public wealth beyond living expenses.[13] Eulogies record extreme measures by more pious rulers to avoid offending this principle.[14] Ascetics and mystics pay extreme attention to the lawfulness of their means of support.[15] Similarly, in a report the Prophet states:

> The hand [meaning possession] is obliged by what it takes, until it performs [or fulfills] it.[16]

This suggests a general conception of unjust enrichment.[17]

TRADE BY MUTUAL CONSENT

For contract law, the most significant condemnation of wrongful taking of property is the verse excepting "trade based on mutual consent [*illa an takuna tijaratan 'an taradin minkum*]." This endorsement of trade by consent (*taradin*) is ·made emphatic by an odd contradiction implicit in the verse — seemingly casting trade as an allowed form of *wrongful* taking. Is it too much to read here some implied protection for those transactions, common enough in commerce, which in their outcome seem unfair

---

[12]See Saba Habachy, "Property, Right and Contract in Muslim Law," *Columbia Law Review* 42 (1962): 450-471.

[13]3:161; 'Ali b. Ahmad al-Nisaburi (d. 1075), *Asbab al-nuzul* (Beirut: Dar al-Kutub al-'Ilmiyya, 1980), 84; Isma'il Ibn Kathir (d. 1373), *Tafsir al-Qur'an al-'azim*, 2 vols. (Cairo: Isa al-Babi al-Halabi, n.d.), 1:399.

[14]See, e.g., Muhammad al-Tabari (d. 923), *The History of al-Tabari*, vol. 12, *The Battle of Qadisiyya*, trans. Yohanan Friedman (New York: State University of New York Press, 1992), 204-06 (how much of state's property rulers could use); Nizam al-Mulk (d. 1092), *The Book of Government or Rules for Kings*, trans. Hubert Darke, 2d ed. (London: Routledge & Kegan Paul, 1978), 64-65, 144-48.

[15]E.g., Farid al-Din Attar, *Muslim Saints and Mystics: Episodes from the Tadhkirat al-Auliya*, trans. A.J. Arberry (Boston: Routledge & Kegan Paul, 1966), 57-60.

[16]"*'Ala al-yad ma akhadhat hatta tu'addiyah.*" Abu Dawud, Tirmidhi, Nasa'i, Ibn Maja.

[17]Islamic law includes a law of unjust enrichment, but it is beyond the scope of this chapter.

and leave one party ruing the deal, or which seem to create gain out of nothing?[18]

Trade is given even greater emphasis by being singled out over other lawful means of gain such as gift and inheritance.[19]

Thus two key elements of a general theory of contract are endorsed emphatically in these verses: mutual consent and gainful exchange. These elements reappear in the Sunna, where one finds no echo of the medieval Christian disapproval of trade as morally suspect:

> Asked 'What form of gain is best?' [the Prophet] said, 'A man's work with his hands, and every legitimate sale.'[20]

> [The Prophet gave one of his Companions] a dinar to buy for him sacrifice animals or a ewe. He bought with it two ewes, then sold one of them for a dinar. He brought him a ewe and a dinar, and he [the Prophet] invoked God's blessing for him in his trade. 'For were he to buy dirt he would make a profit in it.'[21]

As for the requirement of mutual assent, there is the mention in the Prophet's Farewell Pilgrimage sermon, already quoted: "For the property of a man is not permissible except by a willing consent from him."[22]

Again, the divine permission — by which property, sacred in its owner's hands, transfers justly and rightfully to another — is made to hang on the single point of the willing assent of the transferring party.

It appears that the assent sought ideally is the real, the inner, state of mind, and no external token for it. A fundamental proposition of Islam,

---

[18]Commentators tarry only briefly over this point, resolving that the term "except" (*illa*) here has the meaning of "but," and that several words have been elided. Fakhr al-Din al-Razi, *Mafatih al-Ghayb* (Istanbul: al-Matba'a al-'Amira, 1891), 3:302: the correct meaning is "but ['eating' property is lawful] by trade based on mutual consent." He notes another interpretation where "illa" means "except" as usual, but after a long ellipsis: "even if with agreement, such as in usury and otherwise, unless it be by trade by mutual consent." Ibid. There are problems with this interpretation as well, and the majority do not follow it.

[19]It is felt that the verse neither impugns nor endorses these latter means, ibid. One theory why trade is favored with mention is that it is the most common and considered the most "manly" of means of gain. Nasir al-Din 'Abd Allah b. Umar al-Baydawi (d. 1286), *Tafsir al-Qur'an* (Istanbul: Dar al-Tiba'a al-'Amira, 1886), 109.

[20]Hakim ("valid"). Another *hadith*: "The truthful, honest merchant is with the prophets . . . and martyrs." Tirmidhi.

[21]Bukhari, Muslim, Abu Dawud, Tirmidhi.

[22]See p. 57 above.

applying in both spiritual and secular spheres of life, is the Prophet's reported statement or *hadith* "Actions are only according to their intentions (*niyyat*, sing. *niyyah*)."[23] The Qur'an states: "Man has only [i.e., is held accountable only for] what he strives for." [53:39]

We shall see below that many of the characteristic doctrines of the Islamic contract law reflect this extraordinary emphasis on consent.

DEBT

The Qur'an shows no disapproval of incurring debt, setting forth in detail how to record a debt in writing. [2:282] The Sunna reinforces this impression. Besides recording the Prophet's purchases on credit, statements of the Prophet almost encourage one to incur debts if for lawful purposes:

> No Muslim incurs a debt and God knows that he wishes to repay it but God repays it for him in this world and the next.[24]

> God is with the debtor until he pays his debt, as long as it is not for something God disapproves.[25]

The last statement led a ruler to incur a personal debt, saying "I do not wish to spend a night without God with me."[26]

The Qur'an and Sunna encourage leniency by those who hold debts.

> If [the debtor] is in difficulty, [then grant] a delay until a time of ease; if you were to remit [the debt] by way of charity it would be good for you — if you but knew. [2:280]

This verse suggests that creditors and Islamic courts should readily grant pressed debtors additional time to pay, that bankruptcy status affords mere delay and immunity from collections, not release, and (especially since the

---

[23]Bukhari relates it in seven places; Muslim; Tirmidhi; and others.

[24]Ibn Maja and Hakim. Cited from Muhammad Anas al-Zarqa and Muhammad Ali al-Qari, "*al-Ta'wid 'an darar al-mumatala fi al-dayn bayn al-fiqh wa-al-iqtisad*," *Majallat Jami'at al-Malik Abd al-'Aziz* 3 (1991): 25-57, 28.

[25]Ibid., citing Ibn Maja.

[26]Ibid.

61

verse occurs in the context of a prohibition of usury) that the creditor's grant of delay is uncompensated.

USURY

We have already noted the Qur'an's association between *riba* (usury, etymologically "increase") and "wrongful devouring of property," and that commentators consider the former one form of the latter. The Qur'an forbids *riba* in the strongest terms.

> Devour not usury [*riba*], doubled and re-doubled.... [3:130]

> Those who devour usury [*riba*] do not stand except as one stands whom Satan has confounded with his touch: for they say, 'Buying and selling [*bay'*] is like usury' — the while God has made buying and selling lawful and usury unlawful. One who becomes aware of his Lord's admonition and desists, may keep his past gains, and his affair is for God [to judge]; but as for those who return to it, they are Companions of the Fire; they will abide in it! God effaces [the gains of] usury, while He makes acts of charity increase.... Give up what remains of usury, if you are believers; for if you do it, take notice of war from God and His Apostle. But if you repent, then you shall be entitled to your principal: you will do no wrong, and neither will you be wronged. [2:275-79; see also 4:161]

Note that these verses do little to explain what *riba* is, or why it is wrongful, except by opposing it to charity.[27] At a minimum, therefore, it applies to the *riba* known at the time of the Qur'an. Prior to Islam *riba* applied to an increase (usually a doubling of the debt) in return for an extension (usually a doubling of the term) granted a borrower who could not make payment when due.[28] This is called the *riba al-jahiliyya*, or the *riba* of the pre-Islamic period. This practice may lie behind the Qur'anic reference to "doubling and redoubling." Some say that the Qur'an refers only to this type of *riba*.[29]

---

[27]See also 30:39.

[28]A ban on such transactions, understood somewhat more generally, is one interpretation of the hadith prohibiting "sale of a debt for a debt" (*bay' kali' bi-kali'* or *bay' dayn bi-dayn*), a term which resurfaces below. Abdullah Alwi Haji Hassan, *Sales and Contracts in Early Islamic Commercial Law* (Ph.D. diss., University of Edinburgh, 1986), 65.

[29]Fazlur Rahman, "Riba and Interest," *Islamic Studies* 3 (March 1969): 1-43.

The question arises, why, if such transactions meet with the approval of both parties (*taradin*), are they divinely disapproved? The Qur'an asks this very question, but in a more penetrating way — why is sale not like *riba*? — and gives the emphatic, if obscure, answer that God has allowed the one and prohibited the other. Given the question and the response, it becomes morally urgent to be able to distinguish *riba* from ordinary trade. What sorts of "increase" or inequality in exchange transform lawful commercial gain into condemned usury, despite both parties' ready consent? In what circumstances does the desire for gain become perverted and corrupt? Unfortunately, the answers to these vital questions have never been easy. The Caliph 'Umar reportedly lamented that the Prophet never spelled out the full scope of *riba*:

['Umar said,] The last verse revealed was the verse of *riba*, and [then] the Messenger of God was taken [in death]. He had not explained it to us. So leave *riba* and doubt [*ribah*].[30]

The Sunna is no less emphatic and inclusive in denunciations of *riba*. One report has the Prophet declaring, "*Riba* is of 73 types. The least of them is like a man having sexual intercourse with his mother."[31] Another states: "The Messenger of God cursed the one who consumes *riba*, the one who makes it be consumed, its inscriber, and its two witnesses."[32]

The Sunna does offer more guidance as to the meaning of *riba* when in several *hadiths* it describes specific instances of it in loans and sale, without however confining *riba* to these cases. We postpone review of these *hadiths* to the next chapter.

GAMBLING AND RISK

Gambling is another type of consensual transaction condemned in the Qur'an, and represents a second major exception to the general approval of trade by mutual consent.

---

[30]Ibn Maja. Others dispute the late timing of the *riba* prohibition. See Rahman, "Riba and Interest."

[31]Ibn Maja, in shortened form. Hakim gives it in complete form and considers it valid (*sahih*).

[32]Muslim. Bukhari has something similar.

Intoxicants, games of chance [*maysir*], [worship of] idols, and [divination by] arrows are but an abomination, Satan's handiwork; avoid it then, so that you might prosper! By means of intoxicants and games of chance Satan wants only to sow enmity and hatred among you, and hinder you from the remembrance of God and from prayer. Will you not, then, desist? [5:90-91][33]

Particularly noticeable here is that the revelation offers a reason for the gambling prohibition — that *maysir* invokes enmity and distracts the faithful from worship. The Sunna takes this prohibition much further, in condemning not only gambling but also sales of *gharar*, a word meaning peril, risk, or hazard.[34]

The Messenger of God forbade the 'sale of the pebble' [*hasah*, sale of an object chosen or determined by the throwing of a pebble], and the sale of *gharar*.[35]

Do not buy fish in the sea, for it is *gharar*.[36]

These and other *hadith*s condemning aleatory transactions (transactions conditioned on uncertain events) are analyzed below. Again, as with *riba*, a legal preoccupation with *gharar* emerges, driven by the urge for moral security in transactions and for divine sanction of the property rights gained thereby. If commercial gain is lawful, despite the risk and uncertainty intrinsic to it, what is the added element that turns gain into condemned *gharar*? When is the parties' ready consent no longer a talisman, presumably because it is corrupted by some human moral weakness and blindness, such as a passion for unearned gain or for tempting fate? On these vital questions the revelation says little beyond what can be gleaned from texts like those above. As with *riba*, *fiqh* scholars have been unable to define the exact scope of *gharar* or reach full agreement among themselves concerning it.

---

[33]Commentators on this verse describe a complex game played in the Prophet's time, by which lots were drawn for parts of a slaughtered camel with those who lost paying for all its cost. Most declare the term here to refer to gambling generally.

[34]The term *gharar* does not appear in the Qur'an. Etymologically related words meaning "delusion" do appear.

[35]Muslim.

[36]Ibn Hanbal. He states that a version ascribing this to the Prophet's Companion Ibn Mas'ud, not the Prophet, is more authentic.

COMMERCIAL ETHICS

Both the Qur'an and the Sunna repeatedly enjoin commercial probity:

> Give full measure whenever you measure, and weigh with the true balance; this will be [for your own] good, and best in the end. [17:35]

> Do not [refrain from milking] camels or sheep [so their milk appears copious to a purchaser]. One who buys them after this may choose either as he sees best after he milks it: if he wishes he may keep it, and if he wishes he may return it with a [measure] of dates.[37]

> The Messenger of God passed by a heap of foodstuffs. He thrust his hand into it, and his fingers encountered dampness. He said, "What is this, O owner of the foodstuffs?" He said, "Rain has stricken it, O Messenger of God." He said, "Why do you not put it at the top of the foodstuffs, so that the people may see it? He who deceives is not of me."[38]

> Do not meet *al-jalab* [i.e., meet outside the town those who drive animals from one place to another for sale]. The master of the one who is met, and is purchased from, has an option when he comes to the market.[39]

> Only an errant one hoards.[40]

As with the last two *hadiths*, the Sunna reflects a heavy reliance on the market. Shortly after emigrating from Mecca to Medina, the Prophet created a market in which his fellow emigrants could trade. His recognition of the market principles of supply and demand is recounted in the following *hadith*. Asked to fix prices in Medina when prices were high, the Prophet said:

> God is the one who sets prices, who takes, who amply gives sustenance, who makes provision. I do not wish that I meet God Most High and anyone have against me a claim of injustice in either blood [life] or property.[41]

---

[37]Bukhari and Muslim, and in Muslim's version, "He has a three days' option."
[38]Muslim.
[39]Muslim.
[40]Muslim.
[41]Bukhari, Muslim, Abu Dawud, Tirmidhi.

Finally, the Qur'an devotes a lengthy passage (2:282-4) to arranging for proof or evidence of transactions on credit.

FULFILLING CONTRACTS

So far we have focused on one aspect of the morality of contract — when the party benefiting from the contract may justly keep his gains, or when the gains reaped from a transaction are lawful. Another aspect of contract morality concerns the disadvantaged party: when is he morally obliged to fulfill his undertaking?

The Qur'an emphatically upholds the moral obligation to fulfill one's contracts and undertakings: "O you who believe! Fulfill all covenants ['uqud]!" [5:1] The term here used, 'uqud, sing., 'aqd, means knot or tie, hence obligation and compact; also it can refer to the conclusion or ratification of a compact ('ahd) or an oath (yamin). As commentators note, the initial address of the verse to "those who believe" indicates that fulfillment of contracts is part and parcel of faith.

Other Qur'anic verses require one to fulfill all pledges and relations of trust:

> Fulfill every pledge ['ahd] — for verily [on Judgment Day] the pledge will be inquired into! [17:34]

> Fulfill your covenant ['ahd] with God whenever you bind yourselves by a pledge ['ahadtum], and do not break oaths [ayman] after you have confirmed them; indeed, you have made God your surety; behold, God knows all that you do. [16:91]

> God commands you to deliver your trusts [amanat] to those entitled to them. [4:58]

The term 'ahd means injunction, pledge, vow, compact, contract, obligation, promise. It is used in the Qur'an for the primordial covenant to worship and obey God made between God and mankind,[42] but also for other undertakings including, according to commentators, ordinary contracts.[43]

---

[42]7:172-73.

[43]Some explain the two as near synonyms, 'ahd conveying the sense of obligation (ilzam), and 'aqd the sense of undertaking an obligation (iltizam).

Indeed, the two usages of *'ahd* are linked in the second of the last three verses, suggesting that to fulfill the divine covenant requires fulfilling one's pledges to all others. The Sunna contains similar injunctions, the most important being: "The Muslims are bound by their stipulations [*shurutihim*]."[44]

A *hadith* condemns promise-breaking as the behavior of a hypocrite: "If he makes a promise [*wa'd*] he breaks it, and if he makes a compact [*'ahd*] he acts treacherously."[45] Another states: "If a man makes a promise [*wa'd*] intending to fulfill it, and then does not do so, no blame attaches to him."[46]

Despite their broad reach and their highly religious and ethical tone, these provisions fall short of a definitive obligation to observe promises.

FREEDOM OF CONTRACT

Despite the general obligation to uphold contracts, not all contractual arrangements are condoned by the texts. *Hadiths* raise a number of specific obstacles to free contract. The most important such *hadith* involves a transaction of the Prophet's wife 'A'isha, who desired to buy and then free a certain slave, Barira. The owners would not agree to the price without reserving for themselves the "right of clientage," chiefly a right to inherit from the slave. This right ordinarily falls to the manumitter, who in this case was 'A'isha.

> [The Prophet advised 'A'isha] "Take her and stipulate in [the sellers'] favor the right of clientage. For the right of clientage is only his who manumits." 'A'isha did [this], then the Messenger of God stood among the people, and praised God. Then he said, "What do you think of men who impose stipulations [*shurut*] which are not in the Writ [or Book] of God Most High? Any stipulation not in the Writ of God is void [*batil*]. Were it one hundred conditions, the judgment of God is more just, and the stipulation of God more reliable. The right of clientage is only his who manumits."[47]

This *hadith* is highly troubling for freedom of contract. It suggests that the very terms of contracts, not to mention contracts themselves, must be pre-

---

[44]Abu Dawud, Hakim, Ibn Hanbal; Tirmidhi, Nasa'i.

[45]Bukhari, Muslim, Abu Dawud, Tirmidhi, Nasa'i.

[46]Abu Dawud.

[47]Bukhari. Muslim, with "Purchase her, free her, and stipulate in their favor the right of clientage."

67

scribed by God's writ. Unless a term is positively allowed by revelation ("in the Book of God"), it is nugatory, the parties' agreement notwithstanding. Contractual terms are treated here as if they were part of fundamental morality, conclusively and exclusively fixed by revelation, like the Qur'an's prescriptions as to the types and degrees of relationship within which persons may marry.

Other *hadiths* raise specific obstacles to free contract, for example:

> [The Prophet] forbade a sale and a stipulation [*bay' wa-shart*].[48]

> The Messenger of God forbade two bargains [*safqah*] in one.[49]

> The Prophet forbade sale of the delayed obligation [*al-kali'*] for a delayed obligation.[50]

These *hadiths*, and freedom of contract, are discussed in greater detail in the next chapter. Whatever might be suggested by the Qur'an, the provisions of the Sunna create a climate inhospitable to freedom of contract. And this is even more the case when the effect of such provisions is compounded with the revelation's categorical, but vague, prohibitions of *riba* and *gharar*.[51] There is the possibility, not apparent from evidence so far, that all restrictions on free consent stem solely out of desire to protect against *riba* and *gharar*. This is the assertion of the great Andalusian philosopher and jurist Averroës or Ibn Rushd (d. 1198), who stated that the causes for the invalidity of sale intrinsic to the concept of sale are four: illicitness of object of sale (e.g., wine); *riba*; *gharar*; and "those terms that conduce to one of the last two or some combination of them."

SUMMARY

The Qur'an and Sunna powerfully enunciate basic tenets of Islamic contract law. What can we observe about those tenets?

---

[48]Abu Dawud. Ibn Hanbal rejects it.

[49]Ibn Hanbal.

[50]Daraqutni, Bayhaqi, Hakim, and others. See Nazih Kamal Hammad, *Bay' al-kali' bi-al-kali' (bay' al-dayn bi-al-dayn) fi al-fiqh al-islami* (Jedda: Markaz Abhath al-Iqtisad al-Islami, Jami'at al-Malik 'Abd al-'Aziz, 1986), 9-10.

[51]Muhammad b. Ahmad Ibn Rushd (d. 1198), *Bidayat al-mujtahid wa-nihayat al-muqtasid* (Cairo: Mustafa al-Babi al-Halabi, 1981), 2:123-4.

Clearly, one tenet is that property is God-created and God-given. The construction of property differs radically from a common modern conception of property as a secular value to be defined and redefined as needed to further utility, or as the aggregate of whatever property claims the legal system chooses to respect. In Islamic law, by contrast, property is irreducible, sacrosanct, and virtually transcendent. The lawfulness of its acquisition and use is grounded on texts whose source lies above reason, and is a matter with which God is minutely concerned.

A second major tenet is that contract is a moral and legal means to gain property. The legitimacy of gain through trade, a vexed issue at the intersection of ethics, economics, and contract law, is resolved in a strikingly liberal fashion. Offsetting this endorsement in the Qur'an are prohibitions on *riba* and *maysir*, and in the Sunna more detailed *riba* prohibitions and the ban on *gharar*. Obviously generalized prohibitions on increase and risk, if expansively interpreted, are arrows aimed at the very heart of the idea of commercial gain.

With this introduction to the Qur'an and Sunna texts on contract and related ideas, in the next two chapters we explore the classical Islamic law itself, which presents itself as the corpus of law which has been authoritatively derived from these texts.

CHAPTER 4

Islamic Laws of Usury, Risk, and Property

This chapter begins our exploration of Islamic contract law by investigating its rules concerning three concepts basic to that law: usury, risk, and property. These concepts are prefigured in Qur'anic verses found in the preceding chapter.

We continue the method introduced at the beginning of the previous chapter, turning our attention for this and the next chapter to the classical Islamic law (*fiqh*). While exposing *fiqh*'s rules, we pose two layman's, outsider's, questions about them. First, admitting that *fiqh* rules are the most authoritative and operative interpretations of the texts of the Qur'an and Sunna we have read, are they impressive and convincing interpretations? Second, do they appear to be rational, in reflecting some persuasive order, logic, or reasoning, whether moral, economic, legal, or all three? Whether or not such a rationale exists, searching for it helps the outsider to learn and appreciate the complex structure of the legal rules.

As we noted above in discussing the Islamic legal method of *qiyas* or analogy, Islamic law and legal interpretation rarely rely, at least explicitly, on general meanings or rationalizing explanations of the texts as the ground for rulings. A great part of the law's interpretation and rulings trace from historical events in the Prophet's era and later that are not exposed here. So it is unlikely that outsiders can answer either of these two questions with complete success. On the other hand, three facts about the Islamic legal tradition make the endeavor not wholly unjustifiable, even in Islamic terms: (i) Qur'anic and Sunna texts do include general statements of morality and law (*qawa'id, maqasid*); (ii) Islamic *fiqh* does exhibit predictable patterns often expressible as general principles (also *qawa'id*); and (iii) theology recognizes that these principles are concordant with and respond to human reason, common sense, and experience.

Our approach means that in this and following chapters we depart from classical Islamic legal method and presentation and pursue what must remain an approximation.[1] But our goal is not to capture the thought process of classical legal scholars, whose method is quite different,[2] but rather to test and compare the rules elaborated by these scholars with the outsider's rationalizing appreciations of them. Among other things this effort demonstrates how often these latter rationalizations fail to capture the complexity and profundity of the classical interpretations.

This chapter often presents the views of only two schools of thought, the Hanbali and the Hanafi, the most influential schools in modern Sunni contract law.[3]

LAW OF USURY (*RIBA*)

The Qur'an; *Riba al-Jahiliyya*

The Qur'an vehemently condemns *riba*, but provides little explanation of what that term means, beyond contrasting *riba* and charity and mentioning exorbitant "doubling." Commentators describe a pre-Islamic

---

[1] It is also to rush in where the truly learned and qualified fear to tread — to making rationalizations and generalizations about Islamic law or even its individual legal schools. The practice involves constant errors and omissions. To gain an authentic sense of Islamic jurisprudential method and content, one should delve into *fiqh* texts, through translations if necessary. See e.g., Ibn Rushd, *The Distinguished Jurist's Primer*, trans. Imran Ahsan Khan Nyazee (Reading, UK: Garnet Publishing Ltd., 1996), 153-231, esp. 158-171.

[2] These outsider's understandings are not at a great remove from *contemporary*, as opposed to *classical*, Islamic thought. Modern reinterpretations of the scriptural texts and of the classical legal corpus, like our own proposed outsider understandings, work to relate the revealed texts and classical Islamic thought, on the one hand, with modern religious, philosophical, economic, and legal ideas, on the other.

[3] The Malikis are a close third in influence in commercial law, and the Shafi'is a distant fourth.

practice of extending delay to debtors in return for an increase in the principal (*riba al-jahiliyya*). Since this practice is recorded as existing at the time of the revelation, it is one certain instance of what the Qur'an prohibits. Hence Ibn Hanbal, founder of the Hanbali school, declared that this practice — "pay or increase" — is the only form of *riba* the prohibition of which is beyond any doubt.[4] Among other things, it includes charging a debtor any penalty for failure to pay when due (although delay by a solvent person is a sin and may be punished as a crime).

The Sunna

The Sunna shows that the divine prohibition of *riba* extends far beyond *riba al-jahiliyya*, but it still leaves much uncertainty about its definition. Several *hadiths* suggest how expansive the notion may be. For example:

> If a man intercedes for his brother, who then gives him a present, and he [that man] accepts it, he has opened a wide gate for *riba*.[5]

Two other *hadiths*, more germane to our concerns, have been the most influential texts in shaping the *fiqh* conception of *riba*:

> Gold for gold, silver for silver, wheat for wheat, barley for barley, dates for dates, salt for salt, like for like, equal for equal, hand to hand. If these types differ, then sell them as you wish, if it is hand to hand.[6]

> Every loan [*qard*] that attracts a benefit is *riba*.[7]

---

[4]Shams al-Din Muhammad Ibn Qayyim al-Jawziyya (known as "Ibn al-Qayyim," d. 1350), *I'lam al-muwaqqa'in 'ala rabb al-'alamin*, ed. Taha 'Abd al-Ra'uf Sa'd (Beirut: Dar al-Jil, 1973), 2:153-4.

[5]Ibn Hanbal, Abu Dawud.

[6]Muslim.

[7]This hadith, not in any of the six chief collections, is related by the most respected scholars only on the authority of Companions, not the Prophet. As a prophetic *hadith* scholars reject it as false. See Muhammad b. 'Ali al-Shawkani (d. 1839), *Nayl al-awtar* (Cairo: Mustafa Babi al-Halabi, n.d.), 5:262.

Note that the first *hadith* covers sales and the second loans. We shall analyze each separately.

The Sunna on *Riba* in Sales

The actual reach of the *riba* prohibition goes far beyond compensation for lending money. Oddly, the core case of *riba* for Muslim scholars is not interest in loans, but sales involving excess or delay in exchanges of certain types of property — for example, foodstuffs and currency. Therefore we need to consider *riba* in sales in order to understand the full meaning of *riba*.

The *hadith* "gold for gold" suggests the rules for most cases of *riba* in sales. The *hadith* establishes that certain goods (technically called *ribawi*, or *riba*-related) can be exchanged for each other as long as the exchange is present barter ("hand-to-hand"). Exchange of goods within a single type (e.g., dates for dates) is permitted only in equal amounts (e.g., one kilogram for one kilogram). These two permissions entail two prohibitions: first, of all sales within a single type with inequality, with or without delay (termed *riba al-fadl*, lit., *riba* of excess); and second, of all exchanges with delay among the listed (*ribawi*) goods, with or without equality or identity of type (termed *riba al-nasi'a*, lit., *riba* of delay).

Due to the first prohibition, on *riba al-fadl*, one cannot sell, for example, good-quality dates for a larger quantity of poor-quality dates. In another *hadith* the Prophet advises conducting such exchanges through the medium of money, one of the parties selling his dates for cash and then buying the other's dates with cash.[8]

The second prohibition, of *riba al-nasi'a*, seems to ban sales with delay of any of these goods for gold or silver. But reports that the Prophet purchased on credit[9] reverse this result: delayed sales are permitted as long as currency is only one of the two considerations. Goods may be sold on credit for silver or gold.

Does this *hadith* apply only to the items mentioned in it? Does it con-

---

[8]"Sell the whole for *dirhams*, then buy the (better quality dates) with the *dirhams*." Bukhari and Muslim.

[9]The Prophet's wife 'A'isha reported: "I said, 'O Messenger of God, so-and-so has come with linens from Syria. What if you were to send to him, and buy from him two robes with delay (*nasi'atan*) to a time of ease?' And he [the Prophet] sent to him, and he refused." Hakim, Bayhaqi.

cern sales of barley or wheat but not rice? Of dates but not raisins? A minor school, the Zahiri, does hold that the named types are literal and exclusive, but the majority use analogy to see a deeper "efficient cause" (*'illa*) for the *riba* prohibition behind each of the named types. An *'illa* is the attribute of an event that entails a particular divine ruling in all cases possessing that attribute; it is the basis for applying analogy (*qiyas*) to the two cases. *Ribawi* goods are therefore goods that exhibit one of the "efficient causes" occasioning application of *riba* rules. The schools define these causes differently. The Shafi'is detect two causes among the six cases of the *hadith*: currency and food. The Malikis add to food additional traits: being basic foodstuff and being preservable. Hanafi and Hanbali schools see only one cause — goods sold by either weight or volume. This *'illa* is divided into three equal sub-causes: measure by weight, measure by volume, and highly precise measure (for the precious metals gold and silver only). All the schools declare that the *hadith's* prohibitions apply to exchanges of items that share a single (sub-) cause. Thus, the Hanafis and Hanbalis prohibit the sale on credit of bread for copper (both measured by weight), but allow the sale on credit of bread for salt (one measured by weight and the other by volume).[10] Malikis and Shafi'is, since they are concerned only with exchanges among food or among currencies, reach results opposite to the other two schools in these cases. To give a more contemporary example, crude oil is a *ribawi* for Hanafis and Hanbalis, but not for Malikis and Shafi'is. For the former schools, whether oil belongs in the weight or volume class (this may depend more on historical than present practice) determines whether it can be traded for either wheat or iron. Note also that according to this *hadith*, if one of the two countervalues is not *ribawi* — a house, a suit of clothes — then no prohibitions arise at all.[11]

As to *riba al-fadl* (*riba* of excess), the *hadith* is read as permitting exchanges even within an *'illa* as long as the genus of the goods differs (e.g.,

---

[10]The Hanbalis and Hanafis define weighables and measureables somewhat differently. See Mansur al-Bahuti (d. 1641), *Kashshaf al-qina'* (Beirut: Dar al-Fikr, 1982), 3:262-63; compare Abu Bakr al-Kasani (d. 1191), *Bada'i' al-Sana'i'* (Beirut: Dar al-Kitab al-'Arabi, 1982), 5:186.

[11]Depending on the school, even non-*ribawi* goods can be subject to *riba* prohibitions, if the genera are identical, sale is with delay (*nasi'a*), and there is an excess. An example is one milk-ewe now for two milk-ewes later.

This paragraph and the next rely heavily on N. Saleh, *Unlawful Gain and Legitimate Profit in Islamic Law*, 2d ed. (The Hague: Kluwer Law International, 1992), 11-43

wheat and dates are both preservable foodstuffs, but of different genus, and therefore can be bartered with excess).[12] Here emerge complex casuistic definitions of genera: for example, for the Hanafis and Hanbalis beef and mutton are different genera, exchangeable with excess, while for the Shafi'is and Malikis they are the same genus and can only be exchanged equally.

In these rules of sale, note that, except for exchanges within a single *ribawi* genus, permission or prohibition does not turn on any calculation of price. Nothing prevents the price in a sale on credit (for currency) from exceeding the price for an equivalent present sale, and thus involving an element of compensation for delay in payment. Whatever the prohibition of *riba al-jahiliyya* means, it does not mean a per se prohibition of a charge for extending credit. In medieval Christian canon law an effort was made to determine the "just price," which would allow one to determine to what extent credit sale prices involved the "selling of time."[13] Classical and modern Islamic scholars, with near unanimity, do not attempt this;[14] they specifically acknowledge that goods sold on credit (*bay' al-nasi'a* or *bay' mu'ajjal*) are priced higher than goods sold for cash, and consider this perfectly natural.[15] A later section will draw out the full consequences of this result, but for now we note that it vetoes a naive understanding of *riba* as simply a ban on compensation for credit.

The law also permits compensation for delay in another form of credit sale, the forward purchase (*salam*), a contract by which goods specified in the contract (usually fungibles) are purchased for later delivery. This contract is invalid if the purchaser does not pay the price immediately on making the contract. An example would be paying a farmer cash now for a certain quantity and quality of wheat to be delivered on a specified future

---

[12]Properly, identity of genus is also part of the *'illa* since both conditions must be met for *riba al-fadl* to exist.

[13]See J.T. Noonan, Jr., *The Scholastic Analysis of Usury* (Cambridge, MA: Harvard University Press, 1957), 82-99, showing how medieval just price theory, while acknowledging market prices, sought to prevent excessive gain.

[14]E.g., Ibrahim al-Shatibi (d. 1388), *al-Muwafaqat* (Cairo: Maktabat al-Tijariyya al-Kubra, n.d.), 4:41-42; Muwaffaq al-Din 'Abd Allah Ibn Qudama (d. 946), *al-Mughni wa-yalihi al-sharh al-kabir* (1972; repr. Beirut: Dar al-Kitab al-'Arabi, 1983), 4:259-264, discussing without disapproval increasing prices in sale for credit risks and delayed payment. See also Rafiq al-Misri, *Bay' al-taqsit* (Beirut: al-Dar al-Shamiyya, 1990), 39-51. The Fiqh Academy has endorsed this position. Decision 53/2/6, sixth session (1990), *Fiqh Academy Journal* 1: 447-8.

[15]Medieval Christianity differed. Noonan, 19. Interestingly, this prohibition proved difficult for later theorists to justify. Ibid., 81, 90-95.

76

date. In such purchases, it is understood that the wheat is sold for less than the spot price of wheat. Thus, in both credit (*nasi'a*) and forward purchase (*salam*), i.e., in sales where the countervalue is currency paid either in advance or after delay, the law allows the parties to agree on price differentials compensating for the delay in contract fulfillment.

The Sunna on *Riba* in Loans

The second *hadith* ("Every loan that attracts a benefit is *riba*") is the most important in modern economic life, since it concerns the contract of loan. By loan is meant the loan of fungibles (*qard*) including money.[16] "Benefit" includes interest on a money loan. The authenticity of this *hadith* is in much doubt, but the ruling it represents is universally accepted by scholars and can be derived from the rules on *riba al-jahiliyya* or on sales. Profit on loans is banned without regard to whether the fungible subject-matter of the loan is also *ribawi*, i.e., is weighable or measurable (for the Hanafis and Hanbalis) or is food (for the Shafi'is and Malikis). Thus, a fungible textile measured by the yard is not *ribawi* for either group, and yet cannot be loaned for consumption with excess.

Plumbing the Rules of *Riba*

What logic drives the rules of *riba*? For example, why restrict the barter of dates to exactly equal quantities? Who would engage in such a transaction? Why should sale of wheat now for salt later be prohibited, while sale of wheat now for silver later is not? Why should the *sale* of wheat now for an equal amount of wheat later be offensive, when the *loan* of wheat for later equal repayment is not? Why should the fact that cotton is measured by weight instead of volume dictate for the Hanafis and Hanbalis

---

[16]The Hanafis require that *qard* goods be fungibles. *al-Fatawa al-hindiyya*, 3:201; Kasani, 7:395. A more common view is to allow *qard* in whatever can be adequately known by description (*mawsuf fi al-dhimma*, capable of *salam* sale). Ibn Qudama, 4:355. The Hanbalis define *qard* even more broadly, including loan of unique objects such as jewelry against return of their value, and this is one Shafi'i view. Ibid.; Ahmad b. 'Abd Allah al-Qari (d. 1940), *Majallat al-ahkam al-shar'iyya*, ed. 'A. Abu Sulayman and M. 'Ali (Jidda: Tihama Publications, 1981), art. 749.

whether it can be sold on credit for iron? For what reason is it forbidden to demand an increase for delay in payment of a debt or a loan, while to demand an increase for delay in paying a purchase price is allowed?

Although the uninitiated may assume that Islamic rules on usury equate with a prohibition of interest on credit, or the denial of the time value of money, clearly something much more complex is afoot. Let us essay various rational explanations for these rules, thus departing from the standard method of classical Islamic law. In doing so, we will find a number of intelligible principles that do appear to animate the law, but none that explains all results; as in many areas of law in any legal system, outcomes do not follow from any single policy, but from many which, by competition and cooperation, seem to give the law its final shape.

Although few classical scholars acknowledge a need to go beyond the usual *'illas* (e.g., measurement by weight, use as currency, repayment of a loan) in order to "understand" *riba* laws or identify their deeper "causes," there have been a few attempts to do so, famous perhaps because of their rarity. We will examine two of them, generating three possible rationales for *riba*. Thereafter we provide two other rationales for *riba* rules emerging from basic principles (*qawa'id*) elicited classically, for a total of five:

- Mathematical equivalency
- Avoiding commercial exploitation
- Minimizing commerce in currency and foodstuffs
- Linking lawfulness of gain to risk-taking
- Using money and markets to allocate and moderate risks

Table 4-a supports the unfolding argument by juxtaposing specific *riba*-based permissions and prohibitions, while showcasing three of the five rationales.

Mathematical equivalency. A first *riba* rationale emerges from a classic statement by the philosopher Averroes, or Ibn Rushd (d. 1198), who was also a great jurist of the Maliki school.[17] Though a Maliki, Ibn Rushd announced his preference for the Hanafi *'illa*, equality of measure. He suggests that behind the *riba* provisions is the goal of exalting fairness of exchange, advanced by insisting on exact mathematical equality of exchange whenever that equality is possible and appropriate. Adequate equality is usually achieved by transacting through the medium of currency, the

---

[17]Ibn Rushd, *Bidayat*, 2:129ff.

purpose of which, he notes, is to provide a neutral measure of respective values. If, however, the two countervalues being exchanged have similar uses *and* are either both measured by volume, both weighed, or both currency, then exact mathematical equality ought to be required. Presumably because delaying one of the two deliveries introduces an uncontrolled element of inequality, the law prohibits all delayed exchanges of goods within these three groupings. Note that for this theory *riba al-fadl* offers the central instance of *riba*.

This theory does account for permission for sales, both present and delayed, where one (only) of the two countervalues is currency (e.g., wheat for money), since these are exchanges between disparate, unequal, types not conducive to equality, and since the purpose of currency is to provide a neutral measure of value. The theory is weak, however, in accounting for the ban on delayed sales among goods measured the same way (volume, weight, or currency), for example, banning sale of iron now for cotton later. Ibn Rushd offers two explanations for the ban on such sales. First, he suggests that a better way to achieve them exists, namely transacting through the medium of currency. Presumably this serves equality and fairness because the market provides reasonably good estimates of future prices in terms of currency, but why should a similar requirement not apply to non-*ribawi* goods (which may be exchanged with delay)? Perhaps an answer is his second argument, that when measured or weighed goods have "similar uses," exchanges should occur only with equality, and commerce in them is due only to "intemperateness" and should be discouraged. How this applies to exchanges of different genera (e.g., iron and cotton), with or without delay, is unclear, since uses may not be "similar," although it is true that most items measured by volume are fungible foods, and most weighed items are industrial materials. Ibn Rushd does not discuss this issue beyond noting his admiration for a certain scholar's view, that *riba* applies only to currency and food items measured by volume.

An interesting side question is why *qard* loans without interest are lawful, when sales with delay of a *ribawi* good for an equal but delayed price in that same good (e.g., ten bushels of wheat now for ten bushels of wheat later) are *not* lawful. Presumably the latter result is because delay introduces an unreasonable inequality into the exchange. Why are loans different? A technical *fiqh* answer is that loans are always presently due, liable to being called at any time, a provision favoring the lender and reducing his market risk. As important is the Prophet's description of *qard* as a charita-

Table 4-a. Chart of *Riba*-Related Transactions

Transaction	Riba al-jahiliyya (pre-Islamic riba)	Loan of fungible with interest or benefit (qard jara manfa'a)	Loan of fungible (qard) without interest or benefit	Riba al-nasi'a (credit exchange of ribawi goods) (Cf. Rationale 5)	Time sale (bay' mu'ajjal)
Example	Postponement of money due now in return for __more__ money later	Two types: A. Wheat now for equal wheat later PLUS BENEFIT B. Money now for equal money later PLUS BENEFIT	Two types: A. Wheat now for equal wheat on demand B. Money now for equal money on demand	A. Wheat now for rice later B. Gold now for silver later	Wheat now for money later
Lawful?	NO	NO	Yes (if exactly equal)	NO	Yes
Does transaction allow for increase for delay?	Yes	Yes	No	Yes	Yes (sale price can exceed price of present or cash sale)
Does law recognize value of use during delay of property or price?	No (money is sterile?)	A. No (why? Because wheat is sterile? See below) B. No (money is sterile?)	No — but calls it a charitable act	?	? — law does not attempt to regulate the sale price
Is seller/lender ordinarily in a stronger financial position (than buyer/borrower)? (See rationale 3)	Yes	Yes	Yes	Yes	Yes — buyer needs wheat, has no money
Does seller/lender evade all risks (except credit risk)? (See rationale 4)	Yes, and gets an increase too	Yes, and gets an increase too. For borrower, loss is inevitable (because fungible is consumed by use). Borrower must restore lost goods AND pay for the use. Pays twice	A. Avoids risk of loss of wheat for duration of loan; assumes market risk B. Yes	A. Yes, avoids risk of loss of wheat, but bears market risks in two commodities [COMPARE WITH TIME SALE FOLLOWING] B. Yes	Evades risk of loss of wheat (money suffers less risk of loss). But bears a market risk on value of wheat
Is mathematical equivalence of the countervalues possible? (See rationale 1)	Yes	Yes	Yes — and it is achieved (disregarding factor of delay)	A. No (having two commodities complicates the evaluation) [COMPARE WITH TIME SALE] B. Almost yes (gold and silver values known and stable in relation to each other)	No. But a market exists for wheat valued in money

Table 4-a. Chart of Riba-Related Transactions, *Continued*

Transaction	Advance sale (salam)	Lease (ijara)	Partnership (sharika)	Riba al-fadl (barter with excess)	Double sale ('ina) (an "artifice" or hila)
Example	Money now for wheat (or other fungible) later	Sale of use of donkey for fixed period for money (rental)	Partners contribute money and/or services for percentage of ultimate profits or losses	A. Wheat now for more wheat now B. Gold now for more gold now	Between two parties, sale and resale of same object, once for immediate payment, once on credit
Lawful?	Yes	Yes	Yes	NO, even if quality differs	Some scholars: morally disapproved but valid; others: unlawful and invalid
Does transaction allow for increase for delay?	Yes	Yes. Rent is compensation for foregoing use of asset. Rent payments may be either prompt or delayed	Only if there is successful investment	N/A	Yes
Does law recognize value of use during delay of property or price?	Yes, very purpose is investment; understood that buyer's money is needed to produce wheat	Yes, very nature of contract. Not permissible for consumables, however, since for them use and destruction are identical	Yes, recognizes value of use for making profits. But compensates only to the extent that use does result in profits	N/A	Not explicitly
Is one of the parties ordinarily in a stronger financial position than the other? (See rationale 3)	Probably: buyer/investor has excess money; understood that seller needs the money to produce goods	Not clear. Usually owner/lessor is stronger	No. Parties may, however, decide within broad limits how to divide profits. In *mudaraba*, worker, though providing no capital, is shielded from capital loss	No	Yes (seller on credit)
Does one of the parties evade all risks (except credit risk)? (See rationale 4)	Buyer/investor bears only market risk; seller obliged to provide wheat if at all possible, even if his own harvest fails	No. Law emphatically requires lessor to bear all risks of loss or harm to donkey (except those caused by lessee) and even the costs of maintaining the donkey	No. All partners bear risk of loss of their investment (whether time or capital). Partnership invalid if partner tries in any degree to shelter his capital contribution from loss	N/A. Neither party suffers risk except as to price	Yes. Seller on credit avoids risk and gets an increase too
Is mathematical equivalence of the countervalues possible? (See rationale 1)	No. But market exists for wheat values in terms of money	No	No. Parties to share unknown profits, losses	Yes	Yes

ble act,[18] implying that the lender's voluntary acceptance of the delay in the exchange is charity.

Avoiding commercial exploitation. The next two rationales for the *riba* prohibition emerge from a statement by Ibn Qayyim al-Jawziyya ("Ibn al-Qayyim," d. 1350), a reformer within the Hanbali school and student of Ibn Taymiyya.[19] The first of these is the fear of the strong exploiting the weak. Ibn al-Qayyim argued that the Qur'an shows the reason for its vehement prohibition of *riba* by contrasting *riba* and charity. The core case of *riba* is "pay or increase," i.e., *riba al-jahiliyya*, where one obligated to pay is given an extension against an increase in the debt. This is exploitation of the needy, he says, since only a needy person would pay more for a mere extension of time. To such a person the rich have a duty to *give* charity, not to *take* something more from him. The prohibition of other forms of *riba*, particularly *riba al-fadl* and *riba al-nasi'a*, which includes even equal exchanges of *ribawi* goods with delay, is to prevent that evil from arising in any form. These prohibitions prevent gold, silver, and foodstuffs (the latter are essential for life, and are often used in lieu of money) from being traded like ordinary commodities. Such trading leads inevitably to exploitation of the poor through hoarding and speculation as well as through loans with interest and increasing debts in return for a delay. Note that for Ibn al-Qayyim, *riba* rules are comprehensible not because each and every act they prohibit is intrinsically unjust, exploitative, or unfair, but because to prevent such acts from occurring God has taken the precautionary step of excluding certain goods from ordinary commerce. Because of the vehement divine disapproval of such situations, the law does not merely enjoin fairness and enforce it in particular cases; instead, it deploys rules designed to prevent the occurrence of unfair situations.

This theory does not, however, directly explain why the rules do not cover sales of fungibles for currency, especially with delay and with increase. Perhaps Ibn al-Qayyim's explanation for this is implied in his statement that those who lack currency and transact by barter especially need protection, compared to those who have currency and access to markets.

A common addition to this rationale is that the *riba* prohibition, by forcing the investor to bear risks, prevents the rich from remaining forever

---

[18]Ibn Maja.
[19]Ibn al-Qayyim, 2:153-164.

rich and the poor poor.[20] Fakhr al-Din al-Razi, a great Qur'an commentator, notes one opinion on the reason for the prohibition:

> God forbade *riba* only because it prevents people from busying themselves for gain, because if the owner of the dirham can by means of a *riba* contract gain an additional dirham whether in cash or credit, it becomes easier for him to win the means of subsistence. He will rarely bear the burden of profit, commerce, and arduous crafts.[21]

Minimizing commerce in currency and foodstuffs. A third rationale, also brought out by Ibn al-Qayyim's exposition, is to suppress the trading impulse with respect to currencies and foodstuffs.[22] If money is to remain a neutral measure of value, it must not be dealt with as a commodity. Because foodstuffs are often used in lieu of money and because they are basic needs of mankind, they should be treated as much as possible as if they also were neutral and stable values, withdrawn from commerce.

Linking lawfulness of gain to risk-taking. A fourth possible rationale for *riba* prohibitions is based on a classical legal maxim influential in many aspects of Islamic commercial law, "Gain accompanies liability for loss,"[23] which suggests that gain is morally justified only when one faces risk to secure it, while riskless gain is unjust. For example, when an investor puts his capital into property capable of producing yield, such as land or a donkey, he may or may not reap a profit, but his capital is exposed to danger of loss: a crop may fail; the donkey may sicken and die. The maxim declares that in such situations the investor is entitled to his gain, if any. In an interest-bearing loan, on the other hand, the lender is shielded from the risk of losing either his profit or his capital — at least as a matter of the borrower's contractual undertakings — and therefore gain is improper.

---

[20]See Qur'an 59:7, often cited for this proposition, which requires distributing booty to, among others, the needy and the orphans "so that it may not [merely] make a circuit among the wealthy of you."

[21]Razi, 2:531. Modern authors often point to interest-taking as accentuating unfair distributions of wealth, while under Islamic profit-sharing and zakat taxes wealth gravitates to the active and skilled entrepreneur and to the investor who assumes risks and adds value. This, they posit, frames the key distinction between the Islamic and the capitalist economic systems.

[22]Ibn Rushd makes this point as well.

[23]"*Al-kharaj bi-al-daman.*" Abu Dawud, Tirmidhi, Nasa'i, Ibn Maja.

This argument is closely linked to an observation that most loans not only shield the lender from risk, but they also involve consumables, goods which yield benefits only through being consumed. Unlike a donkey or a farm, wheat or money produces no fruit or yield (*kharaj*), and are in that sense sterile. A lender who gets compensation beyond exact restitution of his goods is exacting gain from someone in return for nothing, and is therefore unjustly enriched. Gain can fairly be derived from money only when one invests it in property that does yield tangible gain, such as the donkey or the land.[24] Both of these arguments against interest-taking in loans have close parallels in the canon law tradition.[25]

The prohibition of riskless gain is linked to the prohibition of "sale of *gharar*," or the sale of risk. As we shall see later in this chapter, *gharar* rules often bar transactions that involve assuming a significant and unknowable risk for compensation (as in buying a runaway horse or the yield from a pearl diver's next dive). Interest loans give rise to similar concerns, in two ways. First, the borrower makes a payment against benefits he hopes to secure by consuming the property borrowed, but these benefits are highly contingent; he makes a fixed payment but may suffer loss (e.g., he borrows money and spends it on goods in the hope of selling them for a profit).[26] Second, since the borrower also assumes the risk of loss of the borrowed property, he would expect to be compensated for doing so, but instead the very worst situation for him obtains: because the goods are consumables, he derives no yield from the goods (they are sterile); they are certain to be destroyed (through consumption); and yet he pays more to the seller, not less. It is like a wager he is certain to lose. From this viewpoint, *riba* affords an extreme case of *gharar*.

One can derive from this a conclusion that in a situation where one is guaranteed (at least contractually) to obtain a fixed countervalue, concerns about *riba* are accentuated. Given this result, *riba* concerns will be greater for food and other fungibles, because these, unlike non-fungibles, cannot

---

[24]Kasani, 7:395-96 (recognizing that for consumables the thing itself represents the usufruct; hence to exact interest is to take a compensation for nothing).

[25]For Saint Thomas Aquinas's version closely tracking these arguments, see Noonan, 53-57.

[26]Razi, 2:531. As we shall see, for the Hanafi school this point occasions suspicion as to the lawfulness even of the lease of non-consumables.

become totally unobtainable or destroyed, since they will become available sooner or later on the market. Therefore, because they involve less risk, one would expect transactions in them with an excess to come under added scrutiny for *riba*.

Note the subtle linkings of risk and lawful reward. Profits are positively viewed when associated with the risks of ownership of known productive property: risks either of that property's future profitability (due to its yield or to market movements) or of its continued existence. Conversely, when one party escapes risk altogether, profits come under intense scrutiny for *riba*. Lastly, when the property itself is a risk, or is unknown, unrealized, or otherwise highly contingent, the risks borne by the parties cast doubt on the legality of the entire transaction.

Using money and markets to allocate and moderate risks. Why does Islamic law permit compensation for delay in the sale on credit for currency (even for sale of consumables)? If wheat is presently worth $1 a pound, why can one sell one hundred pounds of wheat now for $120 in currency after one year, and not sell one hundred pounds of wheat for one hundred pounds of wheat after one year?[27] Applying the previous rationale ("gain accompanies liability for loss") we see that in both cases, the purchaser, since he gets the wheat right away, assumes the risk of its loss. In the second sale, wheat now for wheat later, the seller is assured of getting his exact wheat back, evading risk (ignoring any change in the value of that wheat), but in the first sale, wheat now for currency later, the seller is exposed to market risk, namely the risk of a market price above $1.20 per bushel. Perhaps this justifies gain in credit sales for money.[28]

In a delay sale in *ribawi* goods which are different (e.g., selling wheat now for any quantity of rice later), again, market risks are inevitable, and there is no equivalence between the goods, so we would expect the transaction to be lawful, as in credit sale for currency, but it is not. Why? Perhaps the argument here would be the reverse, that risks become too great. In this transaction, two highly market-sensitive commodities are exchanged for each other, doubling the risks. As in *riba al-fadl* or unequal hand-to-hand

---

[27]This is a sale, not a *qard* loan, because the time of payment is fixed.

[28]Of course, repayment in wheat also involves market risks, but one at least gets back exactly what one had before in concrete terms. Compare the canonist *venditio sub dubio*. Noonan, 90-93.

barter within a genus, the law forces the parties to transact through the medium of money. Using markets and money, the parties' risks become reasonable, since the parties presumably gain adequate market knowledge to attain reasonable fairness in their exchange, and since the transaction then is denominated on one side in relatively stable money.[29] (We recall from Chapter 3 the Sunna's strong endorsement of the market and market prices.) So this fifth possible rationale is that moderate risk justifies excess, while too much or too little risk incurs a ban, as under the rules of *gharar*.

Clearly, none of the above explanations is wholly satisfactory, but offer something toward comprehending *fiqh* results. For our purposes, the relative implausibility of other explanations is as important as the plausibility of the ones already offered. For example, if we attempt to use modern financial economics to explain these *fiqh* outcomes, we do worse. For example, understanding *riba* as prohibiting interest is only partly true, since in the context of credit sales the rules tolerate recognition of the opportunity costs of money. Credit sales may be made at a premium over cash, without any attempt to regulate that premium in relation to a fair price or to the likely forward market price for the goods sold. Similarly, the oft-repeated idea that Islamic law permits gain only when a party is exposed to risks of loss and has no contractual assurance of gain does not hold true; the seller in a credit sale has contractual assurance of gain without any risk of loss.

Modern financial analysis and terminologies also run the risk of obliterating distinctions that seem vital to the Islamic system, such as distinctions between:

- extending credit in a sale *versus* extending credit in a loan;
- a payment denominated in currency *versus* a payment denominated in some other fungible (a distinction which disregards the volatility of currencies and the question of inflation);[30]

---

[29]A last puzzle is why *riba al-nasi'a* among gold and silver should be prohibited. Here perhaps there is not too *much* risk (as among goods) but too little, and one reverts to demanding equivalency (exact exchange in *qard*) or present exchanges.

[30]Chapter 8 discusses some dimensions of the Islamic legal position on inflation. The OIC Academy earlier declared modern paper currency to be a type of currency like gold and silver. Decision no. 9, third session (1986), in Organization of the Islamic Conference, *Islamic Fiqh Academy Resolutions and Recommendations* (Jedda: OIC, 1989?), 34. The OIC Fiqh Academy studied the issue of indexation of currency debts and declared it against Islamic law. Decision 4, fifth session (1988), 3:2261. The same volume

- contracts with similar economic purposes but with differing legal incidents (e.g., a sale of one hundred pounds of wheat now for one hundred pounds of wheat later *versus* a loan of one hundred pounds of wheat, since in the latter the lender can demand early repayment; or two contracts, one with the price due at once *versus* one with price due later; or contracts that differ as to remedies when promised goods are unavailable; and so forth).[31]

GAMBLING (*MAYSIR*) AND RISK (*GHARAR*)

As we observed in the previous chapter, the Qur'an condemns gambling (*maysir*), stating that by it Satan "wants only to sow enmity and hatred among you, and hinder you from the remembrance of God and from prayer." The Sunna speaks about not only gambling but risk or *gharar*. In the Sunna, *gharar* refers to a number of transactions characterized by risk or uncertainty at their inception. The following *hadiths* are representative of the Sunna's instruction on *gharar*:

> The Messenger of God forbade the 'sale of the pebble' [*hasah*, sale of an object chosen or determined by the throwing of a pebble], and the sale of *gharar*.[32]

---

publishes several studies of the issue. Thereafter apparently the Academy decided to take the issue under reconsideration, spurred by the example of very high inflation in Turkey. See, e.g., Decision 79/6/D8, eighth session (1994), 3:787-88. Classical law, with narrow exceptions, set itself against recognizing losses in real value as to currencies and other fungibles. Relevant classically debated issues are currency that has become debased and token copper coinage (*fulus*). See, e.g., Kasani, 7:395.

[31]A question often asked is whether Islamic law forbids the taking or giving of interest in transactions with non-Muslims. Some scholars declare *riba* permissible under certain conditions in transactions occurring in the "abode of war," or *dar al-harb*, which in medieval times referred to non-Muslim regions not under treaty with Islamic states. The views of the majority Shi'ite school, the Twelvers, are much more extensive, incorporating (in one view) even *riba* gains from dealing with Christian or Jewish residents of Islamic lands. Sami Homoud, *Tatwir al-a'mal al-masrafiyya bi-ma yattafiq wa-al-shari'a al-islamiyya* (Cairo: Dar al-Ittihad al-'Arabi, 1976), 210-220. Non-Muslim regions are not usually described today in terms of *dar al-harb*. In any event, the majority *fiqh* view is opposed to any exception.

[32]Muslim.

Do not buy fish in the sea, for it is *gharar*.[33]

The Messenger of God forbade the [sale of] the covering [copulation] of the stallion.[34]

The Prophet forbade sale of what is in the wombs, sale of the contents of the udders, sale of a slave when he is runaway, . . . and [sale of the] 'stroke of the diver' [*darbat al-gha'is*, sale in advance of the yield of a diver's dive, whatever it was].[35]

Whoever buys foodstuffs, let him not sell them until he has possession of them.[36]

He who purchases food shall not sell it until he weighs it [*yaktalahu*].[37]

[T]he Prophet forbade the sale of grapes until they become black, and the sale of grain until it is strong.[38]

The Spectrum of Risks and Their Prohibitions

Let us arrange the transactions prohibited in these *hadiths* on a spectrum, according to the extent that risk is at the core of the transaction, as in a gambling contract.

The pure speculation. The *hadiths* describe a few transactions that seem intentional gambling, being final sales of wholly unknown values: the "stroke of the diver" or whatever a stone lands upon. Also in this category are other obscure pre-Islamic transactions prohibited by the Sunna which, on one set of interpretations at least, seem rudimentary, playful forms of gambling indulged in by merchants: an example would be to sell for a fixed

---

[33]Ibn Hanbal, indicating that its most correct version is handed down on the authority of Ibn Mas'ud, not the Prophet.

[34]Bukhari.

[35]Ibn Maja, with a weak chain of transmitters.

[36]Bukhari.

[37]Muslim.

[38]Bukhari, Muslim, Abu Dawud, Tirmidhi.

price whatever goods (unexamined) the buyer touches (*mulamasa*). But very little is known about these pre-Islamic contracts beyond their names, with the result that extremely varied interpretations of their nature are offered.

The uncertain outcome. A second group of *hadiths* describes contracts where the countervalue is not only of uncertain value, but may not be realized at all, for example, the sale of a fish in the sea or a runaway slave. Presumably, the sale of goods not yet in one's possession falls in this category. Risk here may seem greater than in the last category, but it is less essential to the transaction. For one thing, it can be easily avoided by making the sale conditional on the relevant risk being eliminated (e.g., the fish caught, the goods obtained, etc.).

The unknowable future benefit. Other *hadiths* describe transactions with still less initial risk, since they transfer valuable benefits which are precisely known and defined, but whose future benefit to the buyer is unknowable, such as the "covering of the stallion" and arguably the "stroke of the diver." Such a transaction could be infected with the evils of gambling, especially if the buyer had false hopes or paid too much; in other circumstances, perhaps where the contract has become customary and occurs between informed parties, such contracts could become wholly innocuous and indeed indispensable.

Inexactitude. A final set of *hadiths* pose the least element of gambling or risk. They seem only concerned with inexactitude, such as in sales of goods before they are weighed. Here again, such sales may involve deliberately blinding oneself to risks, or alternatively may be thoroughly mundane and practical, such as in the sale of a heap of goods which both parties view but neither measures, or a sale by the pound.

How do classical scholars interpret these *gharar hadiths*? Before describing *fiqh* rules, let us consider the possibilities. The reason for these prohibitions would not be avoidance of risk per se, since incurring commercial risks — those of the market or supply and demand — is elsewhere approved and even encouraged. *Hadiths* permit a *salam* contract in which one pays a year in advance for so many bushels of wheat at harvest time — certainly a risky transaction as to price. But they also forbid a *salam* contract tied to the crop of a particular tree or field.

As these rules on *salam* suggest, a possible interpretation of the *gharar hadiths* is that they bar only risks affecting the existence of the object as to which the parties transact, rather than just its price. In the *hadiths*, such risks arise either 1) because of the parties' lack of knowledge (*jahala*, ignorance) about that object; 2) because the object does not now exist; or 3) because the object evades the parties' control. Therefore the scholars might use one of these three characteristics to identify transactions infected by the type of risk condemned as *gharar*.

With such a reading, scholars would insist that valid sales (and by analogy other binding contracts) exhibit two features: *knowledge*, i.e., the parties' full knowledge of all aspects of the sale, including the object itself; and *existence*, i.e., a concrete sale object capable of production (treating (3) above as a special case of (2)). The absence of one of these features cannot be compensated for by the other, and price cannot compensate for the absence of either one. Certainly, such a reading of the texts would ignore the modern custom[39] (especially after the advent of insurance) to see risk, however dire, as merely one factor affecting price.[40] Such a conception of *gharar*, scholars might argue, is needed to achieve the mutual consent (*taradin*) demanded by the Qur'an. How can parties consent to the transfer of that which may not exist, or that as to which they have no knowledge? They could do so only if risk itself is part of the object of the sale. But to prohibit such sales is arguably the precise intent of the Prophet's rejecting "the sale of *gharar*." Therefore, the consent needed for *taradin* is rendered more stringent: it must relate to the specific goods transferred, and be based on certain knowledge. Agreement to risk is excluded, since this is not true consent.

Another reading of the *hadiths* is possible, one which starts from the Qur'anic prohibition of *maysir*, which mentions as its reasons only enmity and distraction from religion. These reasons resemble the grounds on which many societies prohibit gambling contracts, that gambling leads to individual immorality (the compulsion to gamble) and to social harms. A scholar in-

---

[39]Richard A. Posner, *The Economic Analysis of Law* (Boston: Little, Brown & Co., 1992), 12, 102-109. Probability theory easily determines the value of a gambling contract (expected value is possible gain times chance of winning). All contracts binding someone to a future performance can be seen as performing an insurance function, shifting risk for a price. *Fiqh* acknowledged and permitted contracts to serve this function as to many risks (e.g., market fluctuations, credit risks in sale), but not others (e.g., wagers, sale of nonexistent or unknown objects).

[40]Also, by seeking out the assured existence of a concrete thing, and distinguishing the risks affecting that existence from risks of price, this reading ignores how market disasters can wipe out value completely.

spired by the Qur'anic text might read the *gharar hadiths* as intended only to suppress the gambling instinct. As we noted, each of the contracts condemned in the *hadiths* could harbor a gambling transaction, but could also be innocent. If gambling were the criterion for illegitimacy, the law might allow for more uncertainty in contracts, as to both existence and knowledge, and open the door more widely for upholding consent or *taradin*.

These two positions are summarized in Table 4-b:

Table 4-b. Poles of Interpretation of *Gharar*

	Scope for valid consent (*taradin*)?	*Gharar* vs. *maysir*?	Evils to avoid?
Position A	Restrictive	*Gharar* dominant	Ignorance, nonexistence
Position B	Broad	*Maysir* dominant	Enmity, distraction from prayer

Classical *Fiqh* Rules on *Gharar*

Looking now at positions actually taken by classical scholars, we find the vast majority adopting Position A in Table 4-b. Prohibitions of *maysir* and *gharar* generally translate into prohibitions of contracts involving either 1) nonexistence (*'adam*) of the subject-matter; or 2) ignorance (*jahala*) of any material aspect of the transaction.[41] Thus, the majority of scholars as a general rule void sales of nonexistent or uncertain objects without any consideration of the degree of risk involved. Whenever risks of nonexistence or ignorance enter into a contract from its inception, then *gharar* rules threaten to invalidate that contract, regardless of the degree of risk actually involved, and regardless of whether the assumption of the risk is agreed to and compensated.

The schools most characterized by Position A are first the Shafi'i, and then the Hanafi. This has led to highly restrictive rules. For example, the

---

[41]Cf. A.L. Corbin, *Corbin on Contracts* (St. Paul: West Publishing Co., 1960), sec. 728: "An aleatory promise is one the performance of which is by its own terms subject to the happening of an uncertain and fortuitous event or upon some fact the existence or past occurrence of which is also uncertain and undetermined." "Aleatory" is derived from the Latin *alea*, a game of dice.

Shafi'i school prohibits sales of absent specific objects altogether. The Hanafi school permits sale of an absent specific object by description but with the proviso that the buyer can reject the object at inspection even if it agrees with the description. It prohibits sale of things that are present but unviewed. Both schools prevent sales of objects present but invisible (such as carrots underground).[42]

The Hanbali and Maliki schools move slightly toward Position B, admitting as binding, for example, sales of absent objects by description, as long as the description is so complete as to rule out any deviations substantially affecting market price. In such cases the sales are binding as long as the objects when produced agree with the description. The Malikis, though not some Hanbalis, allow sale of present but unviewed items such as undug carrots or nuts in the shell.[43] The Maliki school often distinguishes itself by allowing sales other schools prohibit, when circumstances indicate that *gharar* will be "mild."[44]

Tension thus emerges between the schools on a matter of profound principle, made all the clearer by considering the views of Ibn Taymiyya (d. 1328), who in magisterial treatises sought to refashion *fiqh* contract law. Although his influence on later schools can be traced, his unique positions usually found favor only with his students, foremost among these Ibn al-Qayyim. Moderns, however, find Ibn Taymiyya's positions more congenial to modern law than those of other classical scholars, and have given his views vast new currency.

Ibn Taymiyya argues that rendering the *gharar* rules as barring nonexistence and lack of knowledge restricts contractual freedom too much, resulting in blind legalism and undue obstacles to people's welfare. *Gharar* is that which leads to the evils of *maysir* enumerated in the Qur'an. Seeking to return *gharar* to the meaning of "risk," he renders it as that which "hesitates

---

[42]Kasani, 5:139.

[43]Ibn Rushd, *Bidayat*, 2:157; Bahuti, 3:166. See for a characteristic defense of such sales, Taqi al-Din Ahmad Ibn Taymiyya, *Majmu 'al-fatawa Shaykh al-Islam Ahmad Ibn Taymiyya*, ed. 'A. al-'Asimi (Riyadh: Kingdom of Saudi Arabia, n.d.), 29:225-228.

[44]Ibn Taymiyya, *al-Qawa'id al-nuraniyya al-fiqhiyya*, ed. M. al-Fiqi (Cairo: al-Sunna al-Muhammadiyya, 1951), 122-123. See, e.g., Ibn Rushd, *Bidayat*, 2:147ff.; Muhammad b. Ahmad Ibn Juzayy, *Qawanin al-ahkam al-shar'iyya wa-masa'il al-furu' al-fiqhiyya* (Beirut: Dar al-'Ilm li-al-Malayin, 1979), 282. This position is held all the more strongly by Ibn Taymiyya, as in *Qawa'id*, 133.

between soundness and destruction." Sale of such *gharar* is prohibited since such sales truly involve *maysir* or gambling. *Gharar* is a question of degree: uncertainty cannot be wholly eliminated from contracts, so if a contract involves only minor *gharar*, it should stand. Hence, the sale of an unborn camel fetus is prohibited, but the sale of the pregnant camel is permitted. If a nonexistent object is sold with a condition that the sale will be cancelled if the object does not come into existence, the uncertainty is minor. If people want to sell goods "at the market price" or "at so much per pound," without specifying exact total quantity or price, what is the harm?[45] Similarly he upholds contracts with conditions, even ones that suspend the validity of the contract on contingent future events.[46] In conjoining and forcefully advocating all these positions, Ibn Taymiyya draws apart from nearly all other classical scholars, who in varying degrees use ignorance and nonexistence, and not risk at all, as the touchstones of *gharar*.

The majority positions of classical *fiqh* seem antithetical to a great many modern financial transactions, since they presumptively ban all sales of goods not already both owned and in the possession of the seller, not to mention goods that do not yet exist. This view would prevent a bank from binding another party to a lease of a building not yet built or which the bank does not yet own. Indeed, for the Shafi'is and the Hanafis even sales of goods that are merely absent at the time the parties conclude their sale are not binding. The Hanbalis and the Malikis sensibly allow sales of absent and even nonexistent goods as long as the contract describes the goods precisely. But even they require that all terms of the contract be known and specified, and exclude most forms of conditionality or contingency in the operation of contracts. For example, one could not conclude a modern supply or requirements contract (where the amount of goods ultimately needed and often their unit price is not known at inception). Only Ibn Taymiyya's view approaches a modern one, and it is frequently relied on by modern scholars of Islamic banking and finance. But even his view would not countenance the conscious assumption of risk inherent in many modern financial transactions, such as derivatives or insurance, or, most of all, use of these transactions for sheer speculation.

---

[45] Ibn Taymiyya, *Qawa'id*, 115-133; idem, *Nazariyyat al-'aqd* (Beirut: Dar al-Ma'rifa, n.d.), 220-229; idem, *al-Fatawa al-kubra* (Beirut: Dar al-Ma'rifa, n.d.), 3:415ff.

[46] Ibn Taymiyya, *al-Fatawa*, 3:474ff.

FIQH PROVISIONS ON PROPERTY (MAL)

The definition of property (*mal*) is an essential building block of Islamic contract law. *Mal* is defined as tangible things to which human nature inclines. For something to be the subject of a contract, it must be *mutaqawwam*, meaning that its use is lawful under the *shari'a*. For example, wine is not *mutaqawwam* for Muslims, although it is *mal*, since Christians may buy and sell it. There is dispute whether uses or usufructs (*manfa'a*) are *mal*. Hanafis require that *mal* be physically possessable and preservable. They do not consider usufructs to be property, since they fail this test, and presumably because, existing only instant-by-instant over time, they involve *gharar*. The Hanafis admit, however, as an exception to strict doctrine, that usufructs have legal value after that value is fixed by a lease contract. Other schools differ and consider usufructs fully *mal*, on the apparent ground that existence and custody of the underlying thing suffices as a token for the existence and custody of the usufruct.

Mal may be divided into fungibles (*mithliyyat*) and non-fungibles (*qimiyyat*), and into movables (*manqulat*) and immovables (*'aqar*). While the latter distinction is important in practical details, it does not fundamentally shape the contract law.

Mal is owned (*milk*) as either *'ayn* or *dayn*. *'Ayn* is a specific existing thing, considered as a unique object and not merely as a member of a category ("*this* horse," not "a thoroughbred mare"). *Dayn* is any property, not an *'ayn*, that a debtor owes, either now or in the future; or it can refer to such property only when due in the future. Property owned as *dayn* is usually a fungible, such as gold or wheat.[47] Sometimes non-fungible manufactured goods defined by specification are treated as *dayn*. Although *dayn* literally means "debt," in *fiqh* it refers not to the "obligation" per se, but rather to the property the subject of the obligation, which is considered to be already owned by the creditor. Clearly, since such property is not yet

---

[47]Most fungibles are also consumables, i.e., goods that are consumed on first use, like wheat or money. The chief exception to this would be certain manufactured goods, such as pottery, metal goods, cloth, etc. Mustafa al-Zarqa', *al-Madkhal al-fiqhi al-'amm* (9th revised ed.; Beirut: Dar al-Fikr, 1967-68), 3:143-47, gives a useful analysis of the concept of the "consumable" and its place in *fiqh* contract law. One indication of its importance is that leases are possible only for *non*-consumables.

identified and may not even exist (it is not an *'ayn*), referring to *dayn* as present property is fictive.[48]

Indeed, Islamic law takes the fiction one step further, by imagining *dayn* property as subsisting "in the *dhimma*" of the obligor. *Dhimma* means literally "compact," "bond," "obligation," "responsibility," "protection," or "security," but is used legally for the faculty or capacity in an individual by which he accepts duty and obligation.[49] Its usage often employs a metaphor of a physical place (*mahall*) in the individual. Thus, if one buys property generically or abstractly, such as so many bushels of a particular quality of wheat, one is said to have title to that wheat as a described thing in the *dhimma* of the seller (*mawsuf fi dhimmat al-ba'i'*). The fictions of *dayn* and *dhimma* indicate that Islamic law understands sale not as one or more obligations, but as the consenting present transfer of property.

Having explored these fundamental conceptions, in the next chapter we consider Islamic contract law in general.

---

[48]See Muhammad Tahanawi, *A Dictionary of the Technical Terms Used in the Sciences of the Musalmans* (Calcutta: W.N. Lees Press, 1862), calling the application of the term *dayn* to property metaphorical, since it leads to property only in the future.

[49]Edward William Lane, *An Arabic-English Lexicon* (London: Williams & Norgate, 1893), entry on (*dh,m,m*). As Robert Brunschvig suggests in "Corps certaine et chose de genre dans l'obligation en droit musulman," in *Études d'islamologie*, vol. 2 (Paris : G.-P. Maisonneuve et Larose, 1976), 303-322, 322, the distinction between *'ayn* and *dayn* may be more accurately not whether goods are generic or specific, but "between the object which for now is present and the subject which endures." This remark shows the law's emphasis on an existing, present substratum for contractual rights in both cases.

Brunschvig also points out that *'ayn* has several antonyms: genus, *dayn*, fungible, and "in the *dhimma*," 304. Another usage opposes *'ayn* as the thing itself (Latin, *res*) with usufruct (*manfa'a*).

CHAPTER 5

Islamic Law of Contract

We begin with several observations about Islamic contract law in general, and then consider specific contracts. The previous chapter explored *riba* (usury) and *gharar* (risk) as two sets of rules and principles that cut across all contracts in Islamic law.

FREEDOM OF CONTRACT

As with all legal systems prior to the nineteenth century, Islamic contract law is expressed not as a general theory of contract but as rules for various specific contracts — laws of sale, lease, pledge, and so forth. The closest thing to a general law of contract is the contract of sale (*bay'*), used by Muslim jurists as a prototype and analogy for all other contracts.

From the perspective of modern contract law, which honors virtually any genuine commercial agreement having lawful purposes, this characteristic of Islamic contract law instantly arouses questions. May one create new contracts? How exclusive and binding are the rules of the standard contracts? May one add to or vary from the terms prescribed by *shari'a*? In other words, to what extent does Islamic law admit freedom of contract?

The Qur'an emphasizes fulfilling one's pacts or undertakings. The Sunna is more resistant to free contracting, imposing narrow limits on "stipulations," i.e., terms of contracts other than those dictated by *fiqh*. Recall particularly the "Barira" *hadith* which condemned any term "not in the

Book of God."[1] What position does classical law take on the issue of freedom of contract, and what position is followed in modern Islamic banking and finance? We first discuss new contracts, and then stipulations.

New Contracts

Classical *fiqh* rarely even discussed the idea of contractual freedom outside the standard contract types.[2] The most relevant controversy is whether, in the absence of a specifically applicable revealed divine ruling, contracts and stipulations are presumed to be lawful or unlawful. Ibn Taymiyya takes a strong position:

> The underlying principle in contracts and stipulations is permissibility (*ibaha*) and validity. Any [contract or stipulation] is prohibited and void only if there is an explicit text [from the Qur'an, the Sunna or the consensus] or a *qiyas* [analogy] (for those who accept *qiyas*) proving its prohibition and voiding.[3]

At the other extreme from Ibn Taymiyya is the now-extinct "Literalist" or Zahiri school. This school argued that contracts, as private lawmaking, seek to alter the divine legal status of things, which can be done only with affirmative divine authority. The other Sunni schools reject this narrow view, yet, as Ibn Taymiyya asserts, their position is not that different since, although they profess the principle of permissibility (*ibaha*) as he does, in practice they confine themselves to elaborating contract rules by analogy to revealed precedents.[4]

Regardless of doctrine, classical scholars do not extensively discuss the topic of new contracts, mainly due to the very nature of their scholarly method,[5] which proceeds by measuring each proposed action against an-

---

[1]Chapter 3, p. 67.

[2]M.E. Hamid, "Islamic Law of Contract or Contracts," *Journal of Islamic and Comparative Law* 3:1-11.

[3]Ibn Taymiyya, *al-Fatawa*, 3:474. See also idem, *Qawa'id*, 112; idem, *Nazariyyat*, 226; etc.

[4]Ibn Taymiyya, *al-Fatawa*, 4:470ff.

[5]Hamid, 1-10.

other action or statement that has already been established, both being quite concrete in nature. The scholars' goal is to develop a web of rulings (*furu'*) covering all anticipated events directly or by further concrete analogy. For such a method to operate, a contract must first exist (or be imagined) in its complete form and context; to do otherwise would require the scholars to develop a system of operative abstract rules of contract law, which for various reasons they are unwilling to do. A second reason for their silence about new contracts may be that the prescribed contract types fully met their needs. For these two reasons, therefore, the classical scholars' silence on new contracts may not imply opposition to creating them.

This picture of the issue seems supported by the fact that the few new contracts that did emerge in classical times arose not from scholarly theory but from popular custom or practice. The scholars vetted them in the usual way, by analogy to the standard contracts. They were not named among the basic contract types.

The position in modern Islamic banking and finance is not too dissimilar: contemporary scholars voice strong support for Ibn Taymiyya's position that contracts are valid until shown to conflict with the Qur'an or Sunna, yet the mechanics of Islamic legal method still inhibit innovations. The bans on *gharar* and *riba* have generated a wide web of rulings and principles shaping existing contracts, many considered confirmed by *ijma'* or past scholarly consensus. Few new contracts can wholly avoid this legal web. If a new contract redresses some basic constraint on the old ones, it will probably fall afoul of a standard rule or principle of the law and not be accepted. Indeed, the commercial impulse driving innovation probably was already felt in medieval times, and repulsed even then.

On the other hand, many new contracts can survive review against these various rules and principles: among them are various solutions to novel problems arising under modern social or economic conditions, combinations of earlier contracts under a single name, or more complex implementations of standard contractual relationships. Examples are the modern corporation (*sharika*), a novel mechanism developed out of the laws of partnership; the modern construction contract (*muqawala*) combining the sale of materials and the hire of construction services with a fixed period of performance;[6] or the relationship of an Islamic bank with

---

[6] Ibn Qudama, 6:32; Qari, art. 567 & n.

its depositors developed from the Islamic contract of silent partnership (*mudaraba*). Other examples appear in chapters 6 and 10.

Stipulations

In classical law, debates concerning freedom of contract did not concern new contracts, but rather when standard contracts could be altered or combined. We have already quoted some of the *hadiths* restricting stipulations.[7] Other important ones are:

> Illicit are a loan and a sale [*salaf wa-bay'*], or two stipulations in a sale, or sale of what you do not have.[8]

> The Messenger of God forbade two sales in one [*bay'atayn fi bay'a*].[9]

Stipulations were divided into three types: 1) condition (*ta'liq*, literally "suspending") — the conditioning of a contract on a future event; 2) extension (*idafa*) — delaying the beginning of the contract until a future time; and 3) concomitance (*iqtiran*) — varying the terms of the contract.[10] In all cases, if the law finds the stipulation void, the contract may or may not be void also: the results vary casuistically.

The Hanafis prohibit conditions in contracts conveying property, but the Hanbalis are of two views, one of which allows conditioning of contracts that transfer ownership, citing an opinion of the school's founder.[11] Ibn Taymiyya supports this last position categorically.[12] Both schools allow extensions only for contracts such as lease or agency, where property trans-

---

[7]p. 68.

[8]Abu Dawud, Tirmidhi.

[9]Ibn Hanbal, Nasa'i, Tirmidhi.

[10]Sanhuri, 3:134-172.

[11]Hasan Ali al-Shadhili, *Nazariyya al-shart fi al-fiqh al-islami* (Cairo: Dar al-Kitab al-Jami'i, 1981), 94-104.

[12]Ibn Taymiyya, *Nazariyyat*, 227-29; Ibn al-Qayyim, 3:338-40. Cf. for a Maliki view, Ibn Rushd, *Bidayat*, 2:158, allowing sale of runaway slave with payment conditional on recovery.

fers only over time, if at all, and not for contracts of present transfer, such as sale.[13] Ibn Taymiyya is once again permissive. (The extension term in leases is employed in proposing a new Islamic finance mechanism in Chapter 10.) The roles for both these types of stipulation are considered to be dictated by the rules of *gharar*.

With concomitant stipulations, all schools first consider whether the stipulation agrees or conflicts with an "entailment" (*muqtada*) of the contract. Examples of entailments are that the buyer pay the price and that the seller transfer full title. Not surprisingly, all schools permit stipulations that coincide with an entailment, and they all forbid stipulations that contradict an entailment, such as a stipulation that the buyer never resell the object. All schools allow a third type of concomitant stipulation, one that supports fulfilling the contract, such as a requirement that the buyer pay on day X, or pay in certain coins, or provide a pledge as security. The type of stipulation which poses problems is one by which one of the parties obtains an additional benefit, as when a seller of a house stipulates a right to live in it a year without rent. On these the schools differ, for example the Hanafis allowing stipulations only when sanctioned by custom, and the Hanbalis allowing one such stipulation, but no more than one. The most liberal position is that of the Hanbali Ibn Taymiyya who rejects only those stipulations which contradict a clear provision of either the Qur'an, the Sunna, or the scholarly consensus, or which contradict the very object of a contract, nullifying it; he does not appear to discuss numerical limits on stipulations.[14]

In modern Islamic finance and banking law, in their position on stipulations, scholars once again align themselves with Ibn Taymiyya's view. Here their admiration for him appears to have translated fully into practice. One does not observe scholars analyzing stipulations at all as to type, or counting them; they seem solely concerned with whether a term conflicts with a basic *shari'a* principle.

Combinations of contracts conditioned on each other are open to many objections, chiefly that they confuse the price of the individual contracts and obstruct meting out fair remedies in the event of default, thereby

---

[13]As to the Hanafis, Najib al-Hawawini, ed., *Majallat al-ahkam al-'adliyya* [Arabic version] (Damascus: Matba' Quzma, 1923) [henceforth cited as *Majalla*], art. 408, 440; as to the Hanbalis, Ibn Qudama, 6:6-7; Bahuti, 4:6; Qari, art. 537.

[14]Sanhuri, 3:172.

opening a door to *riba* and *gharar*. Again, Ibn Taymiyya is the most liberal: he objects only to combinations of onerous and gratuitous contracts, such as sale and loan (*qard*), since by such combinations parties can easily hide an illegal compensation for the loan.[15] Modern scholars seem to follow this view, since combinations of contracts occur quite frequently, without being questioned on legality. If a combination seeks to subvert a basic principle, however, scholars may oppose it by citing the *hadiths* against "two sales in one" or "two bargains in one."

An easy alternative, much used classically, is to combine contracts informally, without legally conditioning one on the other. *Tawarruq*, for example, is a transaction whereby a needy person buys something on credit and then immediately, in a separate transaction with another party, sells it for cash. Most scholars declared this permissible.[16] Such a ruling reflects the fact that behavior like this cannot be regulated by law but only by moral injunction. Combinations like this are common in modern practice as well and can be policed through practical means such as simultaneous closings.

THE NOMINATE CONTRACT SCHEME

In the following pages we do little more than define the chief individual contracts and mention a few of their rules which have the greatest practical significance. (We exclude contracts that fall outside Western contract law, such as marriage and appointment to office [*wilaya*].)

Mutually Onerous Contracts

Sale (bay'). Sale, the prototype contract, is dealt with much more extensively in *fiqh* writings than other contracts, which are presumed to be regulated by analogy to it where appropriate. Sale at root is understood as

---

[15]Ibn Taymiyya, *Qawa'id*, 142-48.

[16]Kuwait Ministry of Awqaf and Islamic Affairs, "*Tawarruq*," in *al-Mawsu'a al-Fiqhiyya* (Kuwait: Tiba'at Dhat al-Salasil, 1986). The term is a Hanbali one; others refer to it as a type of *'ina* or double-sale. Ibn Hanbal considered it permissible for the needy. Bahuti, 3:186.

the transfer of ownership of some lawful (*mutaqawwam*), specific, known property for a fixed price (which may be money or other known property), both countervalues present and delivered immediately. Variations from this pattern, such as delay in payment of a countervalue, are handled as special cases. Titles to both countervalues transfer immediately at the time of sale, even if actual payment or delivery is delayed by stipulation or otherwise. The rules on which one can delay delivery or payment are complex, and turn out to be important for the future development of modern banking and finance. Accordingly, we give these lengthy consideration in the next section.

Some types of sale have acquired their own names. The forward purchase, or *salam*, is the contract by which fungible goods are purchased for delivery at a later specified time, and which requires payment of the full price before the parties separate. It is called the "sale of the penniless," since it has the purpose of financing production, usually for agricultural goods. *Sarf*, or currency exchange, is stringently regulated due to *riba* rules. In this contract, both parties must exchange the currency during the session in which the contract is concluded. In *istisna'* or commissioned manufacture, one party purchases goods to be manufactured by the other party, fixing the goods by description. When payment is due under this contract, and the extent to which it is binding, are matters of disagreement among scholars; some schools prohibit the contract altogether.[17] The *'arbun* contract is an option contract, by which the buyer makes a nonrefundable deposit against the price, reserving a right either to confirm or rescind the sale. All four of these sale contracts are of great importance in modern Islamic finance and are discussed in this and subsequent chapters.

In certain special sales, the price is fixed in relation to the sale object's cost to the seller: sale at cost (*tawliya*), sale at percentage discount (*wadi'a*), and sale at a percentage profit (*murabaha*). The law regulates carefully the expenses permitted to be included in the seller's cost for calculating the price. *Murabaha* is discussed in detail in the next chapter.

Lease and hire (ijara, *or* kira', iktira'). *Ijara* is the sale of usufruct, covering both hire of persons and lease of property. For Hanafis, whose definition of property or *mal* excludes usufructs, *ijara* is an exception to general

---

[17]See pp. 146-47 below.

legal principle, permitted only because of the people's need and the Prophet's example.[18] Hanafis therefore view leases rather strictly; for example, leases terminate on the death of either party and either party may rescind if a subsequent event diminishes his subjective value in the usufruct (e.g., a lessee rents a shop but later changes his profession; a lessor suffers financial setbacks requiring him to liquidate property). For Hanbalis, in contrast, leases are more stable: e.g., termination is allowed only if the leased object itself has a defect impairing the lessor's enjoyment of it.[19] Yet even this latter criterion may be broad by modern estimation: the Hanbali Ibn Taymiyya upholds reduction or elimination of a lessee's rental obligation when land leased for agriculture gets less rain than usual and its crop fails.[20]

Both countervalues in these contracts, the usufruct and the rent payment, must be specified precisely, or else *gharar* renders the contract invalid. In a lease, the owner of the property must pay for its upkeep and maintenance, since otherwise the tenant's obligation becomes indeterminate and the contract void.[21] It is a fundamental term of all leases that the lessor bears the risk of loss or destruction of the leased object. In the event of significant harm or destruction of the object, the lessee has the right to terminate the lease. In modern transactions, this means that, if insurance is permitted, the lessor pays the premium.

Reward (ji'ala). In reward the quantity of the work and often the identity of the worker are unknown. Examples are "I'll give anyone who returns my stray horse a dinar," or "I'll pay you $10,000 to develop a plan for a new information system." Most scholars hold that the contract is not binding on either party until the work is completed. If the promisor revokes, some scholars require him to pay for the worker's prior services at a "fair wage." The Malikis bind the promisor to the contract. The Hanafis, characteristically hesitant in upholding contracts in usufructs, invalidate the contract and pay the worker merely a fair wage for his time, up to the

---

[18]See, e.g., *Majalla*, sec. 15. The problem is a genuine one, given *gharar* rigor. How can the parties fairly sell the future, unknown benefit of a leasehold?

[19]N. Coulson, *Commercial Law in the Gulf States* (London: Graham & Trotman, 1984), 83-87; Qari, art. 697; Ibn Qudama, 6:25-31.

[20]Reproduced in *Majallat al-buhuth al-fiqhiyya al-mu'asira* 16 (1994): 182-3.

[21]*Majalla*, arts. 529, 561. Qari, art. 542.

amount of the reward.[22] *Ji'ala* clearly pushes the limits of *gharar* rules, and scholars note that it is valid only because it is revocable (on at least one side), and because it is eminently practical.[23]

Other contracts. Other mutually onerous contracts include compromise or settlement (*sulh*), rescission (*iqala*), offset (*maqassa*), and partition (*qasama*).

Gratuitous Contracts

Gift (hiba). Before actual delivery of the object, a gift is revocable and does not transfer title.[24] Offer and acceptance or their implied substitute are still required. A gift may be rescinded in certain circumstances, involving gifts between family members.[25]

Loan (ariya; qard). Two types of gratuitous loan exist, *ariya* (or *i'ara*) and *qard*. *Ariya* is the gift of a usufruct of property that is not consumed on use. It is like a gratuitous lease, except that the obligations of the parties are regulated differently from lease, for example in being terminable at will by either party and (for Hanbalis and Shafi'is) in imposing risk of loss on the borrower. *Qard* is the loan of fungibles, such as money. A *qard* is repaid with goods of identical description, rather than with the very goods originally borrowed. *Riba* rules require that it be free of any form of compensation, even in kind or services. It is a praiseworthy act; indeed, the Prophet reportedly declared it more meritorious than outright charity, since a borrower is clearly in need.[26] Often, to emphasize that a *qard* is made gratuitously, Muslims (like the Qur'an itself) use the term "*qard hasan*," or "good loan." It is now well accepted that a bank or public lending institution may

---

[22]Ali al-Khafif, *Mukhtasar ahkam al-mu'amalat al-shar'iyya* (Cairo: Matba'at al-Sunna al-Muhammadiyya, 1950), 199-201.

[23]Ibn Qudama, 6:350-353. Some claim Qur'anic support for it.

[24]For an extended analysis, see Chehata, *Études de droit musulman: 2/ La notion de responsabilité contractuelle. Le concept de propriété* (Paris: Presses Universitaires de France, 1973), 61-67.

[25]See, e.g., Qari, arts. 931-39.

[26]Ibn Maja.

charge a borrower for actual administrative costs, including overhead, incurred in extending the loan but not including the opportunity costs of the money lent.

In *qard* the ownership of the goods "lent," not the usufruct, transfers. (Goods that are consumed on use, as most fungibles are, can have no usufruct.) Title transfer occurs only on delivery, and until then the contract is not binding on the lender. Even thereafter, the lender may demand repayment at any time, and any attempt to fix a term is futile.[27] The borrower also may terminate at any time. Repayment is required in the exact quantity lent, regardless of changes in market value.[28] Some scholars forbid even a provision that the loan be repaid in another city. Where repayment of the same *type* of goods is impossible, then the goods' *value* is to be paid, determined, for the Hanafis, as of the time lent, and for the Hanbalis, as of the date of unavailability.

Deposit or bailment (wadi'a). Deposit is the gratuitous safekeeping of property. While charges for out-of-pocket costs in providing safekeeping are permitted, use of the deposit without the depositor's permission is not. The contract may be terminated at any time by either party.

Guarantee (daman, kafala). The Islamic law of guarantee is sophisticated. It is defined as the joining of one *dhimma* to another as to a debt, i.e., making an additional person liable alongside the original debtor. (Again, *dhimma* is the faculty by which a person bears liabilities.) Because it is gratuitous, the contract need not be fully specified, and a relatively high degree of *gharar* is tolerated. Thus one may guarantee payment of "whatever obligations my son undertakes."

Classical law has several drawbacks in supporting modern guarantees; the chief one is that guarantees in Islamic law must be gratuitous. If the rule were otherwise, one could guarantee a financial obligation for a price, later make it good, recoup one's loss from the obligor, and thus end up with compensation for extending credit, which is *riba*. The law does however permit the guarantor to recover out-of-pocket expenses for providing the guarantee (not including the opportunity costs of capital frozen to secure the contingent obligation).[29] These expenses will likely not be proportional

---

[27] The Maliki school differs. Khafif, *Mukhtasar*, 181.

[28] See Chapter 4, n. 30 on indexation of debts.

[29] Decision 5, second session (1985), *Fiqh Academy Journal*, 1209.

to the amount of the guarantee or its duration, and are certainly less than conventional banks would charge. Other difficulties, more easily dealt with, are statements in the classical law that a guarantor can cancel at any time before the obligor actually becomes liable, regardless of a term in the agreement; and that a guarantee does not run with an obligation, but is personal for the obligor.

Another limitation on *daman* contracts is that they are guarantees of payment of another person's obligations, not against contingent losses; in other words, they cannot be used as insurance.

Other. Other gratuitous contracts include alms (*sadaqa*) and personal surety (*kafala*).

Accessory Contracts

Agency (*wakala*). Agency (i.e., the contract by which one person represents another as the latter's agent) is a fully developed and flexible institution in Islamic law, allowing full representation in nearly all contractual situations.[30] It can be gratuitous or compensated, and tolerates many forms of compensation.[31] It recognizes the institution of the undisclosed principal.[32]

The chief weakness of *wakala* from the viewpoint of modern practice is that the contract is revocable at will by either party — for the Hanbalis even without notice. A term setting a fixed duration or goal for the agency cannot change this result. Three rules operate to mitigate this outcome: 1) when a party is damaged by an unfair untimely revocation, such as a revocation occurring just before an event earning the agent a commission, a judge might choose to award the agent compensation for actual losses or expenses incurred; 2) in the Hanafi school, a revocation takes effect only on the agent's learning of it; and 3) in the Hanafi school, if an agency involves the interests of third parties (e.g., a debtor appoints an agent to hold income as security for an obligation to a third person), it is irrevocable.[33]

---

[30]Gamal Moursi Badr, "Islamic Law: Its Relation to Other Legal Systems," *American Journal of Comparative Law* 26 (1978): 187-198, 196-97.

[31]Qari, art. 1201.

[32]Badr.

[33]*Majalla*, art. 1021.

The above weakness is underlined by the absence of any doctrine of apparent or inherent authority.[34] Authority is totally dependent on actual, continued consent. Again, we see Islamic law not countenancing acts against the property of the principal except based on his consent.

Pledge (rahn). *Rahn* affords a sophisticated form of security for creditors. It binds only upon delivery. It may be given to secure an obligation which, though binding, may not yet be exactly determined.[35]

There are two major limitations on *rahn*. It requires that the creditor, or at least an independent escrow agent, take possession of the pledge. The pledgee has no right to use the pledge, except with the pledgor's permission, and then not in the *qard* loan. The other limitation is that upon default, the pledgor does not have the right to sell the pledge to realize his debt without permission either from the debtor or from a court. Here again is the Qur'anic notion that property may not be taken without the owner's consent. The Hanafis, but not the Hanbalis, avoid this inconvenience by permitting the pledgor to appoint the pledgee irrevocably as his agent to sell.[36]

Assignment (hawala). Islamic law very early on developed a highly advanced form of assignment of debts. For example, according to the Hanbali school, a debtor may assign his obligation to another person, i.e., bindingly refer the creditor to that person for payment, without the creditor's consent and without recourse as long as the assignee is solvent. Both debtors and creditors may employ the contract. Assignments may even be for or against third parties who are neither debtors or creditors of the assignor, in which case the transfer operates as an agency to collect a loan or as a request for a loan. The limitations on the *hawala* contract arise chiefly from the need to avoid circumstances liable to *riba* and *gharar*. Thus, the debt must be both determined and due, the creditor's claim must be one for fungibles, and, most notably, both obligations must be identical in denomination and term.

---

[34]These are two doctrines both making A liable for B's acts if B, through an act for which A is held responsible, becomes falsely "clothed" with the appearance of being A's agent.

[35]Qari, art. 948, 954.

[36]*Majalla*, art. 760. This is an instance of a third-party interest rendering an agency irrevocable.

Partnership (sharika). There are many kinds of partnerships, and the rules governing them vary considerably among the schools. One should be aware that different schools employ differing terms, or even the same terms with differing meanings; for example, some consider *mudaraba* not a form of partnership but a separate contract type. The following summarizes partnership rules for the Hanbali school, which offers probably the simplest system.[37]

In partnerships the partners agree 1) to assume relations of mutual agency and at times suretyship; 2) to contribute work, credit, or capital, or combinations of all three; and 3) to share profits in predetermined percentage shares. In all partnerships, losses are borne by partners in proportion to their shares of ownership of the capital. Any uncertainty about the sharing of profit invalidates the contract, including any stipulation by a partner for a fixed sum as income regardless of profit or loss. Each partner is personally liable for any infraction of the terms of the mutual agencies, for conduct deviating from customary commercial standards, or for any wrongful (tortious) damage to property. Apart from such acts, each partner binds all his partners in his dealings with third parties. In principle,[38] partnerships are revocable at will by any partner, and terminate with the death or incapacity of any partner.

There are four major types of partnership. *'Inan* is a partnership where each of the partners contributes both capital and work. The parties may determine profit shares, and these need not reflect precisely their respective shares of working-time or of capital, but losses must be borne in proportion to capital contributions. In *mudaraba* (also called *qirad*), some of the partners contribute only capital and the others only work. The capital owners, inactive in the business, are liable for all the losses, but these are limited to their capital shares. The workers bear no losses, except in losing their labor. They are not entitled to any profit until the capital owners have recouped their investment, and then only in the agreed percentage. In *abdan* partners contribute only work. In *wujuh* partners pool their credit to

---

[37]See Abraham L. Udovitch, *Partnership and Profit in Medieval Islam* (Princeton, NJ: Princeton University Press, 1970), 17-39, for a description of Hanafi rules.

[38]Several regulations attempt to prevent unfair terminations or liquidations, while leaving the basic policy of liquidation at will in place. See Ibn Rushd, *Bidayat*, 2:240; N. Saleh, *Unlawful Gain*, 138-140.

borrow capital and transact with it. In the last two partnerships the partners are free to agree upon their relative shares of ownership of partnership capital, but are obliged to share losses accordingly.

These types of partnership are simple models which can be combined into more complex types. Thus, a partnership in which all partners contribute capital but only some of them work is a combination of *'inan* and *mudaraba*. In such a case each partner who contributes work as well as capital must receive a share of profits greater than that determined by his capital contribution.

From the above rules may be elicited three principles basic to all partnerships, which, the law states, cannot be varied even by the parties' agreement:

1) they are revocable at will;
2) losses fall solely on capital;
3) profits must be shared by percentage, not in fixed sums.

These principles have their origin in *riba* and *gharar* concerns. If not for 1), the partnership would be invalid as a hire contract (*ijara*) which fails to specify the wage; if not for 2), some of the capital investors' principal would be shielded from loss and yet earn profits, which would resemble a usurious *qard* loan; if not for 3), the contract would be guilty of both *riba* (in giving assured payment for credit) and *gharar* (in fixing the value of something inherently unknown and nonexistent).

Of all the Islamic contracts, the partnership contract has been the most fertile for modern Islamic banking and finance. Indeed, the very concept of Islamic banking, and much of Islamic economic thought, take inspiration from the contract of *mudaraba*. Gain in *mudaraba* is free from all the evils identifiable in *riba* and in *gharar*. Following chapters discuss *mudaraba* further.

FOUR PRINCIPLES OF ISLAMIC CONTRACT LAW IMPORTANT IN MODERN FINANCIAL PRACTICE

Four common principles of Islamic contract law come into relief when that law is applied in modern finance:

- the non-binding character of many basic contracts;
- a dual scheme for allocating risk of loss;
- the prohibition of sale of debt for debt; and
- the non-binding nature of the promise.

None of these principles is so clearly rooted in the revelation as are the concepts of *riba* and *gharar*. Their authority emerges instead from the fact that they are constantly upheld across the diverse rules of many contracts. In other words, they have been established not literally from *shari'a* sources but by induction from a great many *fiqh* holdings. Of the four, the first two have largely been accommodated in Islamic financial practice but do continue to have significant effects. The last two are currently the most controversial, and most affect the future of Islamic banking and finance. All need to be understood in order to account for certain peculiarities of Islamic contracting practice, explored in following chapters.

Non-Binding (*Ja'iz*) versus Binding (*Lazim*)

All of the nominate contracts are either *ja'iz*, meaning non-binding or revocable at will, or *lazim*, meaning binding and irrevocable. A contract may be *ja'iz* as to one or both of the parties. If a contract is *ja'iz* as to a party, that party may terminate the contract prospectively at any time, even if the contract declares itself irrevocable or fixes its duration. (Termination does not affect acts already taken under the aegis of the contract.) Indeed, a *ja'iz* contract is so by its very nature (i.e., this trait is an "essential term" or *muqtada*). Examples of the *ja'iz* contract are the agency and partnership contracts just discussed. The *lazim* contract, on the other hand, binds a party both retrospectively and prospectively.

The paired concepts of *ja'iz* and *lazim* afford another way to organize the nominate contracts. Contracts that are *ja'iz* to both parties include partnership (all forms), agency, deposit, loan (*'ariya*), and reward. Others are *ja'iz* for both parties until delivery, including gift, loan (*qard*), and pledge. Still others can be terminated by one of the parties, such as pledge by the pledgee (after delivery), or guarantee by the obligee. *Lazim* contracts include sale, lease, compromise, assignment, and rescission.

That so many basic contracts are treated as *ja'iz*, and that this trait in a contract cannot be amended, shows once again how in Islamic law the parties' consent is the basis for legitimacy. *Ja'iz* contracts require more than agreement at the moment of contracting; they demand the parties' continued satisfaction. Otherwise, the scholars tell us, these contracts would be void, usually for reasons of *gharar*. Conversely, scholars allow greater futurity and indefiniteness in *ja'iz* contracts. Many striking examples exist — such as permission for highly general powers of attorney in agency, or the contract of reward (*ji'ala*).

The phenomenon also underlines how sale and other binding contracts are essentially the immediate exchange of titles (though one of the properties may transfer only "in the *dhimma*").[39] In such a case, the deal being complete, no issue of continuing consent could arise.

That a contract is *ja'iz* often creates problems from the perspective of modern practice, especially for partnerships: how, given partnership's *ja'iz* nature, can one overcome the manifold instability of the partnership contract to create stable companies or corporations? This point is discussed in the next chapter.

Risk of Loss (*Daman*) versus Trust (*Amana*)

A second principle of Islamic contract law fixes the relationship of the contracting parties to any object involved in the contract, particularly as to liability for loss or damage to that object. Islamic law contemplates only two possible such relationships: a party holds the object either as a "trustworthy person" or "trustee" (*amin*), or as a "guarantor" (*damin*).[40] If the former, the party is not held liable at all for injury to the object, unless shown to be in breach of trust. A breach of trust is an act that is Islamically illegal, meaning ordinarily a breach of contract or a negligent or intentional tort. The law tends to favor the trustee in contests with an owner, since it was the owner who chose the trustee and entrusted the object to

---

[39]See p. 95 above.

[40]Although the same word is used, the concept is not that of the surety contract or *daman*.

him.[41] A *damin*, or guarantor, in contrast, bears the same risk of loss as an owner. If the object is destroyed through an act of God or force majeure, the guarantor has no recourse.

These paired concepts again allow us to organize and understand the nominate contract scheme, since all contracts use them to allocate property risks among parties. Again, these conceptions are not optional, but inherent in the contractual relationship. Any attempt to alter them by agreement will fail, and may void the contract itself.

A clue to the operation of these concepts is the maxim already noted, "Gain accompanies liability for loss" (*al-kharaj bi-al-daman*). This maxim has a number of interpretations and applications. One sense is that if a party derives the full benefit from an object, then that party should bear the risks of the true owner. In the gratuitous contract of non-fungible loan (*'ariya*), the borrower reaps all profits from the loaned property. The maxim then suggests (at least to most schools) that the borrower should assume the risks of loss. Other contracts, such as agency, deposit, and pledge, also gratuitous, usually do not permit the party holding property (the agent, the bailee, the pledgee) to derive benefit from it. In such cases, the holder not having the profit also does not bear the risk of loss or *daman*, and remains an *amin*, trustee, liable not for misadventures but only to abide by the contract and to exercise due care. In partnerships the partner is only an *amin* as to partnership property beyond his share.

In contrast, in a lease (*ijara*), since the user has to pay a rental in return for reaping the benefits from property, the owner continues to bear the risk of loss. Here the rent is seen as the profit, and the risk of loss stays with the lessor; thus the maxim "rent and liability for loss do not coincide."[42]

The trustee enjoys his immunities, however, only as long as he acts in accordance with the trust placed in him. Should he violate the *shari'a*, whether by breach of a provision of his contract or by negligently or intentionally causing harm to the goods, then he is no longer trustee but guarantor and liable for damages caused by his act, and in many cases (with casuistic variations) for any harm whatsoever to the property, however caused.

---

[41]Note the inversion from Western law of fiduciaries, which holds trustees to a stricter standard than that applied to one acting in one's own interest.

[42]*Majalla*, art. 86 (*al-ajr wa-al-daman la yajtami'an*).

These rules affect Islamic banking and finance most in leases and in partnerships. If, for example, the working partner in *mudaraba* agrees to guarantee the capital of the non-working capital partners, that agreement is void. Since the capital partners' investment yields profit, then it must be also liable to loss. The working partner risks only his labor. He becomes liable for capital loss only if he is shown to have been negligent or to have breached the agreement between the parties. Since in leases the tenant cannot be made to bear risk of loss of the property, the provision commonly found in conventional financial leases that imposes all risks on the lessee is unacceptable.

Rules Governing Delay in Payment and in Performance — The Sale of *Dayn* for *Dayn*

Of our four basic principles of Islamic contract law the remaining two lie at the developmental frontiers of Islamic banking and finance. Knowledge of them is critical to understanding some of the hesitations, concerns, and controversies that influence present debates, and hence we give them an extended discussion.[43]

The third principle, on the sale of debt for debt, affects when obligations (either to perform some action or to pay money or other property) may be delayed, and when such obligations may be bought, sold, or otherwise transferred. On such matters Islamic law has many complex rules, all designed to avoid *riba* and *gharar*. The restrictions these rules impose were less important in the past, when most contracts were promptly executed on at least one side. But in today's world, future financial obligations are among the most important forms of property; indeed, such obligations are the core of many forms of investment traded in huge volumes in financial markets. Accordingly, Islamic legal restrictions in this general area are very significant in the development of new financial instruments, particularly if these are to be traded on secondary markets.

As explained in the previous chapter, property is either a specific existent object (*'ayn*) (e.g., "this house") or an object defined generically or abstractly by an obligation (*dayn*) (e.g., to pay $1000; to "deliver one hundred bushels of #1 winter wheat"). (We shall often refer to *dayn* property as "ab-

---

[43]The following relies heavily on, and is in great part a restatement and analysis of material from, the able and discerning book by Hammad, *Bay' al-kali'*.

stract," as distinct from the concrete 'ayn.) In sale (and similar contracts) parties may exchange either type of property. One can therefore subdivide sale according to the types of property being exchanged. One may exchange 'ayn for 'ayn, 'ayn for dayn, or dayn for dayn.[44] The first, 'ayn for 'ayn, is barter. 'Ayn for dayn is the most common, and has several sub-cases, depending on whether either or both of the two countervalues, the 'ayn or the dayn, is delayed (nasi'a). The most basic sale is of a present 'ayn, i.e., a present, inspected thing, for a present dayn in the form of cash on hand. The money price here is dayn, even if it is paid promptly, because the contract specifies it abstractly and not as so many unique coins. The buyer gains immediate title to the sold 'ayn, i.e., it becomes his property, and he usually demands it at once from the seller. The seller also immediately "owns" the price "as a dayn in the buyer's dhimma," i.e., as an obligation owed by the buyer. If the contract fixes a term for payment, the seller cannot demand the price until then.

The third subdivision of sale is the sale of dayn for dayn (bay' al-dayn bi-al-dayn). Many restrictions apply to these sales, summed up by a maxim forbidding the sale of "al-kali' bi-al-kali'," meaning literally the exchange of two things both "delayed," or the exchange of a delayed (nasi'a) countervalue for another delayed countervalue. The maxim is also attested as a hadith of the Prophet, but only with weak authentication.[45] In any case, the principle is said to have near universal application, and thus to have earned canonical authority as ijma', or unanimous consensus.[46]

The widespread respect accorded this maxim suggests major insights into the Islamic law of contract. As a first insight, the maxim helps explain why the contract of sale is understood as an immediate exchange of title. As we saw above, in every sale titles to the countervalues are exchanged at once, in at least the fictive sense that the creditor "owns" any delayed sum "in the dhimma" of the debtor. But the maxim requires more than just this imagined transfer. Scholars derive from it two additional rules.[47]

---

[44]See Ibn Rushd, Bidayat, 2:125; Kasani, 5:134.

[45]Hammad, Bay' al-kali', 12-13. Ibn Taymiyya argues that the quoted version of the hadith, and not another prohibiting the sale of "al-dayn bi-al-dayn" alone, has been accepted and followed universally by scholars. Ibid., 24.

[46]Ibid., 9-10.

[47]These two extrapolations from the maxim are not unanimously agreed upon by scholars, although such an agreement is often claimed. Ibn Taymiyya seeks to disprove both that the ijma' extends to sales involving one or more 'ayns (contradicting the first

The first of these rules prohibits exchanges where the contract specifies delay terms, not just for the transfer of titles, but also for actual payment or delivery of the two countervalues, e.g., wheat to be delivered later for money to be paid later. This is termed *al-nasi'a bi-al-nasi'a*, "delay for delay," or, as the Malikis term it, *ibtida' dayn bi-dayn*, "initial *dayn* for *dayn*." So interpreted, the maxim prohibits doubly delayed exchanges even if one or both of the goods are *'ayn* — e.g., it would forbid not only the exchange of abstract wheat for abstract money, but also the exchange of a clock later for a horse later, or a clock later for money later. Thus the maxim excludes the purely executory or future sale — perhaps the most common contract of sale today — i.e., a contract in which the parties exchange only promises or obligations, with the actual sale occurring only when these obligations are satisfied.

The second rule, going beyond the literal terms of the maxim, prohibits the exchange of abstract property for abstract property (*al-dayn bi-al-dayn*). This rule applies (here diverging from the first rule) even when one or both of the two *dayn*s is due presently. Thus, it is forbidden to sell a *dayn*, whether due now or later, for another *dayn* due now or later.[48] (Remember that *dayn* includes even a presently due countervalue if known only abstractly or generically.) To make this lawful one must produce the actual goods owed on at least one side of the transaction. For example, the Hanbalis hold that if X owes Y so many bushels of a type of wheat, then Y cannot sell that obligation back to X for so much money, unless the money is actually paid over when the resale agreement is concluded; or X can produce the actual wheat and then rebuy it.[49] In either case, when produced in concrete form the obligation becomes no longer *dayn* but *'ayn (ta'yin)*,[50] and thus lawful. Similarly, in *salam* or its analogue *bay' mawsuf fi al-*

---

rule) and that the *hadith* applies to a *dayn* due presently (contradicting the second rule). But his exploitations of this initiative are quite limited, not going as far as these claims would suggest, probably because in fact the agreement on these particular results is so widespread. Ibid., 14, 24.

[48]Not surprisingly, since in this falls the infamous *riba al-jahiliyya*. Ibn Taymiyya carves out an exception for parties cancelling mutual debts by exchange, even when the debts are not yet due. Ibid., 24-27.

[49]Qari, arts. 292-3.

[50]The point is underlined by the apparent Shafi'i position that if a sale does not employ the word "salam" and if the price exists and is identified during the contracting session (*ta'yin*), then the price need not be delivered at once. 'Abd Allah al-Sharqawi (d. 1812), *Hashiyya 'ala tuhfat al-tullab* (Beirut: Dar al-Ma'rifa, 1975?), 2:16-17. The Hanafis would not use the term *ta'yin* of money. See Kasani, 5:212.

dhimma, which are both contracts to purchase generic goods for later delivery, it is not enough merely to agree on a present price (*dayn*) in exchange for title to these goods "in the *dhimma*." All schools agree that the buyer must actually pay the price during the contracting session, since, again, the price thereby is effectively realized or made equivalent to an *'ayn* — otherwise the sale is void.

These requirements resemble certain *riba* rules studied in Chapter 4: whenever property that is *riba*-related (*ribawi*) is exchanged within a single *'illa* (weight or volume, food, currency), then the exchange must be "hand-to-hand" to avoid prohibited *riba* of delay. For example, wheat can only be exchanged for rice with present delivery on both sides before the contracting parties separate, or else the sale is void. The most common such contract in practice, however, involves not commodities but currencies, and has the special name *sarf*.

The ban on sale of *dayn* for *dayn* has extensive implications for transactions in obligations. Rules prohibit a person owning *dayn* property in the *dhimma* of another (i.e., holding an obligation from another) however arising (from loan, sale, guarantee, liability for damages, etc.) from selling that property (obligation) to a third party, whether or not the payment is made at once or with delay. In prohibiting such sales even for a price in hand the rule seems to go beyond the maxim. Only the Malikis are lenient in this respect, permitting such sales as long as the debt is not in food, is for a present payment in hand, and does not involve a prohibited *riba*-of-delay exchange (e.g., no exchange of an obligation in gold for gold or silver; allows exchange of an obligation in cotton for present payment in cash).[51] As seen above, schools tend to tolerate sale of an obligation to the obligor himself, at times even for a profit, as long as the price is paid at once and the exchange does not fall within *riba* of delay prohibitions.[52] A controversial holding of a few scholars allows a debtor to prepay his obligation for a discount, even in the same currency (*da' wa-ta'ajjal*, or "reduce and accelerate"). A general exception to all the above rules is the contract of *hawala*, or assignment of debt, which permits transferring a debt as long as, apart from change in the parties' identities, the obligation undergoes no change whatsoever due to the transfer and incurs no added cost.[53]

---

[51]Suhnun, *al-Mudawwana al-kubra* (Cairo: al-Sa'ada, 1905) 87-88, 90-91, 95-96; Ibn Juzayy, 296; Ibn Rushd, *Bidayat*, 2:144-5.

[52]Qari, arts. 293, 1621, 1628. Hammad, *Bay' al-kali'*, 24-27.

[53]See p. 108 above.

All this covers cases where both of the countervalues are contractually delayed or where both are *dayn*. What about cases where (a) at least one of the countervalues is *'ayn*, and (b) one (and only one) of the countervalues is contractually delayed? The two rules of the maxim then have no application. The ordinary credit sale is therefore lawful: one may sell a particular horse now for money due later. Schools differ as to whether it is possible to sell an *'ayn* due on a future date, even against money due now.[54] In credit sale, because one side is *'ayn*, the second rule's requirement that one countervalue actually be delivered or paid immediately has no application. It is enough if the *'ayn* is presently due, such that, if not delivered, the creditor may resort to the courts for enforcement. (We discuss the creditor's various remedies below.) If, on the other hand, the creditor chooses to overlook the delay in delivery, or delays in getting enforcement, the validity of the contract and the parties' various rights continue unaffected. (Let us call this type of delay in contract performance "delivery delay," as opposed to "contractual delay.") Note that in this situation neither party performs at once, but this results more from fact than law.

To complicate matters slightly, the law at times accords one or both parties a right to delivery delay, which then becomes difficult to distinguish from contractual delay. The following are instances of this phenomenon. First, if one party practices delivery delay without legal right, then the other party may delay its performance as well. Second, if a party has one of certain rights to rescind, then one or both of the parties may also have the right to delay delivery. For example, in the Hanbali school if a party has stipulated a general right to rescind for a fixed period of time (*khiyar al-shart*),[55] then neither party is obliged to perform until the right is cancelled or expires. Third, for the Maliki school in particular, if unique goods (*'ayn*) are sold without current inspection but by description or by earlier viewing ("I sell you my black four-year-old horse"), then the seller may delay paying the price until the goods are received and their compliance with the description or earlier viewing is confirmed. Malikis even void any contract

---

[54]Opponents argue that title to an *'ayn* transfers at once in reality; it cannot reside in "someone's *dhimma*," i.e., be delayed. Underlying this may be the idea that an *'ayn* is always exposed to loss or disappearance. Ibn Rushd, *Bidayat,* 2:156. Proponents believe the title to the *'ayn* is transferred with the seller retaining the right to use it for a period. Ibn Taymiyya, *al-Fatawa,* 3:371.

[55]See pp. 155–156 below.

that requires an earlier payment in such circumstances.[56] Various rationales are offered for these results, such as the uncertainty affecting performance at a time when the outcome of the contract remains uncertain. Note that in such circumstances, in apparent contradiction to the maxim's first rule, neither party's performance is due immediately, and both are legally postponed to the future.

But there remain several distinctions from the case of the prohibited exchange of two performances both at delayed terms: first, only one of the delays is stipulated in the contract, while the other arises by operation of law; second, the latter delay is merely the mirror image of the former, accorded to achieve some sort of parity between the parties, and falls due whenever the other performance is rendered; third, delay is optional with the party advantaged by these rights, such that an earlier performance is due performance, not a different performance varying the terms of the contract, such as early payment of a delayed price would be.

Following a suggestion of Ibn Rushd, Table 5-a works out the various possibilities for delay of countervalues.

Delivery delays are policed chiefly by such techniques as imposing on a delaying party the risk of loss of goods, or awarding to the other party rights to the property's yield. For Hanafis, the sold object remains at the seller's risk until delivery. If the object is harmed or destroyed other than by the buyer's fault, the seller does not pay lost value to the buyer, but the sale merely fails. For this reason, the sale is said not to be final (*tamm*) until delivery.[57] Intricate rules govern the parties' rights to take action affecting the countervalues (such as selling them to a third party) pending payment or delivery and pending the duration of any options to rescind.

The foregoing rules influence a sale contract worthy of special mention, *bay' al-istisna'*, or sale by manufacture. To the Hanafis, this is a contract to manufacture a good of a certain description, not yet existent, for an agreed price. The buyer need not pay for the good until he accepts it. While the majority Hanafi position holds that until the goods are accepted each of the parties has a right to revoke, Abu Yusuf, followed by late Hanafi law, holds that both parties are fully bound by the contract. The buyer may re-

---

[56]'Abd al-Wahhab Abu Sulayman, "'Aqd al-tawrid," in *Mawsu'at al-mu'amalat al-fiqhiyya, Majma' al-fiqh al-islami*, forthcoming; Ahmad ibn Muhammad al-Tahawi, *Mukhtasar ikhtilaf al-fuqaha'* (Beirut: Dar al-Basha'ir al-Islamiyya, 1995), 2:74-75.

[57]Chehata gives this point an extended analysis, 1-60.

Table 5-a. TENTATIVE ANALYSIS OF OUTCOMES FOR DISTRIBUTIONS OF 'AYN AND DAYN EXCHANGES

In all cases title shifts at the time of sale — on both sides.	A. BOTH PAID OR DUE NOW	B. BOTH DELAYED BY CONTRACT (NOT DUE NOW)	C. ONE DUE NOW, ONE DELAYED BY CONTRACT
I. 'AYN FOR 'AYN	Lawful barter. Informal delays in delivery ("delivery delays") do not void contract, but create right in other party to demand delivery	Not lawful. But various kinds of rights to rescind (khiyarat) can give rise to a legal right in the buyer to delay payment of price until right to rescind ends	Scholars differ on validity of delaying an 'ayn. Mere delivery delay, however, does not void contract
II. 'AYN FOR DAYN	Lawful. Was the most common type of sale (e.g., horse for money). (A countervalue is a dayn even if owing immediately if defined in the contract generically [e.g., $X, or X bushels of wheat of specified quality].) Delivery delay remains possible	Not lawful. But following situations have similar results: CR (a) Rights to rescind as above (b) Hanafi istisna' rules postpone payment and delivery to later date; majority of Hanafis consider this contract non-binding; goods to be manufactured are treated (exceptionally) as 'ayn though delayed; (c) Maliki cases of sale of absent 'ayn, or of 'ayn by description: price may be delayed until 'ayn delivered; works like a right to rescind (khiyar)	Lawful for (contractual) delay of the dayn side (the ordinary credit sale); scholars differ if it is the 'ayn that is delayed (a) Delivery delay of either side is possible. In fact, the Malikis void contracts for purchase of absent 'ayn if they stipulate immediate payment (b) If the item sold is a fungible, it must become an 'ayn, such as by payment or identification (see III.C. below)
III. DAYN FOR DAYN	Not lawful, since it is dayn bi-dayn, unless one or both countervalues is actually paid in contracting session (thus making the dayn effectively 'ayn) (a) If both are currency, then it is sarf, requiring delivery of both before parties separate (b) If not (a), but between other ribawis of same 'illa, like wheat and rice, same result as (a) (c) If not (a) or (b), then one side must be paid now; see rules on salam below (III.C.)	Not lawful, since it is dayn bi-dayn. Closest thing is an istisna' according to Abu Yusuf, which binds both parties "in the dhimma" to perform at a future date. Another instance is lease (ijara) of a thing by description ("a strong 4-year-old pack camel") that commences at a future date (idafa); payment can be delayed	Not lawful, since it is dayn bi-dayn. But if one of the two countervalues is paid during the contract session, this makes it like 'ayn and the exchange becomes lawful. Hence the requirement in salam and bay' mawsuf fi al-dhimma that one of the countervalues be paid before parties separate, or the contract is void

(as suggested by Ibn Rushd, *Bidayat al-Mujtahid*, 2:125)

voke only if the goods differ from their contractual description.[58] Abu Yusuf's position appears to offend the sale-of-debt rules, perhaps explaining why the Hanafis describe *istisna'* as a sale of an *'ayn*, albeit one which (exceptionally) does not yet exist.[59] In such a sale one observes Islamic law's closest approach to the bilateral executory contract, i.e., one contractually delayed on both sides.[60] Considering it to vary from established rules, Hanafis accept *istisna'* only because of long-established custom and the people's need for it. In contrast, for Hanbalis such an *istisna'* is invalid. They allow buyers to achieve the desired result by other means, either by purchase of raw materials on condition that the seller manufacture them into specific goods, or by purchase of abstractly defined goods in the *dhimma* (*bay' mawsuf fi al-dhimma*). In the latter case the buyer must pay in full at once,[61] and in both cases he is bound as long as the final product agrees with the description.

What aspects of the above analysis of delay in sale most affect modern transactions? First, generically defined goods are vastly more common in modern commercial society than they were in medieval times. Outside of real estate and sales between private individuals, few items are sold as unique. Most goods are to some degree standardized and fungible, and are purchased by description, not identification. This means that Islamic law's degree of tolerance for delay, largely confined to sales of *'ayn*, may prove inadequate in today's society. Second, the bilateral executory transaction is fundamental to the operation of modern economies. Through contracts,

---

[58]*Majalla*, art. 392. See also S. Baz, *Sharh al-majalla*, 3d ed. (Beirut: Dar Ihya' al-Turath al-'Arabi, 1986), 14-15. The OIC Fiqh Academy has endorsed this view. Decision 67/3/7, seventh session (1992), *Fiqh Academy Journal*, 777-78.

[59]Shams al-Din al-Sarakhsi, *Kitab al-mabsut* (Beirut: Dar al-Ma'rifa, 1986), 25:84-85.

[60]Another near approach is the future lease (*ijara bi-al-idafa*) for which both the usufruct and the payment may occur at times agreed upon in the future. The lease may moreover involve the usufruct of something by generic description. Thus, "I rent from you a four-year-old pack camel in good condition for one year commencing one year from now."

[61]Practice as to construction contracts in Saudi courts, which generally apply Hanbali rules, differs. Although these can be seen as *bay' mawsuf fi al-dhimma*, judges demand only partial payment at once. I have been told by a Saudi judge that this is through the logic of *ijara*, with the sale of materials treated as incidental. Alternatively, the contract may be seen as the purchase of raw materials, actually delivered, with a condition (*shart*) that they be constructed into a building.

parties expect to be able to gain security for a future performance without paying fully for that performance in advance. Even with no advance payment or performance, modern laws build a reciprocally secure arrangement; the parties mutually undertake either to perform or to respond in damages for all attendant losses. Modern law would see an advance payment requirement as unfair in denying the paying party the ability to refuse performance if the other party should default. But Islamic law, as summed up in the *al-kali'* maxim (forbidding sale of "delay for delay"), systematically opposes this logic. Third, the rules inhibit the liquidity of financial assets, or assets denominated in money or other generic goods. At best, these can only be sold for a differently denominated asset and only with immediate payment.

How fundamental to Islamic contract law are these various outcomes? To what extent could they be changed by reinterpretation? If they are based solely on the logic of the *al-kali'* maxim, not itself firmly established as a *hadith*, and no other revealed texts, perhaps they can be changed. Note that, given *fiqh* method, if a juristic maxim is not also a *hadith*, it cannot properly be used to deduce other legal rulings; the scholar must erect analogies from the original rulings that gave rise to the maxim.

The *al-kali'* maxim, even if not revealed, remains redoubtable because its rule is upheld so pervasively throughout *fiqh*; its authority stems not from *hadith* but from *ijma'* or the consensus of the scholars, an august source of law in its own right. Ibn Taymiyya sought to diminish the force of the maxim not only by noting the weakness of its *hadith* support but also by claiming that the *ijma'* supporting it was narrower than is usually assumed.[62] Today, the maxim is also undermined by the now-widespread willingness to question juristic conclusions of the four Sunni schools, even when they agree and claim among themselves an *ijma'*. For all these reasons, therefore, even this maxim today is not invincible, unless the modern mind can see it as dictated by, or profoundly concordant with, revealed sources.

One way to determine this is to examine the degree to which the maxim and its attendant rules are dictated by other fundamental principles of the Islamic contract law. *Riba* principles are clearly violated in many sales of *dayn* for *dayn*: examples are the Qur'anically-condemned *riba al-jahiliyya* (a debtor buys back his delayed obligation, paying for it with an-

---

[62]Ibn Taymiyya, *Nazariyyat*, 235; idem, *Majmu' al-fatawa*, 20:512.

other higher, further delayed one); a creditor's discount of delayed money obligations to a bank; and the exchange of currency with delay, by which an element of interest is included in the price.

But other *dayn-bi-dayn* prohibitions are difficult to defend from the *riba* perspective. In a *salam* contract, why not allow the buyer to sell his expectation in goods, such as wheat, to the seller or a third party for cash? Here perhaps one fears added intermediary transactions increasing commodity prices. In any event, the Malikis do allow this for goods other than food.[63] Even more difficult to understand is the ban on bilateral executory sales. In sales like *salam* a reduced sale price reflects an interest-like charge compensating the buyer for advancing money against the goods. This charge would disappear if the buyer could delay the price also. Payment delay would also eliminate the chance that when a *salam* contract is rescinded, it would end up like a loan compensated for by an initial chance for gain.

It seems that the more basic objection to sales of debt for debt is not *riba* but *gharar*. For example, *gharar* easily accounts for the ban on the bilateral delayed sale. First, such contracts encourage speculation, since with little or no capital investment one takes a position as to future prices. With immediate delivery, in contrast, at least one countervalue is delivered on terms then acceptable to both parties and those goods are removed from further market risks. The price calculation becomes complicated by the fact that one party gains the current use of one countervalue and assumes its current risk. Lacking these factors, sales with simultaneous delays are likely to leave one party feeling the loser, creating the "enmity" which the Qur'an associates with gambling. Second, the purchase of generic goods that may not exist or be owned introduces *gharar* on one side of the transaction. If a similar risk were allowed on the other side, the transaction arguably becomes too unstable.[64]

---

[63]See page 117 above. Rules on sales of debt are more restrictive for *salam*. Note that the OIC Academy, in a one-sentence statement in a decision, declines to exploit any opportunity afforded by the Maliki position on sale of salam goods before delivery: "Likewise it is impermissible to sell the commodity purchased by salam before delivery [of that commodity]." Decision 65/1/7, seventh session (1992), *Fiqh Academy Journal*, 711, 716. Presumably, they relied on Ibn Qudama's statement that he knows of "no difference of opinion" on the point (4:341), seemingly ignoring the Maliki view. See p. 146, n. 34 below.

[64]Muhammad b. Ahmad al-Ramli, *Nihayat al-muhtaj* (Cairo: Mustafa al-Babi al-Halabi, 1967-69), 4:184. In classical law three other arguments are made for the ban.

Given these arguments, and given the general agreement among the scholars (including Ibn Taymiyya) against the bilateral executory contract, the force of the debt-for-debt maxim in this matter is unlikely to dissipate soon. Recently, however, two authors have argued for its reversal. One does so on the ultimate ground of necessity (*darura*), i.e., that executory contracts are now so necessary in modern commerce that they should be allowed, just as carrion becomes lawful if a man is starving.[65] Another author offers a more nuanced and challenging argument. He argues that delayed payment should be permitted in supply contracts until the goods are delivered, even for fungible goods or goods sold by description. Pointing to the more liberal rules applying to delay in contracts with an *'ayn* on one side, he argues that, first, the central distinction between *'ayn* and *dayn* should rest not on whether the goods are unique but on whether they already exist; and second, where goods under a supply contract are continuously available on the market, the contract should tolerate the postponement of payment until the goods are received, just as they would if the goods were *'ayn*. The Maliki position requiring payment delay in sales of absent *'ayns* should apply to such modern contracts.[66]

Another argument in support of the result is the fact, already mentioned, that nowadays most goods in commerce are generic in some degree (e.g., red horse versus Buick sedan, tailor-made versus ready-made). The narrow rules applying to future obligations in generic goods perhaps should not apply so broadly to obligations in all the diverse goods of mod-

---

First, an executory transaction charges "two *dhimmas*" without any benefit to either party, not even of the usufruct of one of the considerations (Ibn Taymiyya, *Nazariyyat*, 235). Note that this wholly ignores the value to parties of securing an enforceable obligation to perform in the future, so essential to the intricate workings of modern economic life. Second, even contracts with advance payment on one side, such as *salam*, are objectionable for inherent *gharar* and potential for exploitation. They are allowed because producers of goods such as crops need advances, and if there were no *salam*, would have to turn to loans at interest or sharecropping. Third, *salam* and *salaf*, the names used for forward purchases in the time of the Prophet, both mean "advance" or even "loan." Nazih Hammad, *'Aqd al-salam fi al-shari'a al-islamiyya* (Beirut: al-Dar al-Shamiyya, 1993), 15-16.

[65]Hammad, *Bay' al-kali'*, 28-29.

[66]Sulayman, "'Aqd al-tawrid"; also discussion at Harvard Law School concerning that paper, 16 November 1995.

ern society, many of which do not enjoy the volatility and easy marketability possessed by generic goods of the past.[67]

The Promise (*Wa'd*) in Islamic Law

The fourth general principle of classical Islamic law to be considered is, like the third, thrown into relief by modern financial practices. This is the classical law's position that mere promises are not binding. Obligation arises instead either from the past transfer or destruction of property, which automatically generates reciprocal obligation, present or delayed; or from the oath. When promises are "mere" promises — neither oaths before God nor reciprocity for goods — the law sees them as lacking legal significance, not appropriately compelled by the processes of law. Parallels in Western law are the social promise (e.g., "I will meet you at 2:00 p.m."), or the promise without consideration in Anglo-American law ("Because you're a good nephew, I'll give you a million dollars"). In Western systems breaking such promises may occasion social disapproval or ethical demerit, but not enforcement at law.

In modern finance and banking, a great deal depends on promises. Many transactions bind both parties only in the future, and practically any transaction can be entirely prefigured in binding fashion by promise. Such deals can be entered into at very low cost, because one's own promise supports the promise of the other party; yet, once they are agreed to, each party gains a right to recover any losses caused by the other party's unexcused breach. Many financial interests consist partly or entirely of mere promises. In contrast, under Islamic law almost all contracts become binding only after one party has performed, meaning that the grounds for enforcing the contract or awarding damages relies not just on the notion of promise but also on the powerful grounds of unjust enrichment and reliance.

In the modern legal environment Islamic finance and banking are strongly drawn to incorporate the promise. They often do so when the parties have strong extra-legal incentives to comply, whether the promise is legally binding or not. Examples:

---

[67]This argument is expanded below, p. 148.

A lessor promises to convey title to property at the end of a financial lease; the lessor's concern for its reputation and for the saleability of its financial product will prevent it from breaching the promise.

Correspondent banks mutually promise to enter later into a currency exchange transaction on certain terms. The banks are unlikely to jeopardize their business relationships by breaking the promise.[68]

In other cases, however, the legal enforceability of a promise is vital for creating an effective financial instrument. An example of such a case is a modern implementation of *murabaha* sales, which figures prominently in the next chapter. In this transaction, a customer asks a bank to purchase certain goods on the customer's specifications from a supplier (Sale 1), and promises that, after the bank acquires the goods, he will purchase them from the bank for a markup (Sale 2). Since under Islamic law Sale 2, between the bank and the customer, cannot be bindingly concluded until Sale 1 is complete and the bank has the goods in its possession, the bank is exposed to the danger that, while it is acquiring the goods, the customer will change his mind. The bank would suffer losses in trying to return or to dispose of the purchased goods. To meet this problem, scholars have issued fatwas that the promise of the customer to enter into Sale 2 binds him, at least to the extent that he pay any losses incurred by the bank as a consequence of its reliance on the promise. The OIC Fiqh Academy fatwa to this effect carefully provides that the promise is unilateral, binding only the customer. Were it bilateral, the fatwa recognizes, the result would be a binding future sale without performance due from either side, a result not permitted in Islamic law.[69] While using terms and reasoning suggesting that its position applies to all promises eliciting reliance, the fatwa does not expressly go beyond this particular case of *murabaha*. Other scholars have more broadly examined the issue of promises, and concluded that they should be binding under all circumstances.[70]

---

[68]As discussed in Chapter 2, often Islamic banking agreements include clauses providing for resolution of disputes under the laws and courts of non-Islamic legal systems, which do enforce promises, making it unnecessary as a practical (if not a religious-legal) matter to rely on extra-legal incentives.

[69]Decisions 2 and 3, fifth session (1988), *Fiqh Academy Journal*, 1599-1600.

[70]'Abd Allah bin Sulayman Bin Mani', "al-Wa'd wa-hukm al-ilzam bi-al-wafa' bi-hi diyanatan wa-qada'an," *Majallat al-buhuth al-fiqhiyya al-mu'asira* 16 (1413 H): 6-33;

To appreciate the significance of even the modest Academy fatwa for Islamic contract law, let us examine several hypothetical applications to which it might give rise. If Sale 1 involves an extensive delay, since the buyer is bound, but the bank is not, the result is that the bank has a put — i.e., if after Sale 1 the market price of the goods goes above the sale price of Sale 2, the bank can sell the goods elsewhere. If, however, the market price stays at or below the sale price of Sale 2, then the bank may "put" them to the buyer. If the buyer should refuse the goods, the bank can sue for damages in the amount of its losses from the default — which is the same as enforcing the put.

If the fatwa were applied to *salam* contracts (or other contracts with advance payment and delayed delivery), nothing in its reasoning would bar such transactions as the following:

a. A customer approaches a bank to acquire for him goods from a trading house by a *salam* contract. The customer promises that on date T it will buy the goods from the bank for the bank's price P plus a markup (Sale 2). The bank then enters into a *salam* contract (Sale 1) with the trading house to buy the goods with delivery on date T, prepaying P in full to the trading house as *salam* rules require. Given the binding nature of the customer's promise, the net result between the bank and the customer is, again, a conventional put. The bank is not bound to carry through with Sale 2, but will do so if the market price falls below P plus markup.

b. What if, instead of the customer promising to buy in Sale 2, the bank promises to *sell*? This turns the transaction into a call, not a put. The bank could use this approach to sell call options to customers.

c. If the bank feels obliged to uphold sales even when their price terms turn out to be disadvantageous to itself — i.e., the bank may be obliged never to exercise its put option — Sale 2 becomes identical to a Western futures contract, because the bank and the customer are both bound to a future sale without either performing initially. In other words, the bank could use this mechanism to

Sami Homoud, *al-Adawat al-tamwiliyya al-islamiyya li-al-sharikat al-musahama* (Jedda: Islamic Research and Training Institute, 1996), 62-67; see various studies prepared for OIC Fiqh Academy in fifth session (1988), *Fiqh Academy Journal*, 2:753-929.

sell true futures contracts to customers, evading the prepayment requirements of *salam*.

d. What if the bank and the trading house were not at arm's length, but were merely financial and operational subsidiaries of a single larger entity? Then the bank makes no sacrifice in paying cash in advance in the *salam* contract between it and the trading house (Sale 1); the payment would be a mere accounting entry. Then the overall situation (Sale 1 and Sale 2) comes even closer to a conventional call or futures contract. Again, the bank (and its affiliate trading house) could use this tool to offer options and futures contracts to the market.

The possibility that results so anomalous and radical in Islamic legal terms can flow from the Academy's fatwa shows the dangers inherent in the fatwa's approach. By acknowledging future promises as binding, it risks subverting a basic principle of the Islamic contractual scheme, as it has been known up to now. This risk persists even if the promise is seen as merely unilateral or is enforced only by damages awards.[71]

For these reasons, one should not rely on this fatwa being applied beyond its immediate context of certain *murabaha* transactions. Similarly, one should not be optimistic that the arguments of several scholars in favor of the general enforceability of promises will soon succeed.

---

[71]Concern is augmented by historical parallels. In the history of the common law, an opening wedge leading to the enforcement of bare promises was the doctrine that promises were enforced only to the extent of paying the promisee's damages from relying on the promise, by an action sounding in tort. E. Allan Farnsworth, *Contracts* (Boston: Little, Brown & Co., 1990), sec. 1.6; A.W. Brian Simpson, *A History of the Common Law of Contract: The Rise of the Action of Assumpsit* (Oxford: Oxford University Press, 1975), esp. 53-315.

As a second example of how allowing promises to pay damages can serve as a wedge by which to deflect basic contract doctrine, see al-Siddiq al-Darir, "al-Ittifaq 'ala ilzam al-madin al-musir bi-ta'wid darar al-mumatala," *Majallat abhath al-iqtisad al-islami* 3 (1985): 111-113 (delay penalties for late payment).

CHAPTER 6

The Law of Islamic Financial Institutions and Instruments

In light of the essential concepts of Islamic contract and commercial law explained in the previous three chapters, we now examine the institutions, contracts, and instruments by which Islamic banking and Islamic finance are currently practiced. This provides the necessary legal background for the next three chapters, which analyze Islamic finance from the perspective of corporate finance.

This chapter pursues five main topics:

- The basic model and theory for an Islamic financial institution;
- The Islamic contracts used in Islamic finance;
- Insurance;
- The prospects for Islamically valid derivatives;
- Investment securities and their negotiability under Islamic law.

THE MODEL FOR AN ISLAMIC
FINANCIAL INSTITUTION

How is a modern system of banking and investment to be built, given the rules we have described? Searching deeply in Islamic law for fundamental economic and legal norms, Muslims have seized on the principles of partnership, particularly *mudaraba*, as the model for a non-interest-based economic system.[1] They have given special emphasis to two of these principles:

- return on capital cannot be fixed in advance but must be a proportion of profits;
- capital, not labor, is liable to the financial risks of the venture.

Economists argue that, like interest, *mudaraba* offers the opportunity of pure finance, enabling the owner of capital to invest his capital without himself becoming involved in managing that capital and without exposing himself to liabilities in excess of that capital. Unlike interest lending, however, Islamic partnership, governed by the two basic principles above, maintains a fair balance between the owner of capital and the entrepreneur who uses it. Most importantly, the capital provider cannot claim both a fixed profit and the assured return of his capital, whatever the fate of the investment. He profits only in proportion as the venture profits, and it is his capital that is hostage to the venture's losses, although he will not be liable beyond that capital. ("Profit" is understood to be the increase in the total value of the venture over the initial capital investment — i.e., the total return — rather than just the venture's cash income.) The entrepreneur, the *mudarib*, receives a percentage of profit. In the event of a loss, he loses his labor, but has no other obligation.

Modern Muslim economists use these two partnership principles to justify an Islamic financial system in competition with Western ones. These two principles have become the touchstone of Islamicity in economics.

The Two-Tier *Mudaraba*

After adopting these principles, the scholars' next task was to devise institutions for practicing them. Beginning in 1955,[2] scholars developed a notion of "two-tier *mudaraba*" as the model for the Islamic financial institution.

A first-tier *mudaraba* is created when investors (we shall call them "depositors") place their capital with an Islamic bank, fund, or other finan-

---

[1]Partnership, including *mudaraba*, is discussed below, pp. 109-110.

[2]Mohammad Uzair, *An Outline for Interestless Banking* (Karachi: Raihan Publications, 1955) (with gratitude to Dr. M. Elgari).

cial institution, which here acts as the *mudarib* or working partner. The financial institution or *mudarib* in turn invests these funds with entrepreneurs (the equivalent of a conventional bank's borrowers) by means of second-tier *mudarabas*, in which the Islamic financial institution now has the role of capital investor. Such a practice is possible since classical law permits a *mudarib* to choose not to perform the productive work himself but to invest the partnership capital with other *mudaribs*. The institution's profits then come not from interest income but from a percentage of the profits from the second-tier *mudarabas*.

The bank or fund in this arrangement faces fewer liquidity problems than a conventional bank since it does not guarantee the capital of its depositors. (If depositors want total security for their capital, they may have it, but at the cost of foregoing any profit on their accounts.) The risk assumed by depositors enables the institution to tolerate greater risk on its "assets" side, as it must if it is to make equity investments in *mudaraba* ventures instead of lending on interest.

An Islamic bank can earn additional income by charging fees for banking services (letters of credit, guarantees, credit investigations, and so forth) on the basis of contracts of hire (*ijara*). It may make interest-free loans (*qard hasan*) either as a charitable activity or as a favor to customers, lawfully charging for the actual costs of its services in providing such loans, but not for the opportunity cost of the money.[3]

Islamic Legal Hurdles Facing This Islamic Banking Model

While this adaptation of *mudaraba* is both inspired and simple, many problems in classical law had to be addressed before it could be widely applied. Many of these problems are still not fully solved. We consider three major groups of problems:

- Problems in managing deposits, i.e., first-tier *mudaraba* investments, arising because these deposits are understood as partnership interests under Islamic law;

---

[3]Cf. decision 1, third session (1986), Fiqh *Academy Journal* (fatwa specifically for the Islamic Development Bank).

- Problems in organizing the Islamic bank or fund using conventional legal forms and practices, particularly those of the corporation;
- Problems arising from pressure on Islamic financial institutions to frame deposits and investments to have risk and liquidity characteristics similar to those of conventional commercial banks, in order to compete.

Managing Deposits as Partnership Interests: The Public Mudaraba. According to classical law, partnership profits are knowable only after the venture has ended and all of its assets are liquidated. Prior distributions, if any, are made only on account. A partner withdraws by exercising his right to force the termination and liquidation of the partnership.[4] Classical law says nothing about a party transferring or selling his *mudaraba* interest to another partner or to a third party during the life of the partnership. The investor can impose certain general limits on the actions of the active partner or manager, simply by issuing instructions.

If such legal constructions were to control its deposits, how could an Islamic bank or fund offer depositors different maturities or liquidity options? How could it tolerate inevitable mismatches between the maturities of various deposits or investments and still pay depositors the precise return their money has earned? How would the manager respond to the individual instructions of all investors? In response to such difficulties modern Islamic law has, in effect, created a new type of *mudaraba*, called by Sami Homoud a "public" or "shared" *mudaraba*.[5] This *mudaraba* continues unaffected by changes of membership. Its returns are determined not by actual liquidation but by using accounting techniques (and various assumptions like prorating) to provide a constructive or conjectural equivalent to a liquidation.[6] Another innovation is that of a reserve against loss: depositors agree in advance to "donate" a portion of their gains to a chari-

---

[4]It seems highly unlikely that classically such rules were rigidly followed, since mutual settlement agreements and waivers (*sulh, iqrar, ibra'*), and renewed partnership agreements, might often have overcome the need for actual costly terminations and liquidations. Research on the classical practice in such partnership matters is needed.

[5]"*Mudaraba mushtaraka*." Homoud, *Tatwir*, 420ff. To explain some of the differences from the old *mudaraba*, Dr. Homoud uses the analogy of a public bus, which, unlike a taxi, does not allow riders to direct its route or get off wherever they like. Idem, 440.

[6]Decision 5, fourth session (1988), *Fiqh Academy Journal*.

table fund to be used to meet losses of later investors or, if unused, to be given to charity.[7]

Adapting the Islamic Bank to Modern Legal Forms and Practices. Classical Islamic law knows only partnerships, not modern companies with artificial personality. But since it would be extremely cumbersome to use classical partnership law to structure present-day banks or funds, most modern Islamic financial institutions take the form of modern corporations or stock companies. By permitting banks to be organized in this fashion, scholars have committed themselves to resolving a number of problems under Islamic law. At this stage of development, however, not all of these problems have been fully discussed, much less finally solved.

Mudaraba is the closest classical analogy to the modern relationship between stockholders and bank management. The analogy is not perfect, however. For example, if management corresponds to the *mudarib* and stockholders to capital investors, then *mudaraba* rules would dictate that both be compensated by a share of profits. But if the manager is merely an employee of the bank, who is the *mudarib* and who is entitled to its profit share? The problems such puzzles arouse have been considered mere practical problems, not moral or religious ones, and easily surmounted. Scholars seem to conclude that the old rules of partnership should be consulted only in broad essentials.[8] In other words, the modern company is accepted as a new type of contractual relationship, which owes deference only to the basic principles of Islamic partnership law, not to its every detail.

The relationships between an Islamic bank's management, shareholders, and depositors of various types (such as those carrying differing maturities and risks, those who invest in particular projects, those who forego profits, etc.) give rise to difficult fiduciary issues as well as accounting puzzles. How can equity be ensured between the shareholders who are investors in the bank, on the one hand, and depositors who are investors in *mudaraba* funds managed by the bank, on the other? For example, bank

---

[7]Ibid. For an early attempt to state fair accounting and fiduciary principles, see the Jordan Islamic Bank for Finance and Development Law, no. 13 of 1978, *Jordan Official Gazette* 2773 (1 April 1978), in the drafting of which Dr. Sami Homoud played a major role.

[8]See 'Ali al-Khafif, *al-Sharikat fi al-fiqh al-islami* (Cairo: Arab League, 1962); 'Abd al-'Aziz al-Khayyat, *al-Sharikat* (Beirut: Risala, 1984); Mustafa al-Zarqa, *Madkhal*, 3:256-287.

management may be tempted to shift profits from the bank itself to its *mudaraba* funds, or the reverse, depending on whether it wishes to bolster deposit returns or dividends to shareholders. Which of the bank's costs, both overhead and expenses, pertain to the bank as "person" and thus cannot be charged, like other expenses, against its various investments? If the bank invests its own capital in some of the investment funds, thus mixing its assets with those of its depositors, will it manage its other investments equally well? Will the bank's treatment of all these issues be fully disclosed to all interested? These issues preoccupy a new field known as "Islamic accounting principles." If Islamic banking is to achieve long-term success, obviously progress must be made on such issues. There is an industry-wide effort to generate uniform accounting standards, but it has not as yet fully succeeded.[9]

Two other problems under this heading concern how to justify the conceptions of limited liability and of artificial personality, which do not exist in the classical law. These we postpone to later in this chapter.[10]

Competing with Conventional Commercial Banks. Islamic banks are pressured to mimic conventional interest-taking banks in order to survive. The prevailing environment — the expectations of depositors, entrepreneurs, and regulators, as well as the preexisting legal and regulatory system — dictates that Islamic banks cannot behave fully in accord with the two-tier *mudaraba* theory on which they were founded. Banks feel obliged to provide stable, secure, and competitive returns to depositors. While in theory a year or two of losses is part of the bargain between the bank and its depositors, banks realistically fear that losses would cause a run on the bank's deposit funds, which, though the collapse it would cause falls not on the bank as *mudarib* but on the depositors themselves, would still likely destroy the bank and discredit other Islamic banks. Islamic banks have fewer resources to meet a liquidity crunch, since they cannot lawfully discount debt obligations or borrow from the central bank at interest — some of them may not even be able to count on central bank support.

Given these results on the "liability" side of their balance sheets, Islamic banks fear risky or long-term investments on the "assets" side, in-

---

[9]See publications of the Accounting and Auditing Organization for Islamic Financial Institutions, centered in Bahrain.

[10]See pp. 167-69 below.

cluding the very equity investments in second-tier *mudarabas* that theory requires them to make. Another fact accentuates their fears: a dishonest entrepreneur can easily doctor finances by diverting income or exaggerating expenses, such as by charging personal perquisites, with the result that the business shows losses which fall solely on the bank. The temptation to do so is all the greater if the firm is a small one and not obliged, particularly in developing countries, to make disclosures, submit to audits, or adhere to firm accounting standards. Fears of such behavior were confirmed when the earliest Islamic banks suffered extraordinary losses on profit-sharing arrangements. The remedies for this situation are not attractive. Either the bank must become involved in the day-to-day management of the business (structuring the investment not as a *mudaraba* but as an *'inan* partnership, today called *musharaka*) or it must deviate from the Islamic law of partnership to require the entrepreneur to guarantee the return of the bank's investment (perhaps taking collateral for this as well).[11] Another remedy, mentioned by Muslim theorists surprisingly often, is to await the return of true Islamic morality.

For these reasons Islamic banks have been unable to develop in the way originally projected for them. Forced to compete with interest-based banks, they have developed "assets" and "liabilities" looking roughly like those of commercial banks in terms of return, risk, and maturity, and with the same sort of balance between them. This flies in the face of Islamic law, seeking to achieve what that law makes most difficult. To meet demands, Islamic banks are obliged to turn away from *mudaraba* or other partnerships toward short-term credit sales. Indeed, they have invented and heavily employ a form of *murabaha* or "markup" transaction, to be discussed below, which economically, if not legally, is identical to a form of interest-lending. Banks rely on *murabaha* for some 80 percent of their investments, while *mudaraba* is nearly always below 5 percent.[12]

This pattern, representing a stark deviation for Islamic banks from the theoretical path sketched out for them at their founding, causes distress

---

[11]This has been done by including in the agreement the entrepreneur's expected income level, and a presumption that, if this level is not reached, he has been negligent in management. The stated presumption may be conclusive, or rebuttable before a board of arbitrators, the latter perhaps chosen by the bank. Collateral is taken to assure fulfillment of any obligation arising from such negligence.

[12]See, e.g., Awsaf Ahmad, "al-Ahammiyya al-nisbiyya li-turuq al-tamwil al-mukhtalifa fi al-nizam al-masrafi al-islami," fifth session (1988), *Fiqh Academy Journal* 2:1487-1516.

and concern to Islamic bankers, legal scholars, and economists. Serious efforts are under way to correct it, especially now that the problem is becoming better known to the Muslim public. Several banks have announced programs to reduce or eliminate their reliance on *murabaha*. Progress on accounting standards and financial disclosure would help, but in the long run, banks realize that they need to find alternatives to *mudaraba* and *murabaha* investments and to find ways to exploit these alternative investments without excessive risk or illiquidity. These needs propel the banks toward various forms of lease and sale and toward the formation of funds or pools of diversified sale or lease activities, especially those which can assure liquidity through either offering repurchase or redemption by the fund, allowing transfers of interests among fund investors, or creating a secondary market. The need to find vehicles for diversified and liquid investments is a constant theme in discussions of contemporary Islamic finance.

Another important future trend in Islamic banking results from the fact that rarely could a bank singlehandedly launch and underwrite one of these new diversified vehicles as part of its efforts to invest depositors' funds through second-tier or sub-*mudaraba* projects; instead banks would usually structure these funds as separate entities, outside the bank itself, and seek for them separate capital and additional risk-takers and investors. As these separate funds become more common, Islamic financial institutions may grow to be not only banks (though they would continue to provide basic banking services and offer deposits to risk-averse investors) but also the creators, facilitators, and underwriters of such funds, no doubt through affiliates in larger holding companies. To the extent that these funds become a major vehicle for Islamic investment and savings, much of the current pressure on the banks to deliver depositors high profits with low risk would be alleviated. In other words, Islamic banks may become disintermediated, largely through their own efforts. These changes will take time and require a great deal of development in legal and financial infrastructures. Interestingly, the trend parallels developments in conventional banking and financial markets, as increasingly funds traded on the financial markets replace bank deposits as the preferred investment vehicle for the small saver.

It appears that Islamic financial institutions will increasingly be diversified vehicles or funds that invest not directly in firms but in discrete economic functions or operations conducted by or within firms. The funds will derive their profits from sale (including the financing of manufactured goods and agricultural products through advance purchase; cash purchase of raw materials or inventory for resale to firms on credit; and buying a firm's products for resale to end-users on credit) and from lease (including the leasing of equipment and the hiring and re-hiring of services). Funds may use profit-sharing companies or partnerships as vehicles for such direct and discrete investments, by having these companies undertake sub-activities of firms that allow easy verification of profit margins.[13] A return to reliance on general investments in firms through passive *mudarabas* seems unlikely until fiduciary, accounting, and disclosure requirements improve.

Do such prospective outcomes represent a failure of Islamic banking, a falling from the high goals of Islamic economic theory? No. First, nothing about these developments is a deviation per se from the original economic theory based on profit-sharing. Indeed, the funds to which this trend leads would be organized as *mudarabas* or *mudaraba*-analogues. But with this shift the ultimate source of an investor's profits would not be primarily profits from passive investments in entrepreneurs' enterprises, as the idealizing theory of Islamic banking originally posited, but rather profits deriving directly from sale in its various forms, including lease. Early Islamic economists may have seized on profit-sharing as the ideal for investor profits in order to distinguish themselves clearly and emphatically from conventional banking while yet seeking to fulfill the function of financial intermediary: by this tack they avoided any need to make the subtle arguments by which interest lending is differentiated from credit sale,[14] or to explicate the Qur'anically axiomatic distinction between *bay'* and *riba*.[15] But some Islamic economists doubt this approach can be maintained in the long run.[16] After all, under Islamic economics and law, legitimate gains derive ultimately from risk-bearing commerce in real goods and assets. *Mudaraba* and *musharaka* are just vehicles for investing in such commerce.

---

[13]See discussion in Chapter 7, 192-93.

[14]For recent examples of how this can be done, see M. Fahim Khan, "Time Value of Money and Discounting in Islamic Perspective," *Review of Islamic Economics* 1 (1991): 35-45; Monzer Kahf, "Time Value of Money and Discounting in Islamic Perspective: Revisited," *Review of Islamic Economics* 3 (1994): 31-38, 36; Ridha Saadallah, "Concept of Time in Islamic Economics," *Islamic Economic Studies* 2 (December 1994): 81-102.

[15]"For they say, 'Buying and selling [*bay'*] is but a kind of usury' — the while God has made buying and selling lawful and usury unlawful." [2:275]

[16]See Monzer Kahf and Tariqullah Khan, *Principles of Islamic Financing — A Survey* (Jedda: Islamic Research and Training Institute, 1992), 19-30.

Perhaps theory will shift, as practice already has, to understanding *bay*ʿ or sale to be the fundamental notion of Islamic finance, not *mudaraba* or *musharaka*.

ISLAMIC CONTRACTS AS USED IN ISLAMIC FINANCE

In this section we review the various contracts used in Islamic finance, examining them in theory and, to the extent we have reliable accounts or documentation, in practice.

Mudaraba

Mudaraba, although conceptually a partnership, does not require that a company (incorporated or not) be formally created; without one a bank can make a *mudaraba* investment in any existing enterprise, as long as the profits arising from that investment can be determined separately. For example, a customer could use bank funds on a *mudaraba* basis to purchase automobiles wholesale, agreeing to share the net proceeds of retail sales; or a *mudaraba* advance could be used to add additional capacity to an existing factory, as long as resulting increase in profits could be known.

The "diminishing *mudaraba*" is a newly developed contract by which the investor's share in a *mudaraba* is progressively retired or liquidated. Under this contract, the *mudarib*, in his periodic profit distributions to the bank, pays over to the bank not only the bank's profit share but also a predetermined portion of his own profits, which go to reducing the bank's capital share.[17] The additional funds are either held in an account to purchase the bank's share in a lump sum at the end of the *mudaraba*, or they are applied progressively to reduce the bank's capital share (thereby also reducing the bank's claim on profits). Three theoretical problems are raised by this contract:

- It purports to be a binding future sale of *mudaraba* ownership, which is not valid;

---

[17]Properly this is a *musharaka*, since the entrepreneur also owns a capital share in the venture, which increases steadily.

- In its second form (progressive purchase), it incorporates the concept of transfer from one party to another of a *mudaraba* capital investment, at a price of par, arousing difficult issues of how interests in an ongoing *mudaraba* are evaluated;
- Viewing the second form of the contract in another way, it is a binding agreement to enter into a series of diminishing *mudarabas*, each liquidated by a conjectural final accounting, distributing final profits, and each followed obligatorily by a new partnership with a reduced capital contribution from the bank; the problem in this case is that an agreement to enter into a *mudaraba* in the future may not be valid.

All three issues are serious ones. After extensive discussion, OIC Academy has upheld this contract,[18] as have a number of banks' *shari'a* boards.[19] It is in frequent use.

Bay' Mu'ajjal, or Credit Sale

Bay' mu'ajjal, or sale with delayed payment, is the closest Islamic analogue to interest finance, and accordingly has been universally employed as a vehicle of finance throughout Islamic history. Nothing in Islamic law dictates how the price for such a sale is determined; it is simply whatever the parties agree upon. Therefore, nothing prevents the seller from linking the sale price to the period of time for which credit is extended, and Islamic financial institutions in fact do so, employing formulae using LIBOR and other economic indicators. In their actual documentation, however, banks usually avoid mentioning any such procedure for fixing the price, since it is easily mistaken for a charge of interest.

Note that a late payor cannot be forced to pay penalties due to delay (not only for sale but for all obligations). Delay by one who is solvent is, however, a sin, and therefore a crime. Medievally such a person was subject to lashing and imprisonment to force him to pay, but since such measures are no longer in use (except imprisonment in Saudi Arabia), and since

---

[18]See decision 5 (d4/08/88), fourth session (1988), *Fiqh Academy Journal* 4:2161, 2164, and accompanying discussions and studies.

[19]Cf. Nicholas Ray, *Arab Islamic Banking and the Renewal of Islamic Law* (London: Graham and Trotman, 1995), 185-86, quoting several favorable fatwas.

available court processes are slow, late payment does create serious problems for Islamic banks. Debtors know that they can pay Islamic banks last, since doing so involves no cost. To remedy the situation, scholars have proposed expediting court processes or imposing criminal fines on solvent debtors (these paid to the government and not to the banks). Pending such solutions some banks include terms in their documentation requiring debtors to pay late penalties measured by the profit percentages earned by the bank's own depositors, since the bank presumably could have invested the unpaid sums and earned at least that amount. Some scholars have issued fatwas supporting this approach,[20] overcoming a number of serious objections to it.[21] A spirited journal debate on this procedure has ensued.[22]

Murabaha, or Sale with Markup

As classically defined, *murabaha* is simply a sale contract which fixes the price in terms of the seller's cost plus a specified percentage markup. The seller must disclose all items of expense which are included in the cost if these are not known through custom.

Murabaha is now commonly in use only in a composite form known as *al-murabaha lil-amir bi-al-shira'*, or "the *murabaha* of the one who orders or commissions another to purchase," which, it appears, was also known classically.[23] In this transaction, A requests B (nowadays usually a bank) to purchase goods according to certain specifications and then, after B has obtained the goods, to resell them to A by *murabaha.* Either of these two sales can be on credit (*bay' mu'ajjal*), and in modern practice the second of them always is.

This transaction has many advantages. First, ordinarily no bank engages in trading in goods, finding this enterprise too risky and distracting. But this commissioned *murabaha* enables the bank to avoid the drawbacks of trading: it never purchases unless it already has an assured buyer, who moreover informs the bank how to obtain the goods it wants. Second,

---

[20]E.g., Darir, 111-113.

[21]Classical law does not tolerate damages for lost profits (i.e., hypothetical profits, which would have occurred but for the debtor's actions) but only for actual destruction of property or actual out-of-pocket losses. Damages may include usufructs of which the creditor was wrongfully deprived. Loss of use of money during delay cannot be compensated on this ground, however, since money has no usufruct.

[22]For an overview of the debate, see Zarqa and Qari, 25-57.

[23]Homoud, *Tatwir,* 476-481, citing al-Shafi'i, *al-Umm.*

while the bank's profit (the markup) conceivably derives in part from its services in securing the goods through the first sale, it is far more likely — especially in the present day — to derive from the extension of credit in the second sale. To the extent that the bank's services in carrying out the two sales and the costs and risks of its interim ownership can be minimized, the transaction becomes economically very similar to a conventional commercial loan.

Many question the validity of "*murabaha* with order to purchase" because, conducted cleverly enough, it asymptotically approaches interest lending. How does it differ from a simple loan on interest to a customer who then buys the goods himself? In law, if not in economics, there are substantial differences. The most important of these arise from the fact that, for the interval between the two sales, the bank owns the goods. During that time the bank bears the risk that the goods will be destroyed or harmed, or develop a defect, and that the seller may default. At the time of the second sale the bank faces the risk that the buyer will reject the goods as unsatisfactory or defective. None of these situations impinge on a loan. On the basis of such differences the OIC Academy has approved the contract.[24]

While the distinction from a mere loan is compelling in theory, in practice Islamic banks often employ various stratagems to reduce their risks in *murabaha* almost to zero, particularly in international trade. Practitioners call *murabaha*s using such stratagems "synthetic," meaning "artificial." In actual deals we have seen, the bank and its customer agree in advance that the second sale (bank sells to customer) occurs at the same instant as the bank gains title under the first sale (supplier sells to bank). Thereby the bank's risk of casualty to the goods becomes infinitesimal. The customer also waives all claims on the bank as seller, such as for breach of warranty or defects in the goods. The bank assigns to the customer its warranty or other rights against the supplier of the goods. Usually the bank appoints the customer as its agent to purchase and obtain the goods, reducing any possibility of error as to the goods to be bought and eliminating any burden or costs associated with buying or taking delivery of the goods. Sometimes the *murabaha* agreement is made without even a specific delivery date for the goods, leaving that entirely to the customer to determine. A customer may even contract to purchase goods from a supplier before the *murabaha* is signed. All in all, the bank's connection with the goods becomes merely theoretical.

---

[24]Decision 3,2, fifth session (1988), *Fiqh Academy Journal* 2:1599.

Such arrangements eliminate the risks of ownership, but the bank still faces the risk that the customer will break his promise to purchase, forcing the bank to try to avoid the first sale or, if it has occurred, to dispose of the goods. Under classical Islamic law, in fact, the customer cannot bindingly agree to purchase the goods until the seller already has possession of the goods.[25]

As mentioned in the last chapter, scholars have proposed a solution for this last problem which has won the approval of the OIC Academy. The solution is to construe the customer's undertaking to buy not as a contract but as a promise. Ordinarily, classical law does not enforce promises. But several opinions in the Maliki school hold promises (at least to do a gratuitous act like a gift or loan) binding if the promise has a motive or cause (*sabab*) and the promisee relies on it. For example, if one person promises another that if the latter demolishes his house he will make him a loan to rebuild it, and the promisee demolishes his house, a court will compel the promisor to make the loan.[26] Relying on these Maliki views, the Academy has declared that a customer's promise in a "*murabaha* with order to purchase" is binding. It is specified, however, that the customer is bound only to the extent that he is liable for any actual out-of-pocket losses the bank suffers due to his refusal to buy. These losses would not include the bank's lost profits.

While this answer strengthens all "*murabahas* with an order to purchase," synthetic *murabahas* have not had to rely on it since they avoid the problem by practical means. First, as noted, they arrange closings for both sales simultaneously, so that the bank never assumes ownership unless it simultaneously sells to the customer. Second, if these *murabahas* provide for their enforcement under a non-Islamic law, as they frequently do, that law will likely interpret the customer's initial promise as binding. Third, banks take sizeable down payments toward the second sale, which can then be used to defray any losses from the customer's failure to purchase.[27]

---

[25]In the case of unique goods (*'ayn*), the seller in the second sale must have ownership and possession. In the case of generic goods (*dayn, mawsuf fi al-dhimma*), the buyer in the second sale must pay in full in advance, which blocks any use of the transaction for financing.

[26]Harun Khalif Jili, "al-Wafa' bi-al-wa'd fi al-fiqh al-islami," fifth session, *Fiqh Academy Journal* 2:881-908, 902-03.

[27]Saeed, 86; see form contracts, in Ali Ahmad Salus, "al-Murabaha li-al-amir bi-al-shira'," fifth session (1988), Fiqh Academy Journal 2:1060-1087, 1065-1080.

Is a "*murabaha* with order to purchase" then not just like the "devious artifices" (*hiyal*) of the medieval law — superficially legal means to attain substantively illegal ends?[28] Is Islamic law returning to its old tolerance for these artifices? One thing can be said in defense of the modern *murabahas*, even the synthetic ones just described: they link extension of credit to a unique transfer of goods from a third party to the customer, and in doing so they make a meaningful connection with a credit sale of goods, an event for which Islamic law recognizes the time value of money. A conventional loan, by way of contrast, need have no connection with any economic or legal event beyond the customer's undertaking to repay.

No synthetic *murabaha* documents that we saw went so far as to abandon all meaningful connection with this element — for example, by lending money more than once on the same trade. Reportedly, however, some Islamic banks have arrived at eliminating even this element. As explained below,[29] in situations where the goods involved are totally liquid and fungible and can be very cheaply bought and sold, *murabaha* easily becomes nothing but pretense, a mere disguise for interest lending. One wonders whether the *shari'a* boards of banks indulging in such practices are even aware of what is afoot!

In any event, Islamic banking has come under increasing criticism, from its own ranks and from the public, for its heavy reliance on synthetic *murabahas*. Even the OIC Academy's approval of the contract is accompanied by language urging that its use be minimized and replaced by profit-and-loss-sharing investments.[30]

Ijara, or Lease

Since lease is understood as the sale of usufruct (*manfa'a*), its rules follow closely the rules for ordinary sale.

---

[28]On *hiyal*, see pp. 39-40 above. For example, the transaction is similar to the classical *tawarruq*, discussed in Chapter 5, in which a party buys an item on credit from one person and then sells it immediately to another person for cash, with the net effect of a loan. While *murabaha* is similar in some ways, it has more substance in that the customer not only goes into debt but also acquires property.

[29]p. 177 below.

[30]Decision 3,2, fifth session (1988), Fiqh Academy Journal 2:1599.

Leasing, a rapidly growing segment of the Islamic financial market-place, is used chiefly as an alternative to installment sale for financing purchases of equipment. Unlike installment sale, the lessor retains legal title to the property being financed, assuring an effective security interest. In some jurisdictions leasing offers tax savings compared with sale. Other major advantages of leases include flexibility in payment terms and negotiability or transferability, aspects which we discuss in Chapter 10.

Modern Islamic finance often combines leasing with purchase in a single contract called hire-purchase, or *ijara wa-iqtina'*. Under such a contract the tenant pays, in addition to lease, a sum which goes toward buying the leased property. Properly the tenant is given credit for his payments by becoming in ever-increasing degree the owner of the property, with the result that the proportion of his payments that goes for rent also continually reduces. The result is not dissimilar to a mortgage.

The Islamic law of leasing poses three sets of problems for modern Islamic finance all arising from *riba* and *gharar* principles. The first set of problems concerns restrictions on the right of the parties to fix the nature of the right sold, the usufruct, by their agreement. Islamic law understands the usufruct largely as a creature of contract, since only by the *ijara* contract does the usufruct become fixed and known (e.g., for how many years does the usufruct continue?). Still, the law does not give the parties total freedom in this respect. It views some benefits and burdens of the property as belonging naturally and unchangeably to the lessee, and others as belonging to the lessor. For example, the law provides that the duty to repair the goods falls always and solely on the lessor since the repairs benefit him as the owner. A clause purporting to shift repair costs to the lessee is invalid because it unjustly enriches the lessor. Also, if repair costs were imposed on the lessee, they would increase the rent in an amount undeterminable in advance, which is *gharar*. Even a lessee's duty to do everyday upkeep and maintenance is thrown into doubt by this ruling.

The second set of problems arises from the fact that the usufruct of property is not something existent and tangible, but a stream of use extending into the future, and is therefore risky and unstable. What if future events reduce the value of the usufruct to the lessee? Concerned over this, Islamic law gives broad scope to the lessee to cancel the lease if events cause the usufruct to be less valuable to him than expected. For example, as noted previously,[31] even the Hanbali school, which has a narrow view of this right

---

[31]Pp. 103-04.

to cancel, allows reduction or elimination of rent in a lease for farmland if rainfall is less than usual and crops are harmed.

A third set of problems concerns the various types of future sale and option terms that conventional financial leases use to dispose of the residual value of the leased goods at the end of the lease term. Under Islamic law, such terms are invalid as unenforceable future or conditional agreements. We discuss the relevant law later in this chapter, under the heading of futures and option contracts.

Islamic financial practice seems to have sidestepped all three groups of problems. As to problems of repair or destruction of the leased property, many Islamic leases simply adopt the conventional financial lease provision that the lessee remains liable even in the event of the property's total destruction. Other leases, such as that of the Islamic Development Bank, pay heed to Islamic law, acknowledging the lessee's right to cancel in such an event. But often even the latter leases impose on the lessee the obligation to buy casualty insurance naming the lessor as beneficiary. On the second issue, a lessee's right to rescind due to diminished benefit from the usufruct, the present practice seems simply to ignore the problem, allowing lessees to avoid the lease only for conventional legal reasons such as force majeure or a breach of contract or warranty. On the third issue, the unenforceability of terms in leases disposing of the future residual value by options or sales, the solution in practice seems to be to include such terms in the leases, even if unenforceable Islamically, in the expectation that incentives other than the Islamic law will cause the promisor to uphold them.[32]

Salam, or Advance Purchase

The contract of *salam* — the forward purchase of generically described goods for full advance payment — has important potential as an Islamic financing device, particularly for production of agricultural goods. It is not yet used extensively.

Three major problems reduce the *salam* contract's value as a financing vehicle. The first is the risk of default by the seller, made more severe by the fact of prepayment. A partial solution is to take security from the seller, whether pledge or guarantee.[33]

---

[32]This third set of problems is further discussed at pp. 262-62 below.

[33]This is allowed by most, but not all, scholars. See Ibn Qudama, 4:347-352.

The second problem is the bank's need to liquidate the goods after delivery, an inconvenience made more serious by the Islamic legal rule that a *salam* buyer cannot sell the expected goods before actually taking possession of them.[34] To address this problem the idea has surfaced of a "parallel" or "back-to-back" *salam*. After buying goods of a certain description from a seller and paying the full purchase price (*salam* sale 1), but before the seller is due to deliver on that contract, the bank, in a separate and formally unconnected *salam* contract (*salam* sale 2), sells goods of exactly the same description and with the same due date to a third party, receiving full advance payment from that buyer. The net result is that the bank has reversed its position, fixed the profits it will earn from the two trades, and assured a purchaser for its goods. Reportedly classical authors have mentioned this transaction without disapproval. An extensive proposal based on this idea is offered in Chapter 10.

The third problem is that, according to most scholars of the four schools, Islamic law requires that if at the time of delivery the seller can neither produce the goods nor obtain them elsewhere, the buyer has only two choices: either take back his price, without increase, or await the goods becoming available later, with no compensation permitted for the delay.[35] In either case, the buyer loses all or much of the profit from the use of his money.

Istisna', or Commissioned Manufacture

In *istisna'*, or "commissioned manufacture," one party buys goods that the other party undertakes to manufacture according to specifications given in the contract. *Istisna'* exists only in the Hanafi school.[36] The majority view in that school allows the contract only on condition that it binds neither party until the goods are made and accepted by the buyer. But a mi-

---

[34]See decision 65/1/d7, *Fiqh Academy Journal* 1 (1992): 711, 716. Ibn Rushd, *Bidayat*, 2:205-07; Ibn Qudama, 4:343-44; Bahuti, 3:306-07. Under the Maliki school, the buyer may sell his expectation of the goods back to the original seller or to another, as long as the purchased goods are not food. See Ibn Rushd, supra.

[35]Ibn Qudama, 4:333-34.

[36]In other schools, the manufacture of goods was secured either by *salam* or a contract of sale (of the raw material) combined with a contract of *ijara* (hire) by which the seller agrees to process the raw material into a finished product. Kasib al-Badran, *'Aqd al-istisna'* (Alexandria, Egypt: Dar al-Da'wa, 1980), 63-73. An issue must arise in those schools as well as to when *salam*, and when the latter contract, applies.

nority view, now followed in Islamic finance, holds that it is binding on both parties from the start, even though (exceptionally in Islamic law) neither party has to perform immediately. As in all sales, the parties are free to fix the price as they wish, using for example a cost-plus or markup approach or even an explicit reference to the opportunity costs of money (e.g,. LIBOR rates). Since payments can be delayed until delivery, or even beyond, it is also permissible to arrange a schedule of progress payments.

In practice, Islamic banks frequently employ *istisna'* to finance manufacture and construction. Classical Islamic law allows the manufacturing party in an *istisna'* to do the manufacturing, not by itself, but by contracting a second *istisna'* with a third party. Islamic banks have used this structure, called a "back-to-back *istisna'*," to finance purchases of major manufactured goods such as ships or airplanes. Under the first *istisna'* the bank as seller accepts a long-term schedule of payments from its customer, while under the second *istisna'* the bank as buyer pays the manufacturer over a shorter period with progress payments. The difference between the present value of payments under the two contracts is the bank's compensation for the finance. The mechanism is analogous to a *murabaha* with order to purchase.

What is the distinction between *istisna'* and *salam*, especially in view of the more favorable payment rules available for *istisna'*?[37] It seems that classically the distinction has to do with the nature of the goods being bought and sold, i.e., unique, manufactured goods versus generic, fungible goods.[38] Ordinarily in *istisna'* the purpose of a buyer is to obtain the manufacture of goods that otherwise would not exist (e.g., a pair of shoes to fit the customer's feet), while by *salam* a buyer seeks to fix the price for future goods that are virtually assured to exist anyway (e.g., $X for so many bushels of a specific grade of wheat).[39] A last distinction is that the rules of *salam* forbid tying the contract to any particular production process (e.g., the crop of a particular farm) since that exposes the parties to risks; in *istisna'*, on the other hand, a unique manufacturing process is involved. In *istisna'* there is a deliberate encounter with the risks of a particular source

---

[37]Strictly speaking, this issue arises only in the Hanafi school, which alone recognizes *istisna'*.

[38]Bank al-Tadamun al-Islami, Idarat al-fatwa wa-al-buhuth, *'Aqd al-istisna' fi al-fiqh al-islami* (City unspecified: Bank al-Tadamun al-Islami, 1992), 14-15.

[39]Dr. M. Fahim Khan aptly put the point: by *salam* one assures demand; by *istisna'* one assures supply. Workshop, Islamic Research and Training Institute, Islamic Development Bank, Jedda, 23 September 1996.

and process, and, one may argue, the rules of the Hanafi school are that school's attempt to modulate the legal relationships accordingly.

How do these distinctions operate when a contract finances the manufacture of *fungible* (generic) goods? Should the contract financing this production be *salam* or *istisna*? The question takes on special significance due to the fundamental transformation in the nature of goods in commerce since the Industrial Revolution. Most goods, other than currencies and raw material, were once unique. Only a few manufactured goods achieved a degree of fungibility, such as cloth, rope, pottery, or processed raw materials such as flours or oils. In contrast, nowadays most goods are fungible to some degree.

The question arises, therefore, whether this vast shift toward generic goods should cause a shift in Islamic commercial law. Should that law become stricter — subjecting most contracts for manufactured goods to the rules for *salam* (including full advance payment), so as to avoid speculation and disguised interest? Or should such transactions' ties to specific processes of manufacture (even if the goods produced are fungible to some degree) permit them the more liberal rules of *istisna*?

After all, in the past almost all generic goods had the following characteristics:

- they were basic commodities essential to human life, whether foodstuffs or essential raw materials;
- because they were so basic, active markets existed for them;
- because active markets for them did exist, one could use investments in them for speculation, if not *riba* lending.

Perhaps the restrictions on sales of generic goods, as in *salam*, should pertain to goods having all three characteristics. To the extent that modern generic goods do not fit this profile, it would seem that trading in them should be made *easier* than in the past, and thus come under the more lenient rules of *istisna*. (Indeed, the point has significance beyond the *istisna* context, as an argument for limiting the reach of *fiqh's* restrictions on the sale of debt [*dayn*].)[40]

In current Islamic legal circles little attention is paid to the issue of distinguishing *istisna* and *salam*, meaning that Islamic finance likely now

---

[40]See pp. 124-25 above.

follows a rule of thumb that if a transaction involves manufacture it may employ the favorable rule structure of *istisna'*.[41] A series of proposals based on this result is put forward in Chapter 10.

Ji'ala, or Reward

Ji'ala is a contract of reward by which someone offers a certain amount of money or property as a reward to any person who brings about a desired result. For example, "I will pay ten dinars to anyone who returns my lost camel." For those who uphold it and consider it binding, this contract evades the usual obligation in hire contracts to fix the exact services to be performed and to identify the person by whom they are to be performed.

Several characteristics of this contract are attractive from the viewpoint of innovation in Islamic investment. It allows contracting on an object not certain to exist or to come under a party's control. Indeed, *ji'ala* can cover the runaway horse or the fish in the sea, which, were these to be sold, would be proverbial cases of *gharar*. Thus the contract shifts important risks to the worker, since he earns nothing if the horse or fish cannot be recovered. The contract also requires neither that the offeror own an object sought by the reward nor even that he have a pecuniary interest in the performance.

On the other hand, the contract has constraints. One is an implicit requirement that the act sought must flow to some degree from the efforts of the offeree, and not be a mere gamble or alien event. For example, one cannot simply promise a reward to one's friend if the local baseball team wins the pennant. But can one offer such a reward to the star pitcher of the team? Presumably not, since one pitcher's efforts alone cannot decide such an outcome, meaning the contract would still involve too much *gharar*, or gambling.

A second constraint is that the offeror cannot pay in advance of the act, which would prevent the offeror from making progress payments or otherwise financing the performance (unless a series of rewards were contemplated). Another constraint is that (again unless rewards for part performance are stipulated), the act sought must not be of any use to the

---

[41]Consensus of Workshop on the Harvard Islamic Finance Project, Islamic Research and Training Institute, Islamic Development Bank, Jedda, 23 September 1996.

offeror unless fully performed; otherwise the latter could be unjustly enriched. Lastly, one cannot leave the amount of the reward uncertain or conditional on later events (such as a percentage of the ultimate market value of goods recovered), but must define it at the time the offer is made.

Useful applications of this contract would be rewards to employees for developing patents or for solving particular problems. Another application, reported from practice,[42] has employed the contract to compensate lessees for maintaining property they hold under lease. As we have seen, terms in leases requiring the lessee to maintain are void under classical law, because the term benefits the owner and is of indefinite value. Arguably, a reward contract meets both objections. That a reward contract is not binding on the promisee poses scant difficulty, since the lessee in most situations also benefits from the maintenance.

A proposal based on *ji'ala* is offered in Chapter 10.

TA'MIN, OR INSURANCE

Insurance became known in the Muslim world only in modern times and has no counterpart among the classical contract types. Insurance has aroused a great deal of controversy since it involves an obvious high degree of *gharar*, but despite the controversy, it is now in common use in Islamic banking and finance. Avoiding the details of the debates surrounding insurance, we concern ourselves only with two matters: first, the *manner* in which the industry has effectively overcome the Islamic legal objections to insurance; and second, the *impact* that the present availability and common use of insurance may have on other areas of Islamic finance, both in theory and in practice.

The Problem of Insurance and the (Tentative) Solution

As a single contract, insurance violates *riba* and *gharar* rules. One party pays cash premiums in return for the promise of the other party to pay a cash sum on the occurrence of a contingent future event. So viewed, it resembles a bet. Moreover, most insurance companies invest their premiums in forbidden interest-bearing investments.

---

[42]Conversation with Mr. Al-Tayeb Al-Dajani, Cambridge MA, 7 October 1997.

Muslims commonly object to life insurance on the grounds that it reflects disbelief that God has decreed the moment of one's death, or distrust in God's providence. This objection may have powerful religious underpinnings, but lacks an apparent legal foundation. What is being insured against is not death, but the adverse material consequences of it on the living. No tenet of the law prevents one from addressing or relieving those consequences, such as by laying aside savings or arranging for others to care for one's children.

Influential Islamic scholars have defended the insurance contract: Mustafa al-Zarqa', in particular, valiantly advocated its legality in a book published in 1962.[43] His chief argument was that, through the law of large numbers, insurance contracts in the aggregate involve very little uncertainty. The parties are transacting in something — coverage for a certain risk — which can be known and valued quite precisely. The situation is not unlike hiring a guard who provides a known and easily evaluated service, even though the ultimate utility of that service cannot be known. This defense, interestingly, shifts the focus from any particular contract and bilateral relationship to insurance viewed in the aggregate and as an institutional form. While individual contracts appear to lead to gross disparities of consideration determined by random events, in the aggregate they involve no unfairness, gambling, excess risk, or contention. Insurance is also economically highly beneficial to society and to individuals.

Despite its persuasiveness, this line of argument did not vanquish opposition to insurance. In the 1970s, another tack was found, which also involves a shift to viewing insurance as an institution, but with an added twist. Proponents of a new "Islamic insurance" proposed that insurance be offered, not as a bilateral contract transferring a known risk, but as a charitable collective enterprise by which Muslims pool resources to aid each other in the event of casualty or loss. This approach invokes a remembered practice, considered Islamically inspired, by which cohesive social groups provide mutual support in the event of catastrophic loss: e.g., if a shopkeeper loses his shop through fire, guild members pitch in to restore the shop. Some proponents of this approach to insurance also approve of conventional mutual insurance, since it is also based on mutual self-help. Employing this new justification, a new form of insurance company called *takaful* (lit., "solidarity") has been devised, offering a "*takaful* contract." By

---

[43]Mustafa Ahmad al-Zarqa, *Nizam al-ta'min* (Damascus: Matba'at Jami'at Dimashq, 1962).

this contract, members in the company promise to make periodic payments, which the company maintains in accounts in their names and invests Islamically. Members agree that if one of their number should suffer a covered loss, each will make a proportionate gift from his account to cover that loss. The legality of this contract seems to depend on the general principle that gratuitous acts tolerate relatively high degrees of *gharar*, and also on a Maliki view that gift promises can be binding.[44]

Takaful insurance has gained the support of many traditional scholars[45] and has led to the creation of numerous Islamic insurance companies. This in turn has enabled Islamic banks to use insurance regularly in their operations. Indeed, it appears that banks employ even ordinary commercial insurance without qualm, if Islamic insurance is unavailable.[46] Commercial insurance can be justified as a *pis aller*, to be superseded by Islamic insurance when the latter becomes more widely available.[47]

The important point for our purposes is how this result came about. Despite obvious illegality as ordinarily practiced, a commercial insurance practice became approved in the end through two conceptual shifts: first, viewing it not as a solitary contract but at an aggregate or institutional level; and second, giving it an entirely new conceptualization which invokes certain positive Islamic values. Other Islamic financial needs could be met in this fashion, and we suggest this approach in several instances in Chapter 10, particularly as to risk management or hedging. Such approaches use the power of modern positive laws and legal systems (including those of Muslim states) to create not just new rules but also new institutions to embody, enforce, and adapt those rules. For good reasons, including distrust of executive power and of man-made laws, classical Islamic law rarely deployed new formal institutions to support legal change. But the availability

---

[44]Despite this rather neat solution, some scholars harbor doubts. The justification for the contract is tenuous, since the contract is not really a gratuity and since support for the bindingness of promises is slender.

[45]See, e.g., decision 9, second session (1986), *Fiqh Academy Journal*, 2:731; Decision of the Council of Senior 'Ulama' of Saudi Arabia no. 51 (4/4/1398/1978), quoted in *Fiqh Academy Journal*, 2:643-651.

[46]Even the Islamic Development Bank follows this practice.

[47]In a conversation with Mr. Al-Tayeb Al-Dajani, Cambridge MA, 7 October 1997, we learned that some recent fatwas condone all commercial insurance since, reducing it to its Islamic-legal conception (*takyif*), it is a "gratuitous" arrangement, i.e., these scholars declare it the functional and legal equivalent of *takaful* itself.

today of stable, accountable, regulated institutions to embody legal relationships represents a profound and permanent social change in Muslim societies, which now may be fully understood and exploited by Islamic law and finance.[48]

Possible Impact of Insurance on Islamic Financial Theory and Practice

Now that insurance is an everyday feature of Islamic finance, one must consider its possible effects on the system of Islamic commercial relationships. The matter takes on importance considering the pervasive influence of the maxim "Gain [*kharaj*] accompanies liability for loss [*daman*]." This maxim provides a powerful rationalizing account of *riba* and *gharar* principles and their myriad influences on particular contracts. Chapters 4 and 5 used this maxim to explain a number of rules of the classical law. For example, the maxim explains why, in *mudaraba* partnerships, the active partner or *mudarib* cannot agree to assume the risk of loss of the capital of the passive investor. Since the investor gets a profit share, he must also bear a risk of loss. If the result were otherwise, it would be like a compensated money loan (*qard*). What if, using insurance, banks in the future begin to shift their risk of capital loss to a third party for a fee? What if, instead of guaranteeing return of the capital, a *mudarib* purchases insurance for the bank's capital, perhaps even charging the bank's profit account for the premium? Thereby the bank wholly avoids risk of loss by foregoing a part of its profits. Certainly, this does not sound immoral; yet it defeats the force of the old maxim, and with it one of the key criteria distinguishing *mudaraba* from *qard*. The difference between partnership and interest-lending becomes that much more theoretical or formal. In the medieval Christian canon law, a transaction nearly identical to the one just described — the "triple contract" — was the catalyst through which a similar distinction between equity investment and interest-lending was erased, leading ultimately to widespread acceptance of interest-taking in late medieval Europe.[49] (Interestingly, canon law lacks Islamic law's prohibition on *gharar*.)

---

[48]Some of the innovations suggested in Chapter 10 involve institutions.

[49]Noonan, 202-229. The triple contract provided that the active partner in a partnership "insured" the passive partner's capital share plus profits at a fixed and predeter-

A similar concern that insurance erases important legal distinctions arises elsewhere. A key distinction between *murabaha* and interest-lending is that, in the former, the bank assumes the risk of loss of the goods for the period between the two sales, often while goods are in international transit. Most Islamic banks now obtain insurance for that risk. Similarly, lease requires as a basic term that the lessor bear the risk of destruction or harm to the property. Today banks investing as lessors obtain insurance for that risk, and pass the costs of the insurance to the lessee through the rent.

PROSPECTS FOR ISLAMICALLY VALID DERIVATIVES

Islamic finance now manages risk in several ways (see Chapter 9), but Islamic financial institutions state that they need more techniques to manage risk of various kinds, particularly market and currency risks, in order to compete with their conventional counterparts. The chief problem is that the conventional tools for risk management, hedges and derivatives of various kinds (futures, forward contracts, options, swaps, etc.), are presumptively invalid under Islamic law.

As the previous two chapters show, Islamic legal rules, particularly bans on *gharar* and on the sale of "*dayn bi-dayn*," place myriad obstacles in the way of finding Islamic alternatives to these mechanisms. Islamic law may even be fundamentally opposed to the entire enterprise: hedging, the protecting of a profit position from risk, may offend the law's basic principles linking reward with risk; and derivatives, which transfer a risk from one person to another for a payment, seem to fall literally within the Prophet's prohibition of the sale of *gharar*, literally, the "sale of risk." Derivatives can easily be used for gambling in various degrees, and the Qur'anic condemnation of gambling (*maysir*) may be viewed as so vehement as to rule out any consideration of the economic benefits of risk management.[50]

Clearly, scholars seeking Islamic risk management devices face serious challenges, likely to tax all the methods of *fiqh* innovation mentioned in Chapter 2. Of course, the most direct way to achieve the goal of risk man-

---

mined rate, in return for the passive partner's giving up all potential profits above the fixed rate.

[50]Indeed the Qur'an states: "They will ask thee about wine and *maysir*. Say, In both there is great sin, also benefits for man; but their offense (or sin) is greater than their benefit." [2:219]

agement would be a bold redirection in *fiqh* thinking (*ijtihad*) drawing on new interpretations of the revealed sources and of basic principles. This *ijtihad* would declare what about risk management is legitimate in Islamic law, and what is illegitimate. But, as mentioned in Chapter 2, it is ordinarily the more conservative, literal, and legalistic approaches that are followed in Islamic finance, and accordingly, in this chapter and Chapter 10, we explore only such approaches. While doing so, however, we should try not to lose sight of the larger issues just sounded — the proper scope, if any, for risk management in Islamic law.

This section explores the two conditional contracts in Islamic law that are closest to the option contract, the most basic building block of conventional derivatives.

Khiyar al-Shart, or Stipulated Option

Islamic sale contracts may include a "stipulated option" (*khiyar al-shart*),[51] legitimated in several *hadiths*. This option, which can be stipulated by one or both parties, is an unconstrained right to rescind an otherwise binding contract. The option must have a fixed duration, and, while the standard Hanafi view restricts it to three days, the Hanbali view, and a second Hanafi view, allow it to be of any duration.[52] In the Hanbali school, while neither party is obliged to perform during the term of the option, the titles to both of the countervalues transfer immediately upon concluding the contract. Because titles transfer, until the option expires neither party may change the condition of, or dispose of, his own countervalue (e.g., the seller cannot sell to a third party). If a party who holds an option does so, he is held to have rescinded the contract. Meanwhile, either or both of the parties may deliver his countervalue to the other if he so wishes. By way of contrast, for the Hanafis title does not pass from either party (or both) who holds the option, but title and a right to take possession does pass from a party who has no option. (E.g., if a party buys a car but reserves an option for a week, the Hanafis, but not the Hanbalis, would compel the seller to deliver the car at once.)

---

[51] See generally Yvon Linant de Bellefonds, *Traité de droit musulman comparé* vol. 1 (Paris: La Haye, Mouton, 1965-73), 312-323.

[52] The two companions of Abu Hanifa differed with him on this. Their view is adopted in Majalla, art. 300, 313; see Baz, introductory preface, 14.

Since, for all schools, the stipulated option allows a party with an option to suspend its own contractual performance while holding the other to the contract, the option might readily lead to evasions of the *riba* and *gharar* prohibitions.[53] Therefore, for example, the Hanbali school provides that the option is invalid in exchanges of *riba*-related (*ribawi*) goods, in advance purchase (*salam*), and whenever the intent is to profit on a loan.[54]

The stipulated option has little apparent significance in and of itself for the creation of Islamically valid derivatives, if only because the party giving the option cannot be compensated for doing so; the option right itself is not paid for. Its significance is rather as a vital analogy, and a background set of rules and principles, for the next contract, *'arbun*.

'Arbun, or Down Payment

A second conditional sales contract allowed in classical law is the *'arbun* contract, literally "earnest money contract." By it a buyer ("B") concludes a purchase and makes an advance of some sum ($a) less than the purchase price ($p), stipulating that if he decides to take the goods, he will pay the price minus the advance ($p-$a), but if he decides not to take the goods, the seller ("S") keeps the advance. A lease also (as a sale of a usufruct) can be concluded by *'arbun*. Surprisingly, classical law did not require the parties to fix a time limit for the option.

Of all Islamic contracts, *'arbun* offers the closest analogy to an option (a contract by which one party buys the right to purchase from the other party specified goods for a specified price on [or in some versions by] a certain date). If Islamic law is to tolerate options, it will likely be through the medium of the *'arbun* contract. We therefore give the *'arbun* contract an extended analysis.

Most schools declare *'arbun* a void contract, on numerous grounds. A *hadith* reports that the Prophet forbade the contract. *'Arbun* makes a gift

---

[53]An example would be a sale of land, with the buyer (lender) reserving an option and paying the price. During the option, the buyer has title to the land, if not possession, and thus gains both security and separable increases in the property, such as fruit borne after the contract. The buyer (lender) revokes just before the termination of the option, and receives back the full price. The result is a loan paid for by the profits from the land.

[54]Qari, art. 398.

conditional on a sale, and therefore offends a principle against combining gratuitous contracts with onerous ones. It adds to the standard sale contract more than one additional term (*shart*), which a *hadith* forbids. It partakes of gambling. The seller gets the advance for nothing, and is unjustly enriched (*akl al-mal bi-al-batil*). Finally, the buyer need not fix a time limit for the option, so the contract is fatally indefinite.

Only the Hanbalis uphold *'arbun*. Declaring the supposed *hadith* against it invalid, they cite a story from the time of the Caliph 'Umar, in which an official purchased a house for a prison, giving an advance to hold the house pending Caliph 'Umar's approval.[55] Another *hadith* recounts a famous early judge's approval of an individual's reserving a lease on an animal in a caravan and promising to pay a penalty if he failed to take it.[56] Some Hanbalis require a time to be set for the option, but most do not. The OIC Academy has endorsed *'arbun*, but only if a time limit is specified.[57]

Even Hanbali sources tell us little about the other legal incidents of the *'arbun* contract (such as when title passes, when delivery is due, on whom is the risk of loss). But since *'arbun* is akin to a sale with a stipulated option in favor of the buyer, the incidents of the two contracts are probably the same. This means, for example, that for Hanbalis in an *'arbun* sale, title passes, the seller may not transact in the goods, and the purchaser bears the risk of loss of the goods (unless they are fungibles). Also, since all schools hold that the stipulated option is not allowed in forward sales (*salam* or *bay' mawsuf fi al-dhimma*) of abstractly defined goods (*dayn*, in contrast to specific, existent, identified goods, *'ayn*), the same result should be expected for *'arbun*.

It is instructive to analyze the *'arbun* sale in terms of four model contracts in Western law. The first, the "pure option model," is an option contract (a "call" option) which gives a party, in return for paying an "option price" ($x), the right to purchase certain goods at a fixed price ($p) during a fixed period of time. Anglo-American common law understands this as the "firm offer," or an offer to sell which cannot be withdrawn for a certain time, which must have consideration. In financial theory such an option has a value calculable in several ways. This model differs from the *'arbun* contract in two ways: the amount paid for the option is earned even if the

---

[55]Ibn Qudama, 4:289; Muhyi al-Din al-Nawawi (d. 676), *Kitab al-Majmu'* (Jedda: Maktabat al-Irshad, 1992), 9:408.

[56]Bukhari, 2:124.

[57]Eighth session (1994), *Fiqh Academy Journal* 1:794.

buyer proceeds with the sale (i.e., it is not deducted from the purchase price as in 'arbun); and the time at which the option expires is fixed.

The remaining three models do not involve options at all, but instead nonrefundable earnest-money arrangements. In all of them the buyer binds himself to buy, and as security makes an earnest-money deposit which will be forfeited if he breaches the contract, but otherwise will be applied to the purchase price. The earnest-money deposit serves several purposes:

- it indicates the buyer's seriousness, encouraging the seller to take property off the market;
- it compensates the seller for risks assumed and for opportunity costs or other losses incurred while pursuing a failed contract;
- it gives the buyer an incentive to perform the contract, and gives the seller leverage to secure that performance.

As in any sale, the buyer has an implicit option to forego the sale if he is willing to breach it and accept the consequences of breach, which in this case are at a minimum the loss of the deposit.

The earnest money $a includes an amount compensating the seller S for the buyer B's implicit option right — paying S for the opportunity costs ($y) of committing to a price and holding property off the market plus an additional sum ($d) toward meeting any other damages caused by B's breach and as deterrence against that breach. In other words, $a = $y + $d. Since (unlike the pure option case) B is obligated to perform and can only evade the sale through a default, S expects and relies on B to perform, and therefore needs the additional sum $d as security against damages he may incur as a result of his reliance and expectation.[58] Indeed, the damages may

---

[58]This section relies on the line of thought on contract damages initiated by the seminal article by L.L. Fuller and Willam R. Perdue, Jr., "The Reliance Interest in Contract Damages: 1," *Yale Law Journal* 46 (1936): 52-96, 52-57, which utilizes three damages models: *restitutionary damages*, which require a person who took something of value from another person without compensating for it to return that thing or its value; *reliance damages*, which require that a breaching promisor make good to his promisee any losses the latter suffered as a result of relying on the promise, restoring him to his position before the contract; and *expectation damages*, which require a breaching promisor to pay damages putting the promisee in the same economic position he would have been in had the contract been fully performed.

exceed $a and be recoverable only through a lawsuit. Let us call this model the "earnest-money model."

The third and fourth alternative models are special cases of the earnest-money model. The third, the "liquidated damages model," is an earnest-money contract that provides that the deposit liquidates, or fixes in advance, the total sum that S can demand by way of damages for breach. In other words, total losses and damages are fixed at $a, whether in actuality they are less or more. In this contract, S would be unwise to incur additional reliance damages or to entertain expectations worth more than $d. While B is contractually and morally obligated to proceed with the contract, in practical terms he is free to do otherwise as long as he is willing to forfeit $a.

The last model, the "nonrefundable deposit model," is an earnest-money contract that allows B to terminate or avoid the contract at will, though with forfeit of the deposit $a. It differs from the liquidated damages model only in that B is not under even a moral obligation to perform. Again, S will avoid incurring damages greater than $d. This model is virtually identical to the 'arbun contract.

In the last three alternatives, $d both gives B an incentive to perform and provides security to S for damages S may incur from a default. Calculating $d is complex. For example, the more serious B's commitment, the more likely that S will incur reliance costs, suggesting a higher $d, and the more willing B will be to pay a higher $d. On the other hand, to the extent that $d is meant to operate as an incentive, the need for it decreases as the seriousness of B's commitment increases. But it is probably uneconomic for S to enlarge $d beyond the likely amount of his damages merely to provide an incentive. Therefore, and to determine how far the models may serve as approximations to the pure option model, let us disregard any use of $d purely as incentive and define $d only as S's estimate of his likely damages from reliance on or expectation of B's non-performance.

If this is the case, then in the fourth model, where B is contractually free to decline, $d approaches zero, and $a (which equals $y + $d) approaches $y. (Again, $y is the earnest money needed to compensate S for the opportunity costs of keeping the property off the market pending B's performance or decision to purchase.) The amount $d could easily equal zero if S does not rely on any particular contract going through, such as in over-booking situations or where the objective is genuinely to give B the equivalent of an option.

What is the relationship between $y and $x, i.e., between the earnest-money deposit (with $d = 0 and $a = $y) and the price of a pure option?

On the one hand, $x and $y are similar, in that both are compensation for holding goods off the market for the duration of the offer. On the other hand, $y is deducted from the sale price in the event of a sale, while $x is not. To solve the problem, consider a nonrefundable deposit contract where $d = 0$ and $p is the purchase price. Let p_1 be the price in an otherwise equivalent pure option contract. Then, since these two contracts are economically identical and should give S the same compensation,[59] $y equals $x and $p equals $p_1 + $x, since with these values S receives exactly the same compensation under either contract.

Notice that the outcome $y = $x can be generalized to all other cases of the four models. These models differ among themselves only as to the amount of $d. But $d has no effect on the value of $y, since the role of $d is only to compensate S for additional damages if the sale does not go through, while if the sale goes through, S refunds $d through deduction from the price.

From this analysis we reap two important results, useful below and in Chapter 10:

- 'Arbun is identical in form to the binding sale with earnest-money deposit that we called the "nonrefundable deposit" model; this model involves no explicit option at all.
- Under certain conditions ($d = 0$), the operation and pricing of an 'arbun contract are identical to the operation and pricing of a pure option contract or call option.

Ibn Qudama, an immensely influential fourteenth-century Hanbali scholar, conducts an interesting discussion of 'arbun, in which, with ambivalence, he endorses it.[60] He does so only because of the story about 'Umar's prison, and because of a statement from Ibn Hanbal, "There is no harm in it," which in turn, he asserts, came only because of the report from 'Umar. Otherwise, Ibn Qudama mentions only misgivings. Legal reasoning (qiyas), he says, would at least demand that the period for the buyer's option be fixed.

He suggestively compares 'arbun with two similar transactions. One is a transaction by which a buyer asks the seller to rescind a sale and offers the

---

[59]The only apparent difference between a nonrefundable deposit contract and a pure option contract as to pricing seems to be that, in the former, S has the use of $d during the period of the option. Here we assume $d = 0$. But even if $d is positive, this factor is irrelevant if the time factor is taken into account in fixing $d.

[60]Ibn Qudama, 4:289-90.

latter a sum of money to do so. This is a rescission, valid either as a resale or as a settlement (*sulh*), which, being post-hoc, involves no option. He quotes Ibn Hanbal as saying that *'arbun* "is in the same category." He seems to be arguing that in 'Umar's case, 'Umar or his official did not have unfettered discretion to reject the contract, and that they must have been bound beyond loss of the deposit, either with an added moral obligation (liquidated-damages model) or with that plus a legal obligation (earnest-money model). (Note that some contemporary authorities declare a liquidated-damages term valid under classical Islamic law.)[61]

Ibn Qudama underlines the point by comparing *'arbun* to a second transaction, in which a potential buyer pays a potential seller of goods a sum in return for the latter's agreeing not to sell the goods to anyone else. (This would be a pure option contract, except that the exercise price is not fixed.) Later the buyer returns and buys the goods by final sale, deducting the initial payment from the price. The latter sale is valid, since it is free of any condition. Ibn Qudama then hints that if the precedent from 'Umar were interpreted as having occurred in this fashion, then not even the Hanbalis would have approved of *'arbun*. He declares that, in this second transaction, the advance payment would be unearned gain if the final sale were not concluded, and would have to be returned on demand. It is not lawful, he says, to pay money only for "waiting and delay" in making a sale. In other words, he rejects the idea of paying for a pure option, although the terms he uses overlook any idea that the seller could incur actual opportunity losses while waiting. He reasons that if such a payment were permitted, it would be earned by the mere delay, and could not be deducted from the price. In other words, if options were allowed, they would be lawful also in the pure option form, which they are not. But having shut the door, Ibn Qudama then equivocates slightly, letting in some light. He says that if such a payment for mere waiting were permitted, the period of the delay would have to be fixed, "as in lease." Given that the fixing of a period is one Hanbali view,[62] he may be acknowledging here that some may recognize the

---

[61]An authoritative Saudi fatwa supports it for government construction contract delay penalties. Lajnat al-Buhuth al-'Ilmiyya, al-Riyasa al-'Amma li-Idarat al-Buhuth al-'Ilmiyah wa-al-Ifta', "al-Shart al-jaza'i," *Majallat al-buhuth al-Islamiyya* 1 (1975-6): 61-144. The OIC Academy did so in the similar context of *istisna'*. Decision 67/3/7, seventh session (1992), *Fiqh Academy Journal* 3:777.

[62]'Ala' al-Din Abu al-Hasan 'Ali b. Sulayman al-Mardawi (d. 1481), *al-Insaf fi ma'rifat al-rajih min al-khilaf 'ala madhhab al-imam al-mubajjal Ahmad b. Hanbal*, ed. M.H. al-Fiqi (Beirut: Dar Ihya' al-Turath al-'Arabi, 1980), 4:357-359.

pure option right. Moreover, his last point about "lease" suggests the possibility of "renting" the right to use property for a time, the use being merely its not being sold. This is the closest we find any classical author come to discussing the pure option.

Ibn Qudama's discussion finely hones the issue of the Hanbali acceptance of the 'arbun sale. Our scale of alternative models allows us to calibrate various interpretations of that permission. Ibn Qudama himself resists any 'arbun not involving a commitment to buy at a fixed time. This rejects the pure option model, but allows the earnest-money model and the liquidated damages model. Does it also allow the nonrefundable deposit model, in which there is no express commitment to buy, although the deposit not only offsets opportunity costs ($x) (which, to Ibn Qudama, are just "waiting") but may also add something for security and incentive ($d)? The point is very fine. In any event, as he recognizes, other interpretations of Ibn Hanbal's views exist, and some of these give some ground to the attempt to equate 'arbun with the pure option. Ibn Qudama's rental suggestion also deserves investigation, but it would be difficult to imagine its use as a conventional option. It would work only for existent, specific ('ayn) property, and even then might require some form of possession of the property, such as escrow of its title.

This discussion shows how closely the 'arbun contract can be analogized to the pure call option. It also shows how, given the right market or institutional framework, an 'arbun contract could be devised with results and pricing identical or nearly identical to the call option. It suggests several Western-law contracts that elucidate the classical 'arbun and might serve as Islamically acceptable alternatives to it. Chapter 10 explores several such possibilities.[63]

Note that analyzing the 'arbun contract on the model of one of these alternative contracts could lead to accepting an 'arbun as option to sell, i.e., a put (which we might call a "reverse 'arbun"). Usually B pays the 'arbun as a deposit against a further sum B will pay, not S. What if the contract provided that S agrees to sell property to B for $p, S paying $a to B as security that S will perform? Again, $a covers B's opportunity costs ($y) for giving S a "put" right, plus something for damages ($d) for S's potential breach. If S follows through on the sale to B, B will return the deposit along with the

---

[63]See proposals for a "default option" in a *salam* commodities market, and an 'arbun contract in *istisna'* contracts in Chapter 10, pp. 253-38, 281-82.

price (will pay $p + $a). (Repeating the arguments above yields $y = $x and $p = $p_1 - $x.)

So far, however, our discussion has not addressed using the *'arbun* for anything but specific unique property (*'ayn*). Classical law, as we so far understand it, rules out *'arbun* for such generically defined goods as commodities or company shares, which are the mainstays of conventional options. However, an understanding of *'arbun* based on either the liquidated damages model, the nonrefundable deposit model, or Ibn Qudama's example of a post-hoc payment to secure rescission, encourages applying the *'arbun* contract far more broadly. Indeed, it could lead to applying *'arbun* not only to all sales, even of fungibles, but to all mutually onerous contracts (*mu'awadat*). Rafiq al-Misri has argued for such a general use of *'arbun*, even for *salam*, in a paper submitted to the OIC Academy.[64]

Why does classical law bar using options to rescind (*khiyar al-shart*), and by analogy *'arbun*, in *salam*? The reason may be simply that both forms of option ordinarily involve postponing payment of part of the price, while *salam* requires full payment in advance.[65] But if, as perhaps for Ibn Qudama, the important point about *'arbun* is its provision for liquidated damages, not when payment is made, then why not require the salam buyer to prepay in full as always but in the event of default receive back the price *less* the *'arbun*? No insurmountable issue of *riba* enters in, since here the *salam* seller has the use of the price but does not pay for that use. Rather he returns *less* than he received.

It is likely, however, that the classical objection is a more general and basic one, that of *gharar* and fear of speculation, since allowing *'arbun* or stipulated options in purchases of fungible goods in the *dhimma*, or as *dayn*, would permit speculating on the value of those goods without any binding financial obligation and without taking possession of them.[66] If this general objection controls today, then the search for hedges may be altogether doomed and misguided.

---

[64]Eighth session (1994), *Fiqh Academy Journal*, 2:707-743, esp. 736.

[65]It may be relevant that the Maliki school allows *khiyar al-shart* in *salam* during the period of three days that that school allows to the buyer before full payment is required.

[66]In response one might ask why, if this logic is correct, classical law allows a creditor to sell a debtor's obligation to the debtor or reach a compromise (*sulh*) on it with him. (Of course in *salam*, as mentioned above pp. 117, 123, 146, most schools do not allow such settlements.)

Prospects for Approval of the Option as a New Contract Type

If the option cannot be brought under 'arbun, using one of the extensions or analogies just discussed,[67] classical law gives very little hope for approval of the option contract. Rather it poses a series of objections, of which the following are the most important.

- An option requires payment for something that is a mere intangible "right" (haqq), not property (mal) in the usual sense (i.e., a tangible good or a utility taken from a tangible good), as to which alone compensation can be demanded. This is one basis for the objection of some scholars that the option price is "unearned." It is also the position taken by the OIC Academy in declaring the illegality of the option contract.[68]
- An option arguably involves gambling. At the time of exercise only one party can gain from the contract, while the other must lose. Whether a party will gain or lose depends on an unknown future market price. In most actual option contracts, moreover, the parties have no intention to take delivery, but only to liquidate their contracts against the price differentials. In every lawful Islamic sale, on the other hand, the parties fix their exchange fully and finally in the present, and the entirety of at least one of the countervalues is at least presently owing, even if not immediately paid. Of course, whenever an obligation to pay over one of the countervalues is postponed, the bargain may in retrospect turn out poorly for one of the parties depending on market values, but the exact exchange (e.g., so many bushels of wheat for a certain price) was at least fully known and agreeable to both sides at the beginning, with one or both countervalues actually owing or paid.
- An option incorporates the idea of a future sale, itself impossible under classical law. Islamic law seeks to understand even conditional sales as present transfers of title. As for fungible goods ab-

---

[67]The OIC Academy has declared that the option contract is not subsumable under any of the contracts known to *fiqh*, including the 'arbun contract. Decision 65/1/7, seventh session, *Fiqh Academy Journal* 1:711, 715.

[68]Ibid.

stractly defined (*dayn*), it allows forward sales only with present payment in full.

- If the option is in currencies, not even forward sales are allowed, since currencies may be exchanged only at spot.
- Conventional options are bought and sold. Even if an option contract were deemed lawful, the contract is itself an intangible, and not *mal* (property), and could not be bought and sold. It may also involve the selling of *dayn*, which is highly restricted, especially when to a third party.
- The price of an option compensates lost opportunity. Opportunity costs are by definition conjectural, involving sales that do not occur. Damages in Islamic law do not include conjectural losses.
- Options may involve selling what one does not own.

For all these reasons, unless justifiable as '*arbun* or on analogy to '*arbun*, the option contract in conventional form is unlikely to be accepted. If so, and if Islamic finance remains intent on finding means to manage risk, it must approach the problem from other angles. One possible angle is to invent a new legal or financial institution — such as an Islamically regulated market of hedges provided by licensed brokers — within which management of risk takes an entirely different form than merely the private purchase or sale of option rights. This is analogous to the manner in which problems of insurance were overcome. This and other approaches to the option problem are explored in Chapter 10.

INVESTMENT SECURITIES AND THEIR NEGOTIABILITY

The Islamic finance industry has so far taken only tentative steps in the direction of Islamic investment securities, particularly those open to trading.[69] Even less has been achieved in the direction of an Islamic capital market, although a few countries have issued legislation useful for creating and regulating Islamic financial instruments. Only a handful of exchange-traded Islamic financial securities exist, at least outside the prescriptively

---

[69]A recent article describes existing Islamic securities, negotiable or redeemable, and several Middle Eastern stock markets. Abdul Rahman Yousri Ahmed, "Islamic Securities in Muslim Countries' Stock Markets and an Assessment of the Need for an Islamic Secondary Market," *Islamic Economic Studies* 3 (1995): 1.

"Islamic" economies of Pakistan and Malaysia.[70] In Pakistan, *mudaraba* company shares created pursuant to a special law are extensively traded,[71] as are certain "profit-loss-sharing" (PLS) certificates. Several Islamically dubious terms afflict the PLS certificates, including a guarantee of capital backed by a foreclosure right and fixed prior distributions of profit, making them somewhat irrelevant as a model. In Malaysia, many securities are traded in relatively large volumes, but the legal terms of these have been criticized by Islamic scholars elsewhere.[72]

Elsewhere Islamic financial institutions appear eager to launch public markets for securities. Their most severe problems seem to be practical, not legal: they need to gather enough risk capital to do so, and they need to develop an adequate volume of investments that are tradeable. Islamic legal requirements for negotiability (i.e., tradeability), as we shall see below, deny negotiability at market value to funds consisting chiefly of *murabaha* investments, which constitute the overwhelming bulk of banks' investments. We shall analyze the legal issues presented by securitization and negotiability under two headings: first, creating and issuing securities (primary market), and then trading them (secondary market).

Primary Market Instruments Islamically Lawful

Raising large pools of capital through primary (new issue) markets is an everyday practice worldwide, and Islamic finance is rapidly developing new techniques to do this. Most important at present are *mudaraba* funds, common shares in corporations, and non-interest-paying Islamic revenue bonds.

Mudaraba Funds. The mechanism of the *mudaraba* creates an opportunity for investors to come together to finance large projects, sharing both

---

[70]See ibid; 'Ali Muhyi al-Din al-Qura-Daghi, "Bahth al-aswaq al-maliyya fi mizan al-fiqh al-Islami," seventh session (1992), *Fiqh Academy Journal* 1:144-145, 150-51, describing the Tawfiq Company for Investment Funds and the Amin Company for Financial Instruments founded in the 1980s in Bahrain.

[71]Tariqullah Khan, *Practices and Performance of Modaraba Companies (A Case Study of Pakistan's Experience)* (Jedda: Islamic Research and Training Institute, 1996).

[72]This because the trading of these instruments usually depends on a permissive interpretation of the ban on sales of "debt for debt" or a permissive legal interpretation in the primary instrument itself (such as the sale and buy-back artifice, or *qard hasan* investments compensated "voluntarily" from time to time by the issuer).

the profits and the risks. This should be the role of Islamic banks, but these banks have shunned major or risky projects in favor of short-term credit-sale finance. They have, however, floated a number of special-purpose funds, sometimes taking positions in them, at other times merely managing them.

Funds can be created to conduct business using any of the lawful contracts. For example, they may be formed to carry out *murabaha*, *ijara* for services or for leasing, *salam*, or *istisna'*.[73] Such funds have been used as a vehicle for bank syndications for large financings and to engage in ventures too risky or too large for any single institution to take on alone, such as holdings in oil tankers or real estate projects. Recently, funds have been created to hold portfolios of U.S. equity securities — these securities having first been vetted to ensure that their issuers meet certain criteria: e.g., that they hold debt below a certain percentage of their assets, that interest income they receive falls below certain percentages total of income, and that they are not invested in forbidden activities such as gambling or the production of liquor or pork.

Companies with Common Shares. The creation of investment securities has been facilitated by the custom, mentioned earlier in this chapter, of using conventional companies which issue common stock as vehicles, even substitutes, for Islamic partnership. The OIC Academy has approved of share companies as long as they are not formed for Islamically invalid purposes, such as liquor production.[74] This result has required accepting two Western legal concepts: artificial personality and the limited liability of investors. That the stock company is so common in modern Islamic finance bespeaks the potential of the field to adapt modern institutions to its needs. It is an example of how a major institutional and contractual innovation in Islamic law can be accepted without extended debate when no conflict is detected with basic Islamic legal principles and rules.

---

[73]Homoud, *al-Adawat.*

[74]Decision 65/1/7, seventh session (1992), *Fiqh Academy Journal* 1:711, 712. The decision declares that owning shares in share companies formed for unlawful purposes is entirely improper. But owning shares in companies that only sometimes engage in forbidden activities like *riba* is unlawful only "in principle," a term that leaves open the availability of occasional excusing circumstances. Such circumstances are the basis on which fatwas have permitted Muslims to make investments in conventional equity funds. Several studies on the subject appear in the same volume.

Finding affirmative proof for artificial personality among classical precedents is difficult. The classical law did occasionally treat the public treasury (*bayt al-mal*) and the charitable trust (*waqf*) as parties to contracts in their own right. Objections stemming from religious-legal principles have proved weak and the innovation has come to be seen as little more than a practical convenience. It is now widely accepted.[75]

Limited liability offers more serious problems. Islamic partnership law does exhibit a form of limited liability. Without the permission of the passive investor (*rabb al-mal*), the *mudarib* or managing partner may not transact on credit for amounts in excess of the partnership capital;[76] if he does so, he is liable and the inactive partner is not. Thus, without his permission, the passive investor is not liable for more than his capital share. From the viewpoint of the company as a whole, however, there is no limited liability, since one or the other partner (or both) is always fully and personally liable. More fundamentally, one may argue that limited liability conflicts with a basic Islamic moral and legal principle, that obligations are, as it were, irreducible and indestructible without agreed release or forgiveness from the creditor. (This traces to the Qur'anic notions of sanctity of property and of its transfer only by consent.) Even bankruptcy does not extinguish but only suspends claims, which revive when the debtor regains solvency. Similarly, default judgments do not extinguish the debtor's defenses, which can always be raised later, regardless of the passage of time.

In view of such results, how could a mere statutory provision creating an artificial person and anointing that person with limited liability shield the shareholders of that company from claims, especially considering that these very shareholders reaped profits when the company was healthy and would have reaped profits had all gone well? The chief argument supporting limited liability is that by law the names of such companies warn third parties of their limited capacity for liability, so that those who deal with them presumably consent to its character. The OIC Academy, in its brief

---

[75]To Imran Nyazee, the concept, while in itself unobjectionable, affects the legal structure of corporate shares so that they become un-Islamic financial interests in debts purely. His reasoning is that, because the company, being a person, owns its own assets, the ownership of shareholders therefore can only be a purely financial interest. Nyazee, 184-87. This reasoning gives much importance to a legalistic, theoretical notion of title, overlooking a more commonsense appreciation of ownership.

[76]Imran Nyazee makes the point that the capital partner can become liable in excess of his share if a partnership obligation, validly incurred within the limits of the capital, ends up exceeding the capital due to a subsequent loss in the latter. Ibid., 203.

and highly general statement approving of the conception, noted this as the justification.[77]

More study on this issue may be needed. Imran Nyazee points out that the maxim "gain accompanies risk of loss" indicates that profits gained from exercising credit in excess of the capital of the company would be illegal.[78] Misgivings over limited liability still surface in Saudi Arabian courts, where the interpretation and application of a statutory provision creating limited liability companies is unsettled. Very likely Islamic law will evolve doctrines narrowly limiting excessive debt or leveraging and vigorously piercing the corporate veil, but for now, little concern is voiced in Islamic financial practice.

Given these innovations, the vehicle of the modern company or corporation is fully available for Islamic finance, and indeed is in widespread use.

Bonds. So far we have discussed equity interests in profit-making ventures. What instruments can substitute for Islamically forbidden interest-bearing debt instruments? The most notable effort has been the so-called *muqarada* bond, which resembles a revenue bond. (The word *muqarada* is synonymous with *qirad*, which is synonymous with *mudaraba*.) This financial instrument has earned the approval of the OIC Academy.[79] *Muqarada* bonds are issued by an existing company (which acts as *mudarib*) to investors (who act as silent partners, or *rabb al-mal*) for the purpose of financing a specific money-making project or function separable from the company's general activities. The profits of this separate activity are split according to agreed percentages. The contract may provide (non-bindingly) for future retirement of the bonds at their then market price, and often provides that a specific percentage of the *mudarib's* profit share is paid periodically to the bond-holders to retire their investment in stages.[80] For example, in Jordan, bonds called *muqarada* have been issued to evidence shares in investments in commercial real estate projects on land owned by Islamic charitable trusts.[81] According to Dr. Sami Homoud, a

---

[77]Decision 65/1/7, seventh session (1992), *Fiqh Academy Journal* 1:711.

[78]Ibid.

[79]Decision 5 (D4/08/88), fourth session, *Fiqh Academy Journal* 3:2161.

[80]This is the *mudaraba* or *musharaka mutanaqisa*, discussed above, pp. 138-39.

[81]The 1981 law permitting such bonds is described in Qura-Daghi, 141-42. The OIC Academy issued a fatwa concerning aspects of these bonds. Decision 5 (D4/08/88), fourth session, *Fiqh Academy Journal* 3:2161. They aroused the controversial issue of a guarantee of the bondholders' capital by the Jordanian government. The Academy ap-

similar bond offering was used by the Turkish government to finance the building of a toll bridge in Istanbul.[82]

Primary Market Instruments Islamically Unlawful or Questionable

The strictures of Islamic law make some Western primary market instruments either unlawful or questionable: for example, conventional interest-bearing bonds. But what about other financial instruments? Here we consider three mainstays of conventional finance: preferred stock, forward contracts, and options.

Preferred Stock. Many problems beset the creation of preferred stock in Islamic finance, and indeed attack two of the most important characteristics of such stock: fixed income and priority in the event of liquidation. Fixed income runs afoul of one of the unchangeable tenets of Islamic partnership (and company) law: that income is proportional to profits. As described earlier, guaranteed, fixed income — or even priority in partnership income distribution — offends *riba* and *gharar* prohibitions in several ways. By contributing service or good will, an investor can earn a greater share of profits than his capital contribution would dictate, but his profits must always be defined as a proportion of actual profits.[83] Priority in liquidation offends another basic Islamic legal principle: that losses fall on partners in proportion to their capital contributions, without regard to profit shares. In Islamic companies, therefore, losses must fall equally on all contributors of capital regardless of rank or class, all losing so many cents for each contributed dollar.

---

proved the third-party guarantee against *muqarada* capital losses, as long as the guarantee is offered separately from the *muqarada* instruments themselves, by a wholly unrelated party, and gratuitously. The Jordan Islamic Bank is entitled to issue *muqarada* bonds as a form of investment for its depositors. Law of Jordan Islamic Bank, no. 13 (1978), Official Gazette no. 2773, sec. 14.

[82]Private seminar conducted for Islamic Finance Project, Cambridge MA, 1995.

[83]Interestingly, in conventional finance a common shareholder is usually prepared to accept a *lower* profit share and lesser priority in return for voting rights. In Islamic finance, on the other hand, voting rights suggest a role in management, and thus in work, which justifies a *greater* profit share, not a lesser one.

These objections seem to be insurmountable obstacles to creating an Islamically acceptable conventional preferred stock share.[84] The point is indirectly proved by an article by Muhammad Anas Zarqa which proposes "preferred shares" built on the idea, acceptable to *fiqh*, that a class of shareholders enjoy a higher share (e.g., 80 percent) of profits up to a certain level (e.g., 7.5 percent of capital, so as to yield these shareholders 6 percent of profits as dividend), and then a lower share (e.g., 30 percent) of profit beyond this level. He provides data showing that these shareholders enjoy a slight advantage in risk differentials.[85] He proposes nothing that would create liquidation preference.

Forward Contracts. The previous chapter explained how the prohibition on sales of *dayn bi-dayn* (debt for debt) bars the bilateral executory contract, the contract made binding solely by the exchange of promises without performance on either side. This bar prevents the conventional forward or futures contract, since such contracts are purchases of commodities at a future date with payment due only on the date of delivery. As described in the previous chapter, this objection to forward contracts may not be insurmountable, and several scholars have proposed ways to overcome it. For now, however, it is firm, and the only Islamic alternative to the forward contract is *salam*. The prospects for an Islamic forward market based only on *salam* are discussed in Chapter 10.

Currencies futures arouse particularly powerful objections in classical law, since currencies may be traded only at spot, with actual delivery. Islamic banks and investors would very much like to have a valid means to hedge against currency fluctuations. Some banks do achieve a degree of hedging by so-called swaps, in effect forward contracts achieved through the informal cooperation of Islamic and other financial institutions. Some may employ a "non-binding" promise, perhaps even a binding one. Plausibility is lent by a statement of al-Shafi'i that mutual promises in currency exchange are unobjectionable. If considered mutually binding, however, these contracts could hardly be valid since they would then be pure *riba* of delay. Notice also that if one party to such a transaction is a non-Islamic institution, it can easily hedge its exposure with conventional derivatives.

---

[84]The OIC Academy has declared that preferred shares with these two characteristics are invalid. Decision 65/1/7, seventh session, *Fiqh Academy Journal* 1:711.

[85]Muhammad Anas Zarqa, "Shari'a Compatible Shares: A Suggested Formula and Rationale," *Third International Conference on Islamic Economics*, 29-30 Jan. 1992, 21-35.

Options. Earlier in this chapter we discussed how slim the prospects are for offering option contracts in the fashion of conventional finance. Such options are not now, to our knowledge, being offered or traded by Islamic financial institutions.

Secondary Market

The most interesting aspect of the Islamically valid securities proposed in the last section is their potential to be traded, ideally on organized securities exchanges. Developing securities tradeable on secondary markets would enable Islamic financial institutions to turn a crucial corner toward a new success. Islamic banks desperately need to overcome the liquidity hurdles which, as we explained above, tend to accompany an Islamic effort to imitate conventional commercial banking. Developing longer-term investments that can be securitized and traded would enable Islamic financial institutions to move away from commercial banking, where Islamic law is constraining and uncongenial, toward other sectors, where Islamic law can be much more permissive and approving.

Securitizing and trading Islamic financial interests will not be easy, however, and potential conflicts loom with deeply ingrained habits, if not principles, of Islamic law. Speaking very generally and imprecisely, while Islamic law encourages trading and markets in all tangible goods and properties, it systematically restrains, if not prevents, the trading of financial interests. As we saw in the last chapter, the law blocks trading in monetary obligations (understood Islamically as *dayn*, currency, or equivalents of currency), obligations demarcated in generic goods (e.g., so many bushels of a particular grade of wheat [also *dayn*]), and even contingent or future rights generally. Even for existent unique goods (*'ayn*), the law ordinarily will not allow trading until the goods first are owned by and in the physical possession of the seller.

The easier advances in this field, therefore, will come in the securitization and trading of interests in tangible, known property. Many investments potentially qualify. For example, one could gather investors to buy an office building jointly and lease it for twenty years, issuing securities representing their interests. Because these interests represent co-ownership of a building, they could be freely traded. Similarly, investors could join to purchase an automobile dealership consisting of buildings owned outright, vehicles held for sale, and a facility providing repair services.

But one cannot progress far in imagining a secondary market in these securities without worrying about the restrictions on sale of debt for debt described in the last chapter. In the office building example, one cannot securitize the lease itself and validly make a market in those securities, since to own a lease is to own only a future stream of rental payments (*dayn*), not actual property. Or, in the dealership example, if the dealership sold cars on credit, it could not securitize and negotiate its rights to consumer installment payments.[86] As additional examples, while one may issue securities in a fund to purchase cotton by *salam*, once that purchase is made one cannot re-sell the securities until the cotton is actually delivered. After taking delivery, trading again becomes possible because the investors possess their own cotton. Similarly, if one securitizes the purchase by *istisna'* of an airplane, the trading of the securities to third parties is forbidden until the plane is delivered.

Returning to the dealership example, what if the dealership owns buildings, cars, and equipment, but also cash and some installment sales obligations? Does the dealership's holding of cash and obligations, however minimal, bar trading of interests in the dealership? What if the dealership owes money on a mortgage on one of its buildings? The OIC Academy in 1988 issued a fatwa that as long as the assets represented by the securities are in greater part (*al-ghalib*) by value real assets (*a'yan wa-manafi'*) as opposed to cash or obligations (*dayn*), then trading of the securities becomes permissible.[87] (We shall use the term "real assets" for property other than cash and obligations: i.e., real estate like land or buildings, other existing, known chattel goods and equipment [*a'yan*], and usufructs like leased

---

[86]Or rather one could, but only using one of three approaches. The first is to comply with rules for sale of debt, which generally bar sales of debt except to the debtor, and then only for cash in hand. The second approach is to assign the debts by the contract of *hawala*, but this would allow compensating for the debts only by creating new debts of equal tenor from the newly admitted security holder. The third approach is to arrange a conjectural liquidation and accounting on the occasion of every incident of transfer, reimbursing the withdrawing investor's principal together with his share of income already earned from installments paid in. This perhaps can be justified as a conjectural sale "to the debtor." The last stratagem alone is practical, and may be in use, since it appears that some funds composed entirely or chiefly of *murabaha* income are being traded. Indeed, the everyday transaction of liquidating or withdrawing Islamic banking deposits, even those whose term expires, may rely on this idea. But even it raises serious doubt, since taken to extremes it could legitimate any sale of debt for debt.

[87]Decision 5 (d4/08/88), fourth session (1988), *Fiqh Academy Journal* 3:2161, 2163.

property and hired services.) This opinion is justified by the many classical rulings permitting one to ignore something impermissible when it is mixed with a greater quantity of something permissible, such as prohibited wine mixed with water, or impure substances in water used for ritual purification. It is also justified by rulings allowing an impermissible transaction to occur when it is a component of a larger permissible transaction (e.g., selling a camel fetus in the womb is invalid, but one can sell a pregnant camel).

This fatwa is of far-reaching importance since it makes possible the trading of interests in real-world businesses. As the fatwa suggests, an investment in a start-up business may go through stages: first, one contributes cash to buy an interest in a future venture, and one's interest can only be sold for an equal amount of cash; second, the contributed cash is used to buy a building, equipment, and inventory, whereupon one can trade the security freely; third, inventory worth more than half the capital is sold on credit, whereupon one again cannot trade interests; and finally, the business settles down to a pattern of holding a majority of its capital at any time in inventory, equipment, and buildings, and their usufructs, and its securities can once again be freely traded.

This fatwa has been used to legitimize trading in funds holding portfolios of conventional equity securities, when the debt/equity ratios of the companies whose shares are held fall below a certain fraction.

Sami Homoud proposes taking the fatwa yet another step: he suggests that portfolios of securities be created such that in the aggregate the value of the securities in the portfolio that may be lawfully traded exceeds the value of those which may not, so that the whole may be freely traded.[88] He suggests that by this approach adequate means can be created by which to trade even debt securities. Reportedly, the Islamic Development Bank's unit trust uses this approach, mixing lease with installment sales investments.

Trading of Mudaraba Capital Interests, Whether Embodied in Partnerships or in Share Companies. For the securities we have discussed so far, we have ignored the issue of the vehicle for the securities or their issuer, proceeding as if the securities were merely undivided co-ownership shares in the enterprise or property. Ordinarily, of course, investment securities take the form of interests in companies which in turn own the investment. The natural vehicles for such ownership in Islamic law are *mudaraba* or

---

[88]Homoud, *al-Adawat*, 112.

musharaka companies. If securities are issued as interests in such companies, may these interests be traded?

Classical law holds that no partner may withdraw or be replaced without a termination and liquidation of the partnership, presumably in order to determine finally and exactly the withdrawing partner's share and to allow other partners a point of decision whether to continue the partnership with or without a new partner. But in modern times, accounting procedures are used as a substitute for the liquidation requirement. As for the partners' consent to a new partner, nowadays this is properly secured in advance by including a provision to that effect in the company's charter. In any case, the identity of a new partner seems largely beside the point if the partner is a mere contributor of capital playing no role in the business.

Two more difficult issues concern the terms on which the securities are traded:

- What kind of a sale is a trade in securities — is it like selling currency, debt (*dayn*), or real assets?
- If it is like a sale of real assets, will the price of the security be simply its liquidation value as shown on the company's books ("book value," the value to which the logic of the previous paragraph leads), or can it be determined by negotiation between the parties, by supply and demand, or by the broader market?

To answer both these questions, scholars made a major innovation, which now seems fully accepted. They began to see securities representing capital interests in *mudaraba* partnerships (and *a fortiori* shares of stock companies) as reflecting not personal partnership interests but shares in the ownership of the enterprise. Ownership of the enterprise is in turn equated with ownership of the company's "assets." After making these associations, the scholars could leap to understanding the buying and selling of these securities on the model not of partnership in the enterprise, but of undivided co-ownership of the company's assets.[89] This construction is advantageous since co-owners may sell their interests to third parties without the permission of other co-owners. In other words, securities (and shares in companies) become place-holders for undivided ownership in the com-

---

[89]This leap may have been facilitated by the fact that Islamically both co-ownership and partnership are called *sharika* — *sharikat milk* (ownership) and *sharikat 'aqd* (contract), respectively.

pany's assets, and the assets become place-holders for the commercial enterprise as a whole.

In Islamic terms, can one justify looking at partnership interests sometimes in terms of the mutual agreement of the parties and sometimes in terms of simple co-ownership? In this context the question may resolve to another question: why does classical Islamic law demand that partnerships be liquidated before any interest in them is transferred, even with all partners' consent? Is this due only to uncertainty as to the value of the assets of the partnership, so that, if they were known exactly and valued, trading in the constituent assets at a market price would be allowed at any time? The analogy here is to the sale of goods before they are weighed — a classical case of unlawful *gharar*. Alternatively, is the requirement of liquidation due to the fact that the partnership venture is seen as a whole, the success or failure of which cannot be known just from its assets at any one time, but only in its final outcome? Sale of an interest during the partnership's life is then like selling a fish in the sea or a crop before its soundness appears — two other instances of prohibited *gharar*. But if the latter explanation is correct, then why does the law (with rare exceptions) allow partners to force termination of the partnership at any time, possibly causing a premature and costly liquidation and harming the other partners?

The first analogy, to goods before they are weighed, seems better. Nowadays this analogy is all the more persuasive, after the development of companies of indefinite duration, with multiple ventures and projects. The objection of *gharar* can be overcome by relying on modern accounting techniques and modern practices of disclosure to shareholders of financial records. Arguably the values a modern partnership or company represents are sufficiently well known to the purchaser, and to the market at large, to permit them to be bought and sold fairly at a market price. Indeed, their market value is likely a fairer valuation of their worth than the books of the company.[90]

With this result, the question of whether the trade of securities is like

---

[90]What about intangible values that contribute to a company's worth, such as good will? Since property in Islamic law usually ignores intangible values, does including such values in the assets of a company spell defeat to the conception of securities as ownership interests in the company's assets? First, Islamic law is increasingly recognizing intangible property as *mal*, and thus arguably "real" for this purpose. An example is intellectual property rights, broadly endorsed by the OIC Academy, decision 5, fifth session (1988), *Fiqh Academy Journal* 3:2571. Second, the price of tangible assets nearly always reflects a great many associated intangible values, and conversely, a great many

a sale of cash, debt, or real assets becomes easy. According to the OIC Academy fatwa mentioned above, if the majority of the value of the enterprise is in real assets, then shares or interests in that enterprise are as freely tradeable as are those assets. The second question above is also easily answered: it is nowadays well accepted that, if tradeable, shares in the capital of *mudarabas* or of companies may be bought and sold at a market price.

After this extraordinary achievement of Islamic legal thought, one of the most striking in modern Islamic finance, one is reluctant to point out how the solution may lead to future difficulties. Although the analogy to ownership of underlying assets is effective as to issues of negotiability, in other contexts it may need to be restricted or abandoned. In particular, if shares can be the equivalent of real assets, are all Islamic sales contracts (and their rules) applicable to shares? Are there situations where such a conception of shares must give way to another conception, that shares represent mere financial instruments, i.e., that they represent cash investments in return for which the company grants certain rights to income, control, and security? What about the obvious extreme fungibility and liquidity of shares, making them the sort of property that attracted *riba* restrictions classically? Should shares still be treated as if they were an ownership share in a concrete, unique venture?

As an example, consider *murabaha* of shares. An investor requests a bank to purchase for him a quantity of IBM shares on a markup basis, payment to be made at a certain later time. The investor might pledge the shares with the bank. The result is very similar to buying shares on margin. As a second example, an Islamic bank, wishing to invest excess liquidity for one week, could approach a large conventional broker offering to finance the broker's purchase of a large volume of IBM shares by *murabaha*, allowing it one week to pay. Or it might in reverse obtain liquidity by asking the broker to finance the bank's own purchase of shares. The shares themselves, of course, could be bought and sold instantly, and after the *murabaha* is over, just as instantly disposed of. In practice the temptation would be strong not even to bother with actual transfers, which would attract fees; or the broker might just do the "sales" in house, or with one of its subsidiaries, not charging any fee beyond the markup.[91] As a final example, if shares represent real assets, what are dividends? Are they like the yield of agricultural

---

intangible assets, valuable in and of themselves, can be bought only in association with the real assets to which they are indissolubly linked.

[91]Conversation with Mr. Al-Tayeb Al-Dajani, Cambridge MA, 7 October 1997.

land, the benefits of which may go to a tenant? If so, may shares be rented, in effect accomplishing a sale of contingent future dividends for a price, the latter payable now or with delay? This would permit speculation on dividends.

Trading of Obligations, Futures, Options, and Other Contractual Rights. Due to the strictures against the sale of debt (*dayn*), the idea of trading in various rights to future payments or commodity deliveries is extremely problematic. For example, one could not buy or sell a right to delivery of goods in *salam* or to a delayed payment in *murabaha*. Similarly, if an option right could be created, perhaps by the *'arbun* contract, then the contract itself could not be traded. Thus, even if a market in options or futures contracts could be created, this seems unlikely to be more than a primary market. Chapter 10 presents several proposals to deal with this problem, chiefly the parallel or back-to-back *salam* contract.

Toward Islamic Financial Markets. Even if useful Islamic financial instruments are devised, and their capacity to be traded assured, problems will remain concerning the shape and function of a market in which these instruments can be traded. The question arises: if Islamic institutions and investors are already trading on the conventional financial markets, such as through the above-mentioned equity security portfolios, why not either continue to use conventional markets or set up new ones modeled after them? The answer seems to be that use of these markets is just a measure forced on the industry while it awaits Islamically correct markets of adequate volume to emerge. The OIC Academy has called for the extensive research needed to mount such markets.[92] Establishing them is made all the more daunting by the need for the government to cooperate by passing the extensive supportive legislation and regulation required to establish a securities market.

---

[92]Decision 61/10/6, sixth session (1990), *Fiqh Academy Journal* 2:1725.

PART II

A Financial Analysis of Islamic Banking and Finance

Samuel L. Hayes, III

CHAPTER 7

Islamic Financial Instruments: A Primer

Businesses in every modern culture are faced with the same set of financial challenges. They must finance inventories and credit sales, and they must keep a certain amount of cash on hand. Productive assets such as land, equipment, buildings, and ongoing research programs also must be financed. Whether the business operates in the West, the Middle East, or the Far East, whether it follows the practices of conventional commerce or those sanctioned by the Qur'an, funds under reasonable terms must be found and deployed. Those who supply capital — the investors — likewise share common concerns that transcend borders and culture: risk, return, liquidity, and the purposes for which their capital will be used. This chapter examines the instruments that Islamic finance has developed to meet these universal requirements.

A central preoccupation for anyone examining Islamic finance is understanding how the religious rulings of Islam affect the operations of a business in the contemporary commercial setting. Even if one sector operates according to a different set of religious (or other) constraints, it still must be able to meet with reasonable economic efficiency the basic requirements of both the commercial enterprise and the investors who supply its financial requirements. These "basic requirements" do not imply a carbon copy of conventional financial arrangements, but there are certain financial operations and protections which have to be accomplished by any business or investor. These may be handled in alternative ways.

FINANCING WORKING CAPITAL

The need to pay for inventories and receivables is universal. In Western finance, a straightforward way to finance inventory is through a line of credit provided by a financial intermediary, such as a commercial bank. The lender may hold a specific lien on the inventory as security for the loan. The underlying philosophy is that the size of the loan will vary with the amount of carried inventory, and provision for an annual "cleanup" (liquidation of the loan) assures that this credit does not become a long-term funding source.

The *Murabaha* Contract

In Islamic finance, where interest-bearing lines of credit are forbidden, a close substitute to the line of credit is found in the *murabaha* transaction, which involves the sale of goods with a profit markup built into the price. For example, if a builder needs to finance $10,000 of raw materials, he can arrange for an Islamic bank or other investor to purchase the goods on his behalf, add a profit margin, and then resell him the goods for, say, $11,000, with payment to be delayed for three months.

The added profit margin is completely acceptable according to Islamic religious law.[1] It can cover anything which the seller chooses to incorporate in it, with no questions asked or justification required. Thus, in addition to actual costs incurred in processing the deal, the seller can load in a charge for such things as the risk that the buyer won't ultimately pay for the goods, the risk that payment in another currency will leave him disadvantaged, and, very importantly, the seller's opportunity cost in having his funds tied up until the buyer actually pays him. This last charge — for the tie-up of the investor's capital — represents a very subtle distinction from the charging of straight interest.

---

[1] Abdul Halim Ismail, "The Deferred Contracts of Exchange in al-Qur'an," in *An Introduction to Islamic Finance,* ed. Sheikh Ghazali Sheikh Abod, Syed Omar Syed Agil, and Aidit Hj. Ghazali (Kuala Lumpur: Quill Publishers, 1992).

The *'Ina* Contract

Another form of inventory financing that is generally frowned upon but nonetheless used in Islam (particularly in Pakistan) is *'ina* (double sale). Here, a businessman offers to sell some of his inventory to a bank for an immediate cash payment. He then buys back the inventory on an installment basis. While there is a sale and a purchase, this transaction has far less substance than a *murabaha* credit sale, where a genuine movement of goods and title is intrinsic to the transaction.

A variation on this *'ina* deal is for a party in need of funds to find a transaction and then insert itself into the loop. For example, if A needs money, he identifies B, who is intending to buy a good, such as cement, for cash from cement producer C. Party A gets an Islamic bank to buy the cement and sell it to A on a *murabaha* installment sale basis. A then immediately sells the cement to B for cash. A then has the use of that cash until it is depleted by the *murabaha* installment payments to the bank. This maneuver is a classic example of what is known in Arabic as a *hila* (trick).

The *Salam* Contract

An alternative Islamic arrangement for financing in-process inventory is a *bay' al-salam* contract (or the more generalized form *bay' fi al-dhimma*: "sale by description").[2] Here, an Islamic financial institution or other investor pays immediately to the producer the value of goods to be produced and delivered at a given point in the future.

A risk to the lender is that there will be no market for the goods even after delivery. Because of this, Islamic banks seldom enter into such *salam* arrangements in the absence of a third party's promise to buy the delivered goods.

The *salam* deals uncovered in our research were for the most part simple and straightforward. In several deals, however, an implied currency

---

[2]S.M. Hasanuz-Zaman, "Bay' Salam: Principles and their Practical Applications," in *An Introduction to Islamic Finance,* ed. Sheikh Ghazali Sheikh Abod, Syed Omar Syed Agil, and Aidit Hj Ghazali (Kuala Lumpur: Quill Publishers, 1992).

forward contract was built into the arrangement. For example, suppose the trading arm of an Islamic bank in country A makes a *salam* contract with a domestic cotton producer to deliver cotton in six months in exchange for a payment in country A currency now. The bank will simultaneously arrange for the sale of the cotton (perhaps in the form of another *salam* contract) to a foreign buyer in country B at the expected time of the cotton's delivery for a set price in country B's currency. In pricing the *salam* contract, the bank will include not only the credit risk and the expected increase or decrease in the price of the asset over the intervening period, but also a premium or discount reflecting the forward exchange rate between the currencies of the two countries.

The *Istisna'* Contract

A variation of this particular inventory financing method is an install-ment payment arrangement called *istisna'*. This is similar to a *salam* con-tract, except that it is used in cases of specific goods to be produced, such as trousers or shirts of a certain description, rather than a generic class of goods for which there are fungible substitutes, such as wheat. There is usu-ally a provision for periodic installment payments on the total purchase price, oftentimes keyed to the actual progress in the manufacture of the items. Thus, a shipbuilder might obtain from the ultimate buyer a contract to purchase a vessel for a certain price with installment payments spread over the period during which the ship is under construction. This is quite similar to a Western construction loan or other bridge financing.

As with a *salam* arrangement, the *istisna'* contract can be made di-rectly between the manufacturer and the end user. An intermediary, such as a bank, may also act for the end user. In these cases, the bank might enter into an *istisna'* contract — either with a lump sum payment up front or with installment payments — with the manufacturer on the one hand and an installment payment *murabaha* with the ultimate user on the other. The gross profit earned by the bank is represented by the present value of the installment payments received from the end user minus the combined pre-sent value of the progress payments paid to the manufacturers, plus what-ever administrative costs the bank incurs. With the bank in the middle, the manufacturer is free of the customer's credit risk. The cost to the manufacturer for insuring itself against this credit risk is equal to the gross profit earned by the bank.

Drawing an example from the deals we analyzed, an Islamic bank contracts with a manufacturer to produce certain items for delivery in six months. An *istisna'* arrangement made with the manufacturer calls for a series of progress payments on the manufacture over the six-month period. A buyer for the goods has already been located by the manufacturer and the bank has made a contract which requires this buyer to make immediate payment to the bank. The buyer will not take delivery of the goods for six months. The bank's contract with the manufacturer is an *istisna'* deal, whereas the bank's contract with the goods buyer is a *salam* arrangement. The pricing of the *istisna'* will reflect the risks of nonperformance by the manufacturer as well as the bank's opportunity rate for capital. The pricing of the *salam* transaction between the end user and the bank will reflect both the credit risk of the bank's guarantee as well as the end user's own alternative use for money during the period between cash payment and delivery of the goods.

FINANCING RECEIVABLES

Accounts receivable financing is stickier in Islamic finance than in its Western counterpart. Retail customers cannot use credit cards because they incorporate an interest charge, so an Islamic retailer can't pass over his customer credits to a conventional credit-card provider, such as Visa or American Express. However, a debit card, which immediately withdraws the specified amount of money from the buyer's bank account, is acceptable because it does not involve an interest charge. The downside for the customer is that he or she gets no credit "float" to use interest-free for a period; it is the same as paying with cash. It is worth noting that debit cards are also used to perform a number of payment operations and fund transfers where interest payments are not even an issue. The *shari'a*, or religious law, does not forbid remuneration for such efforts and services; in fact, Islamic law *requires* remuneration for services at their just value.

Conventional financing of an account receivable via factoring is not permitted under Islamic law because the receivable is considered to be a debt instrument, something which Islamic banks and other Muslim investors are generally forbidden to buy. The rule of thumb for Islamic religious acceptability is that an investment must represent an ownership claim on real assets, such as inventory, plant, or equipment.[3]

If the seller is willing to commit his or her capital, the same *murabaha* transaction mentioned earlier can be structured to extend credit to a business customer. If an inventory item is sold to a customer, the seller can, of course, add to the price a profit markup sufficient to allow the buyer to take more time to pay for it. For instance, if an auto dealer sells a car to a customer, the transaction can be structured as a credit sale, with installment payments reflecting the time, effort, and profit expectations of the auto dealer for the period over which the installment payments are scheduled to be made.

If the dealer doesn't want to tie up its own money in the credit sale financing, it can arrange for an Islamic bank to perform that service in the manner of a conventional consumer credit company. An Islamic bank can arrange to buy the car and then resell it to the customer, incorporating its own markup to cover any items it wishes, including, but not limited to, its various costs and profit expectations for the repayment period. If the car buyer doesn't meet his payment obligations, the credit supplier is in a difficult position. Under Islamic law, the creditor is forbidden to charge an extra fee for any delay in payment beyond the originally specified payment date; one cannot levy a markup on the markup already built into the contract. Not surprisingly, Islamic credit suppliers in *murabaha* transactions often press aggressively for prompt payment, resorting to the appropriate courts where feasible, and even salary assignments.

In *murabaha* arrangements for financing inventory or facilitating a credit sale, the borrower may ask to prepay the installments and receive a negotiated discount on the face amount of the obligation: the amount of the discount usually bears a close relationship to the prevailing rate of interest for money for that class of risk and maturity. The reasoning behind this accommodation is that, in Islam, any creditor has the right to forgive part or all of a debt at his discretion. As long as there has been no prior

---

[3]Michael Grahammer, "Islamische Banken: Ausweg aus dem Finanzierungsdilemma für Nahostgeschäfte?" in *Forschungergebnisse der Wirtschaftsuniversität Wien,* ed. Edgar Topritzhofer (Vienna: Swervice Fachverlag, 1993).

agreement and no "common practice" precedent is established, this is considered religiously acceptable. It is another means for incorporating a de facto cost of capital into an Islamic financial contract.

The credit supplier, on the other hand, cannot *demand* early payment except when the customer has defaulted on an installment, in which case the entire amount typically becomes immediately due and payable. This feature of the payment terms makes the instrument akin to a conventional debt instrument: the creditor has essentially purchased an I.O.U. from the credit user. A provision for installment payments will, like conventional home mortgage payments, also include a component of principal repayment. The capital user's right to early repayment of a *murabaha* contract is similar to any consumer loan. In the case of *murabaha* and its derivatives, the factors that would influence the capital user's possible early payment would include his liquidity position, the attractiveness of the discount being offered relative to other refinancing contracts, the capital user's opportunity cost for money, and whether or not the creditor had a lien against the goods.

If a customer defaults on the payment terms of a *murabaha* contract (e.g., account receivable), the creditor's first move is usually to go to court and sue for payment, both from the customer's company as well as from the individual owners of the company. There is a clear legal and moral obligation to pay up. If this fails, the creditor can repossess if he has obtained a pledge of the item purchased. The creditor then would have to sell the item in the open market to retrieve as much of its investment as possible. This feature would appear to give the customer a de facto put option alternative. If at any time the value of the good in question falls below the present value of the total installment payments, it could be economically advantageous for the customer to forfeit the item and withhold any remaining unremitted payments. However, in *shari'a* law, this kind of opportunistic default would not be permitted. The customer may only default if he is experiencing genuine financial difficulties.

Another sticky aspect of *murabaha* transactions is the requirement that the credit supplier not simply purchase but also take physical possession of the item before it is resold to the end user. This would not be an issue for a retail store selling, for instance, refrigerators from its on-premises stock, but if an Islamic bank is to provide the end user with the credit to make the purchase, the bank must take physical possession of the refrigerator before shipping it to the customer, which may require the bank to maintain its own warehouse and shipping facilities. This becomes problematic in the case of inventory financings done on behalf of large corporate customers. If ABC Oil Company wants to finance five million gallons of jet fuel which it has refined but not yet sold, it might come to XYZ International Bank's "Islamic window" and seek *murabaha* financing for that inventory. To be Islamically correct, XYZ Bank must take physical possession of that fuel before selling it back to ABC Oil Company on a delayed payment basis. In actual practice, the physical transfer is often omitted, except on paper. A number of Islamic scholars have condemned these transactions as "synthetic" *murabahas* with the result that at least one leading Islamic bank has phased out such transactions over a two-year period.

Long-Term Financing

In conventional corporate finance, longer-term needs are met with a variety of debt and equity instruments and their derivatives.

- *Secured debt,* which often occupies a senior position in a corporation's capital structure, typically has a direct claim on assets with independent value.
- *Financial (full payout) leases* are another form of secured lending, since until the full payout has been accomplished, the lessor holds legal title to the leased asset. Because leases are regarded as alternatives to direct loans, generally accepted accounting principles require that they be capitalized as though they were direct loans. Operating leases (leases in which there is no expectation of full payout to the lessor) are another secured financing technique through which to gain capital structure leverage.
- *Unsecured debt* is junior to secured debt (at least to the extent of the collateral's value) and has only a general claim on a borrower's assets after secured claims have been satisfied.
- *Subordinated debt,* depending on the terms set forth in its contract, typically stands even lower in the hierarchy of claims for the cash flow and assets of a borrower. It can nonetheless further expand the debt-carrying capacity, and thus the financial leverage, of a company.

- *Preferred stock*, a hybrid of debt and equity, is another instrument of Western finance. It usually stands junior to the company's debt obligations but senior to the common stock and receives a fixed dividend that is paid before any common stock dividends. In a liquidation, it typically has a priority claim on assets before anything goes to common share owners.

Each of these categories of debt or quasi-debt instruments has the capacity to enhance the profitability of the enterprise and its owners — the common shareholders — if operating results are favorable. In corporate strategy formulation (and in textbooks used to teach financial management), considerable attention is given to ways to optimize that capital structure to the benefit of shareholders.[4]

In Islam, the notion of a hierarchy of capital suppliers is repugnant; the idea of giving one source of capital a preferential position over others as to profits or claims on assets is not in the spirit of the partnership approach to business structure. The optimal arrangement is an assemblage of collegial investment partners who all do well if the enterprise prospers, and who share the pain if the venture stumbles.[5]

This underlying philosophy of *pari passu* partnership, very much in evidence in many of the Islamic deals examined, does not, however, prevent financial leveraging.[6] When a company avoids tying up expensive equity capital and obtains goods on credit from a supplier in a *murabaha* transaction, it gains financial leverage. Leasing, an Islamically acceptable financing vehicle, also produces financial leverage. It is likewise possible to use a revenue bond (called a *kirad* bond, discussed below) as a means of obtaining an advantage for a business's owners. In sum, there are a number of religiously acceptable avenues by which an Islamic firm can create financial leverage.

---

[4]See, for instance, Richard Brealey and Stewart Myers, *Corporate Finance* (New York: McGraw-Hill Book Company, 1996).

[5]See, for instance, Sami Hassan Homoud, *Islamic Banking*, pt. 2 (London: Arabian Information, 1985).

[6]Muhammad Mohsin, "Assessment of Corporate Securities in Terms of Islamic Investment Requirements," in *An Introduction to Islamic Finance*, ed. Sheikh Ghazali Sheikh Abod, Syed Omar Syed Agil, and Aidit Hj. Ghazali (Kuala Lumpur: Quill Publishers, 1992).

Leasing (*Ijara*)

For intermediate- to longer-term financing of equipment and real estate, a leasing arrangement (*ijara*) is an attractive Islamic financing form. Islamically valid leases are almost identical to conventional leases since, as has already been noted, it is perfectly appropriate under Islamic law to pay rent for the use of a real asset. They can be either operating leases (where the lessor takes back the equipment when the lease ends) or full-payout financial leases (where the lease payments cover one hundred percent of the value of the equipment or property and where title may pass to the lessee at the conclusion of the lease).[7] As a mode of finance, leases have the advantage of not requiring the same intensity of investigation and audit of the lessee's affairs that would be the case were an outright investment being made in the lessee's enterprise.

Islamically valid leases may provide that the lessee may purchase the leased asset at different points in the life of the lease, adding an early termination option for the lessee. There have also been reported instances of *ijaras* being terminated and renegotiated during the life of the lease. These have received the sanction of a *shari'a* board, despite the general *shari'a* admonition that the terms of a financial arrangement must be fixed and known at the time of the formulation of the original contract. Citibank set up a ship lease in which the implicit interest rate in the lease was reset each year to provide what was essentially a floating-rate interest component (something which would normally be unacceptable in Islam).

As an example of an *ijara* contract, consider this scenario: Banque Mercantile enters a lease contract with American Security Company to lease for $1,000 per year a theft control system worth $10,000 today. The lease contract is to run for fifteen years although the expected life of the equipment is twenty years. At the end of the fifteen-year contract, Banque Mercantile has the option either to purchase the equipment for $2,500 (its depreciated value at that point) or to return it to the lessor. The present value of the lease payments plus the present value of the salvage value at the end of the lease should equal $10,000 at the lessor's desired annual opportunity rate of return on capital.

The Islamic leasing deals we researched are very similar to conventional leases. Many are operating rather than financial leases, i.e., they do

---

[7] *New Horizon,* February 1995, 7.

not involve an option to purchase the equipment for a nominal sum at the end of the contract. One major difference is found in the responsibility for such things as maintenance and insurance in Islamic contracts. In many conventional operating leases, that responsibility is with the lessee, but in the Islamic operating leases we examined, the lessor bears these upkeep responsibilities.

Capital to fund Islamic leases is often raised using a *mudaraba* transaction. (This financing form, further discussed below, couples an entrepreneur — the *mudarib* — with passive capital suppliers.) Third-party insurance coverage is often included to cover any damage sustained during the lease period. The cost of this insurance is passed on to the lessee via the lease payments. The leasing fund of one leading Islamic bank employs just such a mixture of *mudaraba* and *ijara* structures. The bank pools its investors' money to purchase equipment to be leased exclusively within the United States. Insurance is also included. A 6 percent return, paid semiannually, is guaranteed by the bank to its investor pool. (On its face, however, this guarantee does not appear to be in accordance with *shari'a* jurisprudence.)

Revenue Bonds

A financing arrangement backed by the revenues of a particular project is referred to as *qirad* bond (or *muqarada* bond) financing. An example would be a bridge or tunnel project with revenues from tolls collected from users. A portion of this income (after meeting direct expenses) would be paid out to the bond holders as their participation in the profits of the facility. Oftentimes the municipality claiming jurisdiction over the facility will guarantee the return of the face value of the bonds at the conclusion of the contract life. There may also be a provision for declining participation in the ownership of the facility through periodic repayment of the principal of the bonds during the contract life.[8]

Qirad bond financing thus bears a close resemblance to conventional revenue bond financing, which likewise may incorporate a standby guarantee of principal from a sponsoring authority and a schedule of sinking fund payments designed to retire the bond principal in part or in total by the end of the contract.

---

[8]*New Horizon*, Dec. 1994, 8.

While *qirad* bond financing is religiously acceptable, examples of its application are few; one example is a 1980 offering of *qirad* bonds to renovate *waqf* properties (endowments) within the Kingdom of Jordan.[9]

One writer has also raised the possibility that *shari'a* sanction could be obtained for a financing contract whose cash payments to investors would be tied to an overall measure of enterprise profitability, along the lines of a conventional "income bond."[10] This financing instrument would also bear a close resemblance to a conventional participating preferred share, with a major variable being the differing tax treatments accorded the distributed income of the two securities in a number of countries. It is not clear whether this contract would receive *shari'a* approval, however. It would be neither a *qirad* bond with a dedicated stream of revenue, nor a straightforward equity security. It would presumably have some preferred position (such as a claim on assets) and would probably have a capped rather than an open-ended claim on a share of earnings.[11]

Another conventional financial instrument that bears a striking resemblance to the *qirad* bond is the "equipment trust certificate" commonly used to finance railroad boxcars. Here, a specific asset generates income that can be distributed, and in the event of a default, the asset can be readily retrieved by the investor. The *qirad* bond also bears some resemblance to a conventional project financing. A project financing is designed as a stand-alone arrangement that insulates its ultimate sponsors from liability beyond their actual investment in the project. While most project financing packages include several layers of debt in addition to the equity contributed by the sponsors, there is no reason why the financing couldn't be set up in a *mudaraba* or a *musharaka* form (where both parties contribute capital) to meet *shari'a* requirements.

The *qirad* bond offers attractive possibilities for expanding the range of Islamic investment instrument forms.[12] In instances where one could carve out a revenue source or a discrete activity with its own profit-and-loss responsibility, a *qirad* bond could be created to finance that activity. Even if the

---

[9]Homoud, *Islamic Banking.*

[10] S.L. Hayes, "New Interest in Incentives," *Harvard Business Review* (July-August, 1966).

[11]We also came across a "participation term certificate" used in Pakistan. While this instrument is supposed to employ the same principle as a *qirad* bond, its structure defines the profit so narrowly that it is actually a debt contract with an interest rate.

[12]A detailed discussion of innovative Islamic contract possibilities is presented in Chapter 10.

surrounding organization did not conform to Islamic principles, the targeted portion of the business financed with *qirad* bonds could be judged to be in accordance with *shari'a*, in the opinion of some scholars.[13] Cash profits paid to the bondholders (along with a possible amortization of the original capital) could permit the investors to obtain a payback of their original capital in a relatively short time and thus provide an attractive containment of both credit and market risk, even if the bulk of the profit return had to await the ultimate liquidation of the activity at the end of the contract period.

EQUITY-LIKE INSTRUMENTS

Every business requires risk capital, and businesses in the Muslim world are no exception. Risk capital is expected to take the first buffeting from adverse operating results that hit many businesses.

The bar against conventional debt financing in the Islamic world would seem to result in relatively heavy reliance on equity funds to finance business activity. In keeping with the "partnership" philosophy that governs business relationships in the world of Islam, an enterprise makes cash distributions to its owners strictly as a function of operating performance and the need to retain profits to finance further growth. Investors thus participate in both the up and down sides of the company's fortunes. If the company's affairs suffer, shareholders may receive no dividends and may also see the value of their shares decline. Islamic businesses can, as in some conventional markets, repurchase their own shares from investors, since this conforms with the declining-equity participation form of Islamic finance mentioned in connection with revenue bonds.

The *Mudaraba* Contract

One important Islamically valid form of equity investment is the *mudaraba* profit-sharing arrangement.[14] Capital is contributed by one party and the managerial oversight and entrepreneurial push is provided by an-

---

[13]Conversation with Dr. Abdul Wahab Ibrahim Abu Sulayman, Boston, 15 November 1995.

[14]Muhammad Akram Khan, "Types of Business Organization in an Islamic Economy," in *An Introduction to Islamic Finance,* ed. Sheikh Ghazali Sheikh Abod, Syed Omar Syed Agil, and Aidit Hj. Ghazali (Kuala Lumpur: Quill Publishers, 1992).

other (called the *mudarib*). Any profits are shared according to a predetermined formula. In the event of loss, the passive capital suppliers lose all or part of their money, and the entrepreneur loses the time and energy (the "sweat equity") he committed. These *mudaraba* arrangements can be used to finance well-established and mature businesses as well as new ventures with greater risk and profit potential.

Suppose an inventor of a new high-tech milling machine needs capital to bring the prototype to the point of actual manufacture. An Islamic venture capitalist might agree to put up the $1 million in estimated cost, on the condition that any profits will be shared, 60 percent to the capital supplier and 40 percent to the entrepreneur. If the project is successful, both parties will be well rewarded; if the project is unsuccessful, the venture capitalist loses his money and the entrepreneur loses his sweat equity (and pride!).

Some *mudaraba* arrangements closely resemble Western limited partnerships. The contractual arrangement between the two parties may be restricted to a particular investment proposal or line of business, or it may be unrestricted. This latter case closely resembles the "blind pools" organized by some Wall Street investment houses to invest in venture capital deals and leveraged buyouts.[15] Safeguards are needed to ensure the targeted investments' religious acceptability, and it is common to see contract provisions requiring *shari'a* approval for each proposed investment by the pool. Additionally, there are often provisions for periodic audits to certify that all activities, investments, and expenditures in connection with these portfolio investments are fully in accord with *shari'a*.

Among the actual deals we have examined are the following:

- *A real-estate fund.* In this *mudaraba* deal the pooled funds are invested in various real estate projects. The *mudarib* gets a 2 percent management fee. The investor receives a 6 percent cash dividend per year, if earned, with any additional profits being reinvested. The *mudarib* receives 20 percent of any return in excess of 8 percent. The 8 percent return is guaranteed by a third-party Islamic merchant bank which organized the fund and employs the *mudarib* as the fund manager.
- *A commercial bank mudaraba with a car dealer.* A bank agrees to invest two hundred million Saudi riyals in a venture with a car dealer

[15]See, for instance, the terms of the 1987 Investment Pool raised for Kohlberg, Kravis, and Roberts.

(the *mudarib*) who, in turn, will use the money to purchase cars and resell them to retail buyers using a *murabaha* installment sale contract. The car dealer represents to the bank (but does not promise) an expected bad debt loss and minimum profit and agrees to make monthly profit remittances to a sequestered bank account. In the event of a default, the bank has the right to recover its funds by debiting one of the *mudarib*'s other bank accounts or any other of the *mudarib*'s assets.

- *A Lebanese reconstruction fund mudaraba.* Investors' money is pooled in a *mudaraba* to be committed to a specific real estate development on the outskirts of Beirut. The returns to be earned fall into two categories: operational profits and capital gains. The target returns to the passive investors are 10 percent per year from operating profits and 15 percent from capital gains. The *mudarib* participates in the cumulative operating profit to the extent of 10 percent of total project returns up to 12 percent. The *mudarib* gets 20 percent of cumulative operating profits from 12 percent to 14 percent in total returns, and 30 percent on operating profits above 14 percent. On the capital gains side, the *mudarib* receives 20 percent of the cumulative gains up to the investors' targeted 15 percent, 25 percent of the gains on total capital appreciation of 15 percent to 18 percent, and 30 percent of capital appreciation above 18 percent in total gains.

The *Musharaka* Contract

Another important type of equity arrangement is called *musharaka* and involves two or more parties in a project where each contributes both capital and management. The decision-making process for the disposition of the funds is shared, usually proportionate to the relative sizes of the investments.

Two such *musharaka* deals surfaced in our research:

- *An oil and gas company musharaka.* Outside investors commit capital while the oil and gas company contributes the rights to drill at specific locations. Any profits or losses from the drilling operation are shared, 40 percent to the outside investors and 60 percent to the oil and gas company, after the deduction of administrative fees for managerial oversight of the operation. The outside investors' capital commitment is represented by *musharaka* certificates that can be transferred from one investor to another, since they represent claims on real producing assets.[16]

- *An Islamic bank contract of partnership with a capital supplier for imports.* The bank pays in foreign currency a certain percentage of the cost of goods being imported and also issues a guarantee for the purchase price of the goods to the partner. The partner puts up the rest of the capital. The cost of insuring the commodity is deducted by the bank from the revenue before sharing the profits of the resale of the imported goods. The profit/loss distribution follows the proportion of capital each contributes, net of expenses.

PREFERRED STOCK

In conventional finance, preferred stock is sometimes used to finance a portion of the long-term equity needs of a business. As noted earlier, a preferred share typically enjoys a claim on assets senior to that of the common shares and a preference over the common in the distribution of any profits earned by the enterprise.

It is impossible to generalize about whether preferred stocks are religiously acceptable,[17] because the term "preferred stock," whether in an Islamic or non-Islamic context, is a generic label for securities which can be constructed with many different provisions. Although it is not Islamically acceptable to offer certain shareholders either a higher or a more senior fixed dividend than that made available to others, it is acceptable to offer them a higher *payout ratio*. An example of this would be a company that has sold equal amounts of two classes of common stock, one of which has the right to receive twice the share of dividends as the other class. If a company earns $6 million in a particular year, and determines to pay out half of these earnings ($3 million) to its shareholders, one class of common stock

---

[16]Note that this establishes circumstances in which a secondary market for investment securities can be promoted. As is emphasized elsewhere in this book, the potential for creating enhanced liquidity through such a public market is one of the most important factors affecting the future of Islamic finance.

[17]Discussion with Dr. Mohammed Elgari in Boston, 3-6 January 1996.

would get $1 million and the other class would receive $2 million. Presumably the class of common stock getting the higher payout would either pay a premium for that privilege or would sacrifice some other desirable feature in exchange, such as its right to have a vote on corporate affairs.

Such "participation shares" were legalized in the state of Bahrain in the late 1980s.[18] A legislative decree currently permits two types of shareholders to exist in a joint stock company. The first class has conventional common stock rights and privileges. The second class of shares has the right to participate in the profits without the right to interfere in management or vote in elections. In this case, the motivation has been to maintain management control in the hands of Bahraini nationals while at the same time attract growth capital from outside the state. This conforms closely to a *musharaka* contract in which one party puts up capital but remains a silent partner in the enterprise while the other party also puts up capital and is the active manager of the activity.

ATTITUDES TOWARD RISK

In the business world, there is a natural and universal concern for maximizing profitability while containing risk. The contemporary field of financial engineering has focused considerable effort on developing investment instruments that address that concern — in effect extending the efficient frontier of risk and reward. A host of arrangements have been devised to increase economic efficiency and have spawned myriad strategies employing such derivatives as calls, puts, forward contracts, and swaps. The employment of these devices has, in turn, had an important impact on the pricing and cost of financial contracts around the world. A broad array of manufacturing and commercial activities have also been affected worldwide by strategies used to hedge such important cost components as commodities.

The Islamic business sector is in no way immune to these economic forces. Islamic investors and capital users react to the same array of concerns as everyone else — concerns such as illiquidity, credit risk, capital structure risk, currency risk, and overall economic risk — and a variety of protections are built into their financial contracts.

---

[18]Discussion with Dr. Sami Homoud in Jedda, 22 September 1996.

Illiquidity Risk

Illiquidity is at or near the top of the list of concerns for most institutional and individual Islamic investors. This is reflected in our estimate that 80-90 percent of all Islamic funds are employed in short-term (and, therefore, more liquid) *murabaha* transactions. Since these "markup" sales typically liquidate themselves in no more than a few months, it is understandable that Islamic banks are drawn to these investments — after all, they obtain most of their funding from current account and investment deposits with short-term withdrawal rights and they have no central bank discount window to which they can turn to meet unanticipated liquidity needs. Many individual investors, too, are naturally averse to risk or have serious personal or political preoccupations that lead them to prefer greater liquidity to higher returns.

As noted, illiquidity in the Islamic financial sector is exacerbated by the absence of an organized secondary market for Islamic investments. *Shari'a* jurisprudence bars trading in financial assets; a Muslim can only trade in real assets such as commodities, plant and equipment, and other tangible goods. Many Islamic scholars hold the view that shares of stock are evidence of undivided ownership of a company's *real* assets and thus may be traded as long as those assets themselves are suitable for trading.[19] Much scholarship is being devoted to developing Islamic rules for the establishment of secondary markets in those instruments.[20] In the meantime, Islamic investors have essentially been locked into a hold-to-maturity strategy.

Credit Risk

Credit risk is also a natural preoccupation of Islamic investors and capital users. Many demand a recognizable international "name" with a qual-

---

[19]See, for instance, the term sheet for the Wellington Management Company's Islamic oriented stock mutual fund, entitled "NCB Global Trading Equity Fund" (Boston, 1997), 1.

[20]Nublan Zaky Dato' Yusoff Zaky, *An Islamic Perspective of Stock Market — An Introduction,* ed. Sheikh Ghazali Abod (Kuala Lumpur: Dian Darulnaim Sdn. v. Bhd, 1992); see also M.A. Mannan, *Understanding Islamic Finance: A Study of the Securities Market in an Islamic Framework* (Jedda: Islamic Development Bank, 1988).

ity image. Most *salam* and *istisna'* deals we have seen include a third-party performance guarantee (usually from a bank) on the part of both the producer and the ultimate goods purchaser. In *murabaha* transactions, a third-party guarantee in the form of an Islamic letter of credit is also common.

Currency Risk

Field interviews suggest that although country risk appears not to be as much of an issue for Islamic investors as for many other investors, currency risk is a hot button. To protect against currency risk, deals are often either denominated in dollars, or currency value is guaranteed by a third party.

Limiting currency risk is much more difficult for Islamic investors than for their non-Islamic counterparts, since risk-curbing measures commonly used in conventional finance theoretically aren't available to Islamic investors. Forward currency contracts are proscribed because both the price and the monetary exchange are postponed to the future. Put and call options are unacceptable because they involve speculation. Interest rate and currency swaps are forbidden because interest (*riba*) is built in.

Capital Structure Risk

Capital structure risk is another preoccupation of Islamic investors and capital users. This is particularly noteworthy because, in contrast to conventional practices, Islam promotes a flat structure in which all invested capital is committed on a partnership basis, and profits and losses of the enterprise are shared proportionately. While there is no doubt that the capital structures of Islamic enterprises are less hierarchical than those of conventional businesses, we have already identified how significant financial leverage is nonetheless employed. The short-term part of the right-hand side of the balance sheet typically includes considerable accounts payable (oftentimes referred to as "spontaneous credit" in conventional finance) in the form of credit sale contracts with suppliers. There may also be *salam* or *istisna'* contract obligations.

In the realm of longer-term financing, we have pointed out that Islamic businesses can utilize both operating and full-payout leases (*ijara*), another form of de facto debt. Islamic investors in leases protect their capital through the governing lease terms. In full-payout Islamic leases, for in-

199

stance, ownership of the asset remains with the lessor (investor) until the purchase option is exercised (if ever). We have also noted the use of "floating-rate" leases which protect the lessor from being locked into an unfavorable investment return in the event of an upward future shift in interest rates.

The next chapter explores these capital structure considerations in greater depth.

CONCLUSIONS

An obvious conclusion from this survey of Islamic financing practices is that investors and capital users the world over are motivated by many of the same concerns, no matter what their religious convictions. They will reach for profit but go to great lengths to limit risk. They prefer liquidity if the cost is not too high. They value cash that comes to them sooner rather than later, depending on how lucrative their alternative uses are for the money. Islamic finance will grow only to the extent that it can respond in a reasonably efficient way to these basic economic motivations.

It is therefore essential that the current gaps in the portfolio of Islamic financing tools be filled — and quickly. These gaps are evident from the machinations and contortions we have noted in the existing Islamic financial instruments. Filling these gaps will require the development of options to allow for legitimate risk hedging (as opposed to speculation), mechanisms to contain the risk of cross-currency transactions, development in the use of profit-participating "carve-outs" where something akin to *qirad* bonds can be used, and the establishment of a viable secondary market for many of these Islamic instruments so that liquidity can be assured.

Ultimately, no financial system can survive in the contemporary world unless it is in harmony with the dominant global financial market forces. As the world economy becomes increasingly integrated, the financial systems, markets, and practices of its participants have to respond. Nations whose financial practices stand apart from this integrating evolution, for either political or cultural reasons, will find it harder to tap into the global market for capital as borrowers or lenders. In the following chapters, we attempt to identify means by which progress in this area can take place.

CHAPTER 8

The Opportunity Rate of Capital and Islamic Capital Structure

Much ink has been spilled in the literature of finance over the question of the optimum capital structure for a business — its mix of debt and equity — and the impact of that structure on the business's overall cost of capital. The ultimate objective of capital structure selection is obviously to achieve the mix of capital funds with the lowest sustainable cost. Low cost of funds, in turn, contributes to maximizing profit and shareholder wealth.

How do these concepts manifest themselves in the Islamic context? After all, loans with interest charges are forbidden in Islam. And whereas conventional capital structure is hierarchical, composed of equity owners and creditors with various priorities of legal claims, the Islamic business is based upon the concept of partnership. But the equity owners of an Islamically-run business are just as interested as everyone else is in maximizing profit, provided Islamic rules are observed. They are not really barred from enhancing those profits through the judicious use of "other people's money," and their opposition to interest-bearing loans does not mean that they are oblivious to the time value of money and the costs of various forms of capital.

INTEREST AND USURY

Recall that a central Islamic tenet holds that it is usurious either to charge or to receive interest on loans of capital. A saying of the Prophet specifically

---

Note: Research Assistant Indrajit Garai made important contributions to this chapter.

forbids interest on loans: "Any loan that attracts a benefit is *riba*."[1] Many would argue, however, that it is a practical impossibility to conduct commerce (Islamic or otherwise) in any reasonable manner without the ability to reflect period charges for capital in many pricing decisions. The previous chapter's examination of Islamic financing contracts confirms that practitioners of Islamic finance do, in fact, consistently incorporate such period charges, although under different labels. Based on this evidence, some outside observers have been quick to dismiss the concept of Islamic finance as so much window dressing, regarding Islam's prohibition on interest as akin to proclaiming that the laws of gravity are suspended! They point out that Islamic capital users do act as though money has a cost over time.

Many Islamic scholars do not in fact believe that Islam denies the time value of capital,[2] but they take pains to distinguish between the interest rate on a loan for a fixed period of time and the anticipated (but uncertain) rate of profit that a person might hope to achieve by employing capital in a business for a given period of time.[3]

We have seen that an "opportunity rate" for capital can legitimately be factored into such Islamic contracts as *murabaha* (credit sale), *salam* (delayed receipt) and *ijara* (leasing) deals. Islamic scholars make a sharp distinction between a sale made on credit and the extension of a loan. Although it can be argued that a credit sale involves two transactions, one pertaining to the article being sold and the other to the time for which credit is extended (a loan), Islamic scholars choose to view it as a single transaction. In their view, when time is *joined* to property — whether cash or in kind — it acquires a legitimate value as part of that single sales transaction. The Prophet used the example of an unborn animal to illustrate the

---

[1]See, for instance, the discussion and references in Muhammad Umar Chapra, "The Nature of Riba and its Treatment in the Quran, Hadith and Fiqh," in *An Introduction to Islamic Finance,* ed. Sheikh Ghazali Sheikh Abod, Syed Omar Syed Agil, and Aidit Hj. Ghazali (Kuala Lumpur: Quill Publishers, 1992).

[2]Muhammad Akram Khan, "Time Value of Money," in *An Introduction to Islamic Finance,* ed. Sheikh Ghazali Sheikh Abod, Syed Omar Syed Agil, and Aidit Hj. Ghazali (Kuala Lumpur: Quill Publishers, 1992.)

[3]Saadallah, 81-102. See also Kahf, "Time Value of Money," 31-38. See also Muhammad Anas al-Zarqa, "An Islamic Perspective on the Economics of Discounting in Project Evaluation," in *An Introduction to Islamic Finance,* ed. Sheikh Ghazali Sheikh Abod, Syed Omar Syed Agil, and Aidit Hj. Ghazali (Kuala Lumpur: Quill Publishers, 1992.)

general idea: the price of a pregnant sheep could be increased in consideration of what it carries, even though the unborn animal itself could not be sold separately. Thus, time may be considered in setting a price, but it is not separable from the sold article, and the compensation for time is therefore included as part of the price of the article being sold.

Although the Qur'an and Sunna forbid a fixed or predetermined return (*riba*) on financial transactions, they view trade as a positive virtue; profits are applauded. A *murabaha* transaction between a willing seller and a willing buyer involving the extension of credit could, as already discussed, include in the marked-up price compensation for denying the seller the use of the asset and extending to the buyer the use of that asset before he or she has actually paid for it. (It is also assumed that the price markup will include other non-time-related elements, including administrative costs, compensation for credit risk, and the profit that would normally accompany a cash sale.)

Similar reasoning applies to a *salam* contract, where the buyer provides money immediately but doesn't receive delivery of the product from the seller until an agreed-upon point in the future. In the case of leases, there is also well-established backing from the prophetic Sunna for compensation to an owner from someone who is using that asset. In this case, an asset is anything that can generate a usufruct: a benefit from use.[4] Clearly, if an owner leases an asset to someone else, he is entitled to an offset for the profit that would have been expected had the owner retained the asset for his own benefit.

In a markup or other delayed payment transaction, the seller estimates the *potential* profit he will sacrifice by giving up the item for the indicated period of time. He must also assess the possibility of default (the risk of non-payment), or of a buyer dragging his feet so that it would be necessary to go to court to obtain payment. The buyer must also make an assessment of what he could gain by receiving the use of the item in advance of payment. The actual amount built into the markup on the sale will represent a reconciliation between the asking and offering prices. Scholars stress the importance of this mutual consent to the contract.[5] In the West, this is the process through which the interest charge is hammered out. The

---

[4]Abbas Mirakhor, "Short-term Asset Concentration and Islamic Banking," in *Collected Papers*, Waqar Masood Khan and Abbas Mirakhor (Washington, DC: International Monetary Fund, 1987).

[5]See pp. 59-61 above.

process is not dissimilar under Islamic jurisprudence, which does not seek to control how the markup is actually determined. If the markup includes a period charge for tying up the capital, so be it!

THE ISLAMIC COST OF CAPITAL

Time is money in financial markets. Instruments are priced as a function of the cash flow connected to them as well as the risks which surround them. All things being equal, an investor would rather obtain money sooner than later, and a capital user would rather delay payments to which it is obligated.

These commonsense preferences have been formalized in a system for handicapping cash flows as a function of the time that they occur. This "discounted cash flow" (DCF) analysis systematically reduces the value of cash inflows expected to be received at certain points in the future. It makes the same kind of adjustment for investments where the outlay of the money can be delayed for a specified period of time.

The size of the annual discount used is determined by the business risk associated with the investment as well as the means by which it is financed. Some businesses are more risky than others and therefore would require the prospect of annual returns higher than those of lower risk projects. Furthermore, the more of "other people's money" (e.g., debt) that is employed, the higher the risk of a financial default. This would also drive up the minimum acceptable return on the capital, thus dictating a higher discount rate.

Another element embedded in the discount rate is the expected erosion in purchasing power due to inflation. Conventional financial theory recognizes an inflation premium embedded in the risk-free rate of return on government securities. Since all other (risk-laden) return expectations are based on this risk-free rate, these expected returns are automatically adjusted for an anticipated rate of inflation.

Islamic scholars have thus far been unwilling to permit a component of investment return to be explicitly labeled as a compensation for the erosion of purchasing power. They do not recognize a difference between nominal and real rates of return, even though it has been much discussed in recent meetings of the Fiqh Academy and in the literature. Nonetheless, in articulating an expected rate of profit for the assumed risks of an investment, Muslims end up incorporating an implicit inflation assumption when they set the profit expectation as a function of other conventional capital market returns of comparable risk.

THE COST OF EQUITY

It is obviously important, in light of the foregoing, for both investors and capital users in the Islamic world to determine appropriate annualized benchmark profit returns for the commitment of funds. The task is, however, much more challenging than in the West, where liquid and deep financial markets, as well as the use of the Capital Asset Pricing Model (CAPM) and the Arbitrage Pricing Theory (APT), often make it straightforward to determine appropriate returns for equity investments with different risk characteristics. To what extent can these models be utilized in setting the cost of equity funds in Islamic finance?

Capital Asset Pricing Model

The CAPM assumes that return on a security is proportional to its risk. Here the risk of a particular security is compared to the risk of the market as a whole. The investor seeks to minimize risk per unit of return (or, equivalently, maximize return for a given level of risk) by allocating savings into 1) a risk-free security and 2) the market portfolio — a weighted average of all the available risky securities. The proportion allocated to each of these two categories will be different for every investor, depending on his individual tolerance for risk.

The CAPM concludes that the equilibrium relation between risk and return is given by the Security-Market Line (SML):

$$E(R_i) = R_f + \beta_i[E(R_M) - R_f] \, ,$$

where $E(R_i)$ is the expected return on a risky security i, $E(R_M)$ is the expected return on the market portfolio M, R_f is the return on a risk-free asset, and β_i is a measure of the riskiness of asset i:

$$\beta_i = cov(R_i, R_M) / var(R_M) \, .$$

205

An asset's beta measures its contribution to the risk of the market portfolio: a higher beta means that an asset's return is more sensitive to changes in the value of the market portfolio and that the asset contributes more to the risk of the portfolio.[6]

Applying CAPM requires two conditions: 1) the existence of a risk-free rate and 2) the availability of a well-diversified market portfolio. In Islamic finance, neither condition is satisfied. The proxy for the risk-free rate in the West is the U.S. government treasury bill rate. Theoretically, there is no equivalent of this riskless rate in Islamic markets. Even sovereign Islamic governments are not supposed to borrow money on an interest-paying basis.[7] Nor does the well-diversified market portfolio hold in Islamic practice: most countries within which significant amounts of Islamic financing activity take place lack the active or liquid public markets needed to generate a market portfolio. Companies that finance according to Islamic principles are mostly privately held. The difficulty in identifying a riskless rate within the closed Islamic market and the absence of a diversified portfolio benchmark make application of the CAPM to contemporary Islamic finance a dubious proposition.

Our research, however, suggests that Islamic capital markets are not as closed as they would first appear. Pakistan, Sudan, and Iran have converted their entire financial systems to the Islamic form, and Malaysia maintains a dual banking system. But even in Iran, the most closed of these Islamic countries, investors and capital users are much influenced by financial market developments in the rest of the world.[8] Riskless rates, particularly those related to U.S. government securities, are regularly scrutinized, as are the returns earned by diversified securities portfolios, such as the Standard

---

[6]Frederic S. Mishkin, *The Economics of Money, Banking, and Financial Markets,* 3d ed. (New York: Harper Collins, 1992), MA-7.

[7]Certain Islamic governments (e.g. Pakistan, Sudan) have either exempted their own external capital raising from the applicability of Islamic law or issued government securities that are justified as Islamic because their interest rate is not fixed but tied to some measure of national output such as gross domestic product (GDP). In so doing, they have apparently persuaded their *shari'a* scholars to declare these as religiously acceptable profit-sharing arrangements. These government securities could not, of course, serve as proxies for a risk-free rate.

[8]See for instance Said Saffari, "Islamic Banking in Iran," Working Paper of the Center for Middle Eastern Studies, Harvard University (Boston, 1996).

and Poor's 500 and the Morgan Stanley EAFE (Europe, Asia, and the Far East).[9]

As a practical matter, therefore, it may well be possible to determine appropriate required rates of return (e.g., profit targets) and valuation estimates for assets available to Islamic investors in most Islamic countries.

Arbitrage Pricing Theory

Arbitrage Pricing Theory (APT) is also used to determine an appropriate risk-adjusted rate for capital. APT does not try to identify which portfolios are efficient; instead it assumes that each security's return depends partly on pervasive macroeconomic influences and partly on "noise" — events that are unique to that particular company.

APT says the return on an asset i is made up of components corresponding to each of these macroeconomic factors plus a constant unique to the asset (ϵ_i):

$$R_i = B^1_i \text{ (factor 1)} + B^2_i \text{ (factor 2)} + \ldots + B^k_i \text{ (factor } k) + \epsilon_i$$

and the expected return on a security is

$$E(R_i) = R_f + B^1_i [E(R_{\text{factor 1}}) - R_f] + \ldots + B^k_i [E(R_{\text{factor } k}) - R_f]$$

where R_f is again the return on a risk-free security; $B^1_i, \ldots, B^k_i$ describe the sensitivity of the asset's return to each of the factors; and $E(R_{\text{factor 1}}), \ldots, E(R_{\text{factor } k})$ are the expected rates of return due to each of the factors.[10]

Naturally, the success of this model rests upon the ability to find a good list of the factors included in the model. Researchers have argued that, within the scope of diversifiable investments, four principal macroeconomic factors influence a security investment's return:[11]

---

[9]See for instance Cambridge Associates, "U.S. Historical Capital Market Returns: Executive Summary" (Boston, 1997).

[10]Mishkin, MA-8.

[11]Stephen Ross, Randolph Westerfield, and Jeffrey Jaffe, *Corporate Finance* (Chicago: Richard D. Irwin, Inc., 1996), ch. 11.

1. the level of industrial activity;
2. the rate of inflation;
3. the spread between short- and long-term rates;
4. the spread between yields of low- and high-risk corporate bonds.

The first factor, which captures the rate of productivity in an economy and therefore the profit from asset ownership, is relatively easy to measure in Islamic settings, using the rate of gross domestic product (GDP) growth as a proxy. The second factor, the rate of inflation, is also readily measured from the consumer price index.

The third factor, the spread between short- and long-term rates, seeks to capture the investor's relative preferences for near-term versus long-term payoffs. The larger the spread between the two, the more nervous and reluctant an investor is about entering into a long-term commitment. In an Islamic setting, where investments tend to be illiquid because of the absence of viable secondary markets, one would expect an even larger spread than the one we observe in the much more liquid Western financial markets. In the absence of a public bond market in Islamic settings, one would have to refer to the yields embedded in privately-placed instruments. For example, one could turn to an Islamic bank's portfolio of recent deals and compare two *murabaha* deals of different maturities offered by the bank to the same company (or to two different companies judged by the banks to have similar creditworthiness). The markups consist of administrative costs, credit-risk compensation, and the rent of capital. Assuming the administrative cost and the credit-risk compensation are proportionally the same, one could subtract the markup of the shorter-duration *murabaha* from that of the longer-duration one to measure the spread attributable to the difference in maturities.

The fourth factor obviously accounts for the spread in the yields of bonds of different quality grades across time. In the context of Islamic finance, this will be a particularly important variable. Since Islamic investors are not allowed to demand extra return in the event of default, this could mean that capital suppliers would require an appropriately higher initial profit-sharing arrangement with the *mudaribs* (entrepreneurs) for investing in lower credit-rated companies. It is important to note that this is not a company-specific default risk, but a differential risk between two groups of companies with contrasting credit qualities. An individual company's credit/idiosyncratic risk is in the "noise term" of the equation and is assumed to be diversified away. A proxy for credit-spread among Islamic companies, in the absence of traded corporate debt instruments, as in the case of CAPM would have to rely on an examination of private deals done by Islamic banks on behalf of companies with demonstrably different credit profiles. Again, assuming administrative costs and the riskless rent on capital to be the same, the difference between the two markups could reasonably be viewed as compensation for the credit-risk differential.

Although the APT approach to determining a required equity return for an Islamic business may be more feasible than utilizing CAPM, the foregoing discussion suggests that it may not be totally satisfactory. We therefore turn to a third approach to determining appropriate hurdle rates that does not rely on *any* outside market data.

Equilibrium Analysis of a Profit-Sharing Agreement

Even if conventional financial tools are not entirely adequate to the job of estimating cost of capital and expected rate of return for Islamic businesses, we know intuitively that Islamic investors and capital users have ways of factoring them into their business and investment decisions. Envision a *mudaraba* profit-sharing arrangement agreed to by an investor and an entrepreneur. Let us assume that many projects are available for investment, and that many investors are willing to invest in a particular project under consideration. The investor has a lower bound on the opportunity cost of his equity capital, and the entrepreneur has an upper limit on what he is willing to pay for capital. The entrepreneur will use the investor's money if the implied cost of capital to him is less than or equal to his cost from other sources. The investor will invest in the project if the expected return is larger than or equal to the rate of his own risk-adjusted alternative investments. Probability tree analysis can be used to calculate either the implied cost of capital to the entrepreneur or the expected return to the investor.

Even if the entrepreneur publishes sufficient information about the project (e.g., the different stages of its operation and their consequences, etc.) for the investor to make an informed decision, the probability estimates attached to these outcomes will be different for the investor and the entrepreneur due to information asymmetry (the entrepreneur typically has better information).[12] Hence the entrepreneur's estimated cost of capital will differ from the return expected by the investor. The profit-sharing arrangement is only acceptable to both parties if the previously stated conditions are satisfied.

The following highly simplified two-period example illustrates how the investor's return rate and entrepreneur's cost of capital could be calculated. Assume there are only two possible profit outcomes after each period: the value doubles, or is reduced by half. Let p_1 be the probability that the value will double by the end of the first period; $1-p_1$ is the probability that the value will halve during this time. Similarly, let p_2 and p_3 be the probabilities that the value will double in each of the two possible outcomes after the second period. If the initial capital investment requirement is V_0, the project's terminal value is illustrated in Figure 8-1.

The net return to the investor of each possible state is the profit in that state *minus* the original investment V_0. The net return to the investor of the most profitable (top) state on the probability tree is also multiplied by $(1-x)$, where x is the profit percentage taken by the entrepreneur. (In the standard *mudaraba* contract, the entrepreneur participates only in any *profits* of a venture; the passive investor assumes all financial losses.) The expected return to the investor, the sum of all these probable returns, is divided by the amount of the initial investment, V_0, to get the *rate* of return. *Expected return to the investor* in this scenario would be

$$[p_1 p_2 (4V_0-V_0)(1-x) + (1-p_1)(1-p_3)[(V_0/4)-V_0)]/V_0 =$$
$$3p_1 p_2(1-x)-3(1-p_1)(1-p_3).$$

(In this example, the return on the middle state on the probability tree is zero, V_0-V_0, so it does not appear in the expression.) Return to the investor is therefore expressible in terms of probabilities and the entrepreneur's profit percentage taken. The investor will accept this project only if this expected return equals or exceeds his opportunity cost.

The entrepreneur seeks at least the profit participation rate that he could have earned by collaborating with other investors in other projects of comparable risk. At the highest profitable state, the entrepreneur has to give back to the investor an amount equal to $V_0 + (1-x)(4 V_0-V_0)$, i.e., the initial

---

[12]Richard Brealey and Stewart Myers, *Principles of Corporate Finance* (New York: McGraw-Hill, Inc., 1996), 927.

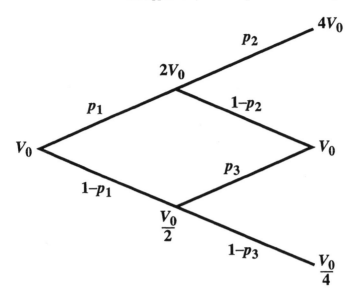

Figure 8-1

investment plus the investor's profit participation percentage. Hence the cost of capital to the entrepreneur for that state is $[V_0 + (1-x) 3V_0]/4V_0$. This is the amount the entrepreneur could have kept if he had supplied the capital himself, divided by the total gross profit of the profitable state. In the other states his cost of capital is zero (ignoring his personal efforts) because the entrepreneur in a *mudaraba* contract does not participate in the investor's capital losses. *Expected cost of capital to the entrepreneur* is then

$$p_1 p_2 [V_0 + 3V_0(1-x)]/V_0, \text{ or } p_1 p_2 [1-(3x/4)],$$

where p_1 and p_2 are the probabilities of profitable operations in each period.

Again, the entrepreneur uses a different probability estimate than the investor because of information asymmetry, and will participate in the project only if the expected cost of capital is less than or equal to the market cost of capital. If L is the minimum profit participation percentage the entrepreneur is willing to accept (i.e., $x \geq L$), and H is the maximum profit percentage the investor is willing to give the entrepreneur (i.e., $x \leq H$), the two parties can only come to an equilibrium agreement if $L \leq H$.

Suppose that the two parties agree that the entrepreneur's profit participation rate x will be $(L+H)/2$, midway between the two parties' minimum requirements. For this value of x, the entrepreneur's cost of equity capital for the two-period project becomes $p_1 p_2 (1-[3(L+H)/8])$, which we will call r. The entrepreneur should use this cost of capital to discount cash flows from the project. If a cash flow occurs at the end of the second period, the discount factor should be $1/(1+r)$. If a cash flow occurs at the end of first period, then the suitable discount factor should be $1/(1+r/2)$.

Cost of Equity Summarized

Conventional asset pricing models such as CAPM and APT offer some assistance in summarizing the cost of equity capital in an Islamic setting, but because relevant data is difficult to obtain, and because so many Islamic firms are privately owned, a more straightforward approach such as the equilibrium analysis just described appears more promising. While the example used here involved a *mudaraba* contract, it would be possible to formulate a comparable analysis for *musharaka*, the other Islamic equity contract.

THE COST OF DEBT

Despite Islamic law's ban on loans with interest, debt and credit instruments nevertheless play a significant part in the capital structures of Muslim businesses (see Chapter 7).

Murabaha

Recall that the *murabaha* contract (credit sale) is a very popular form of Islamic short-to-intermediate-term debt contract. It involves an immediate sale, but on credit terms that specify either a balloon payment at the end point or installment payments at specified interim points. Each installment can be looked upon as 1) a return of capital and 2) compensation for the time value of money. To demonstrate, if x is the administrative cost of obtaining the credit, as a percentage of a loan's face value, and the gross proceeds of a loan are P, the net proceeds to the purchaser are $P(1-x)$. If there are only two semiannual installments of value I for a *murabaha* with a maturity of one year and y internal rate of return (IRR) on an annualized basis, then:

$$P(1-x) = I/(1+y) + I/(1+y)^2.$$

Solving for y will give the estimated cost of capital to the buyer of the *murabaha*.

Salam

The *salam* contract is another form of debt used by Islamic businesses. With this contract a customer agrees to purchase goods which will be delivered at a specified point in the future. The price paid today represents a discount on the price that *would* have been paid if it were a cash sale at the time of the delivery. The internal rate of return on that discount is the cost of that form of debt capital to the business. The magnitude of the discount is a function of the credit uncertainty of the debtor and the time preference of the investor. The implied cost of capital to the *salam* seller is simply the difference between the present value of the future market price of the good and the price that one would receive today.[13]

Istisna'

An *istisna'* contract is similar to a *salam*, except that the goods in question are usually items to be manufactured (rather than generic commodities) and installment payments are often timed to the actual progress made in producing the goods.

In analyzing the cost of debt in this contract, let P be the current market price of the goods to be delivered. Let L be the amount of each progress

---

[13]In a market which is not efficient, the cost of capital incurred to the seller is more fairly represented by $\frac{E(P_T)}{S} - 1$ where $S = $ *salam* price and $E(P_T)$ is the expected terminal price of the commodity.

payment. Again denoting the internal rate of return as y, the implied cost of capital for *istisna'* is:

$$P = \sum_{t=1}^{T} \frac{L}{(1+y)^t}$$

Ijara

Operating and full-payout leases *(ijara)* are still another form of financial leverage applied to the capital structures of Islamic businesses. In an operating lease, payments consist of depreciation, maintenance of the asset, and a profit to the lessor. The lessor's profit is logically the cost of capital to the lessee; if the user had supplied the capital himself, he would not have had to pay this extra charge. For a fixed-payment, fixed-term lease, the internal rate of return can be used as a proxy for the annual average cost of the lease. As an example, let us represent the IRR as y, the market value of the leased equipment as P, the lease payment for each period as L, and the salvage value[14] of the asset as S. Then

$$P = \sum_{t=1}^{T} \frac{L}{(1+y)^t} + \frac{E(S)}{(1+y)^T}$$

where T is the term of the lease.

For full-payout leases, the lease payments consist of depreciation, maintenance of the asset, and a profit to the lessor (e.g., the time value of money). In addition, the lessee usually has an option to purchase the depreciated equipment at a predetermined price (equivalent to a call option). For a fixed-payment full-payout lease of fixed term,

$$P = \sum_{t=1}^{T} \frac{L}{(1+y)^t} + \frac{L-c}{(1+y)^T}$$

where c denotes the value of the option to purchase the leased equipment at time T. Since the lessee owns this option, this effectively reduces the lease payment in the final period.

---

[14]A reasonable proxy for the expected salvage value at the end of the lease would be the current market value for a similar depreciated piece of equipment or other asset.

CALCULATING THE WEIGHTED COST OF CAPITAL

In conventional finance, a business's overall cost of capital is calculated by weighting each component of capital used by the business according to its market value. These weightings are then multiplied by the after-tax cost of the different capital sources. Since there is rarely a reliable market price for most components of Islamic capital, it is usually necessary to rely on the book value of the capital components to obtain the appropriate weightings. The next step is to plug in the appropriate costs for each of the capital components.

Assume a project is funded by all five types of financing discussed above. Denote the component book values as follows — the *mudaraba* part as M_1, the *musharaka* part as M_2, the *murabaha* part as M_3, the *salam* part as S, and the *ijara* part as I. Let their respective costs of capital be r_1, r_2, r_3, r_4, r_5 (as determined in the previous section). Let V equal the total value of the project, $M_1+M_2+M_3+S+I$. In this case the weighted average cost of capital (WACC) would be

$$\frac{r_1 M_1 + r_2 M_2 + r_3 M_3 + r_4 S + r_5 I}{V}.$$

CHOOSING AN APPROPRIATE CAPITAL STRUCTURE

Having described a process for determining the combined cost of capital for a mix of funds employed by an Islamic firm, a logical question is, what *should* be the mix of investment funds utilized by an efficient Islamic business? Recall that the literature often describes the Islamic financial system as equity-based, suggesting that an all-equity capital structure is optimal if sufficient equity funds are available. This flies in the face of much empirical evidence that Islamic firms utilize substantial de facto debt.

One explanation for the observed use of debt funds would be an insufficient supply of Islamic equity funds. Although there *is* excess liquidity in the Islamic savings system, these funds are largely averse to risk and may naturally shy away from equity investments, gravitating instead toward trade financing and other short-term, debt-like investments.

It is also argued that an all-equity structure would only be an efficient solution in an Islamic setting if one ignored the standard reasons why non-Islamic businesses often prefer debt funds over equity. These include the value of the tax shield provided by interest payments in most countries,[15] a reduction in the risk of "moral hazard,"[16] the avoidance of earnings dilution, and the cheaper cost of funds.

Still another explanation for the preference for debt in Western capital structures has been offered by Stephen Ross, who has argued that in a world where there are major variations in a firm's perceived quality and managerial competence, debt confers increased stature.[17] In equilibrium, one would expect a positive correlation between the market value of a firm and the degree of financial leverage which has been successfully sustained over time. Given the high perceived cost of stumbling into default and possible bankruptcy, lower-quality firms will use less debt in their capital structures.

In the Islamic context, the tax shield argument is weak, partly because there is no direct interest expense to deduct (although lease payments, with their implicit interest, would be deductible) and partly because minimal income taxes are paid in many Muslim countries. Similarly, the prospect of bankruptcy should not be as daunting to an Islamic business since religious law does not permit extra charges to be levied as a consequence of default (no "markup on markup" is permitted). However, the prospect of default does increase the risk to lenders and should logically be reflected in higher de facto interest charges built into Islamic debt contracts.

---

[15]An exhaustive series of articles, papers, and books has been directed at the assumptions built into Modigliani and Miller's original proposition that capital structure is irrelevant to the overall valuation of the firm. The prevailing view is that there *is* a value to the tax shield on interest payments that is only partially offset by the increasing risk of default as a business advances further out on the debt limb.

[16]It has also been suggested that if new equity investors are brought into a business (in the Islamic context, this would often be via a *mudaraba* contract), the profits earned by the entrepreneur (*mudarib*) could be diluted along with those of incumbent investors, and there would be an increasing risk that these managers would turn from efforts to maximize the value of the ownership shares to actions designed to enrich themselves by skimming off for themselves a richer package of personal perquisites to the detriment of equity profit maximization. This "moral hazard" argument has been vigorously propounded by Stiglitz (1974), Jensen and Meckling (1976), and Grossman and Hart (1982).

[17]Stephen Ross, "The Determination of Financial Structure: The Incentive Signaling Approach," *Bell Journal of Economics,* Spring 1977, 23-40; idem, "Some Notes on Financial Incentive-Signaling Models, Activity Choice, and Risk Preferences," *Journal of Finance* 33 (1978): 777-794.

216

The "moral hazard" risk is certainly present in *mudaraba* and *musharaka* contracts. A *mudarib* who saw his equity profits declining through the issuance of new shares might well look for other ways to enrich himself through means that would do nothing to enhance the profitability of the firm as a whole.

The suggestion that Islamic firms would seek out debt as an affirmation of their creditworthiness seems less plausible than an argument contending that new debt capital is simply less costly to the firm than new equity. Khan concludes as much when he notes that Islamic firms use debt because it "minimizes the information requirement of a financial contract when the performance of the project is not observable by the financial institution."[18] In other words, the cost of debt funds is lower than that of equity funds because the terms of the debt contract give enhanced protection to the lender, reducing the need for detailed oversight of the borrower's activities.

When all is said and done, there seems little doubt that Islamic businesses should (and do) seek to leverage their capital structures for many of the same reasons that propel financing choices among conventional Western firms.

CONCLUSIONS

This chapter has addressed two central issues in Islamic finance: the time value (or opportunity cost) of money and the cost of business capital. It is evident that Islamic finance practitioners recognize that there is a cost of capital and reflect that cost in their prototype financial contracts.

In the West, determining the cost of capital is made easier by the fact that most major businesses are publicly owned, and secondary markets are often quite liquid; this makes the value of their equity clear. The cost of debt for these companies is likewise explicit. For Islamic businesses, this clarity does not exist. There are very few publicly-owned Islamic businesses, making the calculation of the cost of equity problematic. And while

---

[18]Waqar Masood Khan, "Towards an Interest Free Islamic Economic System," in Khan and Mirakhor, *Collected Papers* (Washington, DC: International Monetary Fund, 1987).

Islamic finance is often described as "equity-based," the use of debt-like contracts is widespread. Therefore, the cost of funds is not fully defined by the cost of equity alone. The conventional method of calculating the *weighted* cost of both debt and equity capital is both possible and the most likely to lead to better investment decision-making within Islamic businesses.

CHAPTER 9

Derivatives in Islamic Finance

There has been a marked effort over the last two decades to expand the variety of products in Islamic financial markets. This has been spurred by a number of forces, foremost of which is the growth in the pool of funds available for Islamically acceptable investments. As already mentioned in Chapter 1, the size of that pool is estimated to be at least $50-100 billion and steadily increasing. These funds are sought by a small but growing group of Islamically-run businesses as well as by conventional capital users who seek a lower cost of funds and are willing to put the necessary effort into deal structuring and documentation to make the financing arrangements religiously acceptable.

The ability of these parties to hedge or eliminate certain types of risk is important. In conventional finance, market and credit risk involving bonds, equity, currency, and commodities can be contained with a variety of arrangements involving derivative securities. The scarcity of these arrangements in Islamic finance has severely impeded risk management, as discussed in Chapter 7. That discussion did however identify certain Islamically acceptable financial contracts, with characteristics that do allow both investor and capital user to contain *some* elements of risk exposure while meeting investment or financing expectations.

This chapter further explores the important religiously acceptable Islamic financial contracts which can serve as partial proxies for some of the derivative securities now commonly used in conventional financial markets. These include *salam, istisna', 'arbun*, third-party guarantee, *khiyar al-*

Note: Research Assistant Indrajit Garai made important contributions to this chapter.

shart, and *mudaraba*. Although introduced in Chapter 5, we once again review the contracts relevant to our discussion of derivatives.

RELEVANT ISLAMIC CONTRACTS

In a *salam* contract, a buyer pays immediately for a commodity or other fungible good which the seller will deliver at a specified future date. For example, a flour milling company might buy from another party a certain number of bushels of wheat at a specified price per bushel to be delivered six months hence. The transaction is final at the time the money is exchanged, but the seller typically doesn't own the promised wheat at that point. The seller can either purchase the wheat at the going price at any time prior to the future delivery date or he can grow it himself.

An *istisna'* contract involves the forward purchase of a good to be manufactured to certain specifications, as opposed to a fungible, generic commodity characteristic of a *salam* contract. The buyer's payment will often be remitted to the seller (e.g., the manufacturer) in installments as progress is made in producing the good. Examples would include a department store ordering the manufacture of a thousand pairs of blue jeans and agreeing to make a balloon payment upon delivery, or a shipping company buying a new freighter and making periodic installment payments to the shipbuilder as construction moves forward.

In an *'arbun* contract, the buyer makes an immediate partial payment for a good and agrees either to pay the remaining balance at a specified point in the future when he takes delivery of the good, or to forfeit the down payment and walk away from the contract (perhaps because in the interim a better deal has been found elsewhere). The seller, however, must stand ready to deliver the good until the date the contract expires, thereby incurring an opportunity cost for the capital tied up in the good. For example, a used car dealer makes an *'arbun* contract with an auto leasing company to purchase one hundred used cars of a certain model and year for $10,000 each, with an immediate payment of $1,000 per car and the $9,000 balance due in three months. If during the intervening three months the market price of that particular car model falls materially below $9,000, the dealer may choose to forfeit the $1,000 down payment and buy the cars on the open market at a lower price. The auto leasing company, however, has had to hold the cars in its inventory during the contract period. If the buyer forfeits the down payment, the seller must find another buyer for its cars – probably at a less advantageous price. The seller can however pocket the $1,000 per car down payment as a consolation.

The *third-party guarantee* is another relevant contract. While Islamic law often disallows guarantees between transacting parties (see Chapter 5), it usually allows a third-party guarantee to be made, and many Islamic contracts include such guarantees. This guarantee can, for instance, relieve one or the other direct parties to the contract of the often laborious and costly process of obtaining and assessing information on the other party's credit standing (this can usually be done more efficiently by a financial institution or other experienced agent). In compensation, the guarantor usually receives a fee as well as a lien on the asset under contract. Since under Islamic law guarantors can charge only for administrative costs (not cost of capital), guarantees are often given by third parties interested in sponsoring a transaction even without a fee (e.g., a government or a parent company).

In a *khiyar al-shart* contract, one party receives an absolute option to confirm or undo a contract. Thereby parties may protect themselves against not only movements in the underlying asset price but also events which may be completely unrelated to the underlying asset. As a (possibly valid) example, an airline company may purchase by *istisna'* one hundred planes for $5 million each on a date five years in the future, giving the manufacturer an option, which it agrees to exercise only if the airline does not source all of its intervening plane requirements from that manufacturer.

In a *mudaraba* contract, an entrepreneurial party (a *mudarib*) is matched with one or more passive capital partners to invest in either a specific project (a "special purpose *mudaraba*") or in a variety of projects (a "general purpose *mudaraba*").[1] Some *mudaraba* funds are similar to conventional hedge-funds, which pool investors' money for investment over a specified time period. If interests in the fund are to be traded, however, it must invest mostly in *tangible* assets, not in financial instruments.[2] The *mudarib* entrepreneurs who develop the concept and then execute the plan

---

[1]Oftentimes similar to a conventional blind pool of capital where the fund manager has total discretion as to the placement of the capital.

[2]In this sense, a *mudaraba* resembles a conventional private equity investment fund.

are compensated in a manner similar to that of conventional hedge-fund managers. *Mudaribs* do not receive a guaranteed annual fee, but are compensated for their annual administrative expenses and also receive a predetermined percentage of the *mudaraba*'s (the fund's) profits (in other words, a "carried interest"). Both Western hedge-fund managers and their *mudarib* counterparts enjoy limited liability — i.e., they participate in the upside profit but are insulated from any capital losses incurred by the pool, unless they have invested some of their own money alongside the other investors.

ISLAMIC CONTRACTS AND WESTERN FINANCIAL PRODUCTS

Derivative instruments such as forwards, futures, and options have become standard tools for risk management in both developed Western financial markets and the emerging markets of Asia, Eastern Europe, and Latin America. They have proliferated despite occasional misuse and abuse because of their effectiveness in managing financial risk. This section analyzes the risk-curbing properties of the Islamic contracts outlined above in the context of conventional finance.

Forward Contracts

The simplest conventional derivative is the *forward contract* on a bond or stock. Assume that a stock is trading today at S_0 and that it pays no dividend. In n periods, the buyer of the forward contract will pay F and receive the stock. To hedge against the possibility that the stock price will rise, the seller borrows S_0 from a bank today at interest rate r, and uses the proceeds to buy and hold the stock for n periods. At the maturity of the contract, the seller receives F and delivers the stock, and owes $S_0(1+r)^n$ to the bank. Hence the forward price F that he receives at maturity should be just sufficient to cover his obligation to the bank at that time; in other words,

$$F = S_0(1 + r)^n.$$

The same argument applies to a forward contract on a bond, if the bond does not pay any interest coupon. For coupon-paying bonds,

Forward price = (bond's spot price)(1 + short-term rate − coupon yield).

In forward contracts, no exchange of securities or cash takes place before maturity. It follows that, at maturity, the instantaneous forward price just equals the spot price at the point when the contract was first made.

A *salam* contract is the closest Islamic approximation to the conventional forward contract. Because the buyer pays the seller money and is promised a fixed amount of a commodity at a specified future date, one might assume that, as with a conventional forward contract, the proper *salam* price is today's spot price. However, two factors can cause the *salam* price to be lower than the spot price. First, unlike a conventional forward contract, where no money changes hands until the contract's expiration, the *salam* buyer's capital is immediately paid over, exposing the buyer to the risk that the seller won't deliver in the future. A discount on the spot price would compensate for this credit risk. The second and less-understood factor is the "cheapest-to-deliver" option. At maturity, the seller of the *salam* contract usually can choose from a limited range of grades of the commodity, and naturally, he chooses the one that is cheapest to deliver. Additionally, the seller typically has a small amount of leeway in timing the delivery. These two factors introduce additional uncertainty for the buyer. While these features are incorporated in futures options in conventional finance, they are not part of a conventional forward contract, which offers the parties no flexibility in performance.

Although the Islamic law of *salam* requires specification of everything that is material to the price and to fulfillment of the contract, there are always some elements which don't get included, and we use a "delivery option" component to cover those. Taking these elements of uncertainty into account,

Salam value = (spot price) − (credit spread) − (delivery option).

From the seller's viewpoint, a *salam* contract is a transaction in which a loan is obtained from the buyer against a promise for future delivery. A *salam* seller can use this loan either to produce the commodity (e.g., grow the wheat) or for other purposes. Consider a *salam* seller who already has the commodity on hand and has written a *salam* contract. This seller bases his decision on two things: any proprietary information about the *expected price movement* of the commodity, and his view of the *volatility* of the future price of the commodity. These relate to two different aspects of the instrument. If the *salam* seller expects the price of the commodity to go down in the future, it is advantageous for him to enter the contract, because by doing so he ensures a floor sale price of the commodity at a future date and hence fully hedges against adverse price movement. Also, by selling a *salam*, the seller has essentially taken a synthetic long position in the cheapest-to-deliver option. We know from option pricing theory that the price of an option is an increasing function of the volatility of the commodity price in the future.[3] Hence, if proprietary information convinces the seller that the price of the commodity will be more volatile in the future than it is now, he would find this delivery option advantageous, especially if he is inordinately averse to risk.

An *istisna'* contract is in some ways similar to a *salam* contract. Because *istisna'* is typically used for nonfungible, customized goods and because installment payments are tied to the progress of the goods being manufactured, there is much less flexibility for undertaking alternative market actions.

Assume a two-month contract with three installments, each represented by I. Let r be the seller's appropriate risk-adjusted discount rate and let V be the present value of the progress payments. Then,

$$V = I + I/(1 + r) + I/(1 + r)^2.$$

If the spot price of the item is S_0, the payoff to the seller in this *istisna'* deal is $V - S_0$. Thus, the buyer typically pays a higher price than the spot price of the item because of both the buyer's credit risk and the time value of money.

The *istisna'* contract is like a forward contract, modified for a progress payment. To make it a fair contract in the conventional sense, the ex-ante payoff of the contract should equal zero for both parties, given the structure of today's yield curve. However, one should be careful in defining what would be a fair contract in the Islamic context. The seller of an *istisna'* contract in an Islamic arrangement usually cannot do anything with the progress payment except use it for the production of the goods; he can't use it for hedging or other market purposes, such as investing in other goods.

---

[3]See John Cox and Mark Rubenstein, *Option Markets* (Englewood Cliffs, N.J.: Prentice Hall, 1985) for further details on sensitivity of options.

Moreover, because the items are customized, the seller can't properly hedge (achieve a riskless contract) by entering into another offsetting contract.

Part of the seller's opportunity cost is also the lack of flexibility. For example, a clothing manufacturer wouldn't be permitted to sell a batch of blue jeans produced under an *istisna'* contract to another garment store at a higher price. On the other hand, this manufacturer does receive the benefit of being able to sell at a fixed price, which would presumably incorporate a fair profit margin, based on the most accurate information about costs and predicted future prices of blue jeans.

Futures Contracts

Conventional futures contracts are similar to forwards, except that they are marked to market each day, with a daily exchange of cash between the two parties to settle the account to that point. Futures prices are reset daily and the contract buyer gains cash if the reset price is higher than the previous day's price, and loses cash if it is lower. Essentially, then, a futures obligation can be equated to a series of forward contracts, each with a one-day maturity. However, the market views futures as a riskier instrument than forwards: in the case of bonds, futures prices go up when interest rates are falling and down when interest rates are rising. The buyer of the contract benefits when interest rates fall because the value of bonds rises. But the overnight reinvestment rate also falls, offsetting some of the gain. Alternatively, a falling futures price corresponds to a higher level of interest rates and, therefore, lower bond prices. The buyer of the contract would sustain losses on the value of the bonds and would have to finance his loss at a higher overnight interest rate.

The net result is that futures contracts are typically priced less attractively than forward contracts. By having to settle a futures position on a daily basis, one has to absorb each day's volatility. In forward contracts, many of these daily fluctuations will cancel each other out by the time of the ultimate settlement date.

There is no direct equivalent of a futures contract in Islamic finance. In addition to the already-discussed problem of forward contracts, where the postponement of both the price of the good and the payment is religiously unacceptable for Muslims, futures contracts require a daily marking to market, which is also forbidden to Muslims. In any Islamic contract, the price of the commodity must be fixed at the outset and not left open to market fluctuation, which might change the contract price thereafter.

However, one could create an Islamic contract with some similarities to a conventional futures contract. It has already been noted that futures are equivalent to a series of one-day forward contracts. In Islamic finance, back-to-back *salam* contracts could be undertaken to roughly replicate a futures contract. That is, a *salam* seller could *sell* a contract now and subsequently *buy* a counteracting *salam* which would essentially close out his position. For example, suppose a trader has good information about the price of a particular commodity over the next two months but no *salam* contract for less than six months is available. If he expects the price of the commodity to fall in the next two months, he can *sell* a *salam* contract for delivery six months from now and plan in two months' time to *buy* another *salam* contract for the same good. If the commodity price does fall in the following two months, he can then buy a *salam* contract for the commodity at a lower price. At the same time, by entering into this "long" contract two months later, he can hedge out any price risk over the following four months, a period for which he does not have confident information. In making these two transactions, the Islamic trader is able to disaggregate the price risks and trade only on that part of the risk for which he believes he has superior information.

Call Options

Conventional financial options, in contrast to Islamic forms, are not obligations but only "rights" to the gains from up or down movements in asset values. Since the buyer has the right not to participate in unfavorable asset price movements, option contracts, unlike forward and futures contracts, cost money which the buyer must pay up front. What should that cost be? The seller of an option contract can construct a dynamic and completely riskless strategy to meet his contract obligation and, like the option buyer, also have the choice of not being exposed to any undue risk. According to arbitrage pricing theory, the price of the option would be equal to the cost of this dynamic replicating strategy.[4]

---

[4]See Cox and Rubenstein for more details on arbitrage-free pricing of options.

Options can be grouped into two categories: call options that pay on the upside of an asset's price movements, and put options that pay on the downside. U.S. financial markets have seen many versions of these two contracts, some with eye-catching names, but they all fall into these two categories.

The closest counterpart to a call option in Islamic finance is the *'arbun* contract, while the Islamic counterpart of a put option is the third-party guarantee. However, pricing these two Islamic contracts by applying conventional option pricing theory is difficult. Conventional option pricing theory, through continuous shifting of position between the underlying security and risk-free bonds, hedges exposure without concern for where the price may go in the future. In other words, for every infinitesimal movement of the price, there is an exact way to match the exposure. This almost instantaneous, yet continuous, hedging ability of the seller of the option relieves him of the need for predicting accurately the trend of future price movements. Additionally, because almost all conventional contracts are settled at maturity with cash, the seller does not have to build up an inventory of the underlying goods to meet the provisions of the contract.

In contrast, an *'arbun* seller cannot trade on the underlying item because he no longer has the right to sell the inventory of the item specified in the contract. Even if he could sell, the secondary market for the specified item itself is likely to be relatively illiquid (assuming its sale was not altogether proscribed because it was classified as a financial security by a *shari'a* board). Furthermore, in Islamic law, the settlement has to involve the exchange of real assets, not cash. All these factors make individual expectations about price movement very important, and the pricing technology is no longer preference-free. Thus, we cannot use conventional option pricing techniques and must look for an alternative approach to determine what an acceptable *'arbun* down payment would be to the seller.

Suppose for simplicity that the item under contract has a spot price of S_0 and can either go up to S_u or down to S_d by the end of the contract life. To fully hedge, the seller of the *'arbun* contract could borrow S_0 on a markup basis (a *murabaha* transaction) to buy the item and hold onto it. In that way, if the price is S_u at maturity, and if the buyer wants to exercise the option, the item is on hand. Let the seller's estimate of the probability of an upside move (to S_u) be p. At maturity, his expected payoff is $p(K) + (1-p)S_d$, i.e., an amount K from exercise of the *'arbun*, and S_d from its not being exercised and the seller of the *'arbun* consequently having to sell the item in the open market at a lower price. This expected sum, along with the down payment collected (assume it was not reinvested) should be enough to cover his loan obligation, i.e.,

$$pK + (1-p)S_d + (\text{down payment})(1 + r) \geqslant S_0(1 + r),$$

where:

p is the probability the price will rise to S_u;
$1-p$ is the probability the price will fall to S_d;
K is the price the buyer must pay to take delivery;
S_0 is the spot price;
S_d is the downside spot price one period into the future; and
r is the appropriate opportunity cost of the seller.

This gives the seller's lower bound for the required down payment.

The owner of a conventional call option has paid for the right to "call" a certain number of securities at a specified price from a call seller during a specified period of time. We can see that the 'arbun contract creates a non-speculative opportunity for a rough Islamic equivalent. Consider the following scenario: an airline company is considering adding to its fleet of aircraft in anticipation of increased travel demand, but hasn't made a final decision. There is a chance that, by the time a decision is made, the price of aircraft will have risen beyond what the company is willing to pay. However, there is also a small chance that the supply of aircraft will exceed demand at that future point, in which case the planes could be purchased on the market at a price lower than that currently offered by the manufacturer. Given these possible developments, the airline might enter into an 'arbun contract with the manufacturer to fix the maximum price it would pay. If the future price of planes turns out to be lower, the buyer can forfeit the down payment and buy the aircraft on the open market.

Put Options

It is common for Islamic banks to provide a *third-party guarantee* for the installment payments of customers who have purchased items from sellers on a *murabaha* basis; in fact, such guarantees are often stipulated as a condition of sale. This is important in the event that a contracting party defaults, because Islamic law does not allow an extra penalty for the defaulting party.[5] Aside from building into the contract the right of collateral offset, the other party is forced to rely on a third-party guarantee, usually from a bank.

The bank in these transactions is compensated by an administrative fee paid by the purchaser of the item. To be Islamically acceptable, this fee cannot be stated as a percentage of the value of the contract. In the case of default, the bank can seize and sell the item to help satisfy the purchaser's remaining obligation to the seller.

From the purchaser's viewpoint, the third-party guarantee can be thought of as a put option obtained from the bank in exchange for a premium. If at some future time the purchaser concludes that the item is not as valuable as the remaining installments, he could theoretically stop paying the installments to the seller and surrender the item to the bank. This is therefore a put option with a strike price equal to the value of the remaining installment payments. (As a practical matter, however, the bank can write in a provision allowing it to recover from the purchaser any loss thereby suffered.)

The third-party guarantee just described can facilitate credit sales to unknown customers in the absence of a credit-checking agency. While a seller might view a sale to an unknown customer in exchange for a premium as too uncertain, a bank offering a third-party guarantee might take a different view. Assuming that the bank sold guarantees to many customers, its aggregate risk would be reduced through diversification, and it could use collected premiums as a reserve fund.

The *Khiyar al-Shart* Option

We have previously described the *khiyar al-shart* contract as a contract where one party holds an absolute option to undo the contract. That party might intend to undo the contract if a particular event occurs. In that case, the option's value is a function of the price of the underlying asset and the probability of the particular event occurring. How would one value such a contract? If we look at the Western market for guidance, one close approximation might be a stock option granted to an employee for as long

---

[5]See, for instance, the discussion in Ziauddin Ahmad, "The Theory of Riba," in *An Introduction to Islamic Finance*, ed. Sheikh Ghazali Sheikh Abod, Syed Omar Syed Agil, and Aidit Hj. Ghazali (Kuala Lumpur: Quill Publishers, 1992).

as he or she remains employed with the company. Typically, these stock options become vested after the employee has been with the company for a certain period of time. In other words, these are similar to forward start-options.

Another example might involve a capital equipment manufacturer, such as an aircraft manufacturer, and an airline which purchases planes to be put into service in its route system. Suppose that an agreement is struck between the two which provides that if the airline fills all its aircraft needs for the forthcoming t periods with that manufacturer, then the manufacturer will not exercise its option to cancel the sale of one plane at the end of period T ($T>t$) at the price prevailing at period t.[6]

Let the price of the plane at time t be S_t, and the price of the plane at time T be S_T (S_t and S_T are both unknown today.) Hence the payoff from holding this contract is max $[S_T - S_t, 0]$, which is the payoff of a standard at-the-money call and would be valued at period t as $C(S_t, S_t, T-t)$.

However, we need the value of this contract today. We know that calls have the property that $C(S, K, t) = KC(S/K, 1, t)$ where K equals the strike price, and S is the spot price; therefore $C(S_t, S_t, T-t) = S_t C(1, 1, T-t)$. But $C(1, 1, T-t)$ is a constant and is known with certainty today, so the present value of this contract is simply $PV(S_t)$ times $C(1, 1, T-t)$. But $PV(S_t) = S_0$,[7] so the present value of this particular *khiyar al-shart* contract is simply the present value of the plane multiplied by $C(1, 1, T-t)$.

The *Mudarib* Call

As already noted, when a project is financed on a *mudaraba* basis, the *mudarib*s (entrepreneurs) receive a fixed percentage of the project's profit.

---

[6]A contemporary example of a Western equivalent of a *khiyar al-shart* option was recently reported in the *Wall Street Journal*: Boeing was wooing airline customers with a package which grants substantial price concessions to airlines if they sustain a sole-source relationship with Boeing, at the expense of rival Airbus Industries. (*Wall Street Journal*, 30 April 1997, B4). Ultimately, Boeing had to negate those agreements as a condition of merging with McDonnell Douglas Aircraft Co.

[7]Assuming an efficient market and the absence of dividends.

In the event of loss, however, the *mudaribs'* liability is limited to their sweat equity. One could argue that the *mudaribs* hold a de facto option on project profits. If the reputation of *mudaribs* were not an issue, *mudaribs* would benefit from increasing the volatility of return from the project by engaging in very risky ventures, because the *mudaribs* hold calls on the project's potential profit return, and the value of an option increases as volatility increases. Thus, there is a built-in moral hazard in such contractual arrangements.

As an example, let us denote the total initial amount of funds in a *mudaraba* by V_0 and denote the unknown end-of-project value of the fund as V. Assume that the *mudarib's* profit participation rate is a. Hence, the payoff to the *mudarib* $= a [\max (V - V_0, 0)]$. This is a call option on the value of the project. However, this is an option on a real prospect rather than a financial option, since the underlying *mudaraba* shares may not be traded. The value of this call is $aC(V_0, V_0, t) = aV_0C(1, 1, t)$, which is a known quantity today.

CONCLUSIONS

While interest-bearing debt instruments are prohibited in Islam, there are some Islamic contracts which result in debt, including *istisna'*, *murabaha*, and *ijara* financing. However, there are no effective derivatives of Islamic debt contracts which replicate conventional risk-hedging and leveraging contracts such as swaps, futures, and options.

Similarly, in the equity security sector, there are no risk-hedging or leveraging contracts in Islamic finance truly comparable to available conventional derivatives. Only recently have favorable *shari'a* rulings made it acceptable to *trade* equity shares in the secondary market. Previously they had been classified as *financial* instruments and were therefore ineligible to be bought and sold. Now a number of Islamic scholars classify them as specific claims on real assets, thus making secondary market trading in them acceptable. This is at least a start toward the future formulation of equity derivatives which are acceptable in the Islamic world.

With respect to commodities and other goods, the *salam* contract is an imperfect Islamic substitute for a conventional forward contract. The related *istisna'* contract for goods being manufactured for a buyer provides another partial Islamic proxy for a forward contract. It is also possible to construct an Islamic contract which partially replicates a conventional futures contract, via back-to-back *salam* contracts.

Third-party guarantees do provide some risk protection in the Islamic context, and one of the characteristics of the *mudaraba* contract provides a de facto call option for *mudaribs* who are party to these arrangements. The *'arbun* contract probably comes closest to providing a substitute for a Western call option, but it has a number of qualifications that limit its use in many real-life situations.

Conventional financial markets provide ample means (i.e., put options and so-called credit-rating options) for managing risks such as deterioration in quality or another party's outright default. In Islam, where default remedies are limited by religious principles (e.g., no interest or penalty can be charged subsequent to a default), the only way to protect against credit risk is a third-party guarantee against such a default.

Currency markets in the West are among the most sophisticated of all financial markets, with a myriad of derivatives to handle all sorts of risk dimensions. Unfortunately, currency is not considered a real asset in Islam and hence there are no generally accepted proxy derivatives in this market to deal with foreign exchange risk.[8]

The next chapter examines some modifications of existing Islamic financial contracts which could meet at least some of the needs of both investors and capital users in the Islamic sector.

---

[8]However, we have come across deals between two countries where the poorer country's central bank guarantees the value of its currency but does not assume any other liability in terms of the traded good. It is considered Islamically acceptable for an intermediary to buy the goods at a fixed price from one country in that country's currency and then sell it to another country for a fixed price in its own currency, thereby assuming the intermediate ownership of the traded good and shouldering the currency exposure as well.

PART III

Case-Studies: Islamic Financial Innovation

Frank E. Vogel

Samuel L. Hayes, III

CHAPTER 10

Innovation in Islamic Financial Products

This chapter builds on earlier ones to generate suggestions for innovation in Islamic finance. Earlier, we identified various demands facing the Islamic finance sector from both capital users (entrepreneurs) and capital providers (investors). Conventional (or Western) finance meets the demands of entrepreneurs by a wide spectrum of techniques, some of which are not offered by Islamic finance. Consider these examples:

- Accounts receivable financing cannot be done in the conventional fashion because Islamic law forbids the sale, hypothecation, or discount of financial obligations.
- Preferred equity, which enjoys more secure income and higher priority in liquidation, also cannot be done conventionally. It is difficult Islamically to invest in a firm (as opposed to one or another of its assets or operations) except with common stock equity risks and returns, yet preferred stock is often desirable or competitively necessary when a firm does not wish to assume additional debt, dilute its equity, or share expected profits with investors.

Islamic investors (often Islamic banks) also have demands that are currently difficult to satisfy. For example, Islamic banks need short-term, high-liquidity investments, since they must match their investments to the short-term nature of their deposits. Currently Islamic banks meet this need largely through "synthetic *murabaha*" contracts, but these now attract mounting disapproval. Because depositors are loath to face losses, banks must also avoid risks, again pushing them toward short-term transactions and *murabaha*, and causing them to seek Islamic equivalents for the risk management devices (options, futures, swaps, and other hedges) used routinely by conventional banks. Banks also need longer-term, higher-return investments to employ their own share capital.

These areas of difficulty in meeting entrepreneurs' and investors' demands through current Islamic mechanisms are where creativity and innovation will bear the most fruit. Which lines of inquiry will best generate the requisite new ideas? Two approaches seem promising: to review the institutions and instruments of conventional finance, seeking concepts that could be of use in an Islamic context; and to identify which Islamic legal vehicles have not been fully exploited for their capacity to meet current needs. The second approach is taken here.

We do not claim that the following proposals are indisputably Islamically valid. Determinations of validity require fatwas from religiously qualified persons or bodies. Neither do we expect that all of our proposals will gain an easy Islamic approval. Most are in markedly gray areas, which is inevitable since we discuss applications that go beyond the ones already tried. To the extent of our knowledge, most of the new methods described here are near to or on the borders of what a *shari'a* board would accept. When they are more controversial than that, we make note of that fact.

Our goal is not to turn Islamic finance into its conventional equivalent. In diagnosing the current needs of Islamic finance, we have tried to avoid assuming that the details of conventional finance are dictated in the very nature of things, that they are inherent parts of any successful financial system. On the other hand, practitioners of Islamic banking and finance often state that Islamic finance must find a way to perform certain functions of conventional finance if it is to compete successfully. Among these are the functions achieved by risk-management devices, marketable securities, accounts-receivable financing, preferred stock, and a futures market. We employ conventional terms to refer to these desired functions below. But by using such terms we do not suggest that these functions have to be fulfilled using the same forms or transactions as in conventional finance, and our suggestions often do diverge from conventional forms. And, even when we do suggest substitutes, we still question whether Muslims will or should adopt them, if their use might possibly lead to conflicts with Islamic legal principles and objectives. For example, as means to manage risks we propose below explicit risk-shifting devices called "hedges" or "options." But we also ask whether, even if these devices pass the literal tests of the classical law, they might lead to undue speculation or gambling.

We do not seek to offer wholly novel solutions, which would call for far-reaching innovative legal thought (*ijtihad*), but try to mimic the more conservative of the techniques of Islamic legal innovation described in Chapter 2. Our approach is daring only in its tendency to project or extrapolate from innovations already under consideration or in use. If our solutions fall within the bounds of Islamic law, then our effort may reveal something about the likely unfolding of Islamic finance. If, on the other hand, they fall outside Islamic law, they may indicate where Islamic finance needs to exert more creativity or *ijtihad*. In this way our proposals serve as case-studies testing the theoretical conclusions of preceding chapters.

We often advocate a shift from viewing an instrument or contract purely on its own terms to viewing it in the context of its larger legal or institutional setting. For example, in several cases below (e.g., concerning hedges, futures, and options) we suggest imposing additional controls on such contracts through institutional and regulatory means.

We seek no devious cures. In these proposals we seek to remain sympathetic to both the detailed rulings and the general principles of the classical law.

THE INTENDED BENEFICIARIES OF INNOVATION

In this section we review the needs of the two groups of participants in Islamic finance: capital users (entrepreneurs) and capital providers (investors).

Capital Users

As discussed in Chapter 7, the needs of capital users divide into two groups: short-term and long-term financing arrangements. In the short-term sector, we have already mentioned that the most important perceived gap is in *financing customer credit sales*. Reliance on owners' equity funds to carry customer receivables is unduly expensive. Inventory financing is readily available through *murabaha* contracts, but when Islamic businesses buy goods forward via a *salam* or *istisna'* contract, a difficulty arises. Having made a firm price commitment and paid all or part of the price at the front end, they need to *hedge against a price change* in the interim period until delivery of the goods.

In the longer-term sector, Islamic capital users need additional financial vehicles that *create financial leverage* in their capital structures. Although interest-bearing loans are forbidden, nothing prevents Islamic businesses from leveraging their equity capital with less expensive and non-diluting funds from alternative sources. One important acceptable source is lease financing, but surprisingly only a small amount of Islamic savings have been committed to lease financing; thus, there is a need to develop tailored lease contracts that are appealing to both Islamic capital users and suppliers.

There is also a need for financing arrangements that can *convert into an equity stake at the investor's option*, particularly important for start-up or early-stage companies that have difficulty attracting either straight equity funds (without a preferred position) or straight debt funds.

Capital Providers

Islamic investors' preference for short-term, liquid investments has channeled them into *murabaha* or markup investments, some of which are criticized as inharmonious with Islamic religious principles. Although all *murabaha* contracts should not be tarred with the same brush that applies to "synthetic" *murabaha* transactions, there is a clear need for more short-term, liquid investment vehicles to supplement bona fide *murabaha* contracts, which are likely to remain an essential source of financing to Islamic businesses.

One means of obtaining liquidity is through the securitization of both short- and long-term Islamic financial contracts. Securitization, in turn, requires the establishment of a *shari'a-approved liquid secondary market* for these securitized instruments.

Because the profit return on shorter-term investments is typically smaller than for longer-term commitments, there is a need for *longer-term, value-added investment vehicles.* Given the risk-averse nature of the typical

Islamic investor, there is a need for ways to disaggregate some of the *shar-i'a*-approved term contracts into components that allow investors to pick and choose among the features they wish to purchase. Once the investment features have been selected, there may still be a need for effective ways *to hedge various dimensions of risk* inherent in the resulting longer-term investments. These could include credit risk, interest rate risk, country risk, and currency risk.

PROPOSALS RELATED TO *MURABAHA* (SALE WITH MARKUP)

Islamic economics literature proclaims that *mudaraba/musharaka* equity investment is the theoretical cornerstone of Islamic banking investment. This conception positions the bank as a passive investor in its customers' business, deriving a profit from operating results. In practice, however, *mudaraba/musharaka* investment has not been extensive, due to such problems as moral hazard and adverse selection (as well as illiquidity). More effective means of enforcing accounting standards, legal and fiduciary standards, disclosure requirements, verification, and so forth are needed before investments of this type will become a truly important vehicle for Islamic banking investment.

Not surprisingly, therefore, *mudaraba* has not been our preoccupation as we have searched for proposals for innovation. But, at the same time, *mudaraba/musharaka* is used frequently in what follows, whenever we are interested in the securitization or negotiability of an investment or whenever a vehicle is needed for ownership of an investment. In most such cases, the risks that have inhibited Islamic banks' use of *mudaraba* in making passive investments in businesses are absent or minimized, usually because the Islamic financing entity is the *mudarib* or has other effective control.

The transaction called "*murabaha* with an order to purchase" has numerous attractions for Islamic banks and investors. (This is the transaction by which a customer asks a financial institution to purchase property which the customer in turn purchases from the institution on credit. Following the usage employed in Islamic banking circles, we shall refer to the composite transaction as "*murabaha*," although technically the term refers only to a sale — here the second sale — in which the price is expressly stated in terms of a specified "markup" over the cost of the property to the seller.) This *murabaha*:

- can be short-term;
- generates an unconditional debt in a fixed amount (unlike an ownership right to share in future profits);
- as a debt obligation, can be collateralized or secured;
- compared to partnership, reduces the need to monitor the customer's business or trust his honesty;
- simplifies calculation of gain by avoiding the need to know the characteristics of any particular industry, market, or pricing structure;
- with its percentage markup, mimics interest-lending, lowering costs of adaptation from conventional banking.

Given these advantages it is understandable why Islamic banks have relied so heavily on *murabaha*: it parallels conventional bank operations, is highly liquid, and entails few risks. Until safe, well-accepted alternatives exhibiting these advantages become available, it is unlikely that Islamic banks will willingly forego *murabaha* in all its forms.

Notice, however, that of the above-listed advantages of *murabaha* only the last two are not common to all forms of investment based in sale or lease, including credit sale, *salam*, *istisna'*, and hire. Even the last two advantages are shared at times by the lease (*ijara*) transaction.

Several Islamic financial institutions are trying to reduce or eliminate their reliance on *murabaha*, at least internationally, but none of the objections to *murabaha* requires its outright ban; rather, these objections argue for trimming away distortions or abuses in its use. *Murabaha* could still be used in sectors to which it is wholly appropriate (chiefly the finance of domestic and international trade) following rules assuring its validity. For example, a *murabaha* would deserve little criticism in Islamic law if the bank itself made the purchase of goods abroad, as opposed to appointing the customer as its agent to do so; assumed the risks of shipment, conformity with description, defects, delivery, taxation, and possible rejection by their ultimate user; and entered into a binding sale to its customer only on the latter's accepting the goods as conforming after shipment. We offer several proposals based on continued use of *murabaha*, but with limitations making it much more acceptable.

Ownership-in-Transit

Company's need: religiously acceptable financing of accounts receivable. If businesses must finance receivables out of ownership funds, the cost of capital is high and availability is limited. Turning to a third party to assume ownership of the merchandise and then sell it to ultimate customers can be cumbersome, is often constricting in acceptable credit profiles, and may result in a significant reduction in the company's profit margins.

Investors' need: high liquidity for their capital. Islamic bank deposits, even when labeled "investment accounts," are nonetheless subject to short-term recall.

Proposed financing contract: The "Ownership-in-Transit" proposal enables the buyer of goods to obtain credit without burdening the seller with large accounts receivable. It avoids any need for the seller to carry inventory until the goods reach the buyer and an account receivable can be issued. It involves a self-liquidating cycle that appeals to investors preoccupied with short-term cash recovery. In this proposal, a manufacturer who must ship finished goods for a lengthy in-transit period sells the goods to an Islamic bank at a discount from the billing price. The bank then sells the goods at a later date to the ultimate customer at a price that compensates it for the tie-up of its money and other costs associated with interim ownership.

So far this is the commonly-used *murabaha* in international trade, one of the mainstays of Islamic banking. To make it more efficient, however, and to enable use of *murabaha* fully in agreement with *shari'a* requirements, we propose a coordinated effort by Islamic banks to enhance volume and streamline arrangements. This financing approach has the potential to generate large volumes of business, thus reducing the higher initial costs of administration and documentation.

Case example: Volvo is shipping new cars to its dealers in the Gulf. The dealers will not pay for these cars until they are landed in the Gulf, requiring Volvo to finance the cars during the several-week transit period from Stockholm to Jedda or Manama. Bahrain Islamic Bank (BIB), under the auspices of a much larger *murabaha* program, is identified to purchase the cars from Volvo as they are being loaded onto ships in Stockholm. BIB continues to own the cars for the period of transit, incurring all shipping and other costs and risks coincident with ownership. The price at which BIB purchases the cars from Volvo is set at a level which will allow the Islamic bank to earn a satisfactory profit, net of all expenses, for the tie-up of its capital until the dealers remit payment for the cars. Because this is part of an ongoing international arrangement to finance trade in huge volumes, BIB is able to offer Volvo a net price for the cars which reflects a competitive financing arrangement for the auto company.

This transaction involves only one contract, that of "*murabaha* with order to purchase," the most commonly used Islamic finance mechanism. In this scheme, however, the contract is employed in its most Islamically pristine form, obliging the financier to own the goods for a period of time and carry meaningful risks as owner.

This proposal suggests the sort of organized international effort the Islamic finance industry will need to make if it is to retain international trade *murabaha* as a key vehicle for Islamic finance, while still satisfying religious scholars and customers. The logic of the proposal is that, if following pristine Islamic rules make *murabaha* more risky and therefore more costly for banks, one way to make it more feasible is through economies of scale. For example, a number of banks (perhaps coordinated by the IDB), or a large banking group, could approach a manufacturer of goods moving in large volumes in international trade — such as automobile exporters like Volvo or Toyota — and negotiate terms for a substantial volume of standardized *murabahas* (see Figure 10-1). These *murabahas* are then drawn up according to stringent Islamic legal standards, on which favorable fatwas have already been secured from prestigious scholars.[1] Through wide publicity given these fatwas, investments in this fund are readily accepted by Islamic bank customers, and would buck the tide of dissatisfaction with *murabaha* and, by association, with Islamic banks.

The banks bear some risks of non-conforming shipments or of rejection by dealers, which would burden the banks with disposing of the vehi-

---

[1]E.g., decision 2 & 3, fifth session (1988), *Fiqh Academy Journal*. Note that, during the substantial period of ownership required by these fatwas, an opportunity exists to securitize the *murabaha* investments.

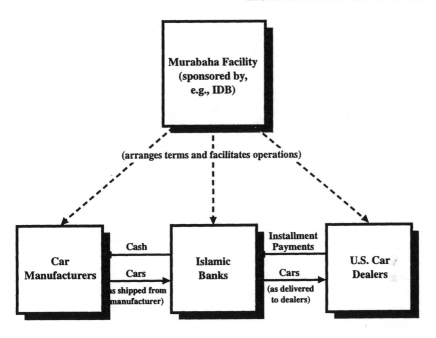

Figure 10-1. Murabaha Facility

cles. However, both dealer credit risk and risk of rejection could be greatly minimized, given the stable nature of the manufacturer-dealer relationship. Risk of loss in transit could be reduced through insurance, which ideally would be purchased through Islamic insurance companies.

This deal structure potentially serves both sides well. The manufacturer is attracted by economies of scale and a lower cost of capital than otherwise obtainable from bankers. (For example, Toyota presently finances its own goods during shipment to dealers.) The banks enjoy a secure investment with low risks. Most of all, banks avoid the high cost of developing their own *murabaha* markets, which requires educating and persuading non-Muslim credit users to accept Islamic banking and its unconventional procedures. Islamic banking customers also gain a higher degree of confidence in the Islamic permissibility of their banks' profits, in which they share.

The bank's intrusion into the usually airtight legal relationship between the vehicle manufacturer and dealer could present problems, but a significant economic benefit could overcome that hurdle.

This approach could be used wherever single manufacturers or sources move large volumes in international trade. The huge trade in crude oil, natural gas, and petrochemicals generated by national oil companies in Islamic countries offers one obvious opportunity.

Cooperative Non-Bank Factoring Firm

Company's need: a source of short-term funds to finance sales, which frees them from case-by-case third-party credit vetoes (control of credit extensions should ideally reside with the business, not the financing source); and maximum preservation of the profit margin for the business, not for the financing intermediary.

Investor's need: low-risk investment opportunities with high liquidity.

Proposed financing contract: A cooperative non-bank factoring firm accomplishes some of the same purposes for a business or group of businesses as a conventional captive finance subsidiary. Passive investors (including possibly some of the client businesses) commit funds to a *mudaraba* managed by a firm of professionals (the *mudarib*) with administrative and collection skills, which is compensated with a share of the profits. Acting as agents of the *mudaraba*, the client business(es) identify and screen credit sale applicants. The *mudaraba* enters into *murabaha* contracts with these applicants, maintaining markups sufficient to provide a reasonable profit to both investors and *mudarib* after expenses and expected bad debts.

Case example: The Mikdashi Appliance Stores Group makes an agreement with Gulf Short-Term Finance House (GSFH) to channel all of its credit sales through GSFH. Mikdashi decides which customers are creditworthy. For each customer sale, Mikdashi sells the relevant appliance to GSFH at a modest discount, which is designed to give GSFH a satisfactory return on its capital after expected bad debt charge-offs. Mikdashi agrees to guarantee a portion of bad debt losses, and some of its profits are used to maintain a reserve for that purpose. At the end of each six-month period, GSFH reviews its actual credit experience with Mikdashi's customers and, after debiting Mikdashi's reserve for its portion of bad debt losses, returns any surplus reserve. Since Mikdashi knows that it will bear losses from poor credit screening, it has an incentive to be careful in its credit judgments. Since GSFH also bears a portion of bad debt loss, it has an incentive to do efficient collections. Expected return-on-investment and bad debt loss figures are renegotiated periodically.

Earlier we highlighted the need for an Islamically acceptable way to finance a business's accounts receivable. Because the sale of a financial asset is forbidden, a business that wishes to conform with religious principles is forced to finance customer credit extensions out of its ownership funds (an expensive source) rather than from some sort of credit line, such as is available Islamically for inventory financing.

A business can, of course, finance an account receivable by selling the good in question to the Islamic bank which, in turn, sells to the intended customer on credit terms. This would not be a satisfactory solution for many businesses, however, since transaction-by-transaction approvals can be cumbersome, and lack of control over credit approvals might, from the perspective of the firm, unduly constrict its growth.

A de facto line of credit arranged on a *mudaraba* or *musharaka* basis for a limited time period is usually not a solution, either. One difficulty of such an arrangement is measuring profitability of the funds. Unless the funds are employed wholly in a separate profit-making activity segregated from the customer's business, it will be unclear what portion of the business's profits stems from whose capital contribution.

Given these difficulties, we believe a non-bank factoring firm holds more practical promise. Close cooperation and an efficient division of labor between it and its business clients approximate the role of a conventional captive finance subsidiary.

The factoring entity is set up as a *musharaka*, with private investors contributing the working capital. Pursuant to an "agency agreement" between the factor and each business client, as agent for the factor the client locates a suitable customer to purchase certain goods on credit. The factor purchases the goods from the client at a discount for cash, and then resells them at full invoice price on credit to the customer. The size of the discount reflects both a reasonable profit return on the capital employed as well as the expected rate of default. Part of the price paid on the first sale is held back from the client business to maintain a bad debt reserve account in its name. The factor and client may choose to protect themselves by increasing the size of the down payment required from certain customers.

The cooperating business agrees to conduct all its credit sales through the factor, thus avoiding the factor's risk of adverse selection (i.e., the risk that the business will funnel only the questionable sales through the factor and keep the top-quality credit sales on its own books). To further ensure that the cooperating business does a satisfactory job of credit screening, a portion of all credit losses is charged to each business's reserve, which to that extent guarantees the obligations of the customers. The factor also has an incentive to exert best efforts since it shares these losses. Any excess bad debt reserve is refunded periodically to the business.

Under Islamic law, establishing the bad debt reserve and refunding savings from the reserve to the business could be structured in either of two ways. One way would be to consider refunds as fees (*ju'l*) earned by the business as agent for locating customers. A problem arises because the compensation is unknown in advance; however, some schools permit compensating an agent by amounts tied to his success, e.g., compensating an agent to sell certain property by the amount, if any, by which the sale price exceeds a certain sum. A second arrangement, probably simpler, is that the business guarantees a percentage of the debts of the consumers, maintaining some of its own funds on reserve with the factor as collateral for these guarantees.

Figure 10-2 illustrates the financial and material flows of the cooperative non-bank factoring firm.

PROPOSALS RELATED TO *SALAM*

Parallel *Salam* Contracts

Company's need: religiously acceptable vehicles that allow Islamic businesses which either consume or produce commodity-like goods to hedge against unexpected adverse changes in the future value of those goods.

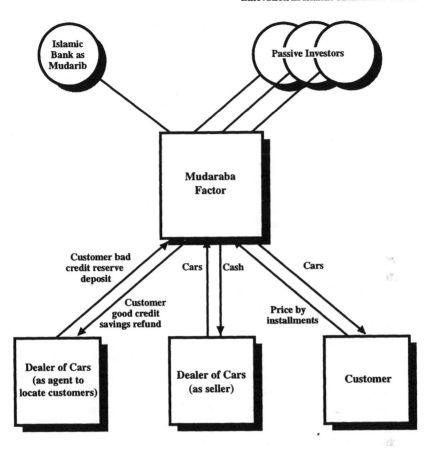

Figure 10-2. Mudaraba Factor Arrangement

Investor's need: to invest in commodities without immediately taking physical possession of the goods and thereby incurring the costs of ownership. If there is a subsequent change in the price outlook for the commodity, investors want to reverse their position.

An owner of a manufacturing venture using a large amount of a particular commodity (e.g., textiles) fears that an adverse price shift in that commodity would depress the venture's earnings and value. An investor might want to take advantage of the opportunity to buy a commodity in bulk and then to parcel it out to smaller repurchasers at a higher price.

Proposed use of salam *contracts:* Islamic business consumers or producers of a certain commodity-like good can buy or sell *salam* contracts on the good and then reassess that position over time. If the price outlook shifts, they can reverse their positions by undertaking a new set of *salam* contracts that are opposite in effect to the first set but are otherwise unrelated. In theory, even further rounds of *salam* contracts can be executed prior to the maturity of the original set if there are subsequent shifts in the outlook for the commodity price.

Case example: The Soufi Cement Co. uses large quantities of lime in its manufacture of cement. Nigeria is expected to restart intensive infrastructure development after a long period of domestic unrest. Anticipating Nigeria's need for cement, management enters into a number of additional *salam* contracts for the delivery of lime in six months' time so it will be able to bid for new business with the assurance of an adequate and reasonably priced source of lime. Three months later, a new outbreak of civil disorder in Nigeria eliminates prospects for enhanced demand for cement there. When the spot price of lime begins falling, Soufi Cement's management worries because it has contracted to purchase a great deal of lime in three months' time at a price that is now higher than the current spot price. Fearing a further drop in the price of lime, to cut its losses it *sells* enough of its original *salam* contracts for lime to exhaust the excess supply of lime it will be receiving three months from now. To be sure, it does sustain a loss in reversing its position, but it has stopped any further losses (as well as any possible recoveries if the price of lime rises before the end of the original contract period).

Possible new intermediary role: The risk-reducing moves just described would be greatly facilitated if an intermediary could act as either agent or principal in arranging for these contracts. Moreover, if the performance of the parties to the contracts were guaranteed by the intermediary, buyers and sellers would not have to undertake, on their own, credit investigations of potential counterparties. These points suggest the establishment of an "Islamic clearinghouse," proposed below.

Recall that a *salam* contract involves purchase of a fungible good, described precisely, for delivery at a specified future time against full payment at the time the contract is entered into. The good does not have to exist at the time of the contract; in fact, many *salam* contracts are for financing crops such as wheat or cotton that are still to be planted and grown. Nor does the seller need to be the actual producer. A *salam* contract resembles a conventional futures contract, the difference being that, in *salam*, cash payment is made at the front end.

For example, a miller could decide to buy wheat from a producer at a certain price for delivery in six months. The wheat producer would consequently be "short" the wheat and the miller would be "long." Ordinarily, the miller would receive the wheat at the end of the sixth month. But let us suppose the miller subsequently comes to the conclusion that the price of wheat is likely to *decline* in value during the prospective period. The miller would then be at a price disadvantage with any competitor who is paying the lower spot price for wheat while he is using wheat purchased at the already contracted higher price. Is there any way to alter his position?

Islamic law restricts the ways a party to a *salam* contract may avoid or undo his contractual obligation. It does not allow the buyer to sell to a third party his interest in the contract, i.e., in the seller's obligation to deliver the goods. Most schools do not permit the buyer to sell the specific goods that he is purchasing under the *salam* contract before they are delivered. As an exception, they permit such sales if sold to the *salam* seller, but only for the exact price originally paid; in other words, they permit the buyer and seller to rescind the contract, with the seller returning all of the price (no less and no more). The Maliki school follows these results as to *salam* contracts in foods, but for non-foods it allows sales of *salam* goods before they are received, either to the *salam* seller (for the original *salam* price *or less*), or to third parties (for *any* price). Sellers face similar restrictions: for example, they cannot pay someone to assume their responsibility under the contract.

An alternative is for the seller or buyer to enter into a wholly separate *salam* contract with a third person, while leaving the original contract intact. The second contract could have the practical effect of reversing the first contract, in whole or in part. For example, the miller-buyer could decide at the end of month two to reverse his position by *selling* a *salam* contract to a third party who had a different view on the likely future movement of wheat prices. The miller would more than likely lose something on the reversal of his position, but he would have executed a stop-loss "short" transaction to prevent any *further* loss. He would be able to take the money he had recouped and use it either to purchase wheat and hold it or to await an even further fall of the market price. Thus, in a very crude way, the miller is able to initially hedge his future raw material needs and then to close out the position part way through the contract period as he perceives a change in price trends.

Classical Islamic scholars reportedly acknowledged this sort of practice as legitimate; indeed, it would be very difficult to enforce a rule to the contrary. Note that parallel contracts have very different effects than a specific reversing or rescission of the first contract, because both contracts survive, and delivery must be made under both. Moreover, at least three parties, with their respective credit risks, are involved. Because of these complications, the transaction does not lend itself as readily or as obviously to reaping a seemingly unearned gain or loss as would simply undoing the initial transaction. (Compare a buyer of wheat forward in a rising market who sells his contract to a third person, exiting cleanly from the transaction with money in pocket, with another buyer who can only reverse his contract by undertaking the obligations of *salam* seller in a separate deal.) In modern times this dual-contract approach is called "parallel *salam*."

How far can this principle be developed in the direction of conventional futures markets? The first step would be for a vendor — possibly a special-purpose *mudaraba* or a subsidiary of an Islamic bank — to establish a *mudaraba* fund to act as broker for one or more particularly fungible commodities.

Suppose a fund is established to buy and sell raw cotton, and enters a *salam* contract with a large cotton producer for a million bales of cotton for delivery in six months. Simultaneously, having lined up in advance a group of smaller cotton users, it sells cotton by six-month *salam* contracts to these users covering the whole million bales of cotton purchased. The fund profits from the spread between the "wholesale" price it paid and the "retail" price at which it sold. These transactions would not refer to each other and are formally unrelated under Islamic law.

The next step toward a viable market is for the fund to make a market in the retail *salam* contracts, publishing "bid and asked" prices for entering into contracts as either buyer or seller. If a cotton user purchases a *salam* contract but thinks better of it, he can come to the fund and sell a *salam* contract for the amount of cotton he is "long," at a price which the fund deems appropriate at that point in time, and regardless of whether the fund has a counterparty lined up.

Alternatively, suppose a cotton producer has sold a *salam* contract for its cotton crop several months earlier to lock in what he thought would be a premium price. If the price then rises further, and he is convinced that the price rise will continue, he can go to the fund to purchase *salam* cotton in the same amount and with the same term as his first *salam* contract, enabling him to benefit from any further price appreciation in that commodity (although he is also exposed to the possibility of a fall in future cotton prices).

The last two cases assume that the fund is itself a party to all contracts arranged for its customers (although it can hardly prevent its customers from making private deals with third parties or even with each other). If it does enter into contracts as a principal, as opposed to merely brokering them, then in some instances the fund will have a net position which is not in balance — either a net long or net short position with capital at risk. Consequently, the fund needs a larger capital base than it would if it confined itself to simply executing simultaneous and equal parallel *salams*. Presumably some passive *mudaraba* investors provide this capital. The fund *mudarib* provides the trading and oversight expertise.

As the next step in development of the concept, the fund brokers deals between customers, and facilitates such deals by guaranteeing the performance of both parties. (This would be a simpler version of the "clearing-house" concept discussed below.) Such credit-enhancement enables the parties to transact readily and anonymously, with a net benefit to the parties on a risk-adjusted basis. The fund can guarantee the parties' obligations, charging, as Islamic law requires, only its administrative costs for doing so and recouping its cost of money from separate sources such as license fees, service fees, etc. *Salam* sellers can post collateral (like "margin") as a pledge (*rahn*) for their performance.[2] A buyer in one *salam* contract can use his investment in that contract as a pledge to secure his position as seller in another.[3] The fund keeps a record of defaulting *salam* sellers.

In a final elaboration, this fund intermediary is replicated until there is a genuine market for *salam* contract transactions.

Note that there are several very important distinctions between the proposed fund and a conventional commodity market. The buyer of a *salam* contract must pay the entire value in cash at the outset, but in a conventional futures contract no cash is paid at once. In a conventional forward contract, only the net difference between the prices of the two goods

---

[2]This is allowed by most, but not all, scholars. See Ibn Qudama, 4:347-352.
[3]Qari, sec. 958.

to be exchanged is paid in a daily settlement of what is in fact a series of one-day futures contracts.

Most importantly, the proposed fund does not allow settlements to occur in cash, as happens in conventional commodity markets. The actual cotton has to pass from party to party through a chain of parallel *salams*, until it reaches a final buyer. Admittedly, the fund can arrange for all these transfers of cotton to occur through a formal mechanism such as a ware-house receipt, so that a party which has reversed its position will experience little inconvenience in settling. The fund may also make a standing offer to buy cotton at the spot price from any ultimate buyer. But even with these mechanisms in place, the result contrasts with the conventional commodi-ties futures contract, which may be settled in cash with no relation whatso-ever to goods actually in the market, and then ceases to exist. In such contracts the price of the commodity serves as little more than an index.

This proposal is a good example of how different Islamic legal ap-proaches can affect evaluation of potential instruments. One approach might ask merely about the literal terms of specific contracts: the arrangement is permissible if the two *salam* contracts comply with *fiqh* rules, do not refer to each other, and are not conditioned on each other; all the other components of the transaction are acceptable contracts of agency, hire, pledge, partner-ship, and so forth. An approach at another extreme, taking a global, system-atic viewpoint, would oppose this proposal because it encourages "speculation." Such abstract misgivings, while important and legitimate, do not decide the issue, since the classical law not only tolerated but encouraged many forms of speculation (e.g., on changing market prices). A medieval Muslim cotton merchant who used *salam* contracts likely engaged in business not fundamentally different from the above. Which kind of speculation — the permitted or the non-permitted — is presented here? The answer may not come until the proposal is set in motion and its results observed.

If the proposed fund does lead to Islamically improper speculation, this is due to its institutional arrangement, not its individual transactions. The solution for such undue speculation must then also be sought institu-tionally. (This shows the importance of seeing transactions not only in dis-crete but also in institutional terms, both to identify problems and to find their solutions.) For example, the market might be closed to all but pro-ducers and users of contracted goods. The market might prescribe the maximum size of positions any single customer could assume, setting these specially for each customer. To prevent the fund itself from taking excessive positions, the maximum number of contracts written could be tied in some way to the size of the wholesale contracts, or to the available underlying commodity goods base.

The Default Penalty Option

Company's need: to hedge its position in a commodity against future price movements.

Investor's need: to take a position in a commodity while reserving the ability to abandon that position depending on subsequent events.

Proposed use of "Default Penalty Option": A buyer in a *salam* contract for a particular commodity negotiates a contract provision permitting him to cancel the contract at an interim point in the contract life on payment of a "default" fee to the seller. This penalty, along with a higher initial *salam* price, compensates the seller for exposure to this downside risk. The seller does not enjoy a default privilege; he could, however, always reverse his position by buying goods in the market.

Case Example: The Middle East Construction Co. has a contract to build a five-mile secondary road. It enters a *salam* contract with a local asphalt company for delivery of 100,000 cubic feet of asphalt in four months at a fixed price. Payment is made immediately. The contract stipulates that if Middle East Construction wishes at any time to default under the contract, the asphalt company will cancel the contract and return the price, less an agreed penalty amount to compensate the asphalt company for its losses due to the default.

The management of risk is an important problem for Islamic finance. This proposal addresses the possibilities for risk-managing options in *salam*. Could a party make a *salam* contract with a condition permitting it to cancel the contract at will, or cancel if the future market price passes a certain figure? Traditional law on these two possibilities is clear. To cancel at will is to posit a "stipulated option" (*khiyar al-shart*) in the contract, which is explicitly ruled out for *salam*. To condition the contract on a future price would be to "suspend" the contract on a condition (*ta'liq*), which for most scholars is not allowed even in ordinary sale contracts, much less in *salam*. Neither of these alternatives is very attractive anyway, since they do not compensate the party who assumes the risk of the option or condition.

In Chapter 6, the many strong Islamic legal objections to the conventional option contract were reviewed, suggesting that Islamic legal permission for conventional options will not be found soon. The contract closest to an option is the traditional *'arbun* contract, approved by the Hanbali school. But classical law very likely bars use of *'arbun* advances in *salam*. Nonetheless, Chapter 6 noted an opinion allowing *'arbun* even in *salam* — *deducting* the advance from the *refund* of the buyer's price if the *salam* is cancelled.[4] Such an approach would lead to results similar to those described here.

We use a different approach here, employing two other contractual arrangements, both of which have been approved by *fiqh* scholars. The first is a contract term fixing or "liquidating" damages. By such a term, the parties agree in advance on the damages that will be paid in the event of default. We discussed the *fiqh* position on this term in Chapter 6.[5]

The second arrangement is rescission. During the term of a *salam* contract a buyer may request a rescission from the seller, offering to compensate him for the privilege. The result would be the return of the buyer's initial payment less the agreed compensation. As we have seen, majority *fiqh* opinion disapproves of this practice in *salam*, permitting rescissions only when without any compensation whatsoever.[6] Malikis do permit compensated rescissions of *salam* contracts, but only when not involving foods.[7]

Combining these last two arrangements — the liquidated damages clause and compensated rescission — suggests the possibility of a contract providing that the buyer may rescind at will on condition of paying a pre-agreed penalty payment as compensation to the seller for his losses from the rescission. In other words, the contract would include a clause such as:

> If the buyer wishes at any time to rescind the contract, he may do so by notice to the seller, who shall immediately refund the purchase price. To compensate seller for any losses from the rescission, however, the seller is entitled to retain $_____.

---

[4]P. 163 at n. 64.
[5]Pp. 159-161.
[6]Bahuti, 3:306.
[7]P. 123, n. 63.

Insofar as this is a pre-agreed, compensated termination of a contract, it reminds one of the widespread Islamic banking practice, also controversial under classical law, by which creditors give discounts to debtors for prepayment of debts (*da' wa-ta'ajjal*). The OIC Majma's fatwa on the subject allows such discounts as long as they are not agreed upon beforehand.[8] But a number of banks, including the Islamic Development Bank, go further and insert binding terms for prepayment discounts in their contracts.

Notice that the proposal here gives a rescission option only to the buyer. No school allows a *salam seller* to pay the *buyer* for a rescission, since then a seller would be paying an additional sum on the occasion of returning money held for a period of time; such an outcome could easily become a subterfuge for interest-lending. But note that the seller in *salam* scarcely needs the protection of an option: to hedge against adverse price movements, he may use the money provided by the buyer to purchase the goods in the present market and hold them. For a seller, hedging against the market is always possible for the price of storage (and the loss of profits from use of the purchase price).

If the "default penalty option" approach described above is legally accepted, then one has achieved the equivalent of a call option — even for a *salam* market in commodities. To imagine how this works, assume parties conclude a *salam* contract for one hundred bales of cotton deliverable in six months at $10 a bale, payable immediately (this is an "ordinary" *salam* contract). The parties add a provision permitting the buyer to cancel for a penalty of $100 (making it a "default penalty contract"). The default penalty contract is like a forward contract plus a put option: the buyer profits as the price rises above $10 per bale; if the price falls below $9 per bale (allowing $1 per bale for the $100 cost of exercising the option), then the buyer will "put" the goods to the seller, avoiding any further losses.

Since a forward plus a put equals a call, the result, apart from the very different payment terms and credit risks, is similar to having a call on one hundred bales of cotton at $10 a bale. The contract would pay according to Figure 10-3.

How would the price of the *salam* contract with default penalty differ from that of an ordinary *salam* contract with otherwise identical terms? A number of factors go into this pricing. Assuming the contract terms just used, an ordinary *salam* contract will cost $1000 ($10 per bale). The price

---

[8]Decision 66/2/7, seventh session (1992), *Fiqh Academy Journal*, 217, 218.

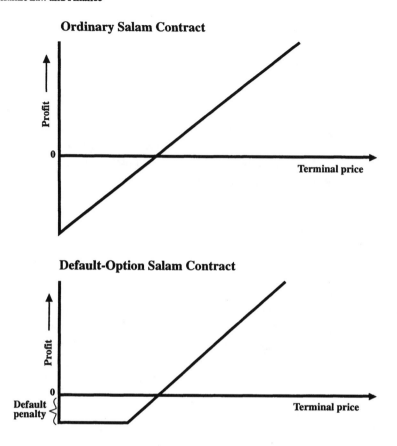

**Figure 10-3. Payment on Ordinary
and Default-Option Salam Contracts**

of a similar default penalty *salam* contract must be higher ($1000 + $X) to
compensate the seller for the risks due to including the default provision.
Note that the penalty amount (of $100) does not compensate the seller for
assuming this risk. It is not paid until there is a "default," and the buyer ordinarily will not "default" until the market has already fallen the equivalent
of the penalty amount plus other costs of exercise. The penalty amount

merely reimburses the seller for what he has already lost from the fall of the market, without any further compensation for the risks he has borne.

That the price for the defaulted penalty *salam* contract should be higher than for an ordinary *salam* contract in the same market should not be Islamically troubling. In *salam* a buyer expects to pay a premium price to contract with a seller with better credit. Similarly, *salam* market prices will be higher, other things being equal, for goods more subject to scarcity. This means that the buyer would be obliged to pay more when the seller incurs greater risks on not only his own production, but on scarcity in the general market, where he would have to go to cover if he lost his own goods.[9] In our case the buyer pays more to compensate for shifting market risks to the seller, although these are risks on the downside, not on the upside.

What would be the impact of *salam* contracts with default options on the *salam* market described under the last heading — the market in which the buyer has the option to cover losses by buying a reversing parallel contract? It seems unlikely that a buyer who enjoyed a perfectly liquid market in *salam* contracts would pay extra for a default option. In either case the buyer pays the purchase price in advance, but the parallel *salam* option is free, while the default option involves both an increased purchase price and a penalty. The default provides added protection only in capping losses at the default penalty amount, regardless of how low the market price falls.

These pros and cons, however, assume a perfectly liquid market without significant transaction costs. In the absence of these conditions, a buyer who is not a trader in the market may find it advantageous to arrange for his potential buyer in advance, by contracting for a put as part of his initial transaction.

If in the end scholars believe this "default penalty" proposal strains classical principles unacceptably, they might consider permitting the arrangement only between licensed traders in an organized *salam* market or clearinghouse. On the ground of trust and solidarity between persons in the same profession and marketplace, and according to regulations adopted jointly by them to control their activities, traders might justifiably indulge in practices which, in unregulated contexts, might lead too readily

---

[9]Offsetting this is the common Islamic rule that when goods are "unavailable" — a term not precisely defined — the buyer has the option of either returning the purchase price or waiting.

to abuses. This is analogous to the manner in which, as discussed in Chapter 6, Islamic insurance came to be accepted after it was portrayed not as a single contract but as an institution organizing beneficial mutual relationships among Muslims.[10]

An Islamic Clearinghouse

The prior two proposals suggest a further one: the addition to the *salam* market (with or without default options) of a clearinghouse to lower the cost and rate of defaults in *salam* contracts. *Salam* sellers become members of the clearinghouse. While sellers have a choice whether to join or to remain independent, becoming a clearinghouse member sends a signal of integrity to the marketplace. As a result, this seller most likely can get a better price than those that offer contracts independently. Buyers averse to risk buy a *salam* through the clearinghouse; the less risk-averse buyers go to independent sellers.

Let us first review the structure of a U.S. options clearinghouse to serve as a model. To trade options in the United States, one must be an exchange member with a financial guarantee from a clearing firm. Members of a U.S. option exchange can be brokers who work as agents for other traders, or market makers trading for their own accounts. Brokers make money through commissions while market makers make money off the bid/ask spread. The presence of these market makers helps keep derivative prices close to their fair prices.

Clearing firms are usually financial institutions that pledge to satisfy any financial obligations incurred by the trader if the trader cannot meet them. Hence the clearing firm must maintain a minimum capital level set by the clearinghouse. The clearing firm charges fees to the floor trader for guaranteeing and processing trades.

The exchange verifies if a trade is good — i.e., it compares the information submitted by the buyer and seller clearing firms. If a trade clears, the clearinghouse receives a report from the exchange and an option position is set for each clearing firm. The clearinghouse collects the option pre-

---

[10]Note that the restrictions faced here affect *salam* in particular, which is Islamic law's characteristic contract for future obligations in generic or fungible goods. These restrictions would likely evaporate in the contract of *istisna'* (see discussion below).

mium from the buyer and passes it on to the seller firm. It also collects margin from the seller firm and guarantees the trade to both clearing firms.

The buyer and the seller of an option have no direct contact in the U.S. option markets. For example, when a buyer firm exercises an option, the clearinghouse randomly assigns the exercise to an outstanding short position. The clearing firm on the short side provides security or cash to the clearinghouse, which then transfers to the clearing firm of the long side.

The clearing firm, which guarantees the trade obligations of its customers and market makers, must minimize parties' incentives to walk away from losing positions. One way it does this is by requiring collateral for each trade position it guarantees. And because the clearinghouse in turn guarantees the financial performance of the clearing firms, it requires from them collateral sufficient to meet the financial obligations of the clearing firm should it fail.

All the attributes and functionalities of the derivatives clearinghouse seem to be Islamically acceptable, and such a clearinghouse would solve the problems of adverse selection and moral hazard associated with *salam*, *'arbun*, and third-party guarantees. *Salam* sellers would become members of the clearinghouse in order to identify themselves with good quality. These *salam* sellers would be required to put up margin and collateral against their obligations. In this environment, sellers' *salam* prices would be higher due to lower default premiums. Also, their delivery options would be much more valuable because they would have better information and access to a greater number of commodity grades of acceptable quality.

If the default option approach of the last section (or substitute) is employed, the clearing party of the seller side would put up collateral to reduce default risk to the buyer. This collateral could be a claim on specifically-identified assets (not necessarily on the exact item on which the default option contract was written). The amount of the collateral could be monitored as a function of the price of the asset under contract, or even as a function of time and the seller's net worth or profitability. Naturally, this would reduce the seller's incentive to walk away from his contract. The buyer's record of exercising in-the-money options (and thereby "providing business" to sellers) would also be helpful in monitoring the buyer's behavior, and would reduce his down payments on subsequent contracts. Ultimately, this structure would make option contracts more efficient and reliable by screening out "bad" (e.g., defaulting) buyers and sellers.

Greater liquidity would be an important by-product of this institutional structure. Though the clearinghouse would match the parties on the buy and sell side of contracts, those parties might never know each other. A pool of buyers and sellers would increase possible pairings and improve the liquidity of default option contracts. The prices of such contracts would also be more competitive. For example, a default option seller who demanded an unreasonable price would not be able to sell his contracts if there were other sellers of the same quality offering similar contracts at a lower price.

In sum, a clearinghouse arrangement offers many benefits:

- A large clearinghouse with access to information can aggregate risks and reduce them through diversification better than a sole intermediary can.
- Collateral mechanisms and access to government funds in case of emergency reduces the risks of individual contracts.
- Derivatives are highly leveraged; a clearinghouse can limit the total leverage of each underlying asset by establishing a maximum number of contracts per unit of underlying asset, resulting in greater market stability.
- The presence of brokers between customers and clearinghouse creates competition that brings the cost of contracts to their fair prices, resulting in a more efficient market.
- An organization of traders, perhaps licensed, can adopt through co-operative means measures that could not be validly imposed through individual contracts.

PROPOSALS FOR INNOVATIONS RELATED TO LEASE AND HIRE (*IJARA*)

Leasing (*ijara*) is growing in importance in the world of Islamic banking and finance, but its full potential for financing long-term business assets is yet to be explored. This section offers a series of ideas for employing leases in an Islamic context.

Leases have four advantages that recommend them to innovators in Islamic finance:

- Leases share the general features of sale (*bay'*) noted in the earlier discussion of *murabaha*, such as yielding a fixed debt obligation, permitting collateralization, and being, if the parties wish, short-term.
- Leases in Islamic finance reproduce a conventional financial technique with little change. In particular, Islamic law freely delegates the pricing of the lease rental to the parties, not imposing restrictions or even guidelines. This makes it possible to determine prices in a fashion similar to conventional practices. For example, Islamic banks routinely use prevailing interest rates and capital amortization schedules to determine a fair lease rental.[11]
- A lease allows one to fix a price now for a future stream of benefits, without assuming the full burdens of ownership. This makes leasing a useful conception in arranging hedges for various risks.
- Leasing is flexible under Islamic legal rules. Since the lease usufruct comes into existence continuously over the life of the contract, it differs from both goods already in existence and goods which do not yet exist, and thus attracts lenient rules. For example, lease rules do not require, as do rules for sales, that at least one of the two performances take place at the time the contract is made. Also, leases may incorporate conditions concerning the future, since the usufruct inhabits the future in any event.

Table 10-a expands on the last advantage by giving examples of some of the lawful alternative forms of leasing.

The full-payout lease. Three items in the table are legally controversial and deserve special comment. One is the "full-payout" lease. Like the conventional financial lease, it is designed to recoup for the lessor the full initial present value of the goods and to afford the lessee at the end of the lease the title — or at least the option of title — to the goods. But two features of the conventional lease are not allowed by Islamic law. First, in conventional financial leases the lessee remains liable for the full rent, even if the leased

---

[11]Some bankers feel that using LIBOR, for example, to set rental rates offends religious principles; others disagree, asserting that LIBOR is simply a benchmark for comparing profit rates with conventional bank rivals.

Table 10-a. Important Dimensions of Flexibility in Lease Terms

Terms open to permutation	Example	Example
Salvage value and other rights	Partial payout lease (significant salvage value, variable final ownership terms)	Full-payout lease (often involving some mechanism to transfer ownership at end)
Rent rate	Fixed (single rent rate throughout life of lease)	Floating (lease is periodic and renewable, rent rate renegotiated with each renewal, may be overarching agreement)
Payment terms	Payable when agreement is signed	Postponed — payable in installments or as lump sum
Time of transfer of usufruct	Commencing at time of agreement	Delayed to commence at a fixed later time (*mudafa*, discussed below)
Number of lessors (diversification ownership)	Single direct owner of leased goods	Multiple owners through undivided co-ownership or partnership
Character of property leased (diversification of leased goods)	Single piece of property	Multiple items leased, of the same or diverse nature

property is destroyed or severely damaged. Under Islamic law, any attempt to shift risks of such damage or destruction to the lessee is void. But if Islamic casualty insurance is permitted, the lessor can simply purchase such insurance, implicitly shifting the costs of the premiums to the lessee in rent. This is done in practice, although some agreements dispense with even this nicety and shift the insurance cost explicitly.

The second problem with the conventional financial lease is that Islamic law does not permit constructing a binding future sale or option of sale for the leased goods. Such a sale would have to be concluded at the end of the lease, not before. More creativity is required to evade this second obstacle than the first. Some Islamic institutions promise to "give" the goods to the lessee provided that the terms of the lease have been met, invoking a Maliki view that a promise to do a gratuitous act is legally binding, but applying that view in a context that is non-gratuitous overall. Another approach is a non-binding promise to sell the goods at the end of the lease for a nominal sum, which the lessee accepts, counting on the lessor's interest in maintaining its reputation and its leasing business.

The OIC Fiqh Academy recommends that the lease include a term allowing the lessee three options: either to extend the lease term, to return the rented property, or to purchase it for the then market price.[12]

In what follows we adopt the term "full-payout lease" to mean a conventional financial lease modified to meet Islamic legal objections.

The floating-rate lease. Islamically, the rent in a lease must be precisely known at the time the lease agreement is concluded. While the rent amounts can differ for different periods of the lease term and may be calculated by reference to the present value of any type of indicator or index, the precise value of rentals must be calculable now, leaving nothing to be determined in the future. Facing this rule, but still desirous of a substitute for the conventional floating-rate lease, Islamic finance has evolved the "periodic" lease, one which expires and is renewed at short intervals over a longer term. Technically the renewals are not binding, and the terms for each new period are open to renegotiation, but in practice the parties execute an umbrella agreement setting out their good-faith or gentlemen's agreement on how lease terms will vary over the period, usually by fixing a new rent against a changing index like LIBOR.

Nothing in Islamic law binds the two parties to the arrangement just described, but concerns for business reputation (or for possible enforcement by a court or arbitration panel recognizing non-Islamic law to some degree) provide enough assurance of performance.

The role of non-binding agreements. Non-binding agreements play a part in both full-payout and floating-rate leases, as well as in other adaptations of Islamic finance. Muslims question such approaches, arguing that if the arrangement were truly non-contractual and optional, businessmen would not enter into it or rely on it. Are they not rather similar to the secret agreements through which parties of the past hatched and managed complex artifices or *hiyal* employing a series of lawful steps to an unlawful end? On the other hand, "non-binding" here does mean that the parties cannot sue but must trust each other. Innumerable phases of cooperation in business are not, and probably could not, be captured in binding agreements. As long as the act being arranged (e.g., a sale of salvage value, renewal of a lease) is not in itself unlawful, is there anything wrong with the parties

---

[12]Decision 6, fifth session (1988), *Fiqh Academy Journal*, 2763.

memorializing a good-faith intention to do business on certain terms? No doubt, the Islamic validity of such arrangements should be reviewed case by case, if not agreement by agreement.

Lease Pools

Company's need: either short- or long-term financing for equipment and other real assets at a competitive cost.

Investor's need: liquid value-added investment opportunities. To minimize risk, investments should be held in a portfolio diversified by maturities and industries.

Proposed contract: Portfolios of *shari'a*-approved leases grouped by common characteristics, such as year-to-year operating leases in the oil service sector, floating-rate full-payout leases for construction equipment, short-term full-payout leases denominated in Saudi riyals, or seven-year, fixed-rate full-payout leases denominated in yen. Each portfolio or "pool" is owned by a company (*mudaraba* or *musharaka*). The company may repurchase the interest of its co-owners, creating liquidity. A super-pool serves as overall organizer and *mudarib* for each of these individual lease pools and possibly also invests in them. The super-pool would be organized as a *musharaka*, with a large Islamic bank or bank group acting as organizer and manager, investing some of its own funds.

Case example: Bahrain Islamic Bank (BIB) sets up a group within the bank to arrange various kinds and maturities of leases to be organized into homogeneous *mudaraba* portfolios. The Government Employees Welfare Society of Brunei has funds it would like to invest for three years at a fixed rate. BIB directs the Society to the appropriate *mudaraba* set up by the bank. A year later, the Society has an unexpected need for liquidity and requests that BIB repurchase its claim on that lease portfolio, which BIB does at its fair price.

In another example, an Islamic bank is lessor in a number of fixed-rate leases and seeks to hedge its exposure to interest-rate shifts by investing in floating-rate leases.

Lease pools already exist as Islamic investment vehicles. For example, a *mudaraba* was formed to purchase a number of tankers and lease them, the proceeds to be divided among the investors. Some of these pools are willing to repurchase investors' interests on pre-agreed terms.

The Islamic legal notions underlying such pools are not controversial: founding a *mudaraba* to hold leases is unremarkable, and the transfer of interests in such a *mudaraba*, even by sale to a third party, is possible. This is due to two principles discussed in Chapter 6: first, that a shareholder in a *mudaraba* may trade his shares if, were he to own the assets of the *mudaraba* directly, he could transfer that ownership interest; and second, that an interest in company assets may be traded if the assets are in greater part neither cash nor debts. Since the pool owns title to actual equipment, both principles are satisfied.

In this section the lease pool idea is developed as a vehicle for fully exploiting all the above dimensions of flexibility in leases. A portfolio of pools — a super-pool — is suggested, which, instead of itself holding leases with the users of the equipment, organizes under itself a number of sub-pools to hold the leases. Each sub-pool specializes in a particular type of lease. The super-pool purchases all the property to be leased, and negotiates and administers all the leases. The super-pool and all sub-pools are set up as *mudarabas* to permit negotiation of interests in them. The super-pool may own interests as a capital contributor to any or all of the sub-pools, and it also serves as a *mudarib* to each. (See Figure 10-4.)

Imagine that a large Islamic bank or bank group launches such a super-pool by first forming a *musharaka* company in which it invests either its own equity capital, some of its deposit liquidity, or both. The bank is then joined by other inactive partners. The bank or an affiliate manages the super-pool, serving as *mudarib* to the inactive co-investors. The super-pool then offers lease financing to customers in as full a range of alternative lease forms as possible, attracting customers for lease investments across the full spectrum of the lease permutations mentioned in Table 10-a — across industries, equipment types, currencies, and tenors (both fixed- and floating-rate, operating and full-payout, etc.). The super-pool only arranges these leases, with actual ownership to be held not by the super-pool but by its various sub-pools. Each sub-pool owns leases of a particular type: sub-pools might exist for three-year fixed-rate operating leases, seven-year floating-rate financial leases, floating-rate leases on airplanes, diversified leases on oil-drilling equipment, three-year equipment leases payable in

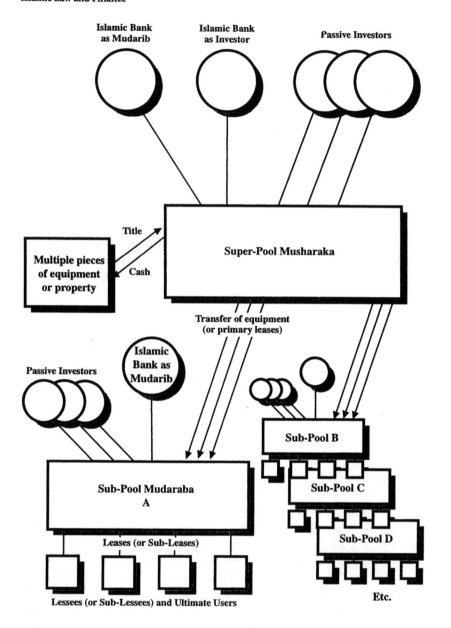

Figure 10-4. Organization of the Leasing Super-Pool

deutsche marks, and so on. (The next section discusses a variation which permits investing in the separate years of a single lease, permitting, for example, a pool to hold the second year of seven-year floating-rate leases, or the seventh year of seven-year fixed leases.) Any variety of lease generated by permuting the characteristics appearing in Table 10-a would be possible. Note that each sub-pool could be diversified to any practical and desired degree, and at a minimum is diversified by holding leases of a number of lessees.

Much of the power of this proposal lies in the risk-focusing effect of a sub-pool receiving *income* with certain financial characteristics (e.g., floating-rate, delayed payment, in deutsche marks, airline industry risks) while bearing *obligations* with different financial characteristics (e.g., fixed-rate, immediate payment, in dollars, no industry risk). This allows the funds to be tailored for certain risks. For example, a pool could be designed as a currency hedge. If the lessee or end-user makes lease payments to the sub-pool in one currency, presumably its home currency (e.g., deutsche marks), and the sub-pool in turn pays installments on the leased property in another currency (e.g., U.S. dollars), then the sub-pool would be hedging the exchange rate between the two currencies. If the opportunity rates used to calculate the lease payments were an accurate reflection of the erosion in the home country's currency vis-à-vis the other currency, then the currency dimension would be a wash, but if such an equilibrium did not hold in that short run, then the sub-pool would generate a currency hedge.

All these lease investments are liquid, since all can be securitized and negotiated. If an investor changes its mind about any one of the components of its investment, it may always transfer its interest to another investor or sell back to the sub-pool itself.

There are three ways in which the super-pool can arrange to transfer the lease investment from itself to the sub-pool, resulting in three different Islamically acceptable legal relationships between the super-pool, sub-pool, and ultimate user:

1. The super-pool enters into the lease directly with the user, and then sells (for present or delayed payment) the leased property (subject to the lease) to the sub-pool.
2. The super-pool arranges the lease, but rather than entering into the agreement as lessor, sells the property to the sub-pool (for present or delayed payments) which then leases it to the user.

3. The super-pool arranges the lease with the user, but rather than leasing the property to the user itself, it leases it to the sub-pool and allows the sub-pool to sub-lease it to the ultimate user.

Each approach has advantages and disadvantages. The third approach permits even the first stage of the transaction to enjoy all the flexibility of the lease relationship. For example, it enables dividing the single lease with the ultimate user into a number of sequential, temporally staged lease investments (as proposed in the next section). It makes it possible to arrange a floating rate for the first-tier transaction and a fixed rate for the second. It also enables interests in the super-pool to be negotiable without difficulty, since the super-pool would hold title to all leased equipment. The third approach, however, causes problems for the trading of interests in the sub-pools, since, once the sub-pool sub-leases the equipment, they own only the financial asset of the future rental stream, which is not Islamically tradeable. This third approach is discussed and illustrated in the next section.

The first and second approaches permit continuous and uncontroversial negotiability at the sub-pool level, since they transfer actual ownership in the goods to the sub-pools. But since the sub-pools do own the property, they become involved in managing it, creating a bias for full-payout leases covering the entire useful value of the underlying goods. These approaches also do not allow floating rates in the first tier of the transaction. This section assumes use of the first and second approaches.

The investment commitment of the super-pool depends on whether the sub-pools pay the super-pool for the equipment immediately or with delay. If they pay at once, then the investment commitment is modest; if they postpone payment, either as a lump sum or as installments, the super-pool needs to be much more heavily capitalized. The negotiability of interests in the super-pool is in some doubt in the latter event, since the super-pool's assets may consist chiefly of debts for equipment purchases, which as financial obligations are not negotiable. If, however, the super-pool held substantial investments in the sub-pools as partner, their value may exceed the present value of the sub-pools' equipment purchase obligations, and thus open the door to negotiability.

The sub-pools assume the credit risk of the end user and the risk of a sudden adverse shift in the demand for the equipment. These risks might be reduced through diversification. The equipment demand risk would be greater for periodic or floating-rate leases since floating-rate leases are based on understandings which are technically not binding and more favorable terms elsewhere might persuade a lessee to abandon the lease. Obviously, the price charged by the primary lessee factors in the negative value of the credit and equipment demand risks in that industry sector.

The super-pool selling or leasing equipment to its sub-pools faces the credit risk of the sub-pools, but these risks are much reduced by the fact that all pools are part of a single organization managed by one *mudarib*, the Islamic bank.

The founding bank (or banks) derives income from its own capital investment in the pool (which can be progressively sold out to capital investors) and from its services as *mudarib*. It can charge an income percentage as *mudarib* of each of the sub-pools, or it can derive its entire profit from its participation share as *mudarib* in the super-pool's income.

The super-pool derives its income from sales to the sub-pools, with prices covering the costs of purchasing the equipment and of negotiating all the equipment leases. It may occasionally have to hold leases for which a sub-pool has not been successfully formed. Sub-pools earn more from their leases than they owe the super-pool for equipment purchase, on a present-value or prorated basis. In other words, the income from the financing is shared between the super-pool and the sub-pool.

Staged Leases and Lease Pools

Company's need: full-payout lease financing at the lowest net cost.

Investor's need: an attractive return without the risks of longer-duration investments. An Islamic investment fund expects to receive a large sum of money two years in the future and wants to lock in today's rate for that particular maturity. A conventional pension fund seeks to maximize yield on the fixed-income portion of its portfolio by purchasing income payments that are at the long-term end of the yield curve.

Proposed contract: A lease pool *mudaraba* managed by a *mudarib* (e.g., an Islamic bank) purchases certain equipment intending to lease it to a particular user for a specified length of time, e.g., five years. The

269

mudaraba enters into five one-year fixed-rate leases, each covering one of the five years, with five investors, each of whom has a preference for one of the years of the lease's income life. Payment may be either immediate or delayed. As arranged by the bank, the investors and the ultimate user sign a formally non-binding understanding that the latter will enter into a one-year sub-lease with each of the investors in turn, entering each sub-lease only as the year commences for which the particular investor owns the lease interest. The ultimate user makes its rent payment either as it enters into each lease or in later installments. Rates for these sub-leases can be either fixed or floating. Interests in the sub-leases are negotiable until the actual lease in each commences, but not thereafter.

As a more complex alternative, the investors in the above can be replaced with sub-*mudarabas*, in which securities are issued that can be bought and sold until the actual lease commences. As a still more complex alternative, this proposal can be included in the super-pool arrangement described in the preceding section.

Case examples: The Bahrain Islamic Bank (BIB) is dissatisfied with its return on short-term trade financing, but liquidity concerns make it unwilling to invest in longer-maturity opportunities. It therefore arranges a full-payout lease with an ultimate user and purchases the requisite equipment. It organizes a *mudaraba* with itself as *mudarib* and sells the equipment to the *mudaraba*, possibly with a markup. The *mudaraba* divides the lifetime of the property into annual tranches and leases them to investors (or sub-*mudarabas* of investors) who each in turn sub-lease to the user. The lease for the first year is taken by BIB for its own portfolio, thus reserving for itself an attractive one-year return in addition to fees earned in selling tranches to other investors.

The Government Employees Welfare Society of Brunei expects a large inflow of funds three years from now from its members as well as from the government on their behalf. The portfolio managers want to "park" those funds for up to a year once they are received, after which they expect to have committed the funds to a portfolio of common stock investments. The portfolio managers predict that short-term profit rates (reflected in the rate of profit they could earn on *murabaha* contracts) will fall in the next several years and they want to capture the favorable one-year profit rates now prevailing, so they approach BIB and acquire an interest in the sub-*mudaraba* that holds the lease for the third year of the equipment's use. Assuming that the credit risk for the ultimate user is low, they thereby lock in today's prevailing yield for cash to be received three years in the future.

This financial structure takes advantage of the fact that, under Islamic law, leases tolerate a greater degree of delay in obligation on both sides since they inevitably involve a good — the usufruct — that comes into existence only gradually. Most schools of Islamic legal thought allow parties to conclude leases that take effect only in the future ("postponed" leases), as when one rents a house for twelve months beginning one year hence. (This lease is called *mudafa*, literally, "extended.") The schools even allow lease payments in postponed leases also to be postponed, even to the end of the future lease term, or on any schedule nearer in term, including prepayment or payment in installments. As a result, the postponed lease is one of the rare cases where Islamic law upholds a contract binding both parties contractually but not requiring either to perform at once ("bilateral executory contract"). This feature in leases allows us to propose an intriguing innovation in lease financing, which might create a means of managing various forms of risk.

In the simplest combination, imagine a bank that secures a five-year lease with a sound commercial "name" which serves both as a drawing card for investors and assures that the terms of the arrangement will be fulfilled. The bank establishes a *mudaraba* to purchase the desired equipment (possibly using *murabaha* financing) and lease it to the user. So far, the pool is a simple form of the leasing pools already available in the Islamic investment market, in which investors take interests in a lease or leases by buying interests in the lessor *mudaraba*.

The next step is to introduce a second tier of investment, as in the previous section's proposal. There, however, the super-pool created the second-tier interests by *selling* the equipment to sub-pools, who in turn *leased* to the ultimate user. Here the first-tier pool *leases* the equipment to the second-tier investors (the "primary lessees") who then *sub-lease* to the end user (the "sub-lessee"). See Figure 10-5. As in the previous section, the primary lessees would likely be financial investors (e.g., Islamic banks).

This two-tier lease arrangement enables the first-tier leases to employ the Islamically acceptable concept of the postponed lease. The pool creates a series of stages, or annual tranches, of interests in the equipment lease, and leases each separately. Each investor or prime lessee enters a one-year

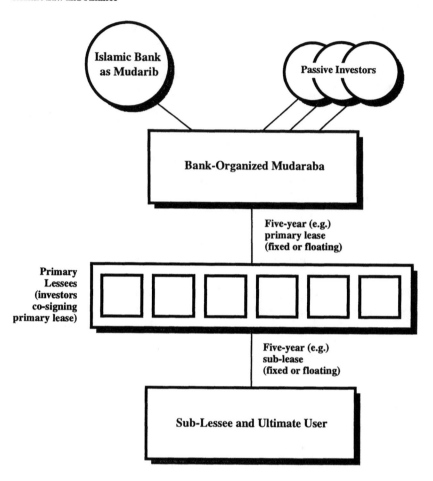

Figure 10-5. Simple Lease Pool (with Subleasing)

lease, all but the first commencing in the future at one-year intervals. Payment for each lease is made either in a lump sum (immediate or delayed) or by installments. The pool obtains an overarching understanding — not enforceable except through the desire of all concerned to preserve their relationship and business reputations — that the ultimate user will enter into

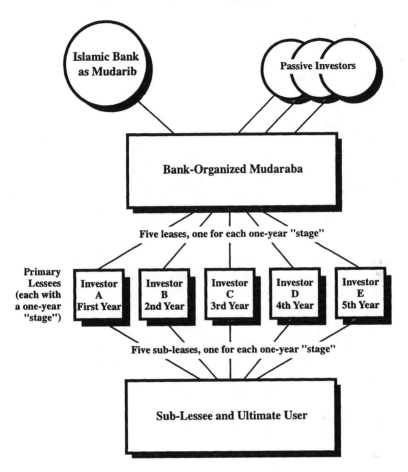

Figure 10-6. Staged Lease Pool

a lease with each of the investors in turn at the beginning of the year for which that investor holds the lease. See Figure 10-6.

Each investor is entitled to sell interests in its lease interest, since it holds a real asset: the usufruct in the equipment. For this reason each investor may be organized as a sub-*mudaraba* in which interests are securitized and then bought and sold. To create this negotiability, the primary leases must be fixed-rate leases, since otherwise the owners of the future

273

tranches of the lease would own not the real asset of a usufruct but only a (technically unenforceable) promise of the pool to lease, which is not negotiable. On the other hand, if negotiability is not needed, a floating rate for the various future primary leases becomes practicable.

Securities for these lease interests may be traded, however, only so long as the investor or sub-*mudaraba* owns the usufruct. Once it sells the usufruct to the ultimate user by entering into a sub-lease with the latter, it no longer owns the usufruct and owns instead the obligation of the user to pay rent. This is a financial debt (*dayn*) in which interests cannot be bought and sold under Islamic law. To cope with this difficulty, the sub-leases are entered into not at once but sequentially as each prime lease commences, in a manner reminiscent of the periodic renewal that underlies the "floating-rate" lease. Again, if negotiability can be dispensed with, sub-leases may be entered into from the start and would be fully binding.

Even the negotiability of the investors' or primary lessees' interests *before* sub-leasing may arouse some controversy among Islamic legal scholars. Two doubts arise as to the nature of the primary lessees' ownership in the postponed usufructs:

- If the usufruct is considered *dayn* (a generic or abstract obligation), not *'ayn* (unique or concrete property), then doesn't trading in it fall under the ban on trading in *dayn*?
- If on the other hand the usufruct is *'ayn*, then isn't re-selling it like selling *'ayn* property that does not yet exist or that the seller does not yet own — both banned?

For reasons explained in Chapter 6, a positive answer to either of these questions would block trading in the usufructs. But these questions may reflect a mistaken view of the situation, for several reasons. First, usufructs in specific equipment (as here) are ordinarily not considered *dayn* but *'ayn*. Second, in any lease the entire stream of the usufruct except for the present instant lies in the future and does not yet exist. It can never be combined in a single package or rendered secure from destruction. Third, no one but the primary lessee owns the usufruct for the future period. If the above doubts posed valid objections, then postponed leases (as sale of future usufructs) would not have been allowed at all, or would have been only with immediate full payment. Fourth, experience shows the good sense of allowing sale and resale of postponed leases — for example, in the sale and resale of airline tickets or of leases on future weeks in vacation apartments.[13] Fifth, leases, due to their natural futurity, are allowed greater degrees of uncertainty (*gharar*) than other transactions. But even if all these arguments in favor of negotiability are rejected, only securitization and negotiability of the primary lease interests is lost, and much of value remains in the proposal.

This mechanism could be an investment device for a single Islamic bank. For example, a bank negotiates a lease with a user, splits the years of the lease into separate sub-leases, takes the earlier maturities for itself — gaining an advantageous rate of return for such maturities — and sells the remaining maturities to its customers.

It may be important for the pool *mudaraba* to make a market in the various primary lease classes. Initially at least this would be a buy-back operation, not a genuine secondary market. Primary lessees might demand such liquidity if they were obliged to pay for their primary leases in advance when entering into them.

A single Islamic bank may wish to develop this proposal in its simplest form, with a single sub-lessee and several primary lessees. But as each component of the scheme is multiplied, the idea could rapidly gain attractiveness through enhanced diversification and liquidity for the investors. The primary lessee could hedge out credit risks at the end-user sub-lessee level by investing in a broad portfolio of such sub-leases. If all the leases were for similar equipment, this would still leave the primary lessee with risks associated with a particular industry (such as the airplane or airline business). If desired, these risks could be reduced by diversifying the equipment portfolio. Similarly, as noted above, one could substitute a sub-*mudaraba* for the primary lessee, which could gather a number of investors. This would make it simpler to provide for liquidity in the primary lessee's investment and would diversify credit risks for the *mudaraba*. The final step would be to incorporate the staged-lease feature into the super-pool conception of the previous section, where it fulfills a particularly powerful and desirable role.

An Islamic Convertible Lease

Company's need: (for a relatively young business enterprise with high growth prospects) financing for real assets while avoiding long-term

---

[13]For this analogy I am indebted to Dr. Munawar Iqbal of IRTI, Islamic Development Bank.

fixed obligations, as well as increasing its equity capital base at favorable prices.

Investor's need: to invest in a small but potentially high-growth business, while gaining some protection by taking a senior position in its capital structure. Conventionally, this situation might call for a convertible bond secured by tangible assets, but such an instrument offends Islamic principles.

Proposed contract: The investor offers the business a fixed-rate full-payout lease with an option for the lessor to convert to equity by exchanging the remaining rent obligation for shares of the lessee at certain points during the life of the lease. The conversion is priced according to the prevailing fair market value of the equity at the time of conversion. Because of the eroding capital investment inherent in the lease contract, the dollar amount of the conversion privilege declines over time.

Case example: The Greylock Management Co., a Boston-based venture capital firm, has been introduced to a recently established Islamically-run electronics business in Kuwait with bright prospects. Greylock is interested in investing but is nervous about patent protection for the company's proprietary technology and about the political stability of the region. The electronics company is unable to sell Greylock a secured convertible debt security because of religious legal restrictions. Instead, it arranges for Greylock to purchase equipment, which the company would itself have purchased with Greylock's capital contribution, and to lease the equipment from Greylock. This provides Greylock with lien protection in the event that the company runs into trouble. In the lease contract, the parties agree that Greylock may convert its remaining capitalized lease value (presumed equal to the equipment's value) into shares of the company either at the prevailing book value or at the price of the last equity financing if one has occurred within the last three months.

Because of the presence of the convertibility option, the annual lease payment is smaller than it would otherwise be. In the event that Greylock does convert into the common, it could materially increase the company's equity base and clear the way for further debt financing from other sources.

A conventional convertible bond gives the bondholder the right to exchange the face value of the debt for equity in the company, usually at a pre-agreed price. The lease arrangement just described is targeted at the same result. To be Islamically correct, however, the lease must have the following characteristics:

- The conversion right is not legally binding on the lessee, but is a matter of honor, a "gentlemen's agreement." Otherwise, the right represents at best a future sale of stock in an unknown quantity and conversion price in exchange for debt (*dayn*), with an option (*khiyar al-shart*) and without present payment. The parties may feel little concern over the unenforceability of the agreement, since the conversion option will be invoked only if the business succeeds and therefore is concerned with maintaining its good faith with investors.[14]
- Valuation of shares purchased on conversion must be the fair value of the shares at the time of the conversion, since otherwise the equity interest of the other capital investors in the lessee would be impermissibly diluted without compensation.

For a publicly traded company, the fair value of the stock is the last trade price. But if, as is more likely, the borrower is not publicly traded, then a proxy for fair market value is needed. We propose that if a private placement offering of equity is done within three months of the conversion date, the conversion should occur at the same price as that offering; otherwise, the book value of the equity on the date of the conversion should be the price reference. Because book value reflects the cumulative investment (including retained earnings or losses) of the incumbent investors, it achieves the capital parity between investors that Islamic law requires. Also supporting this approach is the fact that Islamic financial institutions commonly use accounting methods to evaluate equity interests in *mudaraba*s on the occasion of any change in shareholding or membership.

---

[14]The result is similar to a term, approved by the OIC Fiqh Academy, in a *muqarada* bond by which the issuer (non-bindingly) promises to redeem the bond for a price to be determined at redemption using expert valuation and then agreed to by both sides. Decision 5, fourth session (1988), *Fiqh Academy Journal.*

The valuation of the conversion option could not closely follow conventional theoretical models because the conversion price of an Islamic instrument would be a floating one. However, assuming that the current equity book value was used in determining the conversion price, the value of the option would be considerable in any fast-growing business, for two reasons:

- equity book value typically does not include good will value (which ought to be considerable);
- equity book value would reflect the negative earnings that also characterize many businesses in their "ramp-up" phase of growth.

Even if a round of equity financing has taken place within the suggested three-month period (and substituted as the appropriate price reference point), that price will reflect the latest investors' demands for a future return on their capital, which ought also to satisfy the lessor who is converting into equity at the same time.

A variety of target markets exist for Islamic convertible leases. Two worth special attention are 1) conventional ventures seeking financial leverage at attractive all-in costs and good terms, and 2) Islamic ventures — particularly those in developing countries where this may be the *only* source of investment capital.

For conventional capital users seeking the most attractive funding sources, an Islamically-structured convertible lease could be enticing: in exchange for the conversion option, the lessor could reasonably agree to annual lease payments lower than those of a straight lease. This would reduce the cash flow burden to the enterprise, which is usually strapped for cash during the early phases of growth. Alternatively, an Islamic convertible lease could allow the enterprise to take on more debt (in this case, lease) obligations than otherwise because the annual cash flow burden would be lower per unit of leased asset. This would reduce the need to raise straight equity funds and thus curb the dilution of the existing investors' equity.

Both Islamic and non-Islamic investors would find benefits in Islamic convertible leases. For Islamic investors, Islamic convertible leases with conventional ventures would be a way to diversify their investment portfolios, especially if they could be pooled into a fund of many such leases. It would also offer a practical way to gain access to the conventional economic sector and yet conform to Islamic legal principles. For conventional investors, a pool of convertible leases selected and monitored by professional, well-regarded *mudaribs* could be a welcome opportunity to make equity investments at tolerable levels of risk in emerging countries.

Finally, it would be possible to securitize the contract pools and sell them in a secondary market, thus creating the short-term liquidity which Islamic investors indicate is a priority. Since these securitized "units" would represent direct claims on real assets, they are tradeable under Islamic legal rules.

PROPOSALS FOR INNOVATIONS RELATED TO *ISTISNA'*

This section puts forward a number of proposals using *istisna'*, arranged in ascending order of complication. Several of these proposals are legally unremarkable, or are currently practiced in the marketplace. But others, particularly the last in the series, are unconventional and controversial.

Back-to-Back *Istisna'* Contracts

Company's need: not to pay the full cost at the front end of an expensive, made-to-order product requiring a long manufacturing process. Likewise, the manufacturer finds it burdensome to carry the work-in-process inventory if the payment is delayed until the product is ready for delivery.

Investor's need: longer-term investments yielding returns that are superior to run-of-the-mill trade financing. At the same time, the investor wants to curtail risks.

Proposed contract: Two *istisna'* contracts are employed, involving the manufacturer, a bank, and the firm that is the ultimate purchaser of the contracted good.

Case example: The Saudi Shipping Company is negotiating with Seoul Shipbuilding Group to construct a new 100,000-ton tanker. Saudi Shipping is in a liquidity bind, and Seoul Shipbuilding needs working capital to purchase materials and to pay labor and overhead as construction of the tanker progresses. Saudi Shipping arranges an

279

istisna' transaction, purchasing the tanker from Bahrain Islamic Bank (BIB). Under the terms of this contract, Saudi Shipping will begin making payments to BIB when the tanker is two-thirds completed and will continue these payments for twelve months after the tanker is delivered. BIB, now as buyer, negotiates another *istisna'* contract with Seoul Shipbuilding for the construction of the tanker, with payments paralleling work progress.

Istisna' is flexible as to payment terms, permitting payment either at the time of contract, by installments, by progress payment, at delivery, or over a period of time after delivery. The following step-by-step progression exploits this flexibility.

1. In the simplest case, the purchaser, e.g., a shipping company, buys a tanker from the manufacturer by *istisna'*, making progress payments. The shipping company finances the production of the ship.
2. A bank is introduced into the process with a back-to-back *istisna'*. The shipping company purchases a tanker as before, but from the bank, with payments as agreed. The bank purchases the tanker from the manufacturer by a second *istisna'*, perhaps paying cash. This allows the bank to finance either the purchase or the manufacture, or both. (This practice is already in wide use.)
3. The financing is securitized by replacing the bank in scenario (2) with a *mudaraba* fund, perhaps managed by the bank. The *mudaraba* fund holds the investment until its termination, and then distributes the profits according to the agreed shares. While awaiting the termination, may the capital investors in the *mudaraba* buy and sell their interests to each other or to the fund? Such a result would depend on securing a *shari'a* opinion (highly unlikely at first glance) that the buyer's interest in an *istisna'* contract represents most fundamentally not a *dayn* but an *'ayn*, i.e., not an obligation of the seller to produce a described good, but an ownership right in a tangible thing (the manufactured *'ayn* under production).[15]
4. Back-to-back *istisna'* contracts are multiplied and organized, as in the leasing pool proposal, with various types of *istisna'* obligations

---

[15]Recall that the Hanafis describe *istisna'* as the purchase of an *'ayn*.

assigned to various pools of investors, so that an investor may choose a particular type of *istisna'* investment (a particular industry, term, currency, exposure, etc.). But the payoff from organizing such pools is less than in a lease because the *istisna'* pools lack the float or periodicity feature, and very likely the negotiability feature. The staging feature in leasing (being able to separate out maturity "slices" of the investment), while difficult to mimic, could be done by using contracts for future manufactures, such as the tenth Boeing 777 off the assembly line, or the hundredth mile of a highway project.

Options in *Istisna'* Contracts

Company's need: an option to cancel an order of new equipment that will take some time to produce. This would obviously be a negative from the viewpoint of the manufacturer.

Investor's need: for an investor providing financing to the buyer through a back-to-back *istisna'* arrangement, to give the buyer this option, but only if it can cancel its own *istisna'* contract with the manufacturer.

Proposed contract: An *istisna'* contract is structured with an *'arbun*, permitting the buyer to cancel the contract at will at the loss of a prepaid penalty. If the buyer does not cancel, the prepaid sum is credited to the purchase price. The *'arbun* penalty is fixed at a value that will compensate the manufacturer for the costs of providing the option and for losses in the event of its exercise. In a back-to-back *istisna'*, both contracts have *'arbun* provisions. The first contract's *'arbun* (paid by the buyer to the financing entity) compensates that entity for the costs of providing the failed financing and for the *'arbun* it in turn pays to the manufacturer.

Case example: Kuwait Airways wants to purchase ten new Boeing 777 aircraft for delivery in two years' time. Boeing requires progress payments roughly paralleling the growing value of the partially completed planes and an *istisna'* contract is drawn up. However, Kuwait Airways is uncertain about the level of future demand and wants the right to cancel the order at any time within the first year of the agreement. The purchaser (with or without a back-to-back *istisna'* arrangement providing financing) contracts an *'arbun* with a nonrefundable deposit that will properly compensate Boeing (and any financing intermediary) for losses and inconvenience if the cancellation option is exercised.

One aspect of the *istisna'* contract needing exploration is the extent to which it tolerates options under Islamic law. In the form discussed here, *istisna'* is purely a Hanafi conception, since only that school approves of it. According to the majority Hanafi opinion, the contract is not binding, meaning both parties are free to cancel an *istisna'* at any time until the purchaser receives and approves the goods. Therefore, if we add an option to the minority Hanafi opinion for which *istisna'* is binding, it hardly seems a radical step. For example, the purchaser of an airplane could reserve an option to cancel purchase of a Boeing aircraft up until a specified time (*khiyar al-shart*). Presumably, in *istisna'* logic, this contract is permissible even if the airplane does not now exist and is not uniquely identified, but is simply one of the planes being manufactured that meet the specifications. If this is the case, then it should also be possible for the purchaser to contract an *'arbun*, in which he makes a nonrefundable deposit to support the above option.[16]

Investors could make a hedge on a particular industry (such as the airline or oil industries) by using an *istisna'* with *'arbun* to purchase one or more of the capital goods employed in that industry.

Istisna' Contracts for Manufacturing Streams

Company's need: if a manufacturer, to obtain financing for goods-in-process; if a user of items manufactured by others, to order such items

---

[16]This point was brought to our attention by Dr. Mohamed Elgari during his visit to Harvard in January 1996. This approach might be indictable as *talfiq*, i.e., a "patched-up" combination of school views. Only the Hanbali school allows the *'arbun* option, while only the Hanafi school allows *istisna'* without prepayment. If the bases on which these two schools propound their respective opinions are inconsistent, the combination of their views is improper. This does not appear to be the case here, since the two legal institutions address different problems.

without having to pay the entire cost at the time of order, and also to hedge against unfavorable price changes.

Investor's need: short-term outlets for funds at attractive profit rates, and the ability to hedge against either price or credit risks.

Proposed contract: An *istisna'* contract purchases a piece of the output of a manufacturing or construction process. There could be a series of *istisna'* contracts allowing investors to choose the maturities (the specific segments) they want.

Case example: The Government of Malaysia is building a twenty-mile highway and awards the contract to the Regional Construction Company (RCC). RCC goes to the Islamic Bank of Malaysia (IBM) and negotiates an *istisna'* contract for the construction of the highway in one-mile increments. IBM advances the funds for each individual mile at the time of actual construction. When RCC delivers to IBM the completed one-mile segment, IBM in turn sells the segment to the Malaysian Government in a cash or credit (deferred payment) sale.

Case example: The Indonesian Shoe Company has received an order for three million pairs of shoes to be delivered in six months and needs financing for these shoes while they are being manufactured. The Islamic Bank of Malaysia (IBM) agrees to buy the shoes specified in the purchase order and to make progress payments to Indonesian Shoe as the order is manufactured. IBM will then deliver the shoes to the customer for a cash payment.

In these two case examples, the investor (banker) has moved away from purchasing a specific manufactured item to purchasing part of a production stream: e.g., a particular stretch of highway or a particular stream of manufactured goods coming off an assembly line.

The danger in this arrangement (particularly in the latter example) is that it crosses the line into *salam*, which is the usual contract for purchase of generic or abstract goods for future delivery (*dayn*). If one buys a million shoes off an assembly line, is one not really buying the shoes as future fungible and generic goods, and should one not be following the rules of *salam*? Isn't the fact of manufacture here a rather slim reed, since the shoes may be almost as generic as wheat? We raised this dilemma in Chapter 6: how should one treat contracts for the manufacture of fungibles — as *salam* or as *istisna*?

In the first case example above — highway construction — the thirteenth mile segment (for instance) could easily be taken as not only a manufactured item but as a unique one, making *istisna*ʿ thoroughly appropriate. Real estate always has a high degree of specificity. An alternative approach to the same result is the modern construction contract which, even in Saudi Arabia where Hanbali law is ordinarily applied, is accorded a treatment similar to *istisna*ʿ in allowing delays in payment.

What about streams of manufacture from factories? What if one bought a million pairs of a specific type of shoe from a particular manufacturer, such as Nike? Such shoes no doubt are fungible to some extent, within a particular brand name and model. (Anything can be either fungible or unique, depending on the distance from which we view it.) But in such a contract one is financing a specific manufacturer and a specific process, unlike in *salam* where one may not stipulate any particular production process or source. Are not some of the risks of a single process present in the shoe contract (e.g., loss of shipment at sea leading to cancellation of the contract)? One might make the contract even more specific, by specifying a particular factory or even a particular million shoes of that factory's assembly line (e.g., the third million). Very likely the purchaser is not attracted by the hope of profiting on the market for shoes (which would be assisted by their generic quality if any) but by the opportunity to finance a particular manufacturing process.

As noted in Chapter 6, currently Islamic finance appears to follow a rule of thumb that if a transaction involves manufacture it may treated as an *istisna*ʿ.[17] If such is the rule, we should explore the consequences by taking a further step. What if *istisna*ʿ were used to finance the manufacture of generic items, such as gasoline, for which an active market exists? This is the subject of the next proposal.

Fungible Manufactures and Options

Company's need: if a manufacturer, to find buyers for excess capacity and financing for that production; if the consumer of a fungible, to

---

[17]Consensus of Workshop on the Harvard Islamic Finance Project, Islamic Research and Training Institute, Islamic Development Bank, Jedda, 23 September 1996.

lock in a supply of goods at an attractive price without having to pre-pay the entire order, and to be able to escape from these commitments if business circumstances change.

Investor's need: to take a position in a fungible good but to obtain a hedge in the event that business circumstances change in the future.

Proposed contract: An *istisna'* contract finances manufactured output but with the right of cancellation. An *'arbun* payment at the outset is both a down payment on the *istisna'* and also a fee forfeited on cancellation. Such a contract could be offered on an organized commodities market.

Case example: To secure a future supply of jet fuel and to hedge against price changes, Middle East Airlines approaches the Bahrain National Petroleum Co. with a proposal to purchase a twenty-million-gallon piece of the oil company's future output. A down payment in the form of an *'arbun* is negotiated. The airline can cancel the order at any time prior to the actual starting date for the refining of that particular twenty million gallons.

This *istisna'* proposal combines all the features of preceding *istisna'* proposals, and is therefore susceptible to all their weaknesses and uncertainties. It proposes using *istisna'* to finance the manufacture of highly fungible goods for which an active market exists, and it proposes including an option for the buyer. Combining fungibility and option allows use of the contract to hedge, indeed to speculate, on the market price of the goods under contract. In the example above, if the price of jet fuel moved below the purchase price minus the down payment or *'arbun*, the airline could cancel its order, losing its *'arbun*. The net effect is a call option at the contract price, with no obligation for advance payment other than the *'arbun*.

This result would be impossible under classical rules for *salam*, because these rules do not admit of options of any kind, and require advance payment in full.

Even this proposal can be taken a step further by offering an *istisna'* contract in gasoline on an organized market that brings together suppliers of gasoline (manufacturers or intermediaries for them using back-to-back *istisna'* contracts) with buyers of gasoline.[18] Such contracts would require no advance payment and, as we have seen, may permit an option feature.

It is unknown how far in this progression scholars of Islamic law will be willing to go. If not all the way, then where in the sequence, and with what criteria, will they reinstate the rules applying to *salam*?

JI'ALA (REWARD)

In conventional finance, employee stock options give managers the right to share in, and an incentive to increase, the wealth accruing to the equity owners of the company. In Islamic law, conventional options — including options on stock — are difficult or impossible in most contexts. But reconstruing the issue as employee compensation and reward rather than as a potential stock purchase creates a likely avenue for another Islamic contract, *ji'ala*.

> *Company's need*: to give its employees incentives to meet specific performance goals.

> *The contract*: A company offers an employee a bonus for attaining a certain goal. The bonus is denominated in stock, which presumably gains in value from the employee's achievement.

> *Case examples*: The CEO of a recently-privatized and stockholder-owned national airline is promised a bonus of fifty thousand shares of the company's stock if he successfully enters into certain collaborative agreements with other international airlines. In another example, a company offers its CEO a bonus of a certain number of shares for each percentage point of improvement in the company's productivity.

Relevant to this example are two Islamic contracts, reward (*ji'ala*) and hire (*ijara*). As we have seen, Islamic law allows one to offer a reward (*ji'ala*) to anyone who performs a particular act. As in *ijara*, in *ji'ala* the compensation for services, the reward, must be reasonably well fixed and known in advance. But in *ijara* some scholars have allowed a principal to compensate its employee or agent with a fee (*ju'l*) related directly to the success of the ser-

---

[18]Decision 65/1/7, seventh session (1992), *Fiqh Academy Journal*, 711, 717 suggests possible use of *istisna'* contracts in a hypothetical commodities market run according to Islamic legal principles.

vices the latter provides. For example, a homeowner may tell an agent, "Sell my house for at least $100,000. Your fee will be the amount, if any, by which the sale price exceeds $100,000." Or one may pay a sales agent a certain sum for every unit the agent sells. Or one may compensate an agent with a share in the profits of a venture: for example, a farmer may hire a worker to harvest his fields for a share of the yield; the owner of a truck may hire a worker to do hauling services for others by providing him with the truck and sharing the resulting profits.[19] (Such cases have similarities to *mudaraba*.) Note that in all these cases, while the payment relates to the agent's success, that success is also very closely connected to the agent's efforts or actions. Otherwise excessive uncertainty and risk, even gambling, would result.

Using these concepts, we propose an Islamic contract by which a company would set for an officer a particular achievement goal related causally to his personal efforts, such as obtaining a particular license or achieving a certain level of sales, and reward him with a certain sum of money if the goal is reached. This bonus could also be defined as so many shares of stock, the value of which may have increased because of his success.[20] Alternatively, the bonus could be proportional to the degree of success achieved, such as so much cash or so many shares of stock for each percentage point of improvement. Or where the offeree's control over a venture is considerable, he could be rewarded with a percentage of the profits of that venture.

Note that the conventional executive stock option, by which, in net effect, the employee is granted a cash bonus in the amount of any excess in the value of the company's stock over the exercise price of the option at the time the option is exercised, would probably be Islamically invalid, since the amount of the bonus is currently unknown and because the connection between the executive's personal efforts and an increase in the stock price is too remote.[21]

---

[19]Qari, art. 659; Ibn Taymiyya, *Qawa'id*, 184.

[20]Since the amount of the bonus must be fixed and known from the time of the contract, the shares must be seen as fixed shares of the company's concrete assets and the company must not significantly alter the composition of its assets in the meantime.

[21]This construes an option contract not as a literal option but as a conditional grant of a bonus in the amount of the gain the stock option would yield. To frame a bonus as an option contract arouses additional Islamic legal difficulties, as explained in Chapter 6, 164-65.

CONCLUSIONS

The above proposals are no doubt only a modest sample of the innovations in Islamic finance waiting in the wings. We have presented merely those that occur to us; others closer to the practice than we are can no doubt suggest many more.

Successful and beneficial innovations always share a few common features: they are more useful to users than are existing forms; they allow users to retain many beliefs or practices they value; and they open the door to still greater possibilities. A mundane example of this is the computer-based word processor, an innovation in the development, manipulation, storage, and transmission of text and graphics. The word processor has a greater range of uses and capabilities than the typewriter but does not require users to change valued existing protocols with respect to the content, form, or expression of language; users can carry over acquired skills in typing, editing, and so forth. At the same time, the word processor has made many other things possible, such as desktop publishing; easy incorporation of illustrations, charts, graphs, and even videos; and internet publication.

Successful innovation in Islamic banking and finance may have similar characteristics. It would preserve what is essential about the Islamic heritage in law and economics, while also vastly improving on past commercial techniques, and enabling Muslims to join in, and effectively compete in, world economic and commercial advances.

To us such innovation poses the following challenges for its practitioners:

- To address directly the needs of Islamic finance, viewed as both independent and in competition with conventional approaches, and to understand these needs in conceptual and functional terms;
- To make innovations that concur with the fundamental precepts, ideals, norms, and rules of Islamic law (*shari'a*), not merely those made possible by the coincidence of one or more medieval rulings with the features of a contemporary transaction;
- Yet increasingly to seek changes in Islamic law (*fiqh*) to address the fundamentally different circumstances in which commercial life now occurs, especially where existing Islamic contractual arrangements do not serve the ideals of Islamic law. Of new proposals and of existing Islamic banking and financial techniques it must be asked: is the

technique not only efficient but morally sound — in a broad Islamic sense? If a technique fails this test, then before rejecting it one must ask whether ways exist, such as through systematic or institutional innovations, to constrain or redirect the technique toward justice;

- To strive to convey to both participants and non-participants in Islamic banking and finance not only the economic but also the moral and legal conceptions that shaped classical Islamic law (*fiqh*), and to show how these conceptions survive in the modern theory and practice of Islamic finance. Not only the theories, but also the practices, of Islamic finance must be fully disclosed and understood by both consumers and outside observers.

Conclusion

The objective of this book has been to introduce the subject of Islamic banking and finance, explaining it in terms of both Islamic religious law and secular Western finance and law, and both theoretically and in concrete application.

This task drew us first to the revealed texts of the Qur'an and the Sunna, and then into the religious law and the complex corpus of legal rules derived from those revealed texts, exploring some of the legal principles that lend system and coherence to those rules. We detected a number of underlying goals and values (ethical, economic, financial, legal, religious, and social) that help to explain these rules and principles. Then we compared these texts, rules, and principles with conceptions and practices of modern conventional law and finance. These comparisons afford a dynamic understanding of contemporary Islamic financial institutions and instruments, one that encompasses both their past and their possible futures. The study has given us an appreciation for the richness of the classical Islamic legal heritage in commerce and finance, but also for the challenge Muslims face in applying that heritage to modern life.

Because we have often been submerged in the details, a reminder may be useful of some of the substantive ideals that Islamic finance seeks to fulfill, many of which would also appeal to those of different cultural and religious backgrounds.

- Commerce and profit-making work is encouraged, and property respected. Wealth is a positive good, but from it a portion is owed to the community and those less fortunate.

- Entrepreneurship is encouraged, with work and capital given equal credit for generating wealth. Capital suppliers are to be compensated *pari passu* rather than by the hierarchy of claims that characterizes most Western capital structures.
- If a business fails, the active partner loses his investment of time but capital losses fall only on those contributing capital. Those holding debts of a failed entrepreneur must help bear his misfortune, since they can neither get a binding judgment against him until his situation improves nor impose penalties for his delay in paying.
- While interest-lending is forbidden, suppliers of capital are not prevented from earning a profit on their capital appropriate to the duration of their commitment and its exposure to risk.
- Since exposure to risk is what justifies profit, efforts to shift that risk to another party may be disapproved. Some forms of risk shifting are legitimate, however, but not if they lead to gambling or excessive speculation.

Islamic finance is now on the verge of either major transformation, or a period of frustration and probable decline. If this turning point is negotiated successfully, Islamic finance will enter a new and even more successful era. Until now Islamic finance has largely been confined to the activities of Islamic banks which have tried to practice a Muslim version of conventional retail commercial banking. Elementary knowledge of Islamic law shows, however, that retail commercial banking is one of the most difficult commercial functions to perform in a religiously acceptable manner. Legal rules force Islamic banks to forego two basic features of conventional commercial banking — security for deposits against losses (achieved conventionally through the concepts of depositor seniority in banks' capital structures as well as supplemental deposit insurance) and stability and predictability of returns on the bank's assets (achieved through senior interest-bearing loans to a diversified portfolio of borrowers). Regardless of theory, Islamic banks have found that their competitive and regulatory context compels them to mimic conventional banks in both of these characteristics, pushing them into short-term, low-risk investments in an effort to offer their depositors returns similar in quantity and risk to those obtained by conventional depositors. This circumstance, and others, have prevented them from becoming the profit-and-loss investment intermediaries that Islamic economic theory demands. This in turn causes them both a legal and a financial embarrassment — a legal embarrassment because Islamic banks have survived not on profit-and-loss principles (*mudaraba*) but via markup (*murabaha*) transactions, some of which have been condemned as "synthetic" interest substitutes; and a financial embarrassment because the greater complexity and the shorter term of their investments place Islamic banks at a competitive disadvantage to conventional banks; some are saved only by the loyalty of their base of religious customers.

An answer to both the legal and financial embarrassments is for banks to diversify away from the retail commercial banking mode, toward various flexible forms of intermediation, increasingly common in today's financial environment, that permit genuine profit-sharing. One obvious possibility is the use of various kinds of pooled funds, which by diversification can reduce the risk of profit-sharing investments, even longer-term ones, and which, by being tradeable on secondary markets, achieve a liquidity approaching that of conventional bank deposits. In this scenario, Islamic financial institutions would increasingly concentrate on creating and managing such funds. Islamic banks per se would no longer be the chief medium for Islamic investment; they would exist to help market these funds, to provide highly secure deposits, and to provide certain other banking services of convenience.

The necessary Islamic legal infrastructure for moving in this direction is now being laid. Much of the work is well along — for example, developing the Islamic legal conceptions and rules that govern the creation of new financial instruments and when they can be traded. But much more needs doing — for example, developing doctrines governing the creation and regulation of an Islamic public financial market. If theoretical and practical solutions for these various problems are successfully put in place, Islamic finance will be able to escape some of the constraints on its operations and to compete more effectively with conventional finance.

Much evidence suggests that the pool of Islamically-invested funds is large and growing, and is attracting Western vendors as well as Islamic intermediaries. But at the same time, modern-day Islamic banking arose and persisted because of its religious cachet, by responding to a core group of religious depositors. This remains a fair description of its position today. The question arises: if the industry seeks to expand beyond this niche status and fulfill a larger function in the world financial system, will it have the reserves for innovation and development needed to adapt, and moreover to meet inevitably harsher competition as the world financial system becomes more integrated?

While a final answer to this complex question is not possible at this point, our study suggests several reasons for optimism. We uncovered no insurmountable legal or financial obstacle to the longer-term success of Islamic finance. Islamic law possesses rich resources, many still untapped, for flexibility and development. A few of these resources are exemplified by the financial innovations modeled in Chapter 10.

Islamic finance has several comparative advantages that favor its survival and growth. Most obvious is its religious appeal to Muslim capital providers and users. This advantage is perennial: Islamic propriety in finance is not merely a matter of form or labels, but arouses complex religious, social, moral, and legal issues that will engage Muslims for many years to come. Another advantage is the greater familiarity and comfort of international Islamic financial institutions with Muslim-world and even third-world investment environments, compared with conventional counterparts. A third advantage is that the industry, propelled by Islamic law, is developing specialization and sophistication in several lines of business such as international markup trade financing and equipment leasing.

Does Islamic law (*fiqh*), as elaborated by the scholars and institutions devoted to it, have the potential to meet all the needs of modern Muslims in the commercial and financial sector, in the traditional sense of offering normative guidance for various aspects of daily life? A success in this field would augur well for the law's extending its influence to other aspects of public life in Islamic societies now almost entirely unaffected by it, such as constitutional law, state economy (taxes, social services), public administration, or educational reform.

Contemporary *fiqh* has shown much capacity for development already, in permitting modern Islamic banking and finance to emerge in their present form. The solutions the scholars have reached have been generally accepted by participants as religiously sound. But much concern and even suspicion remain. Participants, both customers and practitioners, are lately demanding that the financial institutions achieve even higher degrees of religious legal compliance. For example, many now demand that the banks eliminate or reduce use of "synthetic" *murabaha* transactions. This new atmosphere of religious strictness now is combining with competitive pressures from the marketplace (such as the need to invest longer-term to improve returns on investments) to push banks and their religious-legal advisory boards into new and uncharted territory.

For these reasons, the Islamic law of finance faces a need for even more ambitious innovation. Difficult issues on the table include developing marketable instruments, organizing financial markets, making future promises binding, and creating tools for risk management. The highly conservative approach of the Islamic legal scholars guiding Islamic banking — for example clinging to past scholars' opinions, categories, and forms of legal reasoning; or failing to deal systematically with the radical change of circumstances in modern times — may not prove adequate for such new challenges and may need to be augmented by bolder techniques. The creation of a number of institutions (such as the Fiqh Academy, associations of Islamic banks, international standards organizations, and others discussed in Chapter 2) increases the capacity for ordered, systematic legal development to meet these challenges, and should aid scholars in overcoming their past cautiousness. They help religious-legal scholars tap the expertise of others, particularly Islamic economists and bankers. Also, these institutions may be able to introduce uniformity of legal opinion where it is needed for Islamic financial development. While the present variations in individual banks' rules and contracts do reflect healthy exploration and experimentation on the part of their shari'a boards, they also retard the emergence of traded financial instruments and of a financial market, which depend on uniformity.

No doubt many of the legal challenges now facing Islamic finance are disquieting and difficult — such as creating derivatives or other risk-hedging devices or encouraging trade in financial instruments. If *fiqh* scholars take too cautious and literalist an approach, backing away from the deeper comparative and functional analysis and bolder legal reasoning or *ijtihad* which is now needed, Islamic finance could languish. Given the record to now, however, we are optimistic about the future.

Glossary

'adam — nonexistence; nonexistence of the object of a contract, often leading to finding of *gharar*

abdān — a type of partnership to which partners contribute only their labor

akl al-māl bi-al-bāṭil — unjust or wrongful taking (lit., eating or consuming) of property; see Qur'ān, e.g., 4:29

'ahd — injunction, pledge, vow, compact, contract, obligation, promise

al-kāli' bi-al-kāli' — see *kāli'*

al-kharāj bi-al-ḍamān — see *kharāj bi-al-ḍamān*

amāna — the status or duty of a trusted person (*amīn*); one of two basic relationships toward property, which entails absence of liability for loss except in breach of duty; compare *ḍamān*

amīn — trustworthy person, trustee; one enjoying the relationship toward property of *amāna*

'aqd — lit., knot, tie; obligation, compact; the conclusion or ratification of a compact or oath; in *fiqh*, juridical act; more narrowly, legal relationship created by offer and acceptance

'arbūn — down payment; a nonrefundable deposit paid by a buyer retaining a right to confirm or cancel the sale

'āriya — gratuitous loan of nonconsumable property; the gift of usufruct

'ayb — defect; defect in goods giving purchaser a right to cancel the sale

'ayn — an existent, tangible thing considered as unique and individual; a thing (Latin, *res*) as opposed to its usufruct (*manfa'a*); thus, antonyms include genus, *dayn*, fungible, thing in the *dhimma*, and usufruct; present coins.

bāṭil — nugatory, void, false, what is wrongful

bay' — sale

bay' mu'ajjal — credit sale, sale with payment of the price at a specified later time

bay' al-wafā' — sale with a right in the seller to repurchase (redeem) the property by refunding the purchase price

bay'atān (or *bay'atayn*) *fī bay'a* — lit., two sales in one sale, prohibited by a *hadīth;* scholars differ as to its meanings

ḍamān — (1) contract of guarantee (also called *kafāla*); (2) one of two basic relationships toward property, entailing bearing the risk of its loss; compare *amāna*

ḍamān al-'aqd — lit., *ḍamān* of the contract; liability for harm to sale object in contract of sale

ḍāmin — one who bears *ḍamān*

ḍarar — damage, harm, loss

dayn — generic property; property defined or contracted for only by its genus, species and other characteristics (usually fungibles); any property, not an *'ayn*, that a debtor owes, either now or in the future; such property when due in the future; compare *'ayn*

dhimma — (lit., compact, bond, obligation, responsibility, protection, security) a faculty in an individual by which he accepts duty and obligation

fāsid — invalid, void, voidable, corrupt, unsound

faskh — termination; cancellation, rescission

fatwā — (pl. *fatāwā*) an authoritative legal opinion issued by a scholar of *fiqh*

fiqh — lit., understanding; the science of law; the corpus juris of classical Islamic law

furū' — (sing., *far'*) lit., branches; the derived rules of *fiqh*

ghabn — lesion (Latin, *laesio*)

gharar — lit., peril, risk, hazard; risk, uncertainty

ghaṣb — usurpation, the invasion of property rights in an open and flagrant manner

ḥadīth — lit., report; historical account of a saying, act, or omission of the Prophet or, secondarily, of an esteemed figure among his companions and early Muslim generations

ḥalāl — lawful, licit

Ḥanafī — one of the four Sunni schools of law, founded by Abū Ḥanīfa

Ḥanbalī — one of the four Sunni schools of law, founded by Aḥmad Ibn Ḥanbal

ḥawāla — contract of assignment of debt

hiba — contract of gift

ḥiyal — (sing., *ḥīla*), legal artifices or stratagems

ḥukm — court judgment; value assigned by *fiqh* to an act

i'āra — same as *'āriya*

'ibādāt — acts of worship; compare *mu'āmalāt*

ibāḥa — permissibility; neutrality of moral value; presumption in *fiqh* that acts are permissible until a revealed proof to the contrary is established

iḍāfa — a stipulation delaying the commencement of a contract performance to a specific time

ījāb — offer; see *qabūl*

ijāra — contract of lease and hire; sale of usufruct

ijmā' — unanimous agreement of all qualified *fiqh* scholars of an age; one of the four roots (*uṣūl*) of *fiqh*

ijtihād — lit., personal effort; the effort by a qualified *fiqh* scholar to determine the true ruling of the divine law in a matter on which the revelation is not explicit or certain

'illa — lit., cause; the basis for an analogy (*qiyās*) between a case as to which the divine law ruling is known and another case the ruling for which is unknown; the characteristic of a case which, when it is found to exist in other cases, justifies applying to those cases the same *fiqh* ruling

'īna — double-sale by which the borrower and the lender sell and then re-sell an object between them, once for cash and once for a higher price on credit, with the net result a loan with interest

'inān — form of partnership in which each partner contributes both capital and work (using the Ḥanbalī definition)

istiḥsān — doctrine allowing exceptions to strict legal reasoning, or guiding choice among possible legal outcomes, when considerations of human welfare so demand

istiṣnā' — contract providing for the manufacture and purchase of a specified item

itlāf — destruction, harm; tort to property

jā'iz — (1) permissible, lawful, licit, valid; (2) term designating contracts as to which one party or both has the right to terminate the contract at any time with prospective effect

jahāla — ignorance, lack of knowledge; indefiniteness in a contract, often leading to finding of *gharar*

ji'āla — contract of reward; a unilateral contract promising a reward for a specific act or accomplishment

kafāla — contract of guarantee (also called *ḍamān;* see)

kāli' — something delayed; appears in a maxim forbidding the sale of *al-kāli' bi-al-kāli'*, i.e., the exchange of a delayed countervalue for another delayed countervalue

kharāj — yield, profit, gain

kharāj bi-al-ḍamān — lit., gain accompanies liability for loss; a *hadīth* and legal maxim and principle

khiyār — a power to annul or cancel a contract; option

khiyār al-majlis — lit., option of the contracting session; the power to annul a contract possessed by both contracting parties as long as they do not separate

khiyār al-shart — a right, stipulated by one or both of the parties to a contract, to cancel the contract for any reason for a fixed period of time

kirā', iktirā' — lease; see *ijāra*

lāzim — (1) binding; (2) term applied to contracts insofar as they bind a party, or impose legal obligations on that party

māl — property; tangible things to which human nature inclines

Mālikī — one of the four Sunni schools of law, founded by Mālik ibn Anas

manfa'a — use, usufruct

mawsūf fī al-dhimma — lit., described in a dhimma; something known only by description and owed by a person

maysir — games of chance; see Qur'ān 5:90

mu'āmalāt — dealings or transactions among human beings; compare *'ibādāt*

mudāraba — (also called *qirād*) a form of partnership to which some of the partners contribute only capital and the other partners only labor (some schools do not treat it as a partnership but as a contract *sui generis*)

mudārib — a partner contributing labor in a *mudāraba*

muqtadā — a term in a contract which *fiqh* considers essential, entailed by the very nature of the contract

murābaha — sale at a percentage markup; one of the sales (*bay'*) in which the price is stated in terms of the sale object's cost to the seller, the others being sale at cost (*tawliya*) and sale at discount (*wadī'a*)

murābaha li-āmir bi-al-shirā' — lit., sale by markup to one commissioning a purchase; a transaction involving two sales: A promises B that, if B buys for A certain specified goods, A will repurchase them from B by *murābaha*, i.e., at a markup

mushāraka — partnership or company; used in modern Islamic law for *'inān* and related forms of partnership

mutaqawwam — things the use of which is lawful under the *sharī'a*

nadhr — vow to God

nasī'a — delay in a sale

niyya — intention

qabḍ ḍamān — possession of property accompanied by liability for or risk of its loss (see *ḍamān*)

qabḍ amāna — possession of property without liability for its loss (see *amāna*)

qabūl — acceptance; see *ījāb*

qaḍā' — religious office or function of the judge

qāḍī — judge

qānūn — law, statute, code

qarḍ — loan of fungible, to be repaid in kind

qarḍ ḥasan — lit., good loan; loan without interest

qawā'id — principle, general rule, maxim

qirāḍ (or *muqāraḍa*) — *muḍāraba*; term for modern bond earning a proportion of the revenues of the project financed by the bond

qiyās — analogy; one of the four roots (*uṣūl*) of *fiqh*

Qur'ān — Koran; one of the four roots (*uṣūl*) of *fiqh*

rabb al-māl — lit., the owner of the property; a partner who contributes capital

rahn — pledge, collateral

ribā — usury as forbidden in the Qur'an; interpreted in classical *fiqh* as including interest and various other forms of gain in contract

ribā al-fadl — *ribā* of excess; an excess in the exchange of *ribāwī* goods within a single genus

ribā al-jāhiliyya — lit., pre-Islamic *ribā*; the *ribā* of "pay or increase," referring to a transaction by which a creditor granted an extension in the term of a debt in return for an increase in the principal owing

ribā al-nasī'a — *ribā* of delay; an exchange of two *ribāwī* countervalues with one due at a later time

ribāwī — goods subject to *fiqh* rules on *ribā* in sales, variously defined by the schools: items sold by weight and by measure, foods, etc.

riḍā — consent, approval

sabab — cause

ṣadaqa — act of charity

salam (also called *salaf*) — lit., advance, loan; purchase of item known by specification or description for delivery at a later specified time, with payment of price in full at time of contract

ṣarf — currency exchange

Shāfi'ī — one of the four Sunni schools of law, founded by al-Shāfi'ī

sharī'a — the divine law known from the Qur'ān and Sunna

sharika — partnership; modern company or corporation; applied also to ownership in common

sharṭ — condition, stipulation

shurūṭ — pl. of *sharṭ*; (1) stipulations; (2) genre of legal formularies

ṣulḥ — reconciliation or settlement of a dispute

Sunna — the Prophet Muḥammad's normative example, as known from the *aḥadīth*; one of the four roots (*uṣūl*) of *fiqh*

ta'līq — lit., suspending; conditioning of a contract on an unknown or future event or fact

tamlīkāt — contracts transferring ownership of property

taqlīd — lit., conferring authority on another; legal conformism; following the opinion of another scholar without knowing the grounds for it; compare *ijtihād tarāḍin* or *tarāḍī* — mutual consent; see Qur'ān 4:29-30

tawarruq — a practice by which a needy person buys something on credit and at once sells it for cash to a third party in a separate transaction

uṣūl al-fiqh — lit., the roots of the *fiqh*; the sources of law; *fiqh* legal philosophy and hermeneutics

wa'd — promise

wakāla — the contract of agency

waqf — charitable foundation or trust

wujūh — a form of partnership to which the partners contribute only their creditworthiness, i.e., by borrowing capital jointly and transacting with it

yamīn — oath

BIBLIOGRAPHY

Abod, Sheikh Ghazali Sheikh, Syed Omar Syed Agil, and Aidit Hj. Ghazali, eds. *An Introduction to Islamic Finance.* Kuala Lumpur: Quill Publishers, 1992.

Abu Dawud, Sulayman Ibn al-Ash'ath (d. 275/889). *Sunan Abi Dawud.* Edited by Muhammad Muhyi al-Din 'Abd al-Hamid. Cairo: Dar Ihya' al-Sunna al-Nabawiyya, n.d.

Abumouamer, Faris Mahmoud. "An Analysis of the Role and Function of Shariah Control in Islamic Banks." Ph.D. diss., University of Wales, 1989.

Abu Sulayman, 'Abd al-Wahhab. "'Aqd al-tawrid." Unpublished paper. In forthcoming *Mawsu'at al-mu'amalat al-fiqhiyya,* Islamic Fiqh Academy, Organization of the Islamic Conference, Jedda.

Abu Zahra, M. *al-Milkiyya wa-nazariyyat al-'aqd.* Cairo: Dar al-Fikr al-'Arabi, 1976.

Aggarwal, A., and T. Yousef. "Islamic Banks and Investment Financing." Ph.D. diss., Harvard University, May 1996.

Ahmad, Ausaf. "Contemporary Practices of Islamic Financing Techniques." *Islamic Economic Studies* 1 (June 1994): 15-52.

_____. "al-Ahammiyya al-nisbiyya li-turuq al-tamwil al-mukhtalifa fi al-nizam al-masrafi al-islami." Fifth session (1988), *Fiqh Academy Journal* 2:1487-1516.

_____. *Contemporary Practices of Islamic Financing Techniques.* Jedda: Islamic Development Bank/Islamic Research and Training Institute, 1983.

Ahmad, Kurshid., ed. *Studies in Islamic Economics.* Leicester, U.K.: The Islamic Foundation.

Ahmad, Ziauddin. "The Theory of Riba." In *An Introduction to Islamic Finance,* edited by Sheikh Ghazali Sheikh Abod, Syed Omar Syed Agil, and Aidit Hj. Ghazali. Kuala Lumpur: Quill Publishers, 1992.

_____. "Islamic Banking: State of the Art." *Islamic Economic Studies* 2 (December 1994): 1-33.

Ahmed, Abdul Rahman Yousri. "Islamic Securities in Muslim Countries' Stock Markets and an Assessment of the Need for an Islamic Secondary Market." *Islamic Economic Studies* 3 (1995): 1-37.

Arab Bankers Association of North America. Proceedings of conference, *Islamic Finance and Investment,* in New York City, May 23, 1996.

Ariff, M. "Islamic Banking." *Asian-Pacific Economic Literature* 2, no. 2 (September 1988).

Asad, Muhammad. *The Message of the Qur'an.* Gibraltar: Dar al-Andalus, 1980.

al-'Asqalani, Ibn Hajar (d. 852/1449). *Bulugh al-muram min jam' adillat al-ahkam.* Beirut: Dar al-Kutub al-'Ilmiyya, n.d.

Attallah, B. *al-Ta'min wa-Shari'at al-Islam.* Alexandria, Egypt: Faculty of Law, Alexandria University, n.d.

Attar, Farid al-Din. *Muslim Saints and Mystics: Episodes from the Tadhkirat al-Auliya.* Translated by A.J. Arberry. Boston: Routledge & Kegan Paul, 1966.

Awan, A. *Equality, Efficency, and Property Ownership in Islam.* Lanham, MD: University Press of America, 1983.

Badr, Gamal Moursi. "Islamic Law: Its Relation to Other Legal Systems." *American Journal of Comparative Law* 26 (1978): 187-198.

al-Badran, Kasib. *'Aqd al-istisna'.* Alexandria, Egypt: Dar al-Da'wa, 1980.

Bahjat, Muhammad. "Nahwa ma'ayir li-al-riqaba al-shar'iyya fi al-bunuk al-islamiyya." *Majallat buhuth al-iqtisad al-islami* 3 (1994): 1-60.

al-Bahuti, Mansur (d. 1051/1641). *Kashshaf al-qina'.* Beirut: Dar al-Fikr, 1982.

Bank al-Tadamun al-Islami, Idarat al-fatwa wa-al-buhuth. *'Aqd al-istisna' fi al-fiqh al-islami.* City unspecified: Bank al-Tadamun al-Islami, 1992.

al-Baydawi, 'Abd Allah (d. 685/1286). *Tafsir al-Qur'an.* Istanbul: Dar al-Tiba'a al-'Amira, 1886.

Bayt al-Tamwil al-Kuwayti [Kuwait Finance House]. *Al-Fatawa al-shar'iyya fi al-masa'il al-iqtisadiyya 1979-1989.* Kuwait: Kuwait Finance House, n.d.

Baz, S. *Sharh al-majalla*, 3d ed. Beirut: Dar Ihya' al-Turath al-'Arabi, 1986.

Brealey, Richard, and Stewart Myers. *Principles of Corporate Finance*. New York: McGraw-Hill Book Company, 1996.

Brunschvig, Robert. "Corps certaine et chose de genre dans l'obligation en droit musulman." In *Études d'islamologie*, vol. 2, 303-322. Paris : G.-P. Maisonneuve et Larose, 1976.

al-Bukhari, Muhammad bin Isma'il (d. 256/870). *Matn al-Bukhari*. With commentary by Abu al-Hasan Nur al-Din Muhammad bin 'Abd al-Hadi al-Sindi (d. 1138/1726). 4 vols. Cairo: Matba'at Dar Ihya' al-Kutub al-'Arabiyya, n.d.

Cambridge Associates. *U.S. Historical Capital Market Returns: Executive Summary*. Boston, 1997.

Chapra, Muhammad Umar. "The Nature of Riba and its Treatment in the Quran, Hadith and Fiqh." In *An Introduction to Islamic Finance*, edited by Sheikh Ghazali Sheikh Abod, Syed Omar Syed Agil, and Aidit Hj. Ghazali. Kuala Lumpur: Quill Publishers, 1992.

_____. *Islam and the Economic Challenge*. Leicester, UK: The Islamic Foundation, 1992.

_____. *Towards a Just Monetary System*. Leicester, UK: The Islamic Foundation, 1985.

Chehata, Chafik. *Études de droit musulman: 2/ La notion de responsabilité contractuelle. Le concept de propriété*. Paris: Presses Universitaires de France, 1973.

Choudhoury, M. *The Foundations of Islamic Political Economy*. London: The Macmillan Press Ltd., 1987.

Citibank. "Exposure Management." Presented in Dubai, March 22, 1995. Bahrain: Citibank, 1996.

Corbin, A.L. *Corbin on Contracts*. St. Paul: West Publishing Co., 1960.

Coulson, Noel J. *Commercial Law in the Gulf States*. London: Graham & Trotman, 1984.

_____. *A History of Islamic Law*. Edinburgh: Edinburgh University Press, 1964.

Cox, John, and Mark Rubenstein. *Option Markets*. Englewood Cliffs, N.J.: Prentice Hall, 1985.

Dallah al-Baraka, Idarat al-tatwir wa-al-buhuth. *al-Fatawa al-iqtisadiyya*. Jedda: Majmu'at Dallah al-Baraka, 1995.

Daoualibi, M. "La Théorie de l'usure en droit musulman." In *Travaux de la semaine internationale de droit musulman*, edited by L. Milliot. Paris: Receuil Sirey, 1953.

al-Darimi, 'Abd Allah bin 'Abd al-Rahman (d. 255/869). *Sunan al-Darimi (al-Musnad al-jami')*. Beirut: Dar Ihya' al-Sunna al-Nabawiyya, n.d.

al-Darir, al-Siddiq. "al-Ittifaq 'ala ilzam al-madin al-musir bi-ta'wid darar al-mumatala." *Majallat abhath al-iqtisad al-islami* 3 (1985): 111-113.

El-Ashkar, Ahmad Abdel Fattah. "Towards an Islamic Stock Exchange in a Transitional Stage." *Islamic Economic Studies* 3 (December 1995): 79-112.

_____. *The Islamic Business Enterprise.* London: Croom Helm, 1987.

El-Erian, M. "Financial Market Development in the Middle East: The Main Issues." Paper presented at workshop, *Development of Financial Markets in Arab Countries, Iran, and Turkey,* in Beirut, Lebanon, July 15-16, 1994.

Elgari, M. "Towards an Islamic Stock Market." *Islamic Economic Studies* 1 (December 1993).

Farnsworth, E. Allan. *Contracts.* Boston: Little, Brown & Co., 1990.

al-Fatawa al-hindiyya. Beirut: Dar Ihya' al-Turath al-'Arabi, 1980.

Fuller, Lon L. *Legal Fictions.* Stanford, CA: Stanford University Press, 1967.

_____ and Willam R. Perdue, Jr. "The Reliance Interest in Contract Damages: 1." *Yale Law Journal* 46 (1936):52-96.

Grahammer, Michael. "Islamische Banken: Ausweg aus dem Finanzier-ungsdilemma fur Nahostgeschafte?" In *Forschungergebnisse der Wirtschaftsuniversitat Wien,* edited by Edgar Topritzhofer. Vienna: Swervice Fachverlag, 1993.

Habachy, Saba. "Property, Right, and Contract in Muslim Law." *Columbia Law Review* 42 (1962): 450-471.

Hamid, M. "Islamic Law and Islamic Banking: Lessons in the Experience of the IDB." Paris: International Bar Association, 1990.

_____. "Islamic Law of Contract or Contracts." *Journal of Islamic and Comparative Law* 3 (1969):1-11

_____. "Mutual Assent in the Formation of Contracts in Islamic Law." *Journal of Islamic and Comparative Law* 7 (1977) :41-53.

Hammad, Nazih Kamal. *'Aqd al-salam fi al-shari'a al-islamiyya.* Beirut: al-Dar al-Shamiyya, 1993.

_____. *Bay' al-kali' bi-al-kali' (bay' al-dayn bi-al-dayn) fi al-fiqh al-islami.* Jedda: Markaz Abhath al-Iqtisad al-Islami, Jami'at al-Malik 'Abd al-'Aziz, 1986.

Hasanuz-Zaman, S.M. "Bay' Salam: Principles and their Practical Applications." In *An Introduction to Islamic Finance*, edited by Sheikh Ghazali Sheikh Abod, Syed Omar Syed Agil, and Aidit Hj. Ghazali. Kuala Lumpur: Quill Publishers, 1992.

Hassan, Abdullah Alwi Haji. *Sales and Contracts in Early Islamic Commercial Law*. Ph.D. diss., University of Edinburgh, 1986.

Hassan, N. "Measurement of Financial Performance of Islamic Banks vis-à-vis Western Type Commercial Banks — Some Conceptual Differences." Presented at seminar, *Development of an Accounting System for Islamic Banking*, May 24, 1994.

Hassan, T. "Islamic Banking: The Need for Uniform Regulation." *Journal of Islamic Banking and Finance* 8, no. 2 (April 1991).

Hawawini, Najib, ed. *Majallat al-ahkam al-'adliyya* [Arabic version]. Damascus: Matba' Quzma, 1923.

Hayes, Samuel L. "New Interest in Incentives." *Harvard Business Review*, July-August 1966.

Hidzir, Y. "The Monetary/Policy Consideration in the Implementation of Islamic Banking in a Conventional Environment." Presented at *Symposium of the Malaysian Experience in Islamic Banking*, March 9-12, 1996.

Homoud, Sami Hassan. *al-Adawat al-tamwiliyya al-islamiyya li-al-sharikat al-musahama*. Jedda: Islamic Research and Training Institute, 1996.

_____. "Progress of Islamic Banking: The Aspirations and the Realities." *Islamic Economic Studies* 2 (December 1994): 71-80.

_____. *Islamic Banking,*. London: Arabian Information, 1985.

_____. *Tatwir al-a'mal al-masrafiyya bi-ma yattafiq wa-al-shari'a al-islamiyya*. Cairo: Dar al-Ittihad al-'Arabi, 1976.

Ibn 'Abidin, Muhammad Amin (d. 1252/1836). *Hashiyyat radd al-muhtar 'ala al-durr al-mukhtar sharh tanwir al-absar*. Cairo: Mustafa Babi al-Halabi, 1966.

Ibn al-Athir, Nasr (d. 637/1239). *Jami' al-usul fi ahadith al-rasul*. Damascus: Maktabat al-Halawani, 1969-1973.

Ibn Hanbal, Ahmad (d. 241/855). *Musnad al-Imam Ahmad bin Hanbal*. Cairo: al-Matba'a al-Yamaniyya, 1895; reprint, Beirut: al-Maktaba al-Islamiyya, 1978.

Ibn Juzayy, Muhammad bin Ahmad. *Qawanin al-ahkam al-shar'iyya wa-masa'il al-furu' al-fiqhiyya*. Beirut: Dar al-'Ilm li-al-Malayin, 1979.

Ibn Kathir, Isma'il (d. 774/1373). *Tafsir al-Qur'an al-'azim*. Cairo: Isa al-Babi al-Halabi, n.d.

Ibn Maja, Muhammad bin Yazid (d. 275/886). *Sunan Ibn Maja*. Edited by Muhammad Fu'ad 'Abd al-Baqi. Cairo: Dar Ihya' al-Sunna al-Nabawiyya, 1975.

Ibn Mani', 'Abd Allah bin Sulayman. "al-Wa'd wa-hukm al-ilzam bi-al-wafa' bihi diyanatan wa-qada'an." *Majallat al-buhuth al-fiqhiyya al-mu'asira* 16 (1413 H.): 6-33.

Ibn Qayyim al-Jawziyya, Muhammad bin Abi Bakr (d. 751/1350). *I'lam al-muwaqqa'in 'ala rabb al-'alamin*. Edited by Taha 'Abd al-Ra'uf Sa'd. Beirut: Dar al-Jil, 1973.

Ibn Qudama, Muwaffaq al-Din 'Abd Allah (d. 620/1223). *al-Mughni wa-yalihi al-sharh al-kabir*. 1972; reprinted Beirut: Dar al-Kitab al-'Arabi, 1983.

Ibn Rushd, Muhammad bin Ahmad (d. 595/1198). *Bidayat al-mujtahid wa-nihayat al-muqtasid*. Cairo: Mustafa al-Babi al-Halabi, 1981.

————. *The Distinguished Jurist's Primer*. Translated by Imran Ahsan Khan Nyazee. Reading, UK: Garnet Publishing Ltd., 1996.

Ibn Taymiyya, Taqi al-Din Ahmad. *al-Fatawa al-kubra*. Beirut: Dar al-Ma'rifa, n.d.

————. *Majmu' fatawa Shaykh al-Islam Ahmad Ibn Taymiyya*. Edited by 'A. al-'Asimi. Riyadh: Kingdom of Saudi Arabia, n.d.

————. *Nazariyyat al-'aqd*. Beirut: Dar al-Ma'rifa, n.d.

————. *al-Qawa'id al-nuraniyya al-fiqhiyya*. Edited by M. al-Fiqi. Cairo: al-Sunna al-Muhammadiyya, 1951.

Ismail, Abdul Halim. "The Deferred Contracts of Exchange in Al-Qur'an." In *An Introduction to Islamic Finance*, edited by Sheikh Ghazali Sheikh Abod, Syed Omar Syed Agil, and Aidit Hj. Ghazali. Kuala Lumpur: Quill Publishers, 1992.

————. *Islamic Banking in Malaysia — Some Issues, Problems, and Prospects*. Kuala Lumpur: Bank Islam Malaysia Berhard, 1986.

————. "The Teaching of Islamic Economics." In *Workshop on the Teaching of Islamic Economics*, at International Islamic University, Malaysia, July 1990.

Jili, Harun Khalif. "al-Wafa' bi-al-wa'd fi al-fiqh al-islami." Fifth session, *Fiqh Academy Journal* 2:881-908.

Johansen, Baber. *The Islamic Law on Land Tax and Rent*. New York: Croom Helm, 1988.

Kahf, Monzer. "The Use of Assets Ijara Bonds for Bridging the Budget Gap." Presented at *International Seminar on Mechanism and Devel-*

opment of Islamic Financial Instruments for Resource Mobilization, May 14-16, 1996, Dhaka, Bangladesh.

_____. "Time Value of Money and Discounting in Islamic Perspective: Revisited." *Review of Islamic Economics* 3 (1994): 31-38.

Kahf, Monzer, and Tariqullah Khan. *Principles of Islamic Financing — A Survey.* Jedda: Islamic Research and Training Institute, 1992.

al-Kasani, Abu Bakr bin Mas'ud (d. 587/1191). *Bada'i' al-sana'i'.* Beirut: Dar al-Kitab al-'Arabi, 1982.

Kazarian, E. *Islamic Versus Traditional Banking, Financial Innovation in Egypt.* Oxford: Westview Press, 1993.

al-Khafif, 'Ali. *Mukhtasar ahkam al-mu'amalat al-shar'iyya.* Cairo: Matba'at al-Sunna al-Muhammadiyya, 1950.

_____. *al-Milkiyya fi al-shari'a al-islamiyya.* Beirut: Dar al-Nahda al-'Arabiyya, 1990.

_____. *al-Sharikat fi al-fiqh al-islami.* Cairo: Arab League, 1962.

Khalil, R. *al-Sharikat fi al-fiqh al-islami.* Riyad University: Dar al-Rashid li-al Nashr wa-al-Tawzih, 1981.

Khan, M. Fahim. "Time Value of Money and Discounting in Islamic Perspective." *Review of Islamic Economics* 1 (1991): 35-45.

_____. "Comparative Economics of Some Islamic Financing Techniques." *Islamic Economic Studies* 2 (December 1994): 35-68.

Khan, Muhammad Akram. "Capital Expenditure Analysis in an Islamic Framework." In *An Introduction to Islamic Finance*, edited by Sheikh Ghazali Sheikh Abod, Syed Omar Syed Agil, and Aidit Hj. Ghazali. Kuala Lumpur: Quill Publishers, 1992.

_____. "Time Value of Money." In *An Introduction to Islamic Finance*, edited by Sheikh Ghazali Sheikh Abod, Syed Omar Syed Agil, and Aidit Hj. Ghazali. Kuala Lumpur: Quill Publishers, 1992.

_____. "Types of Business Organization in an Islamic Economy." In *An Introduction to Islamic Finance*, edited by Sheikh Ghazali Sheikh Abod, Syed Omar Syed Agil, and Aidit Hj. Ghazali. Kuala Lumpur: Quill Publishers, 1992.

_____. "Commodity Exchange and Stock Exchange in Islamic Economy." *The American Journal of Islamic Social Sciences* 5 (1988).

Khan, M., and Abbas Mirakhor. *Theoretical Studies in Islamic Banking and Finance.* Houston: The Institute for Research and Islamic Studies, 1987.

_____. "Islamic Interest-Free Banking." International Monetary Fund Staff Paper. Washington, DC: International Monetary Fund, 1986.

_____. "Islamic Banking." International Monetary Fund Working Paper. Washington, DC: International Monetary Fund, 1991.

_____. "The Progress of Islamic Banking: The Case of Iran and Pakistan." *Economic Development and Cultural Change* 38 (January 1990).

Khan, Tariqullah. *Practices and Performance of Modaraba Companies (A Case Study of Pakistan's Experience).* Jedda: Islamic Research and Training Institute, 1996.

_____. "Demand for and Supply of Mark-up and PLS Funds in Islamic Banking: Some Alternative Explanations." *Islamic Economic Studies* 3 (December 1995): 39-77.

Khan, Waqar Masood. "Towards an Interest Free Islamic Economic System." In *Collected Papers,* Waqar Masood Khan and Abbas Mirakhor. Washington, DC: International Monetary Fund, 1987.

Khayrullah, Walid. "*Al-Muqaradah* Bonds as the Basis of Profit-Sharing." *Islamic Economic Studies* 1 (June 1994): 79-102.

al-Khayyat, 'Abd al-'Aziz. *al-Sharikat.* Beirut: Risala, 1984.

Kotby, H. "Financial Engineering for Islamic Banks." IMES-I.U.J. Working Paper Series, no. 23, November 1990.

Kuwait High Consultative Council for the Completion of the Implementation of the Islamic Shari'a. *Proceedings of Symposium of the Malaysian Experience in Islamic Banking* (5 pamphlets), March 9-12, 1996.

Kuwait Ministry of Awqaf and Islamic Affairs. "Tawarruq." In *al-Mawsu'a al-fiqhiyya.* Kuwait: Tiba'at Dhat al-Salasil, 1986.

Lajnat al-Buhuth al-'Ilmiyyah, al-Riyasa al-'Amma li-Idarat al-Buhuth al-'Ilmiyya wa-al-Ifta'. "al-Shart al-jaza'i." *Majallat al-buhuth al-islamiyya* 1 (1975-6): 61-144.

Lane, Edward William. *An Arabic-English Lexicon.* London: Williams & Norgate, 1893.

Legal Academy of the Organization of the Islamic Conference. Proceedings of conference, *Financial Markets,* in Jedda, Saudi Arabia, March 1990.

Linant de Bellefonds, Yvon. *Traité de droit musulman comparé.* Paris: La Haye, Mouton, 1965-73.

_____. "Volonté interne et volonté déclaré en droit musulman." *Revue internationale de droit comparé* 10 (July-Sep. 1958): 510-521.

Mahmasani, Subhi. *al-Nazariyya al-'amma li-al-mujibat wa-al-'uqud,* 2d ed. Beirut: Dar al-'Ilm li-al-Malayin, 1972.

Majalla: see Hawawini, ed.

Mallat, Chibli. "The Debate on Riba and Interest in Twentieth Century Jurisprudence," in *Islamic Law and Finance,* edited by Chibli Mallat. London: Graham & Trotman, 1988.

_____. "Tantawi on Banking Operations in Egypt." In *Islamic Legal Interpretation: Muftis and their Fatwas,* edited by M. Khalid Masud, Brinkley Messick, and David Powers. Cambridge, MA: Harvard University Press, 1996.

Mannan, M.A. *Understanding Islamic Finance: A Study of the Securities Market in an Islamic Framework.* Jedda: Islamic Development Bank, 1988.

al-Mardawi, 'Ala' al-Din Abu al-Hasan 'Ali bin Sulayman (d. 886/1481). *al-Insaf fi ma'rifat al-rajih min al-khilaf 'ala madhhab al-imam al-mubajjal Ahmad bin Hanbal.* Edited by M.H. al-Fiqi. Beirut: Dar Ihya' al-Turath al-'Arabi, 1980.

Merad, A. "Islah," pt. 1. *Encyclopedia of Islam,* 2d ed.

Metwally, S. "The Aggregate Balance Sheet of and Results of Transactions and Financial Indicators for Islamic Banks and Financial Institutions." *Journal of Islamic Banking and Finance* 1 (April-June 1992).

Mirakhor, Abbas. "Short-term Asset Concentration and Islamic Banking." In *Collected Papers,* by Waqar Masood Khan and Abbas Mirakhor. Washington, DC: International Monetary Fund, 1987.

Mishkin, Frederic S. *The Economics of Money, Banking, and Financial Markets.* New York: Harper Collins, 1992.

al-Misri, Rafiq. *Bay' al-taqsit.* Beirut: al-Dar al-Shamiyya, 1990.

Mohieddin, M. "On Formal and Informal Finance in Egypt." Paper presented at Middle Eastern Studies Association Annual Conference, December 6-10, 1995.

Mohsin, Muhammad. "Assessment of Corporate Securities in Terms of Islamic Investment Requirements." In *An Introduction to Islamic Finance,* edited by Sheikh Ghazali, Sheikh Abod, Syed Omar Syed Agil, and Aidit Hj. Ghazali. Kuala Lumpur: Quill Publishers, 1992.

Mukherji, B. *Theory of Growth of a Firm in a Zero Interest Rate Economy.* Jedda: King Abdulaziz University Press, 1984.

al-Mulk, Nizam (d. 485/1092). *The Book of Government or Rules for Kings,* 2d ed. Translated by Hubert Darke. London: Routledge & Kegan Paul, 1978.

Muslim, Ibn al-Hajjaj al-Nisaburi (d. 261/875). *Sahih Muslim.* With a commentary by Yahya bin Sharaf al-Nawawi (d. 676/1277). Edited by 'Abd Allah Ahmad Abu Zinah. Cairo: al-Sha'b Press, n.d.

al-Nasa'i, Abu 'Abd al-Rahman Ahmad bin Shu'ayyib (d. 303/915). *Sunan al-Nasa'i.* With commentary by Jalal al-Din al-Suyuti (d. 911/1505) and super-commentary by Muhammad bin 'Abd al-Hadi al-Sindi (d. 1138/1726). Cairo: al-Matba'a al-Misriyya, 1930.

Nawawi, Yahya bin Sharaf (d. 676/1277). *Kitab al-Majmu'.* Jedda: Maktabat al-Irshad, 1992.

Nienhaus, V. "Islamic Economics, Finance and Banking — Theory and Practice." *Journal of Islamic Banking and Finance,* spring 1986: 36-54.

al-Nisaburi, 'Ali bin Ahmad (d. 468/1075). *Asbab al-nuzul.* Beirut: Dar al-Kutub al-'Ilmiyya, 1980.

Noonan, J.T., Jr. *The Scholastic Analysis of Usury.* Cambridge, MA: Harvard University Press, 1957.

Nyazee, Imran Ahsan Khan. "Corporations and Islamic Law." Book manuscript on file at Islamic Legal Studies Program, Harvard Law School, 1996.

————. *The Concept of Riba and Islamic Banking.* Islamabad: Niazi Publishing House, 1995.

al-Omar, Fuad, and Mohammed Abdel-Haq. *Islamic Banking.* London: Zed Books, 1996.

Onn, Ismail. "Development of the Islamic Capital Market in Malaysia." In *Symposium of the Malaysian Experience in Islamic Banking.* Kuwait: High Consultative Council for the Completion of the Implementation of the Islamic Shari'a, 1996.

Organisation of the Islamic Conference. *Islamic Fiqh Academy Resolutions and Recommendations.* Jedda: Organisation of the Islamic Conference, 1989?.

Posner, Richard A. *The Economic Analysis of Law.* Boston: Little, Brown & Co., 1992.

al-Qari, Ahmad bin 'Abd Allah. *Majallat al-ahkam al-shar'iyya.* Edited by 'A. Abu Sulayman and M. 'Ali. Jidda: Tihama Publications, 1981.

al-Qura-Daghi, 'Ali Muhyi al-Din. "Bahth al-aswaq al-maliyya fi mizan al-fiqh al-Islami." Seventh session (1992), *Fiqh Academy Journal* 1: 73-194.

Rahim, M.A. Abdur. *Principles of Muhammadan Jurisprudence.* London: Luzac & Co., 1911.

Rahman, Fazlur. "Riba and Interest." *Islamic Studies* 3 (March 1969): 1-43.

_____. "Economic Principles of Islam." *Islamic Studies* 8 (1969): 1-8.

al-Ramli, Muhammad bin Ahmad (d. 1006/1596). *Nihayat al-muhtaj ila sharh al-minhaj.* Cairo: Mustafa al-Babi al-Halabi, 1967-69.

Ray, Nicholas. *Arab Islamic Banking and the Renewal of Islamic Law.* London: Graham & Trotman, 1995.

al-Razi, Fakhr al-Din Muhammad bin 'Umar. *Mafatih al-ghayb.* Istanbul: al-Matba'a al-'Amira, 1891.

Ross, Stephen. "The Determination of Financial Structure: The Incentive Signaling Approach." *Bell Journal of Economics,* Spring 1977: 23-40.

_____. "Some Notes on Financial Incentive-Signaling Models, Activity Choice, and Risk Preferences." *Journal of Finance* 33 (1978): 777-794.

Ross, Stephen, Randolph Westerfield, and Jeffrey Jaffe. *Corporate Finance.* Chicago: Richard D. Irwin, Inc., 1996.

Roy, Olivier. *The Failure of Political Islam.* Translated by Carol Volk. Cambridge, MA: Harvard University Press, 1994.

Saadallah, Ridha. "Concept of Time in Islamic Economics." *Islamic Economic Studies* 2 (1994): 81-102.

Saeed, Abdullah. *Islamic Banking and Interest.* Leiden: E.J. Brill, 1996.

Saffari, Said. "Islamic Banking in Iran." Working Paper of the Center for Middle Eastern Studies, Harvard University, 1996.

Saleh, N. *Unlawful Gain and Legitimate Profit in Islamic Law,* 2d ed. Boston: Kluwer Law International, 1992.

Salus, 'Ali Ahmad. "al-Murabaha li-al-amir bi-al-shira'." Fifth session (1988), *Fiqh Academy Journal* 2:1060-1087.

al-Sanhuri, 'Abd al-Razzaq. *Masadir al-haqq fi al-fiqh al-islami.* Cairo: Dar Ihya' al-Turath al-'Arabi, 1967-1968.

al-Sarakhsi, Muhammad bin Ahmad (d. 483/1090?). *Kitab al-mabsut.* Beirut: Dar al-Ma'rifa, 1986.

Saudi Arabia. Presidency of Islamic Researches, Ifta', Call, and Guidance. *The Holy Qur'an.* Medina: King Fahd Holy Qur'an Printing Complex, 1992.

Schacht, Joseph. *An Introduction to Islamic Law.* London: Oxford University Press, 1964.

al-Shadhili, Hasan 'Ali. *Nazariyyat al-shart fi al-fiqh al-islami.* Cairo: Dar al-Kitab al-Jami'i, 1981.

Shajari, H., and M. Kamalzadeh. "The Interest Rate and the Islamic Banking." *Islamic Economic Studies* 3 (December 1995): 115-122.

al-Sharqawi, 'Abd Allah (d. 1812). *Hashiyya 'ala tuhfat al-tullab.* Beirut: Dar al-Ma'rifa, 1975.

al-Shatibi, Ibrahim bin Musa (d. 745/1388). *al-Muwafaqat.* Cairo: Maktabat al-Tijariyya al-kubra, n.d.

al-Shawkani, Muhammad bin 'Ali (d. 1255/1839). *Nayl al-awtar.* Cairo: Mustafa Babi al-Halabi, n.d.

Shehata, Shawki Ismail. "Limitation on the Use of *Zakah* Funds in Financing Socioeconomic Infrastructure." *Islamic Economic Studies* 1 (June 1994): 63-78.

Shirazi, H. *Islamic Banking: Contracts.* Tehran: Central Bank of the Islamic Republic of Iran, 1988.

Siddiqi, M. *Issues in Islamic Banking: Selected Papers.* London: The Islamic Foundation, 1983.

_____. *Banking without Interest.* London: The Islamic Foundation, 1983.

Simpson, A. W. Brian. *A History of the Common Law of Contract: The Rise of the Action of Assumpsit.* Oxford: Oxford University Press, 1975.

Suhnun, 'Abd al-Salam Ibn Sa'id (d. 269/854). *al-Mudawwana al-kubra.* Cairo: al-Sa'ada, 1905.

al-Suyuti, Jalal al-Din 'Abd al-Rahman Bin Abi Bakr (d. 911/1505). *Asbab al-nuzul.* Cairo: Dar al-Tahrir li-al-Tab' wa-al-Nashr, 1963.

al-Tabari, Muhammad Ibn Jarir (d. 310/923). *The History of al-Tabari.* Vol. 12, *The Battle of Qadisiyya.* Translated by Yohanan Friedman. New York: State University of New York Press, 1992.

al-Tahanawi, Muhammad. *A Dictionary of the Technical Terms Used in the Sciences of the Musalmans.* Calcutta: W.N. Lees Press, 1862.

al-Tahawi, Ahmad ibn Muhammad (d. 321/933). *Mukhtasar ikhtilaf al-fuqaha'.* Beirut: Dar al-Basha'ir al-Islamiyya, 1995.

al-Tirmidhi, Abu 'Isa Muhammad bin 'Isa (d. 297/892). *Sunan al-Tirmidhi (al-Jami' al-sahih).* Cairo: Mustafa al-Babi al-Halabi, 1975-1978.

Udovitch, Abraham L. *Partnership and Profit in Medieval Islam.* Princeton, NJ: Princeton University Press, 1970.

Uzair, Mohammad. *An Outline for Interestless Banking.* Karachi: Raihan Publications, 1955.

Vogel, Frank E. *Islamic Law and Legal System: Studies of Saudi Arabia.* Leiden: E.J. Brill, forthcoming 1998.

_____. "Islamic Governance in the Gulf: A Framework for Analysis, Comparison, and Prediction." In *The Persian Gulf at the Millennium: Essays in Politics, Economy, Security, and Religion,* ed. Gary S. Sick and Lawrence G. Potter. New York: St. Martin's Press, 1997.

Weiss, Bernard. "Interpretation in Islamic Law: The Theory of *Ijtihad.*" *American Journal of Comparative Law* 26 (1978): 199-210.

Wellington Management Company. *NCB Global Trading Equity Fund.* Boston, 1997.

Wilson, Rodney. "Development of Islamic Financial Instruments." *Islamic Economic Studies* 2 (December 1994): 103-115.

_____. *Banking and Finance in the Arab Middle East.* New York: St. Martin's Press, 1983.

_____. *Islamic Financial Markets.* New York: Routledge, 1990.

Zaky, Nublan Zaky Dato' Yusoff. *An Islamic Perspective of Stock Market — An Introduction.* Edited by Sheikh Ghazali Abod. Kuala Lumpur: Dian Darulnaim Sdn. v. Bhd, 1992.

Zaman, R. "The Operation of the Modern Financial Markets for Stocks and Bonds and Its Relevance to an Islamic Economy." *The American Journal of Islamic Social Sciences* 3 (1986): 125-140.

Zarqa, Muhammad Anas. "Financing and Investment in *Awqaf* Projects: A Non-Technical Introduction." *Islamic Economic Studies* 1 (June 1994): 55-62.

_____. "An Islamic Perspective on the Economics of Discounting in Project Evaluation." In *An Introduction to Islamic Finance,* edited by Sheikh Ghazali Sheikh Abod, Syed Omar Syed Agil, and Aidit Hj. Ghazali. Kuala Lumpur: Quill Publishers, 1992.

_____. "Shari'a Compatible Shares: A Suggested Formula and Rationale." Proceedings of conference, *Third International Conference on Islamic Economics,* in Kuala Lumpur, January 29-30, 1992.

_____. "Tahqiq islamiyyat 'ilm al-iqtisad." *Majallat Jami'at al-Malik 'Abd al-'Aziz* 2 (1990): 3-39.

_____ and Muhammad 'Ali al-Qari [Elgari]. "al-Ta'wid 'an darar al-mu-matala fi al-dayn bayn al-fiqh wal-iqtisad." *Majallat Jami'at al-Malik Abd al-'Aziz* 3 (1991): 25-57.

al-Zarqa', Mustafa. *al-Madkhal al-fiqhi al-'amm.* 9th rev. ed.; Beirut: Dar al-Fikr, 1967-68.

_____. *Nizam al-ta'min.* Damascus: Matbaat Jamiat Dimashq, 1962.

Index

Series General Editor
Dr. Mark S. W. Hoyle

The Status of Women under Islamic Law (2nd ed). Jamal J. Nasir
(ISBN 1-85966-084-3)

The Marriage Contract in Islamic Law, Dawoud S. El Alami
(ISBN 1-85333-719-6)

Mixed Courts of Egypt, Mark S. W. Hoyle
(ISBN 1-85333-321-2)

The Theory of Contracts in Islamic Law, S. E. Rayner
(ISBN 1-85333-617-3)

Unlawful Gain and Legitimate Profit in Islamic Law, Nabil A. Saleh
(ISBN 1-85333-721-8)

(Please order by ISBN or by title)